Microsoft®

SQL Server™ 2000
Performance Tuning

Technical Reference

Edward Whalen, Marcilina Garcia,
Steve Adrien DeLuca, and Dean Thompson

PUBLISHED BY
Microsoft Press
A Division of Microsoft Corporation
One Microsoft Way
Redmond, Washington 98052-6399

Library of Congress Cataloging-in-Publication Data
    Microsoft SQL Server 2000 Performance Tuning Technical Reference / Edward Whalen,
    Marcilina Garcia, Steve Adrien DeLuca, Dean Thompson.
        p. cm.
    Includes index.
    ISBN 0-7356-1270-6
    1. Client/server computing. 2. SQL server. I. Edward Whalen, Marcilina Garcia,
    Steve Adrien DeLuca, Dean Thompson.

    QA76.9.C55 M5322   2001
    005.75'85--dc21   2001030647

Printed and bound in the United States of America.

2 3 4 5 6 7 8 9   QWT   6 5 4 3 2 1

Distributed in Canada by Penguin Books Canada Limited.

A CIP catalogue record for this book is available from the British Library.

Microsoft Press books are available through booksellers and distributors worldwide. For further information about international editions, contact your local Microsoft Corporation office or contact Microsoft Press International directly at fax (425) 706-7329. Visit our Web site at www.microsoft.com/mspress. Send comments to *mspinput@microsoft.com*.

Active Directory, ActiveX, Microsoft, Microsoft Press, MSDN, Visual Basic, Visual C++, Visual J++, Windows, Windows NT, and Win32 are either registered trademarks or trademarks of Microsoft Corporation in the United States and/or other countries. Other product and company names mentioned herein may be the trademarks of their respective owners.

The example companies, organizations, products, domain names, e-mail addresses, logos, people, places, and events depicted herein are fictitious. No association with any real company, organization, product, domain name, e-mail address, logo, person, place, or event is intended or should be inferred.

Acquisitions Editor: David Clark
Project Editor: Jean Trenary
Technical Editor: Jack Beaudry
Manuscript Editor: Jan Bultmann

Body Part No. X08-03728

Contents

PART III Configuring and Tuning the System

PART IV Tuning SQL Statements

16 Using SQL Query Analyzer   295

PART V Appendixes and Glossary

Tables

Acknowledgments

Edward Whalen

In writing a book you rely not only on the people who have directly helped during the process, but also on much of the wisdom and experience that others have shared with you over the years. So, it is often necessary to thank those who have helped you get to where you are today.

First I would like to thank those people who helped with this book. This book would not be what it is without the dedication and skills of the great team of editors: thanks to Jean Trenary and David Clark at Microsoft Press, Jan Bultmann, and Jack Beaudry. Without you this book could not have been done. Also, thanks to Damien Lindauer for helping me learn SQL Server years ago. In addition, I would like to thank Bill Gates for making Windows 2000 and SQL Server possible.

I would especially like to thank my friends who worked with me on this book: Steve DeLuca, Marcilina Garcia, Dean Thompson, and Jamie Reding. All of you really made this a great book.

I would also like to mention my good friends and co-workers in Virginia: Geoff, Alex, Shelly, Heather, Arnel, and John. Thanks for helping me with some really tough SQL Server tuning issues.

Finally I would like to thank my wife, Felicia, for putting up with all the time spent writing this book. Without her support this effort would have been much more difficult.

Marcilina Garcia

There are several people whom I would like to thank for their help and support with this book. First, I would like to thank my great friend and coauthor Edward Whalen, who made this book opportunity possible. Thanks for the fourth time, Ed! I would also like to thank my other friends and coauthors of this book—Jamie Reding, Steve DeLuca, and Dean Thompson. Next I would like to thank the editors at Microsoft Press.

In addition, I would like to thank my awesome husband, Luis Garcia, for his support while I was writing this book. I'll never forget Machu Picchu 2001! Also, thanks to my dear step-daughter, Marilyn Nicole Garcia, for her encouragement. I also would like to thank my super-cool parents, Ron and Twila Jean Frohock, for their continued prayers and support, and for always being here for me—and there for me! And especially, I give thanks to God.

Steve Adrien DeLuca

As in any endeavor, there are persons who support the project and contribute in some way to its overall success. I would like to take this opportunity to thank these people.

First, I'd like to thank the people on the great management staff at Microsoft and the Distributed Management Division, including Deborah Black, Israel Gat Naveen Garg, and Ashvin Sanghvi. Special thanks to Steve Ballmer and Bill Gates. Without them, none of this would be taking place in this reality. Thanks to such talented engineers as Dr. Kevin Hodge, Juhan Lee, Paul Darcy, Casey Kiernan and Sally Martin (coinventors with me on other patents), and last but not least Chad Verbowski and Jenny Lehman.

What can one say about close friends such as Ed Whalen and Marci Garcia whom I have worked with and known for many years? I would like to thank other friends who have supported me during this and other projects, such as Pat Beadles, Chef Guido, Tony and Kris Vanacore. And last, but first in my thoughts, thanks to my family, especially my wife, Jean; my daughter, Tina; my sister, Sue; and my brother, Nick; who have always been there to support and help me. Also, I would like to dedicate this writing to the memory of Asta, Lorraine, and my mother Esther—three of the sweetest creatures that ever graced the earth with their presence.

A special thanks to the editing and publishing teams under David Clark and Jean Trenary at Microsoft Press for so often turning my writing into English and making my English understandable.

Michael Dean Thompson

I would like to thank Ed Whalen and Marci Garcia for their patience and assistance; Ed, Mitch and Marci, you are the most talented individuals with whom I have had the pleasure of working. Also, a thanks to Scott Clark, Microsoft BSG Manager in the Gulf Coast District, for your friendship and support during my time at Microsoft. Additional thanks to my parents, Bobby and Gwen Thompson, my children, Christopher, Sara, and Michael, my cousins Clay and Laura, Laura's husband Robert, and my Aunt Jackie for their continued moral support. A special thanks to the Microsoft Press team for their continued patience as deadlines sped past. And a final thanks to my wife, Kristy. I love you.

Jamie Reding

I would like to thank both Ed Whalen and Marci Garcia. As always, it is a wonderful experience working with you. I would also like to thank Steve DeLuca for his insight and contributions to Microsoft and this work. I would also like to extend my admiration and gratitude to my parents, Jack and Karen Reding. Without all your support and love I would not be where I am today. Finally, a very special thank you to my wife, Sharon, and my sons, Alex and Jackson, for their support over the years. Hey guys, you are the best!

Introduction

Since its introduction in 1989, Microsoft SQL Server has steadily gained in popularity. It has gradually moved from the desktop, to the workgroup, and finally to the enterprise computer room. SQL Server 2000 continues the tradition, gaining even greater acceptance into the data center. With SQL Server's growth in popularity comes a greater responsibility for the database administrator and application designer. Because these systems service hundreds or thousands of users in mission-critical functions, the systems need to be well-tuned. In addition, although a workgroup can sometimes get away with a lack of capacity planning, the enterprise cannot. It is unacceptable for a mission-critical enterprise server to run out of capacity with little or no notice. This has led to a new demand for sizing and capacity planning.

SQL Server 2000 is easy to configure and manage, and under many conditions is self-tuning. No matter how smart the database engine is, however, it cannot compensate for an application that is doing unnecessary work or for malformed indexes. Therefore, in addition to showing you how to tune the SQL Server engine itself, this book teaches you how to properly configure your I/O subsystem and tune your applications.

Who Should Use This Book

We have written this book with the intent of appealing to both the seasoned SQL Server administrator and the novice. We hope that for the experienced database administrator the information contained within this book will be a valuable reference and a resource for new ideas. For the novice, we hope that this book will show you how to debug and tune a SQL Server system. Some assumptions were made about the knowledge of the reader, however. Thus, a novice should use this book in conjunction with a SQL Server book, such as the *Microsoft SQL Server 2000 Administrator's Companion*, which was also written by some of the authors of this book.

Regardless of whether you are an experienced SQL Server user, a database administrator, or a consultant, we feel that this book has something to offer you. We hope that you enjoy this book and find the information valuable.

What Is in This Book

Part I, "Basic Concepts," begins with how to tune the SQL Server engine and the server system that it is running on. This section of the book includes the basics upon which the remainder of the book is built. These chapters are intended to give you an insight into how SQL Server works as well as the proper configuration and use of the underlying hardware and OS platform. This section also includes an in-depth tour of the tools available to the database administrator for discovering performance problems and configuring the system.

Part II, "Sizing and Capacity Planning," is a collection of chapters that teach you about the interesting world of sizing and capacity planning. These chapters provide the basics as well as advanced sizing and capacity planning topics as they walk through several sizing and capacity planning scenarios.

Part III, "Configuring and Tuning the System," provides specific information on configuring and tuning the most common types of SQL Server systems. These include online transaction processing (OLTP) systems, data warehouses, replicated systems, and high-performance backup and recovery systems.

Part IV, "Tuning SQL Statements," focuses on creating and tuning applications. This section includes chapters on tuning SQL statements, effectively using indexes and stored procedures, and using hints to improve performance. This section concludes the main portion of the book.

Part V consists of two appendixes designed as quick places to look up useful SQL Server information. Appendix A covers the SQL Server configuration options. Appendix B consists of the SQL Server Performance Monitor counters. This section also includes a glossary of terms used throughout this book.

Some Conventions Used in This Book

The following icons provide you with signposts to certain types of information throughout the book:

Note A note underscores the importance of a specific concept or highlights a special case.

More Info This is a cross reference to another section of the book or other reference material.

Caution This advises readers that failure to take or avoid a specified action could be bad news for their users, systems, data integrity, and so forth.

Tip This element indicates time-saving strategic advice.

Enjoy This Book!

This book has involved a lot of effort by many people, including a great editorial staff. We have striven to make this the best possible book that we could based on the combined experience of SQL Server experts both at Microsoft and in the field. We truly hope that you enjoy this book and that it is useful in your daily work.

Part I
Basic Concepts

Chapter 1
Performance Tuning, Capacity Planning, and Sizing Overview

Performance tuning, capacity planning, and sizing are exciting subjects, offering a great deal of variety and new learning experiences. The tasks are constantly changing, as are the software and hardware. Microsoft SQL Server 2000 includes many new enhancements, improvements, and features designed to allow more complex data analysis, greater scalability, and increased functionality. New central processing unit (CPU) chips or new system designs can complicate the equation.

Performance tuning can be challenging, exciting, and frustrating. Sometimes there is an easy solution to a performance problem; sometimes there is no solution. Another challenge always lies ahead, because your system load and applications are always changing.

Sizing and capacity planning present their own challenges. Not only must you project system capacity needs based on sometimes incomplete and inaccurate data, but you must also project anticipated workloads based on estimates of user needs. Incorrectly sizing a system can cause performance problems that lead to a frustrated and unhappy user community. As workloads and the amount of data stored in the database increase, it becomes much more important to properly size and tune these systems.

This chapter introduces the concepts and rationale behind performance tuning, sizing, and capacity planning. First we define performance tuning and introduce the three components to consider when fully tuning a SQL Server system. Then we talk briefly about sizing and capacity planning. Finally we discuss an effective performance tuning methodology and offer some tuning tips and recommendations.

Performance Tuning and Optimization

Performance tuning is the act of altering the performance of a system by modifying system parameters (software tuning) or by altering a system's configuration (hardware tuning). Performance tuning involves a detailed analysis of the hardware configuration, the operating system and relational database management system (RDBMS) configuration, and the applications that access those components.

One of the main goals in tuning a system is to remove bottlenecks, or performance-limiting components. These components can be hardware or software and can severely affect performance in an otherwise properly configured and tuned system. There might be one or more bottlenecks in your system, or none at all.

To effectively tune a system you must follow a specific set of steps, or methodology. You must also look at all components of the system, including applications, hardware, and SQL Server. We'll start with a look at the various components involved in tuning a system, and turn the focus to methodology later in this chapter.

Application Tuning

Application tuning is usually the first step in tuning a SQL Server system, because an application is the most likely component to cause a performance problem. Also, an application is usually fairly easy to monitor and is sometimes easy to modify to achieve greater efficiency. When you tune an application first, you can then tune the hardware and SQL Server knowing that your application is not using excessive resources. In addition, an application is more likely to change, especially if you develop your own application. Each time an application evolves there is potential for new performance problems, and new opportunities for optimization.

Application tuning involves analyzing structured query language (SQL) statements and determining if the corresponding queries are efficient. Inefficient queries usually use excessive system resources and take an excessive amount of time to run. By tuning these SQL statements and the way the application accesses the database, you can dramatically improve how a system performs. The majority of SQL tuning falls into two categories; modifying the data access method and improving the execution plan.

Modifying the Data Access Method

Modifying the data access method might involve changing the object that SQL Server uses to retrieve the requested data, for example, using a hint in the SQL statement to request the query optimizer to use a particular index; or it might involve modifying the SQL statement itself. For example, by adding predicates to the WHERE clause you might be able to use an index lookup rather than an index scan. You might reduce the number records that SQL Server must search through in order to retrieve the requested data. All of these concepts are covered later in this book in detail.

Improving the Execution Plan

You can also improve the performance of SQL statements by modifying the actual method of execution, for example, by changing the join operation, changing the join order, or both. SQL Server 2000 offers three join operations: nested loops, merge, and hash joins. In many cases, changing the join operation involves a trade-off. For example, the hash join typically executes using many fewer input/output operations (I/Os) than the nested loops join, but at the cost of much more CPU time spent performing the join.

SQL Server Tuning

SQL Server tuning and hardware tuning are closely related. SQL Server tuning involves modifying the way SQL Server allocates resources and how it functions by modifying its configuration parameters. Some of the configuration parameters are related to the use of resources; others are not. Those that are related to resource use are closely tied to the hardware resources available within a system. These parameters must be modified based on the type and number of hardware resources available within the system.

For example, a system with multiple processors, such as a symmetric multiprocessing (SMP) system, might perform better with more SQL Server threads than a single-processor system would. A system with a lot of memory available should have SQL Server tuned to take advantage of that additional memory. The I/O parameters should be modified to take advantage of the type of I/O system present on the system. SQL Server tuning and hardware tuning involve providing sufficient resources for the expected workload.

Hardware Tuning

Hardware tuning, which is the act of providing sufficient hardware resources for the expected workload, lies midway between sizing and capacity planning. To tune system hardware, you must determine which resources can be allocated to SQL Server to provide better performance. This might involve the addition of memory, CPUs, I/O resources, or a combination of all of these. Much of the effort in tuning a SQL Server system involves determining which resources must be added and in what amounts.

Many typical performance problems are caused by insufficient or misconfigured hardware components. The I/O subsystem is a critical component of database performance tuning. By providing sufficient CPU, memory, and I/O resources, you can avoid many performance problems. As we discuss in Chapter 3, "Understanding the I/O Subsystem and RAID" and Chapters 8 through 11 in Part II, "Sizing and Capacity Planning," a poorly sized and configured I/O subsystem can cause severe performance degradation.

Sizing and Capacity Planning

Capacity planning involves planning for the capacity of a system in order to maintain the level of service expected by the user community, and has two parts: precapacity planning and postcapacity planning. *Precapacity planning* involves capacity planning on a system not yet built, and *postcapacity planning* involves capacity planning on a system already in service.

Precapacity planning, or *sizing,* involves anticipating the needed resources for a system based on an anticipated workload. This workload might or might not be accurately represented, depending on the quality of the available data. In some cases you might get very reliable data on the workload, for example, when an existing system is running the same or similar workload. In other cases the data is roughly estimated on paper. The quality of the sizing results depends largely on the quality of the input data.

Sizing is important, since a new system will be expected to meet the terms of a service level agreement (SLA). The SLA is a contract between the service provider (the Information Systems department) and the customer (your users) for a minimum level of service. This contract usually specifies maximum acceptable response times as well as the number and types of users to be serviced. To meet the SLA, you must purchase and configure a sufficient amount of hardware and software to provide for the specified user load, and you must also provide additional capacity for peak utilization periods. An inability to meet the SLA might cost your company time and revenue.

Postcapacity planning, or *predictive analysis,* is a complex and ongoing performance study of hardware and software resource consumption on a system that is set up and running. It is used to project resource consumption to plan for system capacity increases as needed. By anticipating these needs and acting before they become critical, you save both time and money. As with sizing, predictive analysis is only as good as the data used to perform the study. The better the input data, the better the results.

Capacity planning and sizing are complex tasks that can be both frustrating and rewarding. This book will explain what is involved in sizing a system from scratch, as well as how to perform capacity planning on existing systems. We hope that you find capacity planning and sizing as challenging and rewarding as we do.

Server Tuning Methodology

A *performance tuning methodology* is a series of steps that maximize your efficiency at solving performance problems on your system. In this section we introduce a tuning methodology that we use. The process of tuning a system is based on individual preference—you might have your own structured way of tuning, and that's fine. We offer these steps as guidelines and recommend that you adapt them to fit your needs.

Tuning Steps

We follow these steps to improve system performance in an organized manner:

1. Determine the problem.
2. Formulate a potential solution to the problem.
3. Implement the solution.
4. Analyze the results.

With these steps you can identify and solve the performance problems that you might encounter. We also present a few tips and guidelines after discussing this methodology.

Determine the Problem

Before starting to tune a system, you must determine if it has any existing performance problems. It is a waste of time and a bad idea to tune a system that is running well. You can determine if a system has a performance problem in several ways. The easiest and possibly the best way is to listen to the user community, which is a barometer of system performance. Users can tell you if the system performance has slowed and can identify which specific applications or queries are performing poorly.

Note   When interviewing users, take notes. Even if you conclude from the interview that the system is performing well, a record can be valuable. Record the date and time, the applications the user runs, and how the user feels about the performance of the system. Ask pointed questions, such as, "Are response times good? Is the system performing well?" Record this information in a logbook for future reference.

Another good method of determining whether a system's performance is degrading is to use System Monitor in the Windows 2000 Performance console. Data from System Monitor can be captured and saved for future use. By regularly creating performance logs, you can compare performance from one week to the next. Look for changes in key parameters such as CPU usage and I/O usage. An increase in CPU usage could indicate an increased load on the system, which could lead to performance problems.

Another method of checking SQL Server performance is to compile a series of test queries and run them at regular intervals, which allows you to compare a system's responsiveness over time. If the response times increase over time, your system might need tuning or postcapacity planning.

Finally, one of the best ways to determine if performance is degrading is to set up system specific monitoring by storing performance data in a database for long-term analysis. In addition, adding application-specific data collection to your application can provide invaluable information. Changes in the response times of your application can indicate performance problems.

Once you have determined that you have a problem, you must identify what kind of problem it is. Performance problems can consist of one or more of the following:

- **Hardware problems**   Hardware components could be malfunctioning. Faulty components can cause severe performance problems.
- **Hardware capacity**   You might be exceeding the capacity of the system components. You might need postcapacity planning or to reconfigure existing hardware.
- **Software tuning problems**   The system might be mistuned. Tuning SQL Server or Microsoft Windows 2000 might solve the problem.
- **Application problems**   SQL statements might be inefficient, causing excessive usage of system resources.

How to determine if you have one or more of these problems is the heart of this book.

Formulate a Potential Solution to the Problem

Once you've identified a performance problem, it is time to formulate a hypothesis about how to solve it. At this stage you might have an idea how to solve the problem, or you might be creating tests to help further isolate the problem. It is not necessary to know exactly how to solve the problem; in fact, often at this point you will not yet know what the cause of the problem is.

A key element of formulating the solution is to have an idea of what the solution should accomplish, so you will be able to judge its success. Here are a couple examples. Suppose you have analyzed your system and determined that the I/O subsystem is causing a bottleneck. By modifying the I/O subsystem, you should anticipate a change in system performance, which would verify that the problem is actually with the I/O subsystem. If modifying the I/O subsystem does not change the performance of the system, perhaps the problem lies elsewhere.

Similarly, if you determine that the problem lies with the application, you should be able to anticipate how changes will affect the system. It is important to anticipate the effect of a change and verify that it improves or degrades system performance. Not every change that you make will be for the best, and sometimes you will have to reverse your changes to return to the original system performance.

This process doesn't have to be a big deal. Just think about the problem, the proposed changes, and how these changes should affect the performance of your system. This will lead to easier analysis of the results and better tests.

Implement the Solution

Implementing the solution involves putting into action the proposed changes from the previous step and observing the results. It might be difficult to determine how the solution actually affects the system, but by gathering as much data as possible you might be able to infer the results.

Implementing the solution might instantly improve the system or might moderately change the performance characteristics. Documenting any noticeable changes will enable you to determine the long-term effects of the change. We recommend making only one change at a time. If you make multiple changes to a system, improvements and degradations might cancel each other out, preventing you from learning anything from your tests.

Note It is very important to thoroughly test modifications to the application or the system before putting those changes into production. It is much better to spend the time up front testing thoroughly than fixing a problem that has been introduced into the system and making matters worse.

Analyze the Results

The final step in this tuning methodology is to analyze the results of your changes, documenting the changes you made as well as what you expected from each change and how it actually affected the system. This analysis will help you determine whether your hypothesis is correct and whether the change improves performance.

Whether your original hypothesis is correct is important, but equally important is whether you learn anything. An incorrect hypothesis can provide valuable information about the problem. As long as the result of the test provides information, the test is worthwhile.

By following this type of methodology you can effectively tune a system in an organized, structured way. Organization, logical changes, and documentation make the difference between effective and ineffective tuning.

Tuning Tips and Recommendations

In this section we present tips and recommendations for more effectively tuning your system. As we mentioned earlier, organization is the key to effective tuning.

Document Everything

Documentation is an important part of database performance tuning and capacity planning. Documentation should be clear and concise and should consist of the following components:

- **Hardware configuration** This information should be complete so that it is possible to reproduce the system if necessary (this is also necessary for disaster recovery). Include details such as hardware components, redundant array of inexpensive disks (RAID) configuration, and file system layout.

- **Software components** Keep a list of the software components that are installed on the system. This should include software component revisions as well as all service packs.

- **Configuration changes** Whenever you make configuration changes to the hardware, Windows 2000, or SQL Server, keep a record in your server's logbook. You might want to note why the change was made.

- **Performance notes** Log any significant changes to system performance. This might be valuable information, and from it patterns might begin to emerge.

Regularly documenting system changes and logging the system configuration are habits that can really pay off in the long run.

Change One Thing at a Time

It is always a good idea to change only one thing at a time, and it is vital to document your changes. Doing so enables you to determine which changes improve system performance and which changes degrade it. We realize, of course, that this suggestion is often very difficult to follow. If performance has degraded to a critical state, it is often necessary to use what we call a "shotgun approach," in which multiple components are upgraded simultaneously. By upgrading several components at a time you have a good chance of improving performance, but you might not learn anything about what caused the problem. A shotgun approach might also turn out to consist of two or more components that cancel each other out, thus providing no performance improvement at all.

Don't Panic

It is easy for performance problems to escalate into an emergency. By remaining calm, however, you can avoid costly mistakes. Sometimes it is better to walk away from the problem for a few hours and get some rest rather than to make a mistake that might add to the problem. Don't be afraid to solicit help if you need it. Taking on a problem that you are not prepared to handle might lead to more problems. Here are a few tips for getting through emergencies:

- Don't panic, even if others become overexcited.
- Verify the problem. Don't just jump in based on what others tell you.
- Be cautious. Rushing to solve the problem can result in mistakes that can be even worse than the original problem.
- Don't work on little or no sleep. This is a disaster waiting to happen. It is better to fix problems when you are alert and can think coherently.
- Document everything. Documentation might save you in the long run.

Don't Be Afraid to Get Help

Sometimes performance problems can get you into trouble that you cannot get out of by yourself. If that happens, don't be afraid to call in outside specialists. Performance problems can be difficult to solve and might require solutions that you can't implement safely on your own. By leveraging the experience of performance experts, you are most likely to be able not only to solve the problem more easily, but also to learn a great deal. Calling in extra help is not necessarily a sign of weakness, but is often a sign of wisdom.

Summary

This chapter introduced performance tuning, capacity planning, and sizing, giving you a brief glimpse of what this book is all about. Throughout the book we will show you how to accomplish the tuning tasks—application tuning, hardware tuning, and software tuning—that we introduced here.

Each area of tuning is important to the big picture and should be approached using a logical methodology. Keep in mind that not all problems are immediately solvable. Don't forget to document your work and to remain calm. Organization, logical changes, and documentation make the difference between effective and ineffective tuning. Performance tuning in conjunction with capacity planning and sizing will allow you to design, implement, and maintain a smoothly operating, well-running system.

The next chapter provides information concerning the internal architecture of SQL Server 2000 as a foundation for tuning your system.

Chapter 2
SQL Server 2000 Architecture Fundamentals

To best understand Microsoft SQL Server 2000, you need to know its internal architecture—how things work; how it behaves. This knowledge will make you more comfortable with SQL Server and better able to make decisions about its configuration. This chapter explains several important architectural topics that will help you configure, tune, and understand your system.

SQL Server 2000 maintains several major architectural improvements that were introduced in SQL Server 7.0; specifically in memory management, data storage, locking, thread management, the transaction log, and the backup and restore architecture. We discuss each of these topics in detail in this chapter. For information on specific performance enhancements that are completely new for SQL Server 2000, see Chapter 5, "New Features and Performance Enhancements."

Memory Management

Memory management in SQL Server 2000 requires little or no user intervention. By default, SQL Server dynamically allocates and deallocates memory as needed for optimal performance, according to the amount of physical memory available. You can override this behavior if necessary. This section discusses some basic memory concepts, how SQL Server uses memory, and how you can configure memory for SQL Server according to your needs.

Concepts: Physical and Virtual Memory

Your Microsoft Windows NT or Windows 2000 operating system uses the physical memory in the machine, or random access memory (RAM). These operating systems also support *virtual memory*, which allows applications such as SQL Server to use logical representations of memory, or logical addresses, instead of physical memory addresses. The operating system maps these logical addresses to physical memory addresses, which allows the operating system to move code or data around in physical memory as necessary without affecting the application. The intent of virtual memory is to hide the internal management of physical memory from the application.

The operating system also creates a virtual-memory page file (or swap file) located on a disk drive, which it can use as an extension to the physical memory. The amount of physical memory plus the size of the page file equals the total amount of virtual memory available to the system. For example, if you have 512 MB of RAM and a page file on disk of 512 MB, then 1 GB of logical address space is available for use by your applications: half of it resides in physical memory, and half of it resides on disk. The applications do not need information about where their data is stored, whether in physical memory or in the page file—the operating system handles that layer of intelligence.

Data is accessed in memory and on disk in units called *pages*. Eventually, the available physical memory will be filled up with data pages. When that occurs, and the operating system needs space to read a new data page into physical memory, it locates a page of data that has been sitting in memory for a period of time without being referenced by an application (an *aged* page), and writes that page to the page file on disk to free up space in memory for the new page. The aged page is swapped out of memory and stored on disk. If that aged page is referenced later, the operating system reads it back into memory from the page file; that is, it swaps the page from disk into memory.

Moving data between the page file and physical memory is known as *swapping* or *paging* and is handled by the operating system. Since I/O (read or write) operations to disk are more expensive than are accesses to memory, in terms of time and processing overhead, swapping is not desirable. SQL Server is designed to avoid swapping pages, which is discussed later in this section. First, we'll discuss how SQL Server uses memory.

SQL Server Memory Architecture

SQL Server allocates its total virtual memory for two main components: executable code and the memory pool, as shown in Figure 2-1. Executable code includes the SQL Server engine, executable files and dynamic link libraries (DLLs) for Open Data Services, and server Net-Library DLLs. Other components load their own DLLs and allocate memory themselves—these include OLE Automation objects, distributed query OLE DB providers, and extended stored procedures. The *memory pool* is an area of memory from which the following objects are allocated: system-level data structures, buffer cache, procedure cache, log cache, and connection context. System-level data structures hold data that is global to the SQL Server instance, such as the lock table and database descriptors. The *buffer cache* is used to store data and index pages that have been read from the database, so that if those pages are accessed again (either read or written to), they can be found in cache instead of having to be read from disk a second time. The *procedure cache* holds the execution plans, which can be reused, for *Transact-SQL* statements and stored procedures. The *log cache* is used to hold pages read from and written to the log. (There is one log cache for each database's log.) The *connection context* is a set of data structures that record the current state of a connection, such as the parameters used for a stored procedure or the tables being accessed.

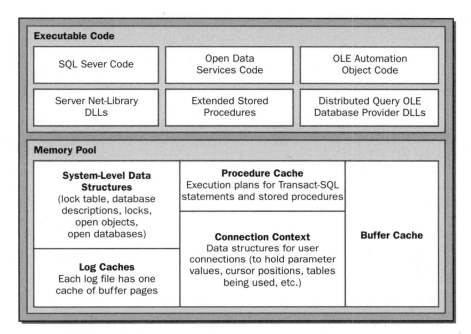

Figure 2-1. *Breakdown of SQL Server address space.*

The size of the data structures and connection context areas of the memory pool are determined by user requests. Data structures are allocated when a new database is defined or when a table or view is referenced. And when a user connects to SQL Server, memory for its connection context is allocated. The other three sections of the memory pool—buffer cache, procedure cache, and log cache—are adjusted dynamically by SQL Server for optimization. For example, if it needs more memory for the procedure cache to hold stored procedure execution plans, SQL Server dynamically increases the total size of the memory pool by allocating more of the available physical memory in the system. If no physical memory is available, SQL Server reduces the size of the buffer cache by freeing up pages to give them to the procedure cache. SQL Server can change the size of the procedure cache, the log cache, and the buffer cache in this manner as needed to optimize performance. It attempts to obtain more space from the available physical memory before taking it from the procedure, log, or buffer caches. Once physical memory is used up, SQL Server adjusts these objects in the memory pool as needed. You do not have to specify a fixed amount of space for each of these objects, although you can specify minimum and maximum limits for the entire memory pool size.

How the Buffer Cache Works

Each instance of SQL Server has a singly linked list that contains the addresses of pages that are initially free—available for use. These pages make up the buffer cache (also known as the *data cache*). When SQL Server first starts up, all pages in the buffer cache are free. As processing begins and SQL Server reads a page from disk, that page is stored in the first page of the buffer cache's free list. If another process (or the same process) must read or modify the same page, it can read the page from or modify it in the buffer cache, instead of performing physical I/Os to the disk. The buffer cache speeds read and write performance by accessing the pages in memory, which is a less resource-expensive operation than accessing pages on disk.

Each buffer page contains header information about the page. This header holds a reference counter and an indicator of whether the page is dirty or not. A *dirty* page is one that has been modified in the buffer cache but whose changes have not yet been written to disk. Each time a page is referenced in the buffer cache by a SQL statement, its reference counter is incremented by one. Periodically, the buffer cache is scanned and the reference counter is divided by four, with the remainder discarded. If the result of the division is zero, the page has been referenced fewer than three times since the last scan, and the dirty page indicator is set for that page. This indicator causes the page to be added to the free list. If the page has been modified, its modifications are first written to disk; otherwise, if the page had only been read, then it will simply be freed without being written to disk. Basically, as more buffer pages are needed for new data pages to be read in, the least frequently referenced pages will be freed.

When SQL Server is running on Windows NT or Windows 2000, the work of scanning the buffer cache is performed by individual worker threads during the time interval between the scheduling of an asynchronous read operation and the completion of that read. The worker threads also write dirty pages to disk and add pages to the free list. These write operations are also performed asynchronously so they do not interfere with the thread's ability to complete its asynchronous read.

Another SQL Server thread called the *lazywriter* periodically checks to see that the free buffer list does not fall below a specific size (depending on the size of the buffer cache). If the free list has fallen below that size, the lazywriter scans the cache, reclaims unused pages, and frees dirty pages with a reference counter set to zero. On Windows NT and Windows 2000, most of the work is done by the individual threads mentioned above, so the lazywriter does not have much work to do. But in very I/O-intensive systems, the lazywriter is needed to help maintain the free list. Because Windows 98 does not support asynchronous write operations, the lazywriter performs all the work of freeing buffer pages and writing the dirty pages to disk. (The checkpoint thread also helps write out modified buffer pages but does not free those pages; see the "What is a Checkpoint?" section later in this chapter.)

Caching describes the process of storing data in memory. Data "gets cached" or it is "in cache." The buffer cache is allocated from the physical RAM in the system. Data access is much faster when the data can be found in the buffer cache; therefore, you want SQL Server to have the most memory possible for its buffer cache. Of course, if you already have enough RAM in your system so that all the database tables and indexes reside in cache, then adding more RAM would not be necessary as it would not improve the performance of SQL Server (although it might help other non-database applications running on the system). SQL Server attempts to use memory in such a way as to minimize costly disk I/O.

Dynamic and Manual Memory Configuration

SQL Server 2000 can manage memory dynamically based on the memory settings you choose, which we describe in this section. Dynamic memory management means that SQL Server automatically allocates and deallocates memory for its memory pool as necessary. As users connect and run queries, SQL Server allocates memory to the memory pool to support the workload. It allocates memory from the available physical memory in the system (if there is any available). SQL Server can also deallocate memory from the memory pool, freeing it for other applications to use. If no other applications are requesting memory, however, SQL Server maintains its memory pool at the current size, even if there are unused pages; it deallocates memory only if it is needed by another process.

To avoid excessive paging (some paging by the operating system is normal), SQL Server maintains its virtual memory space at 4 to 10 MB less than available physical memory, so it is never bigger than physical memory. This allows SQL Server to have the largest memory pool possible while preventing SQL Server pages from swapping to the page file on disk. If the 4 to 10 MB of available memory is consumed by some other application, SQL Server deallocates more of its memory pool to keep 4 to 10 MB free physical memory on the system at all times. If the application then releases some memory, and SQL Server needs it, SQL Server reallocates the memory (still leaving 4 to 10 MB of free physical memory).

If additional applications running on the same machine as SQL Server require memory, SQL Server frees up memory for them from its memory pool. Other applications might attempt to steal memory from SQL Server's total memory pool. To combat this, you can set a minimum size for the memory pool by configuring the *min server memory* option so that SQL Server does not release memory if doing so causes the pool to fall below that size. For example, to ensure that SQL Server always has at least 256 MB of memory, set *min server memory* to 256. (This option is in megabytes.)

You might also want to put a maximum limit on the SQL Server memory pool so that other applications are ensured a certain amount of memory that cannot be used by SQL Server. The option for this is *max server memory*. For example, to tell SQL Server not to use more than 512 MB of memory, set *max server memory* to 512. (This option is also in megabytes.)

When other applications are running on the same system as SQL Server, avoid configuring SQL Server memory settings in a manner that causes excessive paging on the system. For example, if you set the *min server memory* option too high, other applications might have to page. Use System Monitor in the Windows 2000 Performance console to view the Memory object's Pages/sec counter to determine how much paging is occurring on the system. A low number of occasional pages per second is normal (bouncing between 0 and 100, for example), but a continuously high number of pages per second indicates a paging problem that is slowing down the performance of your system. If you cannot avoid excessive paging by adjusting the SQL Server memory options, you need to put more physical memory in the machine.

We recommend that you allow SQL Server to configure its memory usage dynamically by leaving these two memory options unchanged, at their defaults. Again, this is best when you have a dedicated machine for SQL Server and the memory size will not change much. When other applications demand memory on the server, you might need to adjust these options. But even with a minimum or maximum memory size configured, SQL Server dynamically adjusts memory as needed without violating the upper or lower limits. To force SQL Server to allocate a fixed amount of memory, set the *min server memory* and *max server memory* options to the same value. SQL Server allocates memory as needed up to the maximum configured value (or actually, up to the maximum memory available, because you could set the minimum value to a value that is greater than the physical memory the system actually has). SQL Server releases physical memory only if another application needs some, at which point SQL Server has to page to maintain its total virtual memory size (to maintain the *min server memory* size). Again, you do not want SQL Server to page, so do not set the fixed memory size too large for your system. Leave some memory free for other applications when necessary.

Min server memory and *max server memory* are both advanced options in SQL Server. To set them by using the stored procedure *sp_configure*, you must first enable the option *show advanced options* as follows:

```
sp_configure "show advanced options", 1
go
sp_configure "max server memory", 512
go
RECONFIGURE WITH OVERRIDE
go
```

Note   If you change a configuration value for an option that does not require SQL Server to be restarted, you must run the RECONFIGURE statement for the new value to take effect as the *run value* (the value SQL Server will use while running).

Alternatively, you can configure the memory settings through SQL Server Enterprise Manager. To do this, open Enterprise Manager, expand the servers, right-click the server you want, and click Properties on the shortcut menu to open the SQL Server Properties dialog box. On the Memory tab, you can set the minimum and maximum server memory values, or leave them at the default values.

Again, we recommend that you allow SQL Server to configure memory dynamically by leaving the memory options set to their default values if you have a server dedicated to SQL Server. This memory management strategy is designed to improve SQL Server memory usage and to relieve the database administrator (DBA) of memory configuration worries.

Memory Sizes Supported

The Microsoft Windows 2000 operating system is available in several editions—Windows 2000 Professional, Windows 2000 Server, Windows 2000 Advanced Server, and Windows 2000 Datacenter Server. These versions support various memory sizes to be used by SQL Server. The standard address space of 32-bit Windows 2000 supports 4 GB of memory, of which 2 GB is allocated for user processes and 2 GB is reserved for system use. This 2-GB limit represents the maximum amount of memory that can be allocated for SQL Server.

Windows 2000 Professional Edition supports up to 2 GB maximum. The three other editions allow much larger memory sizes, but you must be running SQL Server 2000 Enterprise or Developer Edition to take advantage of the memory with SQL Server. Also, with Windows 2000 Server (as well as in Windows NT 4.0 Enterprise Edition), you can increase the amount of virtual memory for a process to 3 GB. A user process (such as SQL Server) can be allotted up to 3 GB of virtual memory, and the system allocation is reduced to 1 GB. This increase in virtual memory allotted to processes allows you to increase the size of the SQL Server memory pool dramatically (up to nearly 3 GB). To enable this support, you must add the flag */3GB* to the boot line in the Boot.ini file, which you can open through the System icon in the Control Panel.

Windows 2000 Advanced Server supports up to 8 GB of memory, and Windows 2000 Datacenter Server up to 64 GB. See Table 2-1 for the amount of RAM supported by the various editions of the operating system in combination with the edition of SQL Server 2000. This table shows the maximum amounts of memory supported by each operating system, and the version of SQL Server you would need to take advantage of that memory.

Table 2-1. Supported Memory Sizes

Operating System	SQL Server Enterprise Edition	SQL Server Standard Edition	SQL Server Personal Edition	SQL Server Developer's Edition
Windows 2000 Datacenter Server	64 GB	2 GB	2 GB	64 GB
Windows 2000 Advanced Server	8 GB	2 GB	2 GB	8 GB
Windows 2000 Server	4 GB	2 GB	2 GB	4 GB
Windows 2000 Professional	Not supported	Not supported	2 GB	2 GB

To allow applications on Windows 2000 Advanced Server and Datacenter Server to address more than 4 GB, these editions support Address Windowing Extensions (AWE). AWE is a set of extensions to the Microsoft Win32 API that allows memory-intensive applications to address more memory than the 32-bit address space typically allows. AWE allows physical memory pages above the standard 4 GB memory space to be acquired by applications as nonpaged memory and maps views of the nonpaged memory to the 32-bit address space. To allow AWE with Windows 2000, you must add the */PAE* flag to the Boot.ini file. If you have between 4 GB and 16 GB in your system, you can also add the /3GB flag to the Boot file to allow only 1 GB of virtual memory space for the operating system, instead of 2 GB. But if you have more than 16 GB in the system, do not use /3GB in the Boot file, because Windows 2000 needs the 2 GB of virtual memory address space—otherwise it will not use the memory above 16 GB. Table 2-2 shows the Boot.ini flags needed for various memory sizes as examples. See the "AWE Enabled" section in Chapter 4, "System Tuning," for information about setting the SQL Server configuration flags to enable AWE usage. This flag must be set for SQL Server to make use of AWE.

Table 2-2. Flags for Memory Usage

Amount of system Memory	Flag to Add to Boot.ini file
4 GB	/3GB
8 GB	/3GB /PAE
16 GB	/3GB /PAE
Above 16 GB (16 GB to 64 GB)	/PAE

Data Storage

SQL Server 2000 maintains the same data storage architecture that was redesigned for SQL Server 7.0. Files and filegroups have replaced devices and segments that existed in SQL Server 6.5 and earlier. Rows, pages, and extents of data have changed characteristics; tables and indexes have also evolved. All these changes that were geared toward improving the efficiency and performance of SQL Server 7.0 continue in SQL Server 2000. The following sections describe each of these data storage entities in detail.

Data Files and Log Files

SQL Server 2000 maps each database to a set of operating system files, which we simply refer to as *files*. Files can reside on a Windows 2000 file system (NTFS) or file allocation table (FAT) file system (raw partitions are not recommended), but cannot reside on a compressed file system. A file is made up of smaller units of data called *pages*, which we discuss in more detail in the next section. Each file is given a logical name and a physical name when created in SQL Server. The logical name is used to refer to the file in all Transact-SQL statements. The physical name is the path to the location of the physical file. SQL Server uses the following three categories of files for databases:

- **Primary data files** A primary data file contains startup information for a database, points to the other files used by the database, stores system tables and objects, and can also store database data and objects. Each database has exactly one primary file. The recommended file extension for a primary data file is .mdf.

- **Secondary data files** Secondary data files are optional for each database. They can be used to hold data and objects, such as tables and indexes, that are not in the primary file. A database might not have any secondary files, if all its data is placed in the primary file. On the other hand, a database might need one or more secondary files placed on separate disks to spread data across the disks. The recommended file extension is .ndf.

- **Log files** A log file holds all the transaction log information for the database, and cannot be used to hold any other data. Every database has at least one log file, and can have multiple log files. The recommended file extension is .ldf.

A simple, small database might consist of only the primary data file and one log file. A larger, more complex database might consist of the primary data file, three secondary data files, and two log files. See Figures 2-2 and 2-3 for representations of the files that make up a simple and then a more complex version of a sample Accounting database.

Primary Data File = Acct_primary (←Logical Name)
`C:\MSSQL2000\Data\Acct_primary.mdf` (←Physical Name)

Log File = Log_file1
`D:\MSSQL2000\Log\Log_file1.ldf`

Figure 2-2. *A simple Accounting database.*

Primary Data File = Acct_primary (←Logical Name)
`C:\MSSQL2000\Data\Acct_primary.mdf` (←Physical Name)

Secondary Data File 1 = Acct_data1
`E:\MSSQL2000\Data\Acct_data1.ndf`

Secondary Data File 2 = Acct_data2
`F:\MSSQL2000\Data\Acct_data2.ndf`

Log File 1 = Log_file1
`G:\MSSQL2000\Log\Log_file1.ldf`

Figure 2-3. *A more complex Accounting database.*

Note   A SQL Server database can accommodate maximum file sizes of 32 terabytes (TB) for data files and 4 TB for log files.

Filegroups and File Placement

If you create a database with one or more secondary data files, you might also want to create user-defined filegroups for those files. Filegroups provide a way to group secondary files together for data placement purposes, similar to the grouping of database devices with segments in versions of SQL Server earlier than 7.0. You indicate which secondary files are part of each filegroup when creating the database. You can alter the database later to add a filegroup and a new file, but you cannot move a file from one filegroup to another after the file has already been created without recreating the database.

When creating database objects, such as tables and indexes, you can specify in which filegroup to place those objects to locate those objects on specific disks or disk arrays that correspond to the physical location of the files in the filegroup. When you do this, the table or index data is spread across all of the files that are a part of that filegroup. You might have only one secondary file in a filegroup or many files. The purpose is the same in both cases—to place data on specific drives and to optimize disk performance. Figure 2-4 shows a representation of the Accounting database using a filegroup named Acct_fg to group the two secondary data files together.

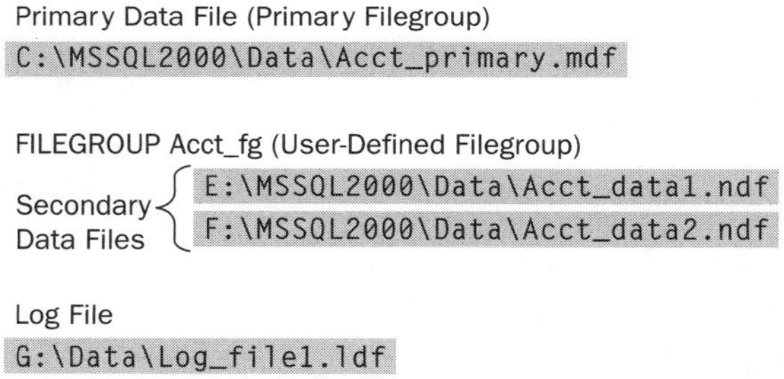

Primary Data File (Primary Filegroup)
```
C:\MSSQL2000\Data\Acct_primary.mdf
```

FILEGROUP Acct_fg (User-Defined Filegroup)

Secondary
Data Files
```
E:\MSSQL2000\Data\Acct_data1.ndf
F:\MSSQL2000\Data\Acct_data2.ndf
```

Log File
```
G:\Data\Log_file1.ldf
```

Figure 2-4. *Using a filegroup with the Accounting database.*

Let's look at another example of working with filegroups. Let's say you have two disk arrays for data—one array of four disks and one array of two disks. (See Chapter 3, "Understanding the I/O Subsystem and RAID," for a discussion of RAID and disk arrays.) You also have two tables to create, Table1 and Table2. Table1 is heavily accessed as read-only data, and that access is sometimes sequential. Table2 is updated only about once a minute, and therefore it is not accessed as often as Table1. You might want to place these tables on separate disks; for example, placing Table1 on the four-disk array and Table2 on the two-disk array. This allows more disks to perform the high number of reads to Table1, and maintain the sequential access, while keeping the writes to Table2 from interrupting. This arrangement also allows two dedicated disks for the updates to Table2.

To perform this kind of table placement, you must create a different filegroup with its own secondary files on each disk array. You can then create the tables on the appropriate filegroup, as shown in Figure 2-5. If the I/O rate is too high on some of the disks, you might need all six disk spindles to achieve better I/O performance for both tables. In this case you could create one filegroup to include both of the files so that the table data is spread across both disk arrays, as shown in Figure 2-6.

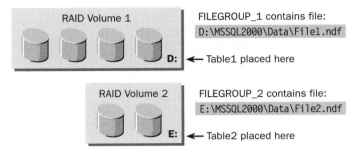

Figure 2-5. *Two different filegroups, each with its own secondary data files.*

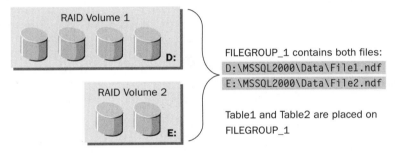

Figure 2-6. *One filegroup that includes both secondary data files.*

Generally, to optimize disk I/O performance on your system, you should distribute data across as many disks as possible to achieve more parallel data access (read and write operations). The use of filegroups can help you achieve more evenly distributed I/O. As mentioned above, when data is loaded or inserted into a table that is placed on a filegroup, the data is spread proportionately across all the files in the filegroup. Next we'll take a closer look at this concept.

SQL Server uses a proportional fill strategy when there are multiple files in a filegroup. That is, SQL Server writes data to each file in an amount proportional to the free space in that file, rather than writing data to the first file until it is full, then filling up the second file, and so on. For example, if file File1 has 400 MB free and file File2 has 100 MB free, then four extents of pages are allocated from File1 and one extent from File2. (In SQL Server 2000, an *extent* is a unit of eight contiguous pages.) Both files become full at about the same time, and data striping is optimized (here *data striping* refers to the distribution of data across files). In our example, one stripe of data (the four extents) is allocated to File1, then a stripe (one extent) to File2, then another stripe to File1 and then

File2 again, and so on. This fill strategy is used whether you create your own filegroup or allow your files to be part of the default primary filegroup—if there are multiple files in the primary filegroup, the data will be spread across those files in the same manner.

The three types of filegroups are as follows:

- **Primary filegroup** This filegroup contains the primary data file and all other files not put into another filegroup. The system tables for system and user databases (such as syslogins, sysdatabases, sysusers, etc.) are always allocated to the primary filegroup.

- **User-defined filegroups** These are any filegroups defined by the user during the process of creating the database or when altering a database. A user table or index can be created in a specific user-defined filegroup.

- **Default filegroup** The default filegroup holds all pages for tables and indexes that do not have a specified filegroup when created. The default filegroup can be switched from one filegroup to another by members of the *db_owner* database role. Only one filegroup at a time can be the default. If no default filegroup is specified, the primary filegroup is the default. You can use the ALTER DATABASE command to change the default filegroup, as in the following command, which sets Acct_fg to the default filegroup for Accounting database:

```
ALTER DATABASE Accounting MODIFY FILEGROUP "Acct_fg" DEFAULT
```

Note Log files are not part of any filegroup and can not be placed in any user-defined filegroup.

All files are part of the primary filegroup by default. The primary data file must be in the primary filegroup—this cannot be changed. Any secondary files you create can be left in the default primary filegroup or created in a user-defined filegroup. If you create all files in the primary filegroup, then all your tables, indexes, and other objects are spread across those files according to SQL Server's proportional fill strategy. Keep in mind that for more specific placement of data, you must use user-defined filegroups.

One of the features of SQL Server 2000 (introduced in SQL Server 7.0) is the ability to back up and restore sections of your database by file or filegroup. You can back up one file at a time or an entire filegroup as one operation. Knowing this might help you decide how many files to create and how to use filegroups to group them for your backup strategy. For example, if you want to be able to back up and restore one table by itself, you can create a file in a filegroup, and then create that table on the filegroup so that you can perform a filegroup backup to back up just that particular table. See Chapter 5, "New Features and Performance Enhancements" and Chapter 15, "High-Performance Backup and Recovery" for more details on backup strategies.

Automatic File Growth

SQL Server 7.0 and SQL Server 2000 have another feature related to files: the ability to enlarge files automatically when needed. This feature is available for both data files and log files. When a file is created, you can choose to allow SQL Server to increase the size of the file when more space is needed for data in that file. We recommend that you choose automatic growth, because it saves the administrator the burden of manually monitoring and increasing file space, and avoids the possibility of an error occurring because the file size limit is hit. This works, of course, as long as physical disk space is available for the file to grow into. This is very useful for log files when, for example, a transaction log backup fails for some reason and the log does not get truncated, which could cause the log to run out of space. With automatic growth enabled for the log file, it will continue to grow, as long as there is physical disk space available on that drive.

A data or log file is created with an initial size. When that initial space is filled up, SQL Server increases the file size by a specified amount. This amount, called the *growth increment*, tells SQL Server how much more space to allocate to the file when the original space has been filled. When this new space fills, SQL Server again allocates more space. The file continues to grow at that rate as needed until the disk is full or until the maximum file size (if specified) is reached.

The *maximum file size* is just that—the maximum size to which a file is allowed to grow. You can specify this size for each file individually at file creation or alter it later. If no maximum size is set for a file, SQL Server continues to increase the size of the file as necessary until all available disk space is exhausted. To avoid running out of space on the disk completely, set a maximum size for each file. If you ever do reach the maximum size, you can add a new file or increase the maximum file size for more space.

We recommend that you use automatic file growth and maximum file sizes. When you create a database, allocate the largest size to which you think the files will grow. If this initial space is filled and automatic growth takes place (which you will know if the current size of the file is larger than its initial size), you should reevaluate the space to determine whether you should add more files or filegroups, or both. This evaluation helps you to avoid running out of space completely, either from reaching the maximum file size or from running out of disk space.

Pages, Extents, and Rows

The basic unit of data storage in SQL Server is a page. A SQL Server 2000 page is 8 KB (as opposed to a 2-KB page size for versions of SQL Server previous to 7.0). The SQL Server data files are made up of pages. (Log files, on the other hand, do not contain pages; they are made up of log records.) The beginning of each data file page contains a 96-byte header that stores information such as the type of page, the object ID of the object (table or index) that owns the page, the amount of free space on the page, and pointers to the previous and next pages for pages in a linked list. The eight types of pages in SQL Server are shown on the next page.

- **Data page** Stores data rows with all types of data except data for **text**, **ntext**, and **image** data types.
- **Index page** Stores rows of index information.
- **Text/image page** Stores data for **text**, **ntext**, and **image** data types.
- **Page Free Space page** Stores information about free space available on pages.
- **Global Allocation Map page** Stores information about allocated extents.
- **Index Allocation Map page** Stores information about extents used by a table or index.
- **Bulk Changed Map page** Stores information about extents that were modified by bulk operations since the last BACKUP LOG statement.
- **Differential Changed Map page** Stores information about extents that have changed since the last BACKUP DATABASE statement, which is used when performing differential backups.

An *extent* is a unit of eight contiguous pages, a total of 64 KB. Space is allocated to tables and indexes in extents. A row on a data page can hold data for all data types except **text**, **ntext**, and **image**. For these data types, a pointer that points to the actual **text**, **ntext**, or **image** data in separate pages is stored in the data row. With this design, the maximum size of one row is 8060 bytes; therefore, a row will never span more than one page, a more efficient method than allowing a row to span pages. If a row spanned two pages, for example, retrieving that row would involve accessing two pages instead of only one, which could cause two disk I/Os instead of one, or two cache accesses if the pages are in the data cache.

Lock Management

The lock manager for SQL Server 2000 maintains the optimizations from version 7.0, which allow lock requests to be completed faster, thus allowing more concurrency for online transaction processing (OLTP) applications, especially when data rows are inserted often. Row-level locking is fully implemented for data and index pages (row-level locking was only partially available previous to version 7.0). Let's take a look at what locks are and how SQL Server manages them dynamically.

What is a Lock?

A *lock* is an object used by internal system software to indicate that a user has a dependency on some resource and therefore has an access right to it. That user is said to own a lock on the resource. Other users are not allowed to perform any operation on that resource if doing so would cause a problem with the original lock or violate the dependency of the user who owns it. SQL Server uses locks to control concurrency for multiple users working with the same database at the same time. Locking ensures that multiple users can read and write to the same database without retrieving inconsistent data and without inadvertently overwriting one another's modifications. Locks are managed on a per SQL Server connection basis.

Lock Granularity and Lock Modes

SQL Server uses multigranular locking; that is, locks can be owned by a user on resources at different levels, from fine to coarse granularity. A fine granularity lock is on a smaller resource, such as a row or page, where a coarse granularity lock is on a larger resource, such as a table or database. The finest granularity level is the row lock. SQL Server allocates a lock on a row of data when this best fits the needs of the user. The coarsest level of lock granularity is the database lock, which locks an entire database. The types of resources that can be locked are as follows (from finest to coarsest level of granularity):

- **Row identifier (RID)** A lock that locks a single row in a table.
- **Key** A row lock within an index.
- **Page** A lock on an 8-KB data or index page.
- **Extent** A lock on a contiguous group of eight data or index pages, or a 64-KB unit.
- **Table** A lock on an entire table, including all its data and indexes.
- **Database** A lock on an entire database.

The finer the granularity of lock, the more concurrency among users to the data is allowed but the more system overhead is incurred. On the other hand, the coarser the granularity, the less concurrency is allowed, but less system overhead is incurred. For example, many row-level locks on a table allow greater concurrency for other transactions to access other rows in the table, but overhead is incurred for each of the individual row-level locks. A table-level lock allows less concurrency to the table, but does not require as much system overhead to manage.

In addition to a lock's granularity, SQL Server allocates a lock in a specific mode. These modes determine how the locked resource can be accessed by concurrent user transactions. The various lock modes are as follows:

- **Shared** Used for read-only operations, such as for a SELECT statement.
- **Exclusive** Used on resources for data modification statements, such as INSERT, UPDATE, and DELETE; ensures that multiple modifications cannot occur on the same resource by more than one user at a time.
- **Update** Used on resources that can be updated.
- **Intent** Used to establish a locking hierarchy; includes intent shared, intent exclusive, and shared with intent exclusive lock types.
- **Schema** Used for operations that perform a table data definition language (DDL) statement, such as adding a column or dropping a table; includes schema modification and schema stability lock types.
- **Bulk Update** Used when bulk-copying data into a table and also when the TABLOCK table hint is specified.

SQL Server dynamically chooses the types of resources that should be locked for a transaction and the lock mode that should be used; you do not need to configure anything for this process to occur efficiently. SQL Server chooses the most cost-effective locks when the query is executed, based on the characteristics of the database schema and the query itself. This design provides ease of administration and improved performance because system overhead is reduced.

SQL Server also dynamically manages lock *escalation*—the conversion of many fine-grained locks into fewer, more coarse-grained locks. This conversion reduces the system overhead incurred when using a large number of fine-grained locks. For example, SQL Server converts many row-level or page-level locks into one table lock when the number of row or page locks for the transaction reaches the lock escalation threshold. The lock escalation thresholds are determined dynamically by SQL Server and do not need to be configured.

The *locks* Option

SQL Server allows administrators to manually configure the maximum number of locks allowed on the system by using the *locks* option. You should not have to change this option in most cases, but we explain it here so you can understand the implications of changing it. Setting *locks* determines the maximum number of locks SQL Server can allocate. When *locks* is left at its default of 0, SQL Server dynamically and very efficiently allocates and deallocates locks according to system needs. Initially two percent of the total memory allocated to SQL Server is allocated to a pool for lock structures. Each lock consumes 96 bytes of memory. When the initial lock pool is consumed and if more locks are then needed, SQL Server allocates memory for them from its memory pool, expanding the memory pool if needed and if memory is available. SQL Server allocates no more than 40 percent of its memory pool to locks. Also, if allocating more memory to locks would cause another application running on the system to page, then SQL Server will not allocate more.

If you do set the *locks* option to a number other than 0, you are setting a limit to the number of locks that can be allocated. If you receive a message from SQL Server that you have run out of locks, increase the number. *Locks* is an advanced option in SQL Server, as are the memory options; you therefore must have the SQL Server option *show advanced options* set to 1 to configure locks, and you must use the *sp_configure* stored procedure. You cannot configure locks through Enterprise Manager.

For details on how to specify in a query which type of lock you want SQL Server to use, see Chapter 19, "Using Hints in SQL Server."

Thread Management

Let's take a look at how threads work with application programs. An instance of an application is managed by the operating system with a unit called a *process*. A process is given a thread of execution to perform the application's programming instructions. A thread can run on one CPU at a time. In a simple application in which the programming instructions can be run serially, there is only one execution path, or one thread, to perform the instructions. In complex applications, the programming logic might be separable into multiple concurrent execution paths, in which case multiple threads are started. Each thread can run independently of the others, and each keeps track of the information unique to it in an area of memory called a stack.

SQL Server uses Windows NT or Windows 2000 operating system threads, and sometimes fibers (see the following discussion), to execute concurrent tasks. (Fibers are not supported with Microsoft SQL Server Desktop Edition.) When not using fibers, threads are started by SQL Server, and then Windows NT or Windows 2000 distributes the threads evenly across the CPUs that are available for use by SQL Server. You can configure the processors that SQL Server can use either through Enterprise Manager or by setting the SQL Server configuration option *affinity mask*.

Most systems perform best by letting SQL Server use all the CPUs in the system. One thread can execute at a time on each CPU in the system. For example, a system with four CPUs can execute four threads concurrently. While one thread might be waiting for an I/O to complete, another thread can run on that same CPU (by switching threads), even in a single-CPU system. More work can be performed because the thread that is waiting on an operation to complete is not blocking the CPU from use by another thread.

Thread management is handled in the Windows NT and Windows 2000 kernel code. When one thread is moved off a CPU and another one is moved on, a *context switch* occurs. Context switching is a moderately costly operation because it requires a switch between the user mode of the application code and the kernel mode of the thread management code. Therefore, fewer context switches are better. Using fiber mode can help reduce context switching in some cases, as discussed in the next section.

Fiber Mode Scheduling and Worker Threads

To reduce context switching, you can enable SQL Server 2000 to use Windows NT and Windows 2000 fibers. Fibers are subcomponents of threads. SQL Server does not use fibers by default, but you can configure it to do so. Fibers are handled by code running in user mode; so switching fibers (to switch tasks on the CPU) is not as costly as switching threads because the mode does not have to change between kernel mode and user mode. Fiber scheduling is handled by SQL Server, where thread scheduling is handled by Windows NT and Windows 2000. In thread mode (when fiber scheduling is disabled), SQL Server schedules one thread per concurrent user command. In fiber mode, SQL Server allocates one thread per CPU, and then allocates one fiber per concurrent user command. Multiple fibers can run on one thread, and fibers can be switched on the thread, while the thread remains in execution on one CPU without switching contexts. This greatly reduces the amount of context switching on the system. Using fibers works best if your system has four or more CPUs. If your system has four or more CPUs, and if your system is performing a lot of context switches (more than 5000 per second), try running SQL Server in fiber mode. To enable fiber mode scheduling, you can either select the option through the Enterprise Manager Server Properties dialog box on the Processor tab by selecting the Use Windows NT Fibers check box, or you can run *sp_configure* and set the *lightweight pooling* option to 1 (setting it to 1 enables fiber mode). *Lightweight pooling* is also an advanced option.

SQL Server maintains either a pool of threads or fibers for user connections. (If fiber mode is set, a pool of fibers is maintained instead of threads.) The threads or fibers in this pool are known as *worker threads*. You can set a maximum limit to the number of threads or fibers that SQL Server can allocate by setting the configuration option *max worker threads*. The default value of 255 is sufficient for most systems and you should not need to change this option. (You can configure it in Enterprise Manager or with the *sp_configure* stored procedure.) SQL Server allocates one thread or fiber per user connection, up to the maximum worker thread limit. When the limit is reached, SQL Server begins thread pooling, so that the next available thread will handle a waiting request. Let's look at this in more detail.

When a SQL statement or batch of statements is sent to SQL Server for execution, SQL Server assigns a worker thread for the statement or batch (or user command) from the thread pool if an existing thread is free in the pool. If no existing thread is free and the maximum number of worker threads has not yet been reached, SQL Server will start a new thread for the user command. If the maximum worker thread limit has been reached and no threads are free, the process must wait for another batch to complete its task and free a thread. This wait is usually very short. If you see an error message from SQL Server saying that you have reached the *max worker threads* limit, try increasing the option value. Remember, however, that the creation of too many threads can cause more overhead and eventually degrade performance. Again, the default value of 255 is sufficient for most systems. For systems that are not under a heavy load, you might experiment by setting this value lower and comparing performance—in some cases the performance will improve because of the reduced overhead.

> **Note** Microsoft SQL Server Personal Edition and SQL Server Desktop Edition do not support fiber mode. Also, Windows 95 and Windows 98 do not support thread pooling. Setting the *max worker thread* option has no effect on those operating systems.

Transaction Log

The *transaction log* stores a sequential record of all *transactions* that make modifications to the database (including updates, inserts, deletes, creating or dropping a table or index, changes to system tables, and DDL statements). A before and after image of the data is recorded in the log for data modification statements, and a record of the logical operation performed is recorded for statements such as CREATE INDEX. A *before image* is a copy of the modified data before the transaction, and an *after image* is a copy of the modified data after the transaction. This log record makes database recovery possible. Either the before or after image is applied during recovery, or the logical operation is rerun or its logical reversal is run. This section covers the function of the transaction log for SQL Server 2000—its characteristics, how it is involved in database recovery, how it grows and gets truncated, and how it is related to checkpoints.

Transaction Log Characteristics

The following enhancements were made to the transaction log in SQL Server 7.0 and preserved in SQL Server 2000:

- **The transaction log is not a table; it is treated as a separate file or set of files in the database.** Thus, I/Os to the transaction log are not written in increments of the SQL Server page size. With SQL Server versions 6.5 and earlier, the log was treated as a database table and all I/Os were done using the SQL Server page size (2 KB in SQL Server 6.5). With SQL Server 2000, the transaction log pages no longer follow the format of data pages. The log writer thread can write to the transaction log using variable-sized writes. Thus, if the log writer thread needs to write only a small amount, it is not necessary to write an entire 8 KB of data (the size of a data page). If the system is performing heavy updates, the log write thread can write using a larger block size (for example, 16 KB or 32 KB). Each database log has its own log cache as well, which is separate from the data cache.

- **The transaction log can be configured to automatically grow as needed.** This option allows more space to be added to the log file as needed, but should be used with care. You do not want the transaction log to grow uncontrollably or you might consume the entire disk drive. Periodic transaction log backups, which also truncate the log when finished, should keep the log size in check.

- **The transaction log can now be implemented across several files.** These files can be configured to grow automatically as well. The transaction log files are not striped; they are used one after another.

- **Log truncation is very quick.** The method used for truncating the log is almost instantaneous and has minimal effect on transaction throughput. Truncation is described later in this chapter.

The transaction log keeps track of when a transaction has committed. When a transaction issues a commit, the operation is not fully committed until a commit record has been written to the transaction log. Because changes to the database are not necessarily written to disk immediately, this log is the only means by which transactions can be recovered in the event of a system failure. If a database is damaged and must be restored from a database backup, all the transactions that occurred since the backup that had performed some type of data modification must be replayed to recover the database to the point just before the failure. This is done by restoring all the transaction log backups taken since the last database backup, including the transaction log backup taken immediately after the failure occurred (if possible). (See Chapter 15, "High-Performance Backup and Recovery" for more specifics on backup and recovery.)

In the event of a system failure in which data files are not damaged, the current transaction log alone is used to recover the database automatically when SQL Server is restarted, because you only have to recover those transactions not yet written to disk. The number of pages you must recover depends on the number of modified (or dirty) pages in the database at the time of the failure, which in turn is governed by the occurrence of checkpoints. A *checkpoint* is a SQL Server operation that writes dirty pages to disk to reduce the time it takes to perform a recovery. Checkpoints and the checkpoint interval are discussed in the "What is a Checkpoint?" section later in this chapter.

As you can see, the transaction log plays an important role in database recovery. Here is a complete list of the types of recovery operations in which the transaction log is used:

- **Recovery of individual rolled-back transactions** When the application issues a ROLLBACK statement, or a failure such as the loss of client connection to SQL Server occurs, the transaction log record is used to roll back any modifications to the database made by that transaction. It applies the before image of the data in this case. This occurs automatically without interrupting other user transactions.

- **Recovery of incomplete transactions caused by a failure** When a failure causes SQL Server to stop without a clean shutdown, such as a loss of power to the system, there might be incomplete transactions—transactions that were committed but whose modifications did not get written from the buffer cache to the data files on disk, or transactions that were not committed yet. Thus, when SQL Server is started again, the transaction log is used to recover all incomplete transactions by rolling forward committed transactions recorded in the log that did not get recorded in the data files (by using the after image of the data), and by rolling back transactions that were in flight (were not committed yet) at the time of failure (by using the before image of the data).

- **Restoring a database to a point of failure** For certain types of failures, such as the loss of data caused by a disk failure on a non-RAID volume, you must restore the database and its transaction logs in order to recover the system. First you must make a backup of the current transaction log if possible. Then to recover, you must restore the last full database backup, the last differential backup if there are any, and all the transaction log backups including the current backup you just made. Restoring all transaction log backups before the current one reapplies all modifications made to the database during those periods. The current log backup rolls forward committed transactions and rolls back non-committed transactions, to bring your database back to the point of failure.

Transaction Log Architecture

SQL Server internally divides each physical transaction log file into multiple virtual files. The size and number of virtual files are determined dynamically by SQL Server when it is creating and extending log files. SQL Server tries to maintain a small number of virtual files for better efficiency during a database recovery. Too many virtual files can slow down recovery. When you create the log file, you can specify a size for the automatic growth increment. If you set this amount too low, SQL Server must extend the log file often, which results in more virtual files being created—the number is chosen dynamically by SQL Server. It is best to create your log files initially at the largest size you think they are likely to grow, and to set the growth increment relatively high as well. This avoids the overhead incurred from SQL Server increasing the size of the file and from having too many virtual files.

The transaction log is a wrap-around log, which is best understood in terms of the logical log and the physical log. When a database is created, log records are written starting at the beginning of the physical log, which at that time is also the beginning of the logical log, as shown in Figure 2-7. When records are truncated from the log file, the pointer for the beginning of the logical log is moved to the point where truncation ended, as shown in Figure 2-8 on the next page. Records continue to be written from the new logical starting point until the end of the logical log reaches the end of the physical log. Now the logical log goes to the beginning of the physical log and continues writing, as shown in Figure 2-9 on the next page. If the end of the logical log ever catches up to the beginning of the logical log, your log file has filled up. If automatic growth is enabled and there is still space available on the disk, SQL Server extends your file. If not, you will get an error and have to manually backup or truncate the log. When there are multiple physical log files, the first log file fills up first, then the logical log moves to the second physical log file and fills it, then to the third, etc. When the last physical log file is filled, the logical log wraps around to the beginning of the first physical log file again.

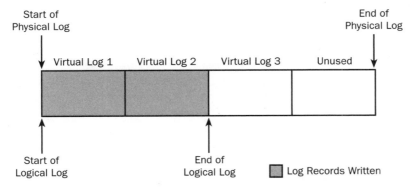

Figure 2-7. *View of the transaction log file with initial records written.*

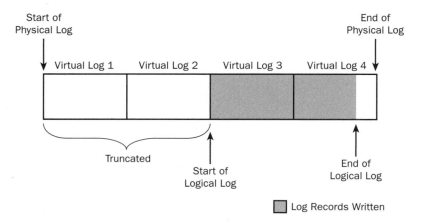

Figure 2-8. *View of the same transaction log file after a truncation.*

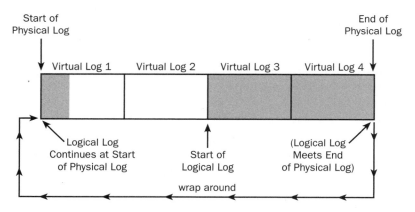

Figure 2-9. *View of the same transaction log file after the logical log wraps around.*

Truncating the Transaction Log

Depending on the number of changes to your database, the transaction log can grow to be quite large. Because the transaction log is a finite set of one or more files, it will fill up eventually and so must be truncated periodically. (If automatic growth is enabled, the log will fill up when the available physical disk space is used up.) Truncation reduces the size of the logical log file. The physical log size is never reduced with truncation, but can be reduced by using the shrink file feature. Truncating the log deletes log records that are not part of the active portion of the log. The active portion consists of the records that have occurred after the last checkpoint, because these records might not have been written to disk yet, plus any transactions that were still active during the checkpoint.

Two methods of recovery determine how you should truncate the log. Use the simple recovery method when you do not want to back up transaction logs, but will use only database backups for recovery in case of a failure. With this method you can only re-store your database up to the point of the last database or differential backup—but not to the point of failure. To avoid filling up of the log file when using this method, you can set the *trunc. log on chkpt.* (truncate log on checkpoint) option, which causes the log to be truncated after each checkpoint. This keeps the size of the logical transaction log in check, but is absolutely not recommended for your user databases. You might use this method for test databases or temporary databases that are not business critical.

For business critical user databases, we recommend the full recovery method, with which in most cases you can recover your database to the point of failure. You must perform an initial full database backup and periodic transaction log backups with this method. You must never truncate the transaction log manually between log backups or you will lose some transactions needed for full recovery. With this method you do not have to worry about manually truncating the log because SQL Server automatically does so after a log backup. You must simply schedule your transaction log backups as often as needed to keep the size of the logical transaction log in check.

> **Note**   You can also truncate the log without backing it up by setting the data-base option *trunc. log on chkpt* to TRUE for that database. This setting forces log truncation at every checkpoint. With this setting you cannot back up the transaction log. It makes the database nonrecoverable and therefore is NOT recommended.

What is a Checkpoint?

A *checkpoint* is a SQL Server operation that synchronizes the physical data and log files with the current state of the buffer cache by writing out all modified data pages in buffer cache to disk. This assures you a permanent (on disk) copy of the data. SQL Server has a thread dedicated to checkpoints. Performing checkpoints reduces the necessary recovery time in the event of a system failure in cases where automatic recovery by SQL Server is possible. This is because checkpoints minimize the number of transactions that must be rolled forward.

The time needed to recover the database is determined by the time since the last check-point and the number of dirty pages in the buffer cache. So decreasing the checkpoint interval—the amount of time between checkpoints, (discussed in the next section)—reduces the recovery time, but with some cost. The checkpoint process incurs some overhead because it performs a large number of writes if there are many modified pages that must be written to disk. These writes could potentially interfere with and slow the user transaction response times.

The Checkpoint Operation

The checkpoint operation involves a number of steps, including the following:

- **Writing out all dirty data and log pages to disk.** A *dirty* page is one that has been modified in the buffer cache or log cache, but has not yet been written to disk. There are two phases for writing out dirty pages with a checkpoint. During the first phase, the checkpoint process marks all pages that need to be written. In the second phase, the checkpoint forces a write to disk of those marked dirty pages.

- **Writing a list of outstanding, active transactions to the transaction log.** This step tells SQL Server what transactions were in progress when the checkpoint occurred, telling the recovery process to go back further in the log than the checkpoint in order to recover those transactions.

- **Storing checkpoint records in the log.** A record marking the start and the end of each checkpoint is written to the log.

Checkpoints occur per database. So for example, if you are connected to SQL Server using the master database and manually run the checkpoint command, the checkpoint operation will run only on the master database. But when SQL Server is shutdown and automatically performs checkpoints, checkpoints are run on all databases. Checkpoints occur in the following cases:

- Whenever you issue a manual CHECKPOINT statement, a checkpoint operation is run on the current database.

- Whenever you shut down SQL Server using a SHUTDOWN statement or using the Windows 2000 Services console, a checkpoint operation is run on all databases.

- Whenever the ALTER DATABASE command is used to change a database option, a checkpoint operation is run on that database.

- Periodically checkpoints are run on all databases as specified by the recovery interval server setting (discussed next). In this case checkpoints are not performed on all databases at the same time, but on each database individually when it needs to be, based on the recovery interval setting.

Configuring the Recovery Interval

The *checkpoint interval*, which is the time between the beginnings of consecutive checkpoints, is determined by the *recovery interval* option and the number of records in the transaction log, not by the system time or size of the log. The *recovery interval* option is set for an entire SQL Server system, not for each database, but checkpoints occur on a per-database basis. Its value is the number of minutes that you want to allow SQL Server for automatic recovery per database in case of a system failure. SQL Server uses an algorithm to determine when it should perform the next checkpoint for each database based on the *recovery interval*. For example, if *recovery interval* is set to five minutes, then SQL Server will perform checkpoints per database often enough that in the event of a system failure, when SQL Server is restarted, no database recovery will take more than five minutes.

The number of transactions in the log file also affects the checkpoint interval. The more records in the transaction log, the shorter the checkpoint interval, which means the checkpoint executes more often. As more data modifications occur, more records are inserted into the transaction log; consequently, SQL Server configures the checkpoint interval to write those changes to disk more often. If few or no changes are made to the database, the transaction log contains only a few records, and the checkpoint interval is long. For example, if the recovery interval is set to five minutes, but only a few modifications have been written to the log in the hour since the last checkpoint, then another checkpoint might not occur for that entire hour or more. This is because the few modifications made will take only a number of seconds to recover, and SQL Server has up to five minutes. On the other hand, if many modifications have occurred in the database, and many log records written, the SQL Server will checkpoint that database more often.

The default value for *recovery interval* is 0—this instructs SQL Server to determine the checkpoint interval for you—usually less than one minute, which is quite often. For systems that have a large amount of memory and a lot of insert and update activity, this default setting might cause too many checkpoints to occur. In that case, you might want to set the option to a larger value. If you can stand a 10-minute recovery in the event of a system failure, you might see better transaction performance, because checkpoints are initiated less often. How you change this option depends on how long you can wait for a recovery and on the frequency of failures.

You can change the *recovery interval* option in two ways: using Enterprise Manager or Transact-SQL. To set *recovery interval* from Enterprise Manager, in the left pane right-click the name of the server that you want to set this option for, and click Properties from the shortcut menu. The SQL Server Properties dialog box appears. Click the Database Settings tab and specify the desired recovery interval, in minutes, in the Recovery Interval box.

To set *recovery interval* using Transact-SQL, use the *sp_configure* stored procedure, as shown here:

```
sp_configure "recovery interval", 10
GO
```

This option does not require restarting SQL Server to take effect. As noted earlier, however, the change does not become active unless you run the RECONFIGURE command. If you are sure of your change, enter the following Transact-SQL statements:

```
RECONFIGURE WITH OVERRIDE
GO
```

The RECONFIGURE command signals SQL Server to accept the configuration changes as the run value.

To ensure that the setting you have made is actually in effect, use the following Transact-SQL statement:

```
sp_configure "recovery interval"
GO
```

The output looks like this (note that the recovery interval has indeed been set):

name	minimum	maximum	config_value	run_value
recovery interval (min)	0	32767	10	10

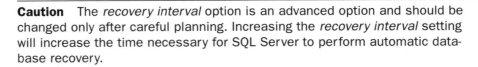

Caution The *recovery interval* option is an advanced option and should be changed only after careful planning. Increasing the *recovery interval* setting will increase the time necessary for SQL Server to perform automatic database recovery.

Summary

This chapter has discussed some of the fundamentals of SQL Server architecture, so that you can better understand your system as a whole and have a better foundation on which to build when learning how to tune your system. The next chapter will help you understand detailed characteristics of disk drives and different RAID levels and how to tune your I/O subsystem.

Chapter 3
Understanding the I/O Subsystem and RAID

The input/output (I/O) subsystem is often the cause of performance degradation in relational database management systems (RDBMSs), which can be due to legitimate I/O needs or to some external problem that causes excessive I/Os. Sometimes the application is efficient and the I/O subsystem is simply overloaded; other times excessive I/Os are not necessary. For example, inefficient SQL statements can cause unnecessary table scans when an index lookup would work better. Too many users on the same system can overload the I/O subsystem. Running large batch jobs on an online transaction processing (OLTP) system can also cause severe performance problems.

When the I/O subsystem is overloaded, the I/O latency (or response time) increases. The term *latency* refers to the time that one component or process is idle waiting for another component to complete some operation. When the I/O latency increases, user response times increase. Also, while SQL statement executions wait for I/Os to return they often hold locks or other system resources. This can cause a cascade effect, where increased I/O latencies cause locking, which causes more locking until the entire system slows down. In this chapter we discuss various latencies, such as I/O latency and subcomponents' latencies.

This chapter starts with an overview of how a disk drive works and why it has fundamental performance limits. Next we cover the various available RAID (redundant array of inexpensive disks) levels and their performance characteristics. We will also cover how RAID arrays can be used in order to protect your system from a disk drive failure by providing fault-tolerance. Since a disk drive is one of the most likely components in your system to fail it is important that you are prepared for such a failure and can keep running. Then we show you how to identify and solve an I/O performance problem. Finally we present a number of I/O subsystem tips and recommendations.

Performance Characteristics of Disk Drives

The disk drive (also called the hard disk) is a fundamental component of the computer system. Amazingly enough, the mechanics of disk drives have not changed much in the last 20 years. They are, of course, much faster and more reliable than they originally were, but fundamentally they remain the same. From a performance standpoint, disk drives are still one of the most important system components to tune. Of course, you can't really tune a disk drive, but you can know its performance characteristics and limitations and configure your system accordingly, and in effect tune the I/O subsystem.

Disk Drive Description

The data storage component of a disk drive is composed of a number of magnetic disk platters. These platters store data magnetically in tracks, much like the tracks of a record (or CD, for those who don't remember records). The track is made up of a number of sectors. The further you get from the center of the disk drive, the more sectors there are per track. Figure 3-1 shows a typical disk platter.

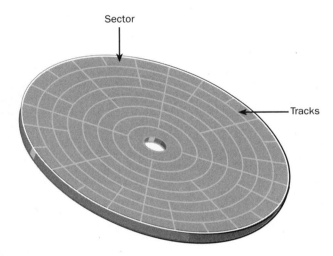

Figure 3-1. *Disk platter.*

A disk drive is made up of many disk platters stacked on top of each other, as shown in Figure 3-2 on the next page. A magnetic head both reads data from and writes data to the disk. Because there are many platters, there are also many disk heads—one per surface. These heads ride on top of an armature that moves in and out of the disk, much like the arm that holds the needle on a record player. These heads and armatures are all connected and move in sync; thus, all heads are over the same X-Y position on all platters at the same time. Because disks operate this way, all heads read and write at the same time, so data is written and read from all tracks simultaneously. We say that data is stored in *cylinders*. The cylinder is the collection of the same track on all disk platters.

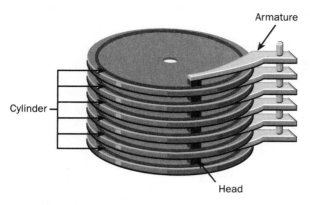

Figure 3-2. *The anatomy of a disk drive.*

Disk drives can be made up of as few as one disk platter or as many as six or more. In fact, the new 72 GB disk drives have 12 platters. The density of the data on the platters and the number of platters determine the maximum storage capacity of a disk drive. Many disk drives have identical mechanical properties, but the number of platters varies, defining the disk drive capacity. A common product line of disk drives includes an 18-GB disk drive with three disk platters, an almost identical 36-GB disk drive with six disk platters, and a 72-GB disk drive with 12 platters.

Disk Drive Behaviors

Now that you have an idea of what makes up a disk drive, let's look at how it works. First we'll discuss the rotational characteristics of the disk drive, and then talk about what *disk seeks* are and how they fit into the performance characteristics of disk drives.

Rotational Latency

Many high-performance disk drives spin at 10,000 revolutions per minute (rpm) and the highest performing disk drives spin at 15,000 rpm. If a request for data caused the disk to rotate completely before it read the data, this action would take approximately 4 milliseconds (ms), or 0.004 second. A rotational speed of 15,000 rpm equates to 250 rotations per second. This translates to 1/250 seconds per rotation, or 4 ms per rotation.

For the disk heads to read a sector of data, that sector must be directly beneath the head. Because the disk drive is always rotating, the disk waits for the sector to rotate to that position. The time the disk takes to rotate into position where the data is available is called the *rotational latency*. The rotational latency can be as long as 4 ms (if the disk has to rotate completely), but on average it is less than the maximum revolution time. For our 15,000-rpm example disk, the average rotational latency published in the spec sheet is approximately 2 ms.

Rotational latency is important to this discussion of disk drive performance because it is this time that contributes to the overall time needed for disk access. When you choose disk drives for your system, the rotational speed is an important consideration. For a 15,000-rpm disk drive the average rotational latency is around 2 ms. Older-generation disk drives on the market run at a rotational speed of 7,200 rpm, in which case one rotation takes 8.3 ms to complete, and the average rotational latency is about 4.15 ms—more than twice as long as the 15,000-rpm disk drive. This can add significantly to your I/O times.

Disk Seeks

In the process of retrieving data from a disk drive, the disk must not only rotate under the heads that read the data, but the head must also move to where the data resides. The disk armature moves in and out between the disk surfaces to move the heads to the cylinder that holds the requested data. The time the head takes to move to where the requested data resides is called the *seek time*. Figure 3-3 represents the concepts of seek time and rotational latency.

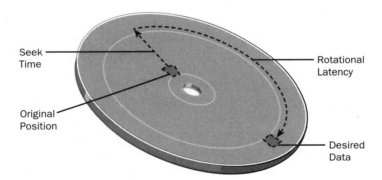

Figure 3-3. *Rotational latency and seek time.*

The time it takes for a seek to occur depends mainly on how far the disk heads need to move. When the disk drives are accessing data sequentially, the heads need to move only a small distance, which can occur quickly. When disk accesses are occurring all over the disk drive, the seek times can get quite long. In either case, by minimizing the seek time you improve performance.

The seek time and the rotational latency both add to the time it takes for an I/O to complete, and so affect the performance of a disk drive. The rotational latency is usually around 2 ms for 15,000-rpm disks. The seek time of the disk varies depending on the size and speed of the disk drive and the type of seek being performed. In addition, there is a slight difference between the seek time for reads and writes, but that difference is minor. Since data cannot be read until the seek has been completed, the rotational latency and seek time do not occur serially. The disk must first seek the requested track, then the disk must rotate from its current position to the sector where the data is held.

Track-to-Track Seeks

The *track-to-track seek time* is the time required to move between adjacent tracks. This type of seek is used when performing sequential I/Os. A typical 15,000-rpm, 18-GB disk drive has a track-to-track seek time of around 0.6 ms. With a track-to-track seek time of 0.6 ms, the rotational latency of approximately 2 ms is a large factor in the disk drive performance. If the I/Os are submitted to the disk drive fast enough, the disk drive might be able to access adjacent tracks or even read or write an entire track at a time. In some cases, however, the I/Os are not requested fast enough and the sequential accesses each incur a disk rotation between them. Whether this happens typically depends on the design and speed of the disk controller.

Average Seek Time

The *average seek time* is the time it takes on average to seek between random tracks on the disk. According to the specification sheet of an average 15,000-rpm disk drive, the average seek time is around 4.2 ms. Because almost all the I/Os that are generated by a SQL Server system are random, your disk drives will be performing a lot of random I/Os.

The maximum seek time of a typical disk can be as long as 9 ms. The maximum seek time occurs from the innermost track of the platter to the outermost track or vice versa. This is referred to as a *full-disk seek*. On average seeks are not full-disk seeks, especially if the disk drive is not completely full.

Disk Drive Specifications

This section discusses how to determine how fast a disk drive can perform I/O operations based on the type of I/O being performed. To make these calculations you must have some information about the disk drive, much of which can be found on the disk drive specification provided by the disk drive manufacturer. In this and earlier sections, we use specifications for a 15,000-rpm, 18-GB disk drive. Some of the specifications for this typical disk drive are given in Table 3-1.

Table 3-1. Disk Drive Specification

Specification	Value	Notes
Disk capacity	18 GB	Unformatted disk capacity
Rotational speed	15,000 rpm	Speed at which the disk is spinning
Transfer rate	40 MB/sec	Speed of the SCSI bus
Average seek time	3.9 ms (read), 4.5 ms (write)	Time it takes to seek (on average) between tracks during random I/Os
Track-to-track seek time	0.5 ms (read), 0.7 ms (write)	Time it takes to seek between tracks during sequential I/Os
Full-disk seek time	7.5 ms (read), 8 ms (write)	Time it takes to seek from the innermost sector to the outermost sector of the disk, or vice versa

These specifications can be useful in determining the performance characteristics of the disk drive.

Disk Drive Reliability

Disks are among the few components in a computer system that are mechanical in nature. The disk drive spins at a high rate of speed and operates at a high temperature. Components include several motors and bearings that can eventually wear out. The disk drive specifications include a figure for mean time between failure (MTBF), which indicates how long a disk is expected to last on average. This figure is only an average, however, and some disk drives might last longer than others. A typical modern disk drive might have an MTBF of 1,000,000 hours, or 114 years. In actuality, some disks will last much longer and some will fail in a relatively short time. It's important to keep in mind that a disk is a mechanical component, subject to wear and tear and eventual failure.

Disk Drive Performance

The time a disk operation takes to complete is made up of a number of smaller time intervals:

- The seek time required to move to the track that holds the data
- The rotational latency required for that data to rotate under the heads
- The time required to electronically transfer that data from the disk drive to the disk controller

The time an I/O takes to complete is the sum of the these intervals plus overhead incurred in the device driver and in Microsoft Windows 2000. Depending on how busy the system is, this operating system overhead can be significant. Remember, the total time for a disk I/O mainly depends on whether the I/O in question is sequential or random. A sequential I/O is dependent on track-to-track seeks. Random I/O performance depends on the average seek time.

Sequential I/O

Sequential I/O consists of disk accesses of adjacent data in a disk drive. Because track-to-track seek time is much faster than random seeks, a disk can achieve much higher *throughput* when performing sequential I/Os. To get an idea of how fast sequential I/Os can occur, let's look at an example.

It takes approximately 0.6 ms to seek between tracks on the disk drive described in Table 3-1 on page 43. Folding in the average rotational latency of 2 ms, it takes approximately 2.6 ms per I/O. This would theoretically allow us to perform 384 sequential I/Os per second (because 2.6 ms occurs 384 times in a second). But with sequential I/Os, other factors come into play, such as the limitation for the transfer rate (40 MB/second is a common limitation) as well as operating system components such as the file system and the device driver. Taking into account that additional overhead, the maximum at which a drive can sustain sequential I/O is around 300 I/Os per second (depending on the size of the blocks of data). As we discuss in the "Queuing Theory and the Knee of the Curve" section in Chapter 8, "Modeling for Sizing and Capacity Planning," if you run a disk drive at more than 85 percent of its capacity, *queuing* occurs; thus, the maximum recommended I/O rate is 255 I/Os per second.

Random I/O

Random I/O occurs when data is accessed from different parts of the disk. This causes random head movement, which reduces performance. Again, let's look at the example described earlier. Instead of seeking between adjacent tracks on the disk for approximately 0.6 ms, it is now necessary to seek to random tracks on the disk. This random seeking takes approximately 4.2 ms to finish (on average), seven times longer than the track-to-track seek.

A random I/O on a typical system takes approximately 4.2 ms (3.9 ms for reads and 4.5 ms for writes) for the disk to seek to where the data is held and an additional 2 ms in rotational latency, for a total of 6.2 ms. This gives a theoretical maximum of 161 I/Os per second (since 6.2 ms can occur 161 times per second). As noted earlier, if you run a disk drive at more than 85 percent of its capacity, queuing occurs. Therefore, the maximum recommended I/O rate is 137 I/Os per second. Taking into account overhead in the controller, a general rule is to drive these disk drives at no more than 125 I/Os per second.

For random disk access, typical disk latency (the time it takes to retrieve I/Os) is around 4.2 ms. When a drive is accessed faster than it can handle, queuing occurs and the I/O latency (response time) increases. As shown in Figure 3-4, the closer the number of I/Os per second gets to maximum capacity, the longer the latencies get. In fact, once you reach 100 percent, queueing is guaranteed to occur and performance degrades dramatically.

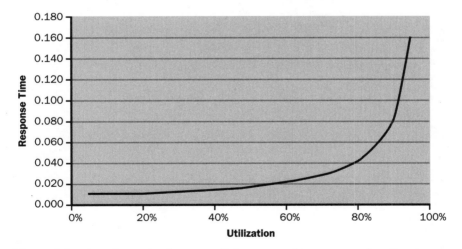

Figure 3-4. *The relationship between I/O latency and percentage of utilization.*

SQL Server is sensitive to I/O latencies. When I/Os take excessive amounts of time to execute, the performance of SQL Server degrades and problems such as blocking and deadlocks might occur. When a thread waits for an I/O, it might hold locks. The longer the I/O takes to execute, the longer the locks are held, causing these performance problems.

Elevator Sorting

When random I/O operations are issued to disks, the heads move in and out between the disk surfaces randomly, which increases latencies. Many RAID controllers support *elevator sorting* to make random seeks more efficient. Elevator sorting is a method of making random I/O operations more efficient. If multiple I/Os are queued on the controller, they can be sorted to reduce head movement, much like the operation of an elevator.

Imagine if an elevator serviced floors in the order that people on the elevator pushed the buttons. The elevator might pass floors where it could more efficiently let people on and off. Just as an elevator is efficient about stopping at floors where it is needed, based on where it is, so do the elevator sorting algorithms achieve efficiency. If more than one I/O is queued at a time, the controller uses an elevator sorting algorithm to choose the most efficient path, as shown in Figure 3-5. Elevator sorting reduces overall disk seek times, although sometimes at the expense of individual seek times.

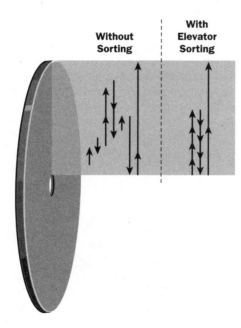

Figure 3-5. *Elevator sorting.*

As you can see, elevator sorting can make I/Os more efficient, resulting in improved performance. Even though the disk manufacturers and the controller manufacturers attempt to make I/O more efficient, the only real way to improve I/O performance is to live within the performance capacity of the I/O subsystem. By understanding the limits of the I/O subsystem and remaining within those limits, you can reduce latencies and optimize SQL Server performance.

Solving the Disk Performance Capacity Problem

So, how do we solve the problem of disk capacity? It is actually straightforward. By following these guidelines you should be able to design a system that performs optimally.

- **Isolate sequential I/Os.** By allocating components that are sequential in nature to their own disk volume, you can maintain their sequential nature. The transaction log is an example of a sequentially accessed file. If you place more than one sequentially accessed file on the same disk volume, the I/Os become random because the disk must seek between the sequential components belonging to different files.

- **Distribute random I/Os.** Because the I/Os are random in nature, the addition of more disk drives should lessen the load on any one disk. By building a system with enough disk drives to handle the random I/O load, you should avoid experiencing any problems. Determining how many disks are necessary and how to configure them are topics addressed later in this chapter and in Part II, "Sizing and Capacity Planning."

Introduction to RAID

As you might imagine, it becomes increasingly difficult to manage a system as you add more disk drives. Instead of adding tens or hundreds of individual disk drives, many users prefer to use RAID. You can implement RAID by using software and existing I/O components, or by purchasing hardware RAID devices. This section introduces what RAID is and how it works.

As the name implies, RAID takes two or more disk drives and creates an array of disks. To the operating system this array appears as one *logical disk*. This logical disk is also known as a *disk volume*, since it is a collection of disks that appears as one disk to the user, the application, and even to Windows 2000 (if hardware RAID is being used). In many cases, however, this single logical disk is much larger than any disk you could purchase. In fact, the number of I/Os that your system can handle depends on the number of disk drives, so in many cases you are better off with a 72-GB logical disk made up of eight 9-GB physical disk drives than with one 72-GB disk.

Not only does RAID allow you to create large disk drives, but many *RAID levels* (configurations) provide you with disk fault tolerance as well. *Fault tolerance* allows the RAID logical disk to survive (tolerate) the loss of one or more individual disk drives. The next few sections explain how and describe the characteristics of various RAID levels.

As mentioned earlier, you can implement RAID by using software; in fact, Windows 2000 comes with RAID software. This chapter is mostly concerned with hardware RAID, however, because of the additional features that it provides. The most common of these hardware RAID features is the controller cache.

Controller Caches

To improve I/O performance, many vendors offer a *controller cache*, which is RAM that resides on the disk controller itself. This cache serves two purposes:

- **Caching data to write** Because there is memory on the controller, the controller can tell the operating system (and subsequently SQL Server) that the I/O has completed as soon as it has been written to the cache, thus making logical write performance very fast. Of course, this data still must be written to the disk at a later time.

- **Caching read-ahead data** Another use of the controller cache is to read data in addition to the data that was requested, in anticipation of that additional data being requested soon. If it is, the response time is very fast. The operation that reads additional data is called *read-ahead* because it reads the next data on the disk, even if it is not currently requested. Remember, the time it takes to perform I/Os is dominated by the seek time. If the disk drive has already moved to the required cylinder, reading a few more sectors does not incur serious overhead.

Write performance is important, especially when using RAID level 5. In most cases the controller cache is of great benefit. There are, however, a few things to be careful of.

- Don't use write caching without a battery backup. Most caching controllers include a battery (or have it as an option). This battery helps retain data in the cache in the event of a power failure. Without the battery the data in the cache is lost and the database could become corrupted. This is especially true of the transaction log. Never use write caching on the transaction log without a battery backup.

- In rare situations in which the RAID array is run near capacity, write caching can actually hurt read performance because of the priority that writes are given within the controller in order to empty the cache. In this case, disabling the write cache could improve performance.

Controller caches can enhance the performance of your disk array. By understanding the various RAID levels and their performance characteristics, you will be better able to configure and size your system.

Internal vs. External RAID

There are two basic types of RAID controllers: internal and external, which refer to where the RAID logic lies in the configuration, as shown in Figure 3-6. With most controllers the RAID logic resides on the controller card, which resides in the chassis that houses the computer system. This is referred to as an *internal RAID controller*. In a second type of RAID controller the RAID logic resides in the cabinet that houses the disk drives. This is referred to as an *external RAID controller*. Each type of controller has its own properties and characteristics.

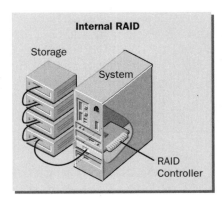
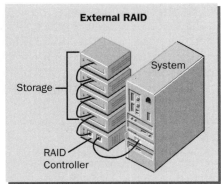

Figure 3-6. *Internal vs. external RAID.*

Storage Area Networks

One of the latest technologies on the market today is the *storage area network* (SAN). A SAN is a large external RAID system that shares the storage among several different systems (hence the term *network*). A SAN offers consolidation of storage and cost savings while allowing centralized management and centralized support.

The concept of a SAN is fairly straightforward. Where an external RAID system has a connection directly from the host bus adapter (HBA) to the external RAID subsystem, a SAN's connection from the HBA goes into a switch. This switch has multiple HBAs connected to it as well as at least one external RAID system. With this setup all the systems on the SAN can access the RAID subsystem. The SAN system is shown in Figure 3-7.

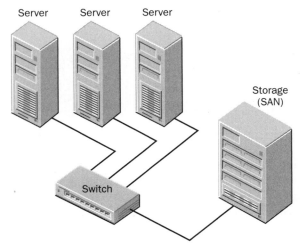

Figure 3-7. *SAN system.*

With SAN systems, multiple systems and multiple storage devices and backup devices can share the same switch, which allows a lot of flexibility. In addition, devices can be shared, allowing you to use your budget elsewhere. Some SAN systems include software and hardware designed to improve the performance of SQL Server backups by using mirror splitting. This concept as it relates to backup and recovery is covered in Chapter 15, "High-Performance Backup and Recovery."

Common RAID Levels

You can combine two or more disks into a RAID array. The main characteristic of a RAID array is that physical disk drives are combined to form a *logical disk drive*, that is, a virtual disk drive. To Windows 2000 (and to System Monitor), this logical disk drive appears as a single disk drive, even though it might consist of many individual physical disk drives. In fact, a logical disk drive in Windows 2000 could appear to be many hundreds of gigabytes in size, even though 100-GB disk drives don't exist (yet!).

Striping

Most of the RAID levels described here use *data striping*. Data striping combines the data from two or more disks into one larger RAID logical disk. Striping is accomplished by partitioning the data and then placing the first piece of data on the first disk, placing the second piece of data on the second disk, and so on. These small pieces are known as *stripes* or *chunks*. The controller determines the size of the stripe. Some controllers allow you to configure the stripe size, whereas other controllers have a fixed stripe size.

If the stripe size is configurable, choosing the right stripe size is important. A stripe size that is too small can split an otherwise single I/O across multiple disk drives, causing multiple seeks to occur when one drive could satisfy the I/O. Under Windows 2000 the largest I/O that is supported is 64-KB, so we recommend using the 64-KB stripe size whenever possible.

The combination of all the related chunks of data across all disk drives is also referred to as a *stripe*, as shown in Figure 3-8. Thus the term *stripe* can describe the piece of data on a specific disk drive (that is, "the disk stripe") or refer to the entire set (that is, "the RAID stripe"), which is helpful to keep in mind during discussions of RAID.

The RAID level itself determines the other characteristics of a RAID array. The *RAID level* is a term used to identify the RAID configuration type. One of the most important characteristics of a RAID system is *fault tolerance*, which is the ability to continue functioning after a disk drive has failed. Fault tolerance is the primary reason for using RAID controllers. Because your data is valuable, you must protect it against a disk failure. This section discusses the most common RAID levels—how they work, what fault tolerance they provide, and how they perform. Some RAID levels are rarely used; only the most popular ones will be covered in this chapter.

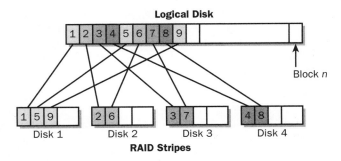

Figure 3-8. *RAID stripes.*

RAID 0

RAID 0 is the most basic of the RAID levels. It offers disk striping only. A chunk (the size of which is defined by the controller) is created on each disk drive. A round-robin method is used to distribute the data across all the disks in the RAID 0 array in order to create a large logical disk, as shown in Figure 3-9.

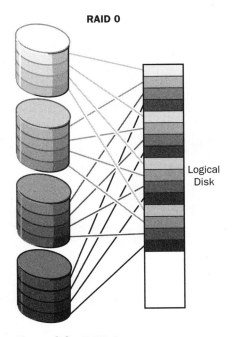

Figure 3-9. *RAID 0.*

Although RAID 0 is considered a RAID level, it doesn't support redundancy. Because there is no redundancy, there is no fault tolerance, so if any disk were to fail in a RAID 0 array, data would be lost. The loss of one disk of a four-disk array, for example, would be equivalent to losing every fourth word in this book. With this portion of the data missing, the entire logical disk is useless; so the entire database on that logical disk is useless.

RAID 0 Recommendations

RAID 0 is not typically recommended for storing SQL Server data files. Because the data in the database is important to your business, its loss could be devastating. A RAID 0 array does not protect you against a disk failure, so we do not recommend using it for any critical system component, such as OS, transaction log, or database files.

Caution A disk drive is a mechanical component. The disk is spinning at a high rate of speed and operates at a high temperature. Because the disk is a mechanical component, it is one of the most likely components to fail. It is important to protect your database against that failure by using fault tolerance on SQL Server data files.

RAID 1

RAID 1 is the most basic of the fault-tolerant RAID levels, as shown in Figure 3-10. RAID 1, also known as *mirroring,* creates a duplicate of your data disk. This duplicate contains all of the information that exists on the original disk. In the event of a disk failure, the mirror takes over; so there is no loss of data. The data is all held on one disk (and stored in the identical form on its mirror), so there is no striping involved. Since RAID 1 uses the second disk drive to duplicate the first disk, the total space of the RAID 1 volume is equivalent to the space of one disk drive. RAID 1 is costly because you must double the number of disks without getting any additional disk space; but you do get a high level of fault tolerance.

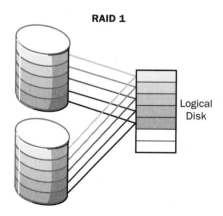

Figure 3-10. *RAID 1.*

When data is written to a RAID 1 volume, the controller must write this data to both disk drives before the I/O is considered completed, because the system is not fault tolerant until both disks have the data. After the data has been written to both disk drives, it can be recovered in the event of a failure in either disk. The latency involved in writing to the disk is the longer of the two disk writes; thus, if one disk takes longer to write than the other disk, the latency of the I/O is the longer of the two individual latencies. For example, if one disk drive takes 0.6 ms and the other takes 0.8 ms, the controller will not indicate to Windows that the I/O has completed until the 0.8 ms I/O has completed.

The fact that the write goes to both disks also figures into the capacity of the disk drive. When calculating how many I/Os are going to each disk drive in the array, you must multiply the number of writes by 2. Reads occur only on one disk. Disks might perform at different rates because the heads on one disk might be positioned differently from the heads on the other disk. This happens because RAID 1 supports split seeks; thus, a seek might take longer on one disk than on the other.

Split seeks allow you to perform reads from either disk in a RAID 1 volume independently. Most vendors support split seeks in order to decrease read latency. By allowing two disks to perform reads, performance increases because the I/O load is distributed to two disks instead of one.

RAID 1 Recommendations

RAID 1 offers a high degree of fault tolerance, as well as good performance. Some recommendations for using RAID 1 are as follows:

- Use RAID 1 when all the data fits on one disk drive.
- Use RAID 1 for your operating system disk. It can be time-consuming to rebuild an OS in the event of a failure. Since the OS usually fits on one disk, RAID 1 is a good choice.
- Use RAID 1 for the transaction log. Typically the SQL Server transaction log can fit on one disk drive. In addition, the transaction log performs mostly sequential writes. Only rollback operations cause reads from the transaction log. Thus you can achieve a high rate of performance by isolating the transaction log to its own RAID 1 volume.
- Use write caching on RAID 1 volumes. Because RAID 1 writes will not finish until both writes have been done, you can improve performance of writes by using a write cache. When you use a write cache be sure that it is backed up by a battery.

There are other fault-tolerant solutions for use when more than one disk is required. RAID 1 is great when fault tolerance is required and one disk is sufficient for all the data.

RAID 5

RAID 5 is a fault-tolerant RAID level that uses *parity* to introduce redundancy to the data. When the data is partitioned into stripes, additional parity bits are computed and stored on one disk in the stripe. If one disk fails, making a stripe unavailable, the parity bits, along with the data stored on other disks in the RAID stripe, can be used to recreate the data on the failed disk drive in the stripe. Thus, a RAID 5 array can tolerate the loss of one disk drive in the array. The parity information is rotated among the different disk drives in the array, as shown in Figure 3-11.

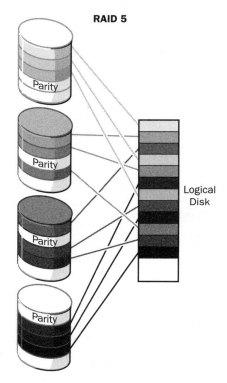

Figure 3-11. *RAID 5.*

The advantage of RAID 5 is that the space available in this RAID level is equal to *N* minus 1, where *N* is the number of disk drives in the array. Thus a RAID 5 array made up of 10 disk drives has the space of nine disks. This makes RAID 5 an economical fault-tolerant choice.

Unfortunately, RAID 5 carries performance penalties. Additional overhead is involved in maintaining the parity. When writing to a RAID 5 array, both the target disk stripe and the parity stripe must be read and the parity calculated, and then both stripes must be written out. Therefore a RAID 5 write actually incurs four physical I/Os.

Parity Explained

RAID 5 computes parity on all the data in all the stripes for all the disk drives. *Parity* is an additional piece of data that is computed by examining all the other bits and determining which value the parity bit must contain to create an even number for even parity, or odd number for odd parity. This parity bit, along with all the remaining bits, can be used to determine the value of a missing bit.

Let's look at an example of how parity works. For this example we will consider a RAID 5 system with five disk drives. Each disk drive is essentially made up of a number of bits, starting from the first part of the stripe on each disk to the end part of the stripe on each disk. The parity is created by looking at the individual bits from each disk drive and creating a bit parity.

In this example the parity is even, meaning that all the bits must add up to an even number. So, let's see how parity works. If the first bit on the first disk drive is 0, the first bit on the second drive is 1, the first bit on the third drive is 1, and the first bit on the fourth drive is 1, then the parity can only be 1 in order for the sum of these bits to add up to an even number, as shown in Figure 3-12.

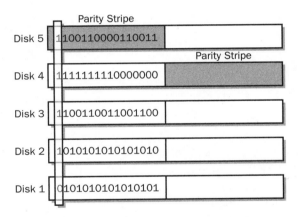

Figure 3-12. *Example: Computing a parity bit.*

Think of the parity as being created on single bits. Even though the disk stripe contains many bits, it is by computing parity on the single bits that the data becomes recoverable. As you can see in Figure 3-12, the parity is actually created on individual bits in the stripes. Even though the disk drives are broken up into chunks or stripe pieces that might be 64 KB or larger, the parity can only be created in a bitwise fashion, as shown in the figure. Of course, the way parity is actually calculated is a little more sophisticated than shown here.

So, let's say for example that disk 3 failed. In this case, you can use the parity bit plus all the other bits from all the other disk drives to recover the missing bit from disk 3, because you know they all add up to an even number.

Computing Parity

As you have seen, the RAID 5 parity is computed by finding the sum of the same bit on all the drives in the RAID 5 array and then creating a parity bit so that the result is even. Well, as you might imagine, it is impractical for an array controller to read all the data from all the drives each time an I/O occurs—it would be inefficient and slow.

Instead, when a RAID 5 array is created, the data is initially zeroed out and the parity is reset. Once this process has been completed, you are left with a set of RAID 5 disk drives with no data but with a full set of parity. From this point on, whenever data is written to a disk drive both the data disk and the parity disk must first be read. The new data is compared with the old data and if the data for a particular bit has changed, the parity for that bit must change. The controller does this using an XOR (exclusive OR) operation. Thus the array controller need read only the data disk and the parity disk, not all the disks in the array.

Both disk drives must be written after this operation has been performed, because the parity operation works on entire stripes. Therefore for each write I/O to a RAID 5 volume, four physical I/Os are incurred: two reads (one from data and one from parity) and two writes (back to data and back to parity). But with a RAID 5 array the parity is distributed, so usually this load is balanced among all the disk drives in the array.

RAID 5 Recommendations

Because of the additional I/Os incurred by RAID 5 writes, this RAID level is recommended for disk volumes that are used mostly for reading. Because the parity chunks are distributed among the different disks in the array, all disks are used for read operations. These characteristics lead to the following recommendations.

- Use RAID 5 on read-only volumes. Any disk volume that does more than 10 percent writes is not a good candidate for RAID 5.

- Use write caching on RAID 5 volumes. Since a RAID 5 write is not complete until two reads and two writes have been performed, you can improve the response time of writes through the use of a write cache. When you use a write cache, be sure that it is backed up with a battery. However, the write cache is not a cure for overdriving your disk drives. You must still stay within the capacity of those disks.

As you can see, RAID 5 is economical, but at a performance price. You will see later in this chapter how high that price can be.

RAID 10

RAID 10 is a combination of RAID 0 and RAID 1. RAID 10 involves mirroring a disk stripe. Each disk has an exact duplicate, but each disk contains only a part of the data, as shown in Figure 3-13. This configuration gives you the fault-tolerant advantages of RAID 1 with the convenience and performance advantages of RAID 0.

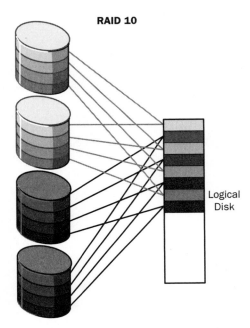

RAID 10

Logical
Disk

Figure 3-13. *RAID 10.*

As with RAID 1, each write operation incurs two physical I/Os, one to each disk in the mirror, so when you calculate the number of I/Os per disk, you must multiply the writes by two. Similarly, the I/O is not complete until both writes are done; so the write latency might increase. Most controllers support split seeks with RAID 10, however, just as they do with RAID 1, so the response time for reading is not increased.

RAID 10 offers a high degree of fault tolerance. In fact, more than one disk can fail and the array can survive. Of course, the loss of both sides of the mirror cannot be tolerated. If the mirror is split across disk cabinets, however, the loss of an entire cabinet can be tolerated.

RAID 10 Recommendations

RAID 10 offers a high degree of fault tolerance and is high performance. RAID 10 should be used when a large volume is required and more than 10 percent of the I/Os are writes. RAID 10 recommendations include the following:

- Use RAID 10 whenever the array experiences more than 10 percent writes. RAID 5 does not perform well with large numbers of writes.
- Use RAID 10 when performance is critical. Since RAID 10 supports split seeks, performance is very good.
- Use write caching on RAID 10 volumes. Since RAID 10 writes are not complete until both writes are done, you can improve the performance of writes by using a write cache. Write caching is only safe when used in conjunction with caches that are backed up with batteries.

RAID 10 is the best fault-tolerant solution, but it comes at a cost. You must purchase twice the number of disks that you would need with RAID 0. If your volume is mostly read, then RAID 5 might be acceptable.

Performance Comparison of RAID Levels

To properly configure and tune your RAID system you must understand the performance differences among the RAID levels. By understanding how the RAID system works and how it performs under various conditions, you will better be able to tune your I/O subsystem. This section compares the different performance characteristics described earlier.

Read Performance

Read performance is not significantly affected by RAID controllers. When you perform read operations on a RAID 0, RAID 1, RAID 5, or RAID 10 volume, you can take advantage of the performance provided by the total of all the disk drives in the system. Because random I/Os are typically the most problematic, they are covered here. You can maximize sequential performance by isolating the sequential I/Os to their own volume. Let's look at random read performance under the various RAID levels.

- RAID 0 volumes spread the data evenly among all the disks in the RAID array, so random I/Os should spread out randomly among all the disk drives in the system. If we use the general rule of 125 I/Os per second per disk drive (random I/O), a RAID 0 array of 10 disk drives should be able to handle 1250 I/Os per second.

- RAID 1 volumes support split seeks, so for read operations both disk drives are used. A RAID 1 volume can support twice the number of reads as a single disk, or 250 I/Os per second, before performance begins to suffer.

- RAID 5 arrays spread the data evenly among all the disk drives in the array. Even though one disk drive is used for parity in each stripe, all drives are typically used for reading because the I/Os are random in nature. As with the RAID 0 array, the read capacity is 125 I/Os per second times the number of disk drives in the array. Running at more than that reduces SQL Server performance.

- RAID 10 arrays, like RAID 1, support split seeks. The read performance is therefore equivalent to the number of disk drives times 125 I/Os per second. Exceeding this limit works, but might cause performance degradation.

As you can see, calculating the read capacity of a RAID array is fairly straightforward. By adding enough disk drives to support your I/O requirements and staying within these limitations, your performance should be excellent.

Write Performance

Write performance is dramatically affected by RAID controllers. Again, random I/Os are typically the most problematic, so let's look at random write performance under the various RAID levels.

- RAID 0 is most capable of handling writes without performance degradation, but at the price of no fault tolerance. Because RAID 0 does not mirror data or use parity, the performance of RAID 0 is simply that of the individual disk drives. A RAID 0 array of 10 disk drives can handle 1250 random writes per second.

- RAID 1 arrays must mirror any data that is written to the array. A single write I/O to the array generates two I/Os to the disk drives, so a RAID 1 array has the capacity of a single disk drive, or 125 I/Os per second.

- RAID 5 arrays are even more demanding on write I/Os. A write to a RAID 5 array actually generates two reads from the disks and two writes to the disks. Thus an I/O to a RAID 5 array generates four physical I/Os to the disks, making the write capacity of a RAID 5 array one-fourth the number of disk drives in the array.

- RAID 10 has the same characteristics as the RAID 1 array. Each write to the RAID 10 volume will generate two physical writes. Thus the capacity of the RAID 10 array is equivalent to the capacity of one-half the number of disk drives in the array.

As you can see, calculating the write capacity of a RAID array is a fairly complex operation. By adding enough disk drives to support your I/O requirements and staying within the limitations described above, you can keep the I/O subsystem from becoming a bottleneck. The next section shows how to calculate the number of I/Os per disk in various situations.

Disk Calculations

To determine the load placed on the individual disk drives in the system, you must perform some calculations. If you are using a hardware RAID controller, the number of I/Os per second displayed is the number of I/Os going to the array. Additional I/Os that are generated by the controller for fault tolerance are not shown. In fact, Windows NT is not even informed that they are occurring, but you must be aware of them.

The following formulas can help you determine how many I/Os are actually going to each disk in the array.

RAID 0

Calculate the number of I/Os per disk drive in a RAID 0 array by adding up all the reads and writes to the array and dividing by the number of disks in the array, as follows:

I/Os per Disk = (Reads + Writes) / Number of Disks

RAID 0 presents a simple and straightforward equation.

RAID 1

With RAID 1 the calculation becomes more complicated. Because writes are doubled, the number of I/Os per disk is equal to the number of reads plus twice the number of writes, divided by the number of disk drives in the array (which is two for RAID 1). The equation is as follows:

*I/Os per Disk = [Reads + (2 * Writes)] / 2*

RAID 1 is harder on writes, but offers a high degree of fault tolerance.

RAID 5

RAID 5 reads are distributed equally among the different disk drives in the array, but writes actually cause four physical I/Os to occur. To calculate the number of I/Os occurring on the individual disk drives, you add the reads to four times the number of writes before dividing by the number of disk drives. The equation for RAID 5 I/Os is as follows:

*I/Os per Disk = [Reads + (4 * Writes)] / Number of Disks*

RAID 5 has a high level of overhead on writes, but offers fault tolerance.

RAID 10

The calculation with RAID 10 is the same as with RAID 1, except that RAID 1 always has only two disk drives whereas RAID 10 supports multiples of two disk drives. Because writes are doubled, the number of I/Os per disk is equal to the number of reads plus twice the number of writes, divided by the number of disk drives in the array. The equation is as follows:

*I/Os per Disk = [Reads + (2 * Writes)] / Number of Disks*

RAID 10 is harder on writes, as is RAID 1, but offers a high degree of fault tolerance.

Choosing the Right RAID Level

To help you determine the best RAID level for you, let's compare them directly. When you compare I/O performance across different RAID levels, one of the most important considerations is the read to write ratio. The different RAID levels perform comparably when performing reads; only the writes have different characteristics. You should also keep in mind whether you need fault tolerance. Finally you should be aware of the different costs involved (for the space you get). Table 3-2 summarizes the characteristics of the various RAID levels. As you can see, your best choice depends on your requirements.

Table 3-2. RAID Levels

RAID Level	Performance	Fault Tolerance	Cost
RAID 0	Best	No fault tolerance	Most economical
RAID 1	Good	Good	Most expensive
RAID 5	Good reads Slow writes	OK	Most economical Fault tolerant
RAID 10	Good	Excellent	Most expensive

Table 3-3 illustrates the differences between RAID 5 and RAID 10 at different read/write ratios. This table shows the load for 500 I/Os per second across 10 disk drives with varying read/write ratios. At about 90 percent reads to 10 percent writes, the disk usage is about even, but for higher ratios of writes RAID 5 incurs much more overhead.

Table 3-3. Comparing Disk Loads

Read/Write Ratio	RAID 5 I/Os*	RAID 10 I/Os†
100% reads; 0% writes	(500 + 0) / 10 50 I/Os per disk	(500 + 0) / 10 50 I/Os per disk
90% reads; 10% writes	(450 + 200) / 10 65 I/Os per disk	(450 + 100) / 10 55 I/Os per disk
75% reads; 25% writes	(375 + 500) / 10 87.5 I/Os per disk	(375 + 250) / 10 62.5 I/Os per disk
50% reads; 50% writes	(250 + 1000) / 10 125 I/Os per disk	(250 + 500) / 10 75 I/Os per disk
0% reads; 100% writes	(0 + 2000) / 10 200 I/Os per disk	(0 + 1000) / 10 100 I/Os per disk

* *[Reads + (4 * Writes)] / Number of Disks*
† *[Reads + (2 * Writes)] / Number of Disks*

This is illustrated in Figure 3-14 below.

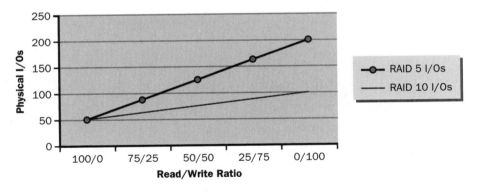

Figure 3-14. *RAID 5 and RAID 10 disk-load comparison.*

I/O Latencies and SQL Server

SQL Server is sensitive to I/O latencies because of the concurrency of transactions within the SQL Server engine. Under typical conditions tens or hundreds of applications run against a SQL Server database, which SQL Server has a complex system of row, page, extent, and table locks to provide for, as you will see throughout this book. When a piece of data or a SQL Server resource is locked, other processes block, waiting for that data or resource to be unlocked.

When I/Os take an excessively long time to finish, the locked resources are held longer than normal. The amount of blocking also increases, delaying other processing in the system. In addition, excessive blocking leads to higher chances of deadlocks. The longer the I/O takes to finish, the longer the locks are held and the greater the potential for problems.

The time a query takes to finish processing significantly increases if an I/O subsystem is overloaded. Take, for example, a case in which long table scans are running on your system. It is not uncommon for this type of query to read hundreds of thousands or even millions of rows to complete the task. If such a large table scan causes one million I/Os to be performed, the time difference between an optimal and suboptimal system is dramatic. On average, one million I/Os at 10 ms each take approximately 2.7 hours to complete. If your system has overloaded the I/O subsystem and each I/O takes 40 ms, however, it will take 11 hours to complete the I/Os associated with this query.

As you can see, SQL Server performance can be severely degraded by a poorly sized or poorly configured I/O subsystem. By designing your I/O subsystem to work within the capacity of the individual components, you can ensure the excellent performance of your database. Some tips and recommendations are provided in the next section.

Guidelines for Configuring I/O Subsystems

This section presents tips and recommendations on how to best use RAID controllers in your system. We hope they help you to better configure and use your RAID array.

- Isolate the SQL Server transaction log onto its own RAID 1 or RAID 10 volume. I/Os to the transaction log are almost 100 percent sequential and almost 100 percent writes. During a rollback operation is the only time the sequential nature of the transaction log is disrupted. If the data needed for a rollback is no longer cached, the information must be read from the transaction log.

- Configure enough drives to keep the data file volumes at fewer than 125 I/Os per second per disk. Simply add more disk drives to the array until you have enough. If the I/Os are random, and they usually are, the I/Os spread out among all the disk drives in the array.

- Configure data file volumes as RAID 5 if write I/Os are less than 10 percent, and as RAID 10 if writes are greater then 10 percent of the total I/Os.

- Regularly monitor the number of I/Os per second per disk. If the disks are nearing their capacity, add more disk drives.

By following these guidelines and carefully monitoring your system, you should be able to avoid performance problems.

Summary

This chapter discussed the basics of I/O tuning. We talked about disk drives and their limitations, so that you can configure your system to work within those limitations. We discussed RAID controllers and the various RAID levels. Knowing the characteristics of the different RAID levels will help you configure your system to its best advantage. We also discussed how a poorly tuned I/O subsystem can negatively affect SQL Server performance. I/O tuning is all about capacity. By working within the capacity of the various components, you can achieve excellent performance. In the next chapter, we discuss how to measure and tune hardware, database layout, and SQL Server configuration parameters.

Chapter 4
System Tuning

You can optimize, or *tune*, many aspects of your Microsoft SQL Server 2000 system to improve performance. Much of this book focuses on tuning different components of your system, such as hardware, SQL Server configuration, database layout, SQL statements, SQL indexes, replication, backup and recovery, and more. This chapter discusses specific tuning issues involving hardware capacity, database layout, and SQL Server configuration options.

First we describe ways to measure performance. Then we discuss how to determine if one or more of your hardware components is causing a bottleneck, which could be holding back the performance of the system. We focus on how you can determine if the hardware you have is sufficient for your needs and if it is performing optimally, and if not, what to do about it. We also discuss how to optimize your database layout using files and filegroups in more detail than we did in Chapter 2, "SQL Server 2000 Architecture Fundamentals." Finally we describe the most common SQL Server configuration options that you might need to adjust from their defaults.

How to Measure Performance

You can measure the overall performance of a system by looking at transaction *response times,* that is, the time it takes to complete a query or task, which is also part of the time the user must wait for the task to finish and possibly return results. (Another part might include the time it takes the application to display the results on the screen.) Slow (long) response times translate into bad performance and frustrated users, whereas quick response times mean better performance and happy users. You should talk with your database users to get feedback on the response times they get when they perform database tasks, which are probably performed through a database application. Try to get specific response times and objective answers—but generally you can get a good idea of which transactions or business functions are taking a long time, such as a query that takes two minutes to respond. On the other hand, you should consider user input along with more concrete data, such as a SQL Profiler trace, to get the most accurate information. It's a good idea to ask a user to run a particular business function through the application while you trace the SQL Server statements for that user in SQL Profiler. This will tell you which statements and/or stored procedures are called for that business function, and also the time it takes for each statement or procedure to finish. Then you can focus on tuning the statements that took the most time to complete or the ones that performed a high number of reads, for example.

You might encounter a transaction that finishes with different response times at each execution. For example, users might wait only 10 seconds for a transaction to finish the first time it is run, and a second time it might take 10 minutes to complete. This can indicate a performance problem, such as a SQL Server blocking issue or insufficient hardware. It also might be related to the time of day when the transaction was run. For instance, if the transaction was first run at 7:30 A.M., before all the users logged on the system, and it was run the second time at 10 A.M., when more users were logged on and lots of processing was going on, then there was more contention for resources on the system in the second instance, and blocking can occur—this alone could affect the response time. Or, a database backup might have been occurring at the latter time, which causes a lot of read activity on the system and can slow down all user transactions.

Your system thus can show faster or slower response times at different times of the day, according to heavy or light user activity. If a user transaction takes a relatively long time to finish, or more time than you think it should based on previous tuning experience, you might have a performance problem that you could resolve, and you should investigate. Some performance issues are impossible to resolve if you are limited in some way. For example, you might need more disks to handle the I/O needs of your system, but not have the budget to buy additional hardware. Be sure to include the costs for new and spare hardware in your budget calculations for the next quarter if you need hardware.

Another way to measure performance is to simply monitor your system on a regular basis. This book discusses what to look for when monitoring and how to interpret what you see. The main method for monitoring hardware performance that we discuss in this chapter is using System Monitor inside the Microsoft Windows 2000 Performance console. System Monitor is similar to the Performance Monitor (PerfMon) in Windows NT. With System Monitor you can view system performance real time or you can collect the performance data in a log file to view it at a later time. The log file option provides an excellent way to compare performance data from different days and times to see how your system has evolved. See Chapter 6, "Monitoring Performance with Windows 2000 System Monitor" for information about how to use the Performance tool. In this chapter we will discuss the counters that are relative to each topic.

Before you conclude that you have a hardware bottleneck, you should investigate your SQL statements, stored procedures, application code, database layout, and indexes, because these areas could also cause performance problems. If a query is performing a table scan, for example, it could be causing more disk I/O activity than if you had an index to cover that query, which could make it appear that you have a disk bottleneck. The main point here is that you should not look at only one area of your system, such as hardware, when tuning. You must look at each area and tune them together. You do not want to end up buying lots of hardware to support a badly written stored procedure that performs many more I/Os than it should.

Tuning the Server with Hardware

When we use the phrase *hardware tuning*, we are referring to tuning the amount, size, and speed of hardware in your system. Hardware tuning involves several components of your system. We discuss the three most common that require tuning in this chapter—the processors, disks, and memory. This section explains how to determine if one or more of those components is causing a bottleneck in your system, and how to solve the problem if you do find one. These methods will also tell you if there is no real hardware performance problem, in which case you don't need to add or upgrade hardware.

Tuning hardware involves examining many interdependent components. You might find a bottleneck in one component, add more of that component to fix the bottleneck, which might allow more processing on the system than before. This could reveal a bottleneck in another component, even though your throughput has improved. We give an example of such a case in the "Tuning the Disk Subsystem" section later in this chapter. We start our hardware tuning discussion with a description of system processor architecture and how to tune your system with the right processors.

Processor Architecture

Processors are also referred to as *CPUs*, although the CPU (central processing unit) is actually only a part of a processor unit. Each processor unit contains a CPU with a level 1 cache, possibly a level 2 cache, and a math coprocessor or other microprocessor chips designed for special functionality, as shown in Figure 4-1.

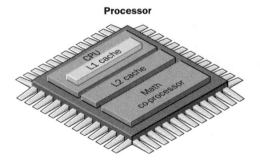

Figure 4-1. *Processor architecture.*

The level 1 (L1) cache is a section of memory located within the CPU, so that the CPU can access it quickly. It is relatively small: in the newer processors, it is 32 KB, of which 16 KB is used for storing instructions and the other 16 KB is used for storing data. This cache is the fastest memory access available to the CPU. The level 2 (L2) cache provides additional space for holding instructions. In some processors the L2 cache is located on the processor unit, and in other processors it is separate from the unit. The L2 cache typically comes in sizes such as 256 KB, 512 KB, 1 MB, and 2 MB.

When data or the next instruction is needed, the processor first checks the L1 cache to see if the data resides there, then checks the L2 cache, then system memory (RAM). It is much faster to access the L1 or L2 caches than it is to read from the system memory. In turn, it is faster to read from RAM than from disk. For the rest of this chapter we use both terms, processor and CPU, to refer to the entire processor unit.

A system with one CPU is called *a single-processor system*; a Microsoft Windows system with more than one CPU is called a *symmetric multiprocessing (SMP) system*, because Windows distributes processing of application threads across all of the CPUs symmetrically. In a single-processor system, only one thread at a time can execute on the CPU, and therefore only one task can be handled at a time. Multiple tasks must take turns processing on the CPU. With an SMP system, the CPUs can process threads in parallel (one thread per CPU), greatly increasing the processing capacity and speed, resulting in increased throughput. The CPUs all share the same system memory (the system RAM) and must take turns accessing that memory by way of the memory bus, as shown in Figure 4-2. The more processors you have in a system, the higher the chances are of collisions on the memory bus when they try to access the memory, causing delays in processing. The L2 cache is helpful in such a case. If the data is in the L2 cache, a processor does not have to access the system memory, avoiding collisions and time spent on the memory bus. Therefore, the more CPUs in your system, the more important a large L2 cache becomes. We recommend that for SMP systems you buy the largest L2 cache that your budget allows.

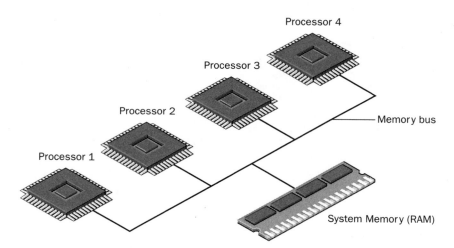

Figure 4-2. *Memory bus utilization with SMP.*

A single processor system will not have the same problem with collisions on the memory bus as an SMP system, but accessing data from the L2 cache is still faster than accessing the memory. Thus a large L2 cache helps performance in any type of system, and does not hurt it.

Tuning the Processor

Whether you have one or more CPUs, how you determine whether you have a CPU bottleneck is basically the same. First you must monitor the CPU activity on your system while work is occurring. Make sure to monitor the system during all times of the day for certain times when processing is heavier than others so that you can configure your system to handle the heaviest load times. To monitor CPU utilization, use System Monitor and choose the following object and counter to monitor:

Processor object, % Processor Time counter Select All Instances to see the processor utilization per processor, as well as the average utilization over all processors (Total).

A general rule is that if your processor utilization stays continuously at 80 percent or above, or if it peaks often at this rate, you might have a CPU bottleneck. See selected sections in chapters 8, 9, and 11 of Part II, "Sizing and Capacity Planning" for more detailed discussions of CPU capacity. If you detect a CPU bottleneck, adding more or faster processors to the system should improve performance. For example, say your system contains one CPU with a speed of 500 MHz, and you find that the CPU utilization is averaging 75 to 80 percent. In this case, you could benefit from adding a second 500-MHz CPU to the system to make it an SMP system with parallel processing capabilities, assuming there is an extra slot in your machine for a second CPU. If not, try exchanging the CPU for a faster one, perhaps a 700-MHz processor. Both solutions will improve performance, but your best bet is to add another processor if possible.

As another example, say you have a system with four processors running at a speed of 500 MHz and an L2 cache of 512 KB. You find that CPU utilization is typically at 75 percent across the four CPUs, and at times utilization hits 100 percent. This high use indicates a CPU bottleneck. You could try adding more CPUs if your system has the capacity; if not, switch the four existing CPUs for four faster ones, such as 700-MHz CPUs. Also, get a larger L2 cache on the processors, such as a 2-MB L2 cache.

When adding CPUs to your system, make sure that the operating system version and your version of SQL Server 2000 supports that number of CPUs. Table 4-1 below shows the number of CPUs supported by the versions of SQL Server 2000 with Windows 2000.

Table 4-1. The Number of CPUs supported by SQL Server and Windows 2000

	SQL Server Enterprise Edition	SQL Server Standard Edition	SQL Server Personal Edition	SQL Server Developer's Edition
Windows 2000 Datacenter Server	32	4	2	32
Windows 2000 Advanced Server	8	4	2	8
Windows 2000 Server	4	4	2	4
Windows 2000 Professional	2	2	2	2

Tuning the Disk Subsystem

Every disk drive has certain mechanical characteristics that determine its speed for handling reads and writes of data. You cannot actually tune the disk itself; rather, you tune the disk subsystem by configuring the type and number of disks needed to meet your I/O needs. Chapter 3, "Understanding the I/O Subsystem and RAID," explained the internal components of a disk drive and how it works. Reading that chapter should help you understand the concepts we discuss here.

You tune the disk subsystem so that your system can process I/Os without experiencing long I/O latencies, and reads and writes occur at an optimal speed. The term *latency* refers to the time that one component is idle waiting for another component to complete some operation; thus, I/O latency is the time it takes for the system to complete an I/O. In other words, you want your disks to have small (short) latencies. Small latencies indicate that you do not have a disk bottleneck. Latency is measured in milliseconds. This section discusses some important concepts about disk drives, how to monitor your disks to determine the read and write latencies on your system, how to tell if you have a bottleneck, and what to do if you have one.

Disk Drive Concepts

The I/O capacity of a disk is the maximum number of I/Os (reads plus writes) that a disk can perform before the number of I/O requests waiting in the queue becomes so large that latencies become exponentially longer, slowing down performance. Chapter 3 discussed how to determine the I/O capacity of a disk in detail, along with the importance of understanding how the different levels of RAID affect the number of physical I/Os that occur on a disk. (You will need to have that information for our examples later in this chapter.)

When the total number of I/O requests that your system needs to perform exceeds the I/O capacity of the disk, each I/O waits longer before it can be completed. An I/O request remains in a wait queue for its turn on the disk. This wait time in the queue results in a longer response time for the task that requested the I/O. Therefore, the essence of tuning disks is determining if you have sufficient disk speed and number of disks to efficiently and quickly handle the number of I/O requests occurring on your system.

As discussed in Chapter 3, disk drives come in a number of sizes and speeds. The size is measured in gigabytes, and the speed is measured in revolutions per minute (rpm). Basically, the faster the disk speed (rpm), the quicker the data can be physically accessed. The size of the disk determines how much data you can store on it. You never want to completely fill a disk with data, however. After a disk hits 85 percent of its capacity, you should consider it full. Chapter 8, "Modeling for Sizing and Capacity Planning," explains the reasoning behind this percentage limit on disk space filled.

Monitoring Disk I/O

Now let's learn how to monitor your disk activity using System Monitor. You use an application called *diskperf* to control which disk counters can be viewed, either the PhysicalDisk object, the LogicalDisk object, or both. So first we'll look at how to use *diskperf.* By default when you install Windows 2000, *diskperf* is enabled to allow counters for physical disk I/O to be viewed, but not counters for logical disk I/O. With physical disk I/O counters enabled you can view the System Monitor disk object called PhysicalDisk, which includes disk counters on a physical disk basis, such as Disk 0, Disk 1, etc. These disk numbers refer to the disk partitions that you created with your disk controller configuration utility. Logical disk I/O refers to the disk drive letter that you created on your physical disk partitions, such as C:, D:, E:, F:, I:, etc. You can view logical disk counters when the logical disk option is enabled by *diskperf.* So for example, you might have two logical disk drives C: and D: created on physical Disk 0. To view the I/O counters on C: and D: separately, you would enable the viewing of logical disk counters through *diskperf* to be able to view the LogicalDisk object in Performance tool. If you do not have logical disk counters enabled, and you view the PhysicalDisk object for Disk 0, you will see the total I/Os for C: plus D: together. You can view your configured physical and logical disks using the Disk Management feature in the Computer Management MMC snap-in. Now, you can change the *diskperf* options or disable all disk counters by running *diskperf* in a command prompt window. The following are the different options for *diskperf*:

- **diskperf** With no parameters reports whether disk performance counters are enabled and, if so, which one—either physical, logical, or both.
- **diskperf -y** Sets the system to enable both physical and logical disk counters when the system is restarted.
- **diskperf -yd** Sets the system to enable only physical disk counters when the system is restarted. This is the default setting.
- **diskperf -yv** Sets the system to enable only logical disk counters when the system is restarted.
- **diskperf -n** Sets the system to disable all disk counters when the system is restarted.
- **diskperf -nd** Disables physical disk counters when the system is restarted.
- **diskperf -nv** Disables logical disk counters when the system is restarted.
- **diskperf \\computername** Specifies the local or remote computer on which to set the *diskperf* options. If none is specified, the local computer is the default.

You must restart your server for your *diskperf* settings to take effect. The following counters under the PhysicalDisk or LogicalDisk object are important for monitoring disk I/O. (Both objects have the same counters, but they refer to either the physical disk or logical disk, depending on which you choose to view.)

- **Disk Reads/sec** The number of read operations performed per second on the selected disk (or disk array)
- **Disk Writes/sec** The number of write operations performed per second on the selected disk (or disk array)

- **Avg. Disk Queue Length** The average number of read and write requests that were queued on the selected disk during the polling interval
- **Avg. Disk Sec/Read** The average number of seconds it takes for a read from disk to be performed on the selected disk during the polling interval
- **Avg. Disk Sec/Write** The average number of seconds it takes for a write to disk to be performed on the selected disk during the polling interval

Select the disk or disks that you want to monitor by clicking the Select Instances From List option and selecting the disk or disks in the list in the Add Counters dialog box, as shown in Figure 4-3.

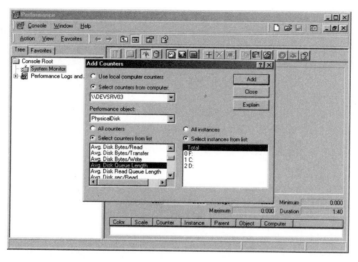

Figure 4-3. *Using System Monitor to select counters to monitor for the PhysicalDisk object.*

Finding Disk Bottlenecks

To illustrate how to use these counters to find disk bottlenecks, we'll walk through some system scenarios. Assume that the disks in these examples are 9-GB/10,000 rpm disks with an I/O capacity of 100 I/Os per second for random I/O. For our first example, assume you have a system configured with a RAID 10 array made up of eight disk drives. That means that each drive has a mirror, so four drives are mirrored to the other four drives, as shown in Figure 4-4. The Windows 2000 disk number for this array is Disk 2.

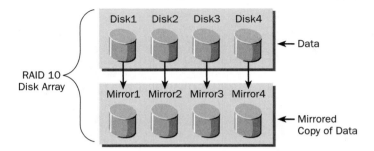

Figure 4-4. *Example with eight disk drives configured as a RAID 10 array.*

Assume that when you use System Monitor to monitor the PhysicalDisk counters discussed earlier, you find the following figures for Disk 2:

Disk Reads/sec	90
Disk Writes/sec	55
Avg. Disk Queue Length	1-2
Avg. Disk Sec/Read	0.009
Avg. Disk Sec/Write	0.007

We know that our drives can efficiently handle 100 random I/Os per second. To find out if we are surpassing that performance limit, we can use the first two values in the preceding list to calculate the number of physical I/Os on the drives because of RAID 10, using the following formula:

*I/Os per Disk = [Reads + (2 * Writes)] / Number of Disks*

Remember that with RAID 10, read requests can be serviced by a disk and its mirrored pair in parallel, and each write requires a physical write to a disk and its mirrored pair (thus we multiply writes times two in the formula). Plugging in the preceding values, we get:

*[90 + (2 * 55)] / 8 = 25 physical I/Os per disk*

Because 25 is well below the determined limit of 100 I/Os per disk per second, we do not have a bottleneck with these disks. Also note that the figures for seconds per read and per write are 9 ms and 7 ms, respectively. These low latencies also indicate that no bottleneck exists.

Now we'll look at this same example using different values for the counters:

Disk Reads/sec	420
Disk Writes/sec	300
Avg. Disk Queue Length	43
Avg. Disk Sec/Read	0.032
Avg. Disk Sec/Write	0.025

Plugging these new values into our formula, we get the following:

*[420 + (2 * 300)] / 4 = 127.5 physical I/Os per disk*

The result, 127.5, is above the limit of 100 I/Os per second; so we do have a slight disk bottleneck in this case. You can also see evidence of a bottleneck by simply looking at the figures for seconds per read and per write: the values should be under 15 ms to get the best performance from your drives. In this case, the figures are 32 ms and 25 ms, which indicate a bottleneck. Also note that the average queue length is 43, much longer than our previous example, which means that more I/O requests are waiting in the queue at one time, thus causing the longer latencies.

To relieve this disk bottleneck, divide the number of occurring I/Os by the I/O capacity per disk to get the minimum number of disks needed to support the amount of I/O. This calculation would look like the following:

*[420 reads + (2 * 300 writes)] = 1020 I/Os*

1020 total I/Os / 100 I/Os per disk = 10.2 disks needed

Because it is impossible to have 10.2 disks, you should round up to 12 disks (we need an even number of disks for RAID 10). Also, you will achieve better performance by adding more disks so that you are not running at the disk I/O limit, but rather below it. Therefore, in this case you would need to add four more disks to the system.

For our next example, we'll use a RAID 5 disk array of four disks that have the same I/O capacity as the disks in the previous examples and assume that random I/O will be performed on these disks. We will use the following numbers for our analysis:

Disk Reads/sec	120
Disk Writes/sec	150
Avg. Disk Queue Length	12
Avg. Disk Sec/Read	0.035
Avg. Disk Sec/Write	0.045

Just by looking at the high latency values for seconds per read and per write, you should realize that there is a disk bottleneck. To calculate how many I/Os are going to each disk, you would use the following formula for RAID 5 (as discussed in the "Disk Calculations" section in Chapter 3):

*[Reads + (4 * Writes)] / Number of Disks in Array = Physical I/Os per Disk*

Plugging in our numbers, we get

*[120 + (4 * 150)] / 4 = 180 I/Os per disk*

180 I/Os per disk is well above the 100 I/O limit. Therefore, you would need to take the total number of I/Os occurring, which is the first part of the equation—*[120 + (4 * 150)]*, or 720 I/Os—and divide that by the I/O capacity of the drive (100), as in the following equations:

*120 reads + (4 * 150 writes) = 720 total I/Os*

720 total I/Os / 100 I/Os per disk = 7.2 disks

Again you should round up to get a minimum of eight disks needed. But again, adding additional disks would be wise to allow for growth.

After you relieve the current disk bottleneck, processes that were waiting for I/O to finish will execute faster, allowing more processing (if there is more to be done), which in turn can cause even more I/O requests per second on the system. This is not a bad thing! It just means that you might need to add even more drives to match the new performance of your system. In any case, the initial addition of disks will improve the performance.

Tuning Memory

Now we'll discuss the third major hardware tuning area—system memory. This includes physical memory tuning and SQL Server memory tuning. You want to have enough physical memory in the system to support SQL Server and any other applications, and you want to allocate as much of that memory as possible to SQL Server without overallocating it, so that you avoid starving other applications of memory. (See Chapter 2 for details on how SQL Server uses its memory.) It is best to dedicate your database server to SQL Server applications only, if possible. That allows SQL Server to use as much memory as possible in the system without having to share it with other applications.

To determine if you have enough physical memory in your system, you must consider several factors. You might need to add physical memory to the system, or you might simply need to adjust the SQL Server memory options to improve performance. You should monitor the following objects and counters through the System Monitor in the Windows 2000 Performance console:

- **Memory object, Available MBytes counter** The amount, in megabytes, of available memory in the system that can be used by processes.
- **Memory object, Pages/sec counter** The number of pages per second that are paged out of memory to disk or paged into memory from disk.
- **SQLServer: Memory Manager object, Total Server Memory (KB) counter** The total memory size, in kilobytes, that SQL Server has allocated.
- **SQLServer: Buffer Manager object, Free Pages counter** The number of free pages available to SQL Server.
- **SQLServer: Buffer Manager object, Buffer Cache Hit Ratio counter** The percentage of pages that were found in the buffer pool (also called the data cache) without having to be read from disk. See Chapter 2 for details on the buffer pool.

- **Process object, Working Set counter** The current number of bytes of memory that the threads in a process have recently touched.

- **Process object, Page Faults/sec counter** The number of times a process references a page in memory that is not in its working set. If the page is still in main memory or being shared by another process, a page from disk will not occur; otherwise, it will.

Now we'll discuss how to interpret these counters. If the value for the Available MBytes counter is very low, meaning there is not much available physical memory left in the system, you should look at the other counters as well to determine whether you need to add physical memory. A low number of available megabytes could mean that your system is too low on total physical memory, or it could mean that an application is not releasing memory as it should when it is finished using the memory. Realize though, that if there is enough free memory in the system, a process is not required to release its memory, which is also known as its *working set*. This working set is the amount of memory, in bytes, that the threads of a process have recently touched. After free memory in the system drops below a certain threshold, Windows 2000 trims working sets to free up some memory.

To find out if a process is holding onto its memory for too long when there is not a lot of free memory available (that is, the value of the Available MBytes counter is low), thus starving other processes, monitor the Process object's Working Set counter for each process instance to determine how much memory each process has in its working set, and the maximum working set size it has used. If a process is no longer running but has not reduced its working set size (it remains at or near the maximum number of working set bytes), there might be a problem because that process is not releasing memory. If this is the case, you should consult with the software developer about fixing this problem before adding memory to the system. If there is no problem with an application holding onto memory, then continue to check the remaining memory counters.

To determine how much memory SQL Server itself is currently using, check the Total Server Memory (KB) counter of the SQLServer: Memory Manager object. This will show you whether SQL Server is hogging most of the memory in the system (this might be what you want if your system is dedicated to SQL Server applications). The value might change as SQL Server allocates and deallocates memory, if it is configured for dynamic memory allocation.

Monitoring the Pages/sec counter is very important. (Paging is discussed in more detail in Chapter 2.) Paging is a costly operation, so you want to reduce it as much as possible. If you see a high number of pages per second occurring, you could be giving SQL Server too much memory and starving other applications of memory, causing them to page. In this case, add memory to the machine or reduce your SQL Server memory by lowering the *max server memory* value. To monitor which process is causing the paging, look at the Process object's Page Faults/sec counter for each process instance. But remember to look at the remaining counters (discussed in the following section) before you reduce SQL Server memory, because you might worsen SQL Server performance.

You should also monitor the buffer cache hit ratio for SQL Server. The *buffer cache hit ratio* is the percentage of data pages that SQL Server requests that are found in the data cache, rather than being read from disk. For most applications (particularly online transaction processing), you want to achieve a cache hit ratio of 90 percent or more. This might not be possible with some applications, such as decision support, because the data and index pages might not be reused often. To achieve this ratio when possible, you need to have enough memory dedicated to SQL Server so that its buffer pool is large enough to support the 90 percent cache hit ratio. If you have allocated as much physical memory as possible to SQL Server and have not reached the 90 percent cache hit ratio, add more physical memory and allocate more to SQL Server if possible. If you can allocate more memory to SQL Server without adding physical memory (because there is still available memory for SQL Server to use), try increasing the *max server memory* option to allow SQL Server to take advantage of more memory. (This suggestion assumes that you do not have the *max server memory* option at its default, 2,147,483,647, which tells SQL Server to use as much memory as possible.)

Another indication of a lack of physical memory is if the number for the Free Pages counter of the SQLServer: Buffer Manager object is consistently well below 5 MB, which is about 640 8-KB pages. (The value is given in 8-KB pages.) If SQL Server cannot maintain 5 MB of free pages, as it is meant to, you are either running low on physical memory or allocating too much to SQL Server. If your cache hit ratio is not at 90 percent or higher, though, generally you need more memory in the system and you have not yet allocated enough to SQL Server. As you can see, you must take all of these System Monitor counters into consideration when forming a conclusion about your memory needs and how to tune memory.

On the other hand, you might have more memory than you need allocated to SQL Server. This can happen if you have a small database that fits completely into memory and there is still memory left over. This does not happen very often. For example, say you have allocated a fixed amount of memory to SQL Server (by setting the *max server memory* and *min server memory* options to the same value). You monitor the system and see that the working set size for the SQL Server process is consistently less than the memory you have allocated to SQL Server (monitor the sqlservr instance of the Process object's Working Set counter). You should then be able to reduce the values for the appropriate memory options to free up memory for other processes.

After you have changed your memory, monitor the system again to see the effects. You might need to make more than one change before you finally get the system tuned well. As a general rule for all types of system tuning, try not to make more than one change at once, or you might never know which one made the difference. Even worse, one change could cause a great improvement in performance, while another change could degrade performance and cancel out the effects of the improvement, and you would never know. While making one change at a time and monitoring it is preferable, sometimes you are very sure that you need to change a couple of things at once. Either way, it is important to keep a record of each change and its effect on the system. Later, if you see the same problem again, you can review your notes to remember what works and what doesn't work to fix that problem, without having to repeat the same analysis.

Optimizing Database Layout

The location and distribution of your data and log files are very important to the performance of your system. Two key guidelines for database layout are as follows: separate files that are accessed sequentially onto dedicated disks, and allow for parallel I/O by distributing data files across multiple disks. This section gives you some general guidelines and concepts about database layout; the next section, "Examples Using Files and Filegroups," provides some examples of how to distribute your data across disks for improved efficiency by using files and filegroups. (See Chapter 2 for a detailed description of files and filegroups.)

Guidelines for Database Layout

SQL Server log files receive mostly sequential writes, and data files can receive either sequential or random I/O. Usually data files receive random I/O because even if a file is accessed sequentially by one user, as soon as a second user begins to access that file, the access is no longer truly sequential. As mentioned in Chapter 3, "Understanding the I/O Subsystem and RAID," you should try to separate sequential I/O onto different disks from random I/O, and separate various sequential I/O files, such as log files for multiple user databases, onto their own disks. Sequential I/Os are much quicker than random I/Os because the seek time on the disk platter is much less. (See Chapter 3 for more details.)

If you place a randomly accessed data file on the same disk as a sequentially accessed log file, the sequential log writes can no longer be accessed sequentially on that disk—the random I/Os interfere with the sequential I/Os, causing the disk read/write head to seek the platter in a random fashion. The same is true if two files that will be sequentially accessed are on the same disk at the same time. One file's data accesses will interfere with the other's, so that neither file is physically accessed on the disk sequentially. Therefore, you should always place each set of user database log files on their own disks (since they are definitely sequential in nature), apart from all data files or other database's log files. This setup is optimal. Figure 4-5 illustrates a database disk layout for one log file and one large data file. This figure shows the log file on a RAID 10 disk array (or volume) and the data file on either a RAID 10 or RAID 5 disk array, for fault tolerance (remember that RAID 5 does not perform as well as RAID 10 if 10 percent or more of the I/O requests are writes). You should always use some type of fault tolerance. See Chapter 3 for details on the different levels of RAID.

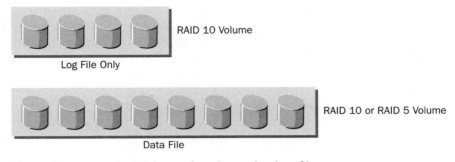

Figure 4-5. *A sample disk layout for a log and a data file.*

Another general guideline when laying out your data files is that you should spread your data across as many disk drives as possible, to allow for more parallel disk access. For example, say your application needs to read and write more than one page of data at the same time, which is typically the case because more than one user runs on the system concurrently. If you have only one disk drive with the data file on it, then each read and write must wait in a queue for access to the disk drive in order to complete its I/O request. Each disk can generally satisfy only one request at a time, as shown in Figure 4-6. The exception is when your application is requesting multiple pages of sequential data, in which case multiple pages can be read at one time with one disk access.

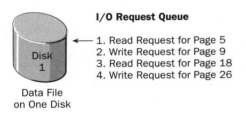

Figure 4-6. *Several I/O requests to one disk must wait in the queue.*

Figure 4-6 shows four I/O requests waiting in the queue. Request 1 will be completed first. Request 2 waits for request 1 to complete; then it will be completed. Request 3 waits for requests 1 and 2 to complete before it can be completed, so it has a longer wait time, and so on. The more I/O requests sent simultaneously to a disk, the longer the wait times for completing each I/O. This is one reason for using multiple disk drives for your data. Note also that I/O requests might not be satisfied in the order in which they were requested. The RAID controller might use elevator sorting (see Chapter 3)—sorting the I/O requests according to the location of the data on the disk platter so that they can be completed with less disk head movement.

When you spread data across multiple disks, it is highly probable that the pages to be accessed will be located on two or more disks. Thus the I/Os can be completed simultaneously (in parallel) on the multiple disks, as shown in Figure 4-7. For this reason, it is generally better to spread your data access across more small disks (such as 9 GB) than across fewer large disks (such as 18 GB or 36 GB), as shown in Figure 4-8.

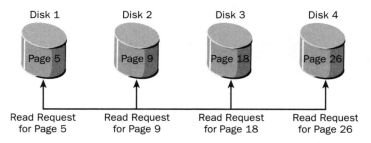

Figure 4-7. *Several I/O requests can be handled in parallel with multiple disks.*

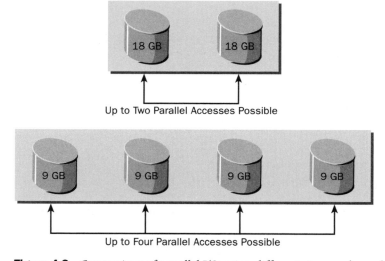

Figure 4-8. *Comparison of parallel I/O using different sizes and numbers of disks.*

Examples Using Files and Filegroups

In order to specifically place your database tables and indexes on certain disk drives, you must create user-defined filegroups. A filegroup provides a way to logically group files together, as well as to isolate single files from the primary filegroup. The primary filegroup is created by SQL Server when you create a database. All files go into the primary filegroup by default if you don't create other filegroups.

To avoid having user database data on the same disk as your SQL Server system tables, you can create a user-defined filegroup on which to later create your user database tables and indexes. If you do not create a user-defined filegroup for your data files, all the files you create become part of the primary filegroup, meaning the primary data file holds user data as well as the system tables. This might be the effect you want, but the recommended method is to separate your tables and indexes from the system tables. In this case, you need to create user-defined filegroups for your files. Figure 4-9 shows a simple example of one secondary data file apart from the primary filegroup that stores user data on separate drives. The figure shows a RAID 10 disk array for the log file; a RAID 1 array for the operating system files, SQL Server code, and system tables; and a RAID 10 volume for the user data tables and indexes.

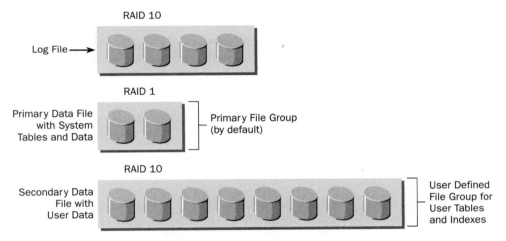

Figure 4-9. *Disk view with one user-defined filegroup.*

Figure 4-9 shows a database layout that locates tables and indexes onto a user-defined filegroup that holds only one secondary data file. Now we'll look at another example to demonstrate creating a user-defined filegroup that includes more than one secondary file. When you create a table or index on a filegroup with more than one data file, SQL Server uses a *proportional fill strategy* to distribute the data between the files, as shown in Figure 4-10 on the following page. With this strategy, SQL Server fills each data file in proportion to its size. For example, if file1 is 400 MB and file2 is 100 MB, then SQL Server allocates four extents (remember one extent is equal to eight pages) of pages in file1 and one extent of pages in file2 to insert data into the files. This way, file1 does not fill up faster than file2, or vice versa, and the data is distributed proportionally between the files. Otherwise, for instance, you could end up with one file completely full of data and the other file only one-fourth full, causing more I/Os on disks holding the full file.

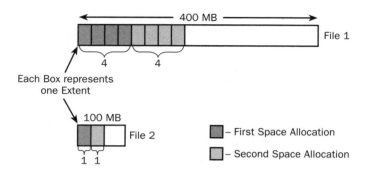

Figure 4-10. *Proportional fill strategy.*

For another database layout example, say you have a larger disk subsystem with two RAID 5 volumes (or arrays) configured for data. (We use RAID 5 here because we are assuming a database in which write requests make up less than 10 percent of the I/O requests—mostly reads are performed). To optimize the distribution of your data and allow for more parallel I/O, you want to spread all your database tables and indexes, which will be accessed randomly, across both disk volumes. To do this, you can create a secondary data file for each volume (make each file the same size for equal distribution) and group them into one filegroup. Then you can create your tables and indexes on that user-defined filegroup, causing the data to be loaded or inserted into the tables in an even distribution across each of the disk drives of the two volumes, as shown in Figure 4-11.

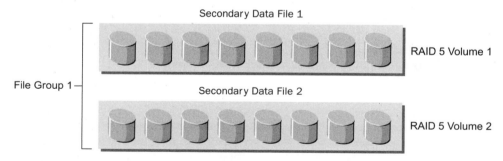

Figure 4-11. *Distributing data between two files within one filegroup.*

Here's another scenario in which using filegroups to place data is necessary. Assume that you have a table, TableS, whose data will be accessed sequentially by one reporting user at a time, and another table, TableR, that will be accessed randomly. To take advantage of the performance benefits of sequential data access on the disk drives, you can place TableS on one set of disks and place TableR on a separate set. That way the random I/Os to TableR will not interfere with the sequential I/Os of TableS. For example, you can create two separate filegroups with one file each, such as FilegroupS containing FileS, and FilegroupR containing FileR. Then you can create TableS on FilegroupS and TableR on FilegroupR, as shown in Figure 4-12.

We have seen how using files and filegroups provides you with different methods to lay out your database optimally on the disks. Now we'll discuss tuning SQL Server behavior through its configuration options.

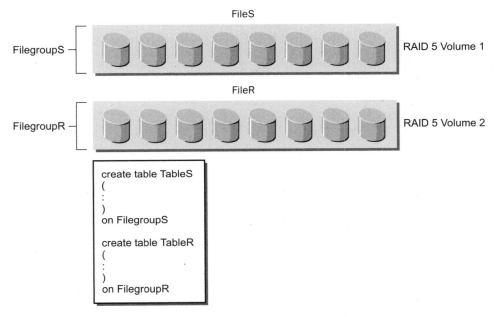

Figure 4-12. *Using filegroups to separate sequential and randomly accessed files.*

SQL Server Configuration Options

You can adjust several configuration options to affect the behavior of SQL Server. Compared with versions earlier than 7.0, SQL Server 2000 requires less manual configuration because it can dynamically configure itself according to the current workload instead of limiting itself to fixed option settings. This section demonstrates how to configure the most commonly adjusted options for performance and explains how they affect the operation of your system. In most cases, changing these options is unnecessary, but knowing what they are and what they do will allow you to make an educated decision concerning whether to modify them.

You can configure most of the options either through Enterprise Manager or with the Transact-SQL *sp_configure* system stored procedure. To use Enterprise Manager, right-click the name of the server you want to configure and then select Properties from the shortcut menu. The SQL Server Properties dialog box appears, with several tabs to choose from for configuring options. Later in this chapter we indicate which tab to use and how to configure the particular options that we discuss.

Many of the *sp_configure* options are defined as advanced options. You must have *show advanced options* set to 1 to view the current values of advanced options or to change an advanced option using *sp_configure*; and *show advanced options* is set to 0 by default. (You do not need to worry about this option when using Enterprise Manager to set advanced options.) To configure *show advanced options,* use the following statement:

```
sp_configure "show advanced options", 1
go
```

As we discuss the options, we will indicate which ones are advanced. In general, to set any option with *sp_configure,* use the following syntax:

```
sp_configure "option name", value
```

Also, we mentioned that most options can be set in one of two ways, but this is not true in all cases. Some options can be set only with *sp_configure* and not with Enterprise Manager. We will identify those options as well in the following sections.

AWE Enabled

AWE stands for Address Windowing Extensions, and is available with Microsoft Windows 2000 Advanced Server and Datacenter Server. SQL Server 2000 Enterprise and Developer Editions use the AWE application programming interface (API) to support large amounts on memory—close to 8 GB with Advanced Server and close to 64 GB with Datacenter Server. See the "Memory Sizes Supported" section in Chapter 2 for more information on allowing AWE with Windows 2000, which you must do before SQL Server can use AWE. The *awe enabled* option is only available for SQL Server Enterprise and Developers Editions. If you have more than 4 GB of physical RAM, then you should use AWE to allow SQL Server to address the memory beyond 4 GB. You must enable the *awe enabled* option by setting it to 1 (its default is 0). Restart SQL Server for the setting to take effect. Then use the System Monitor to see how much memory SQL Server has allocated. Note that the Task Manager counter of memory usage for SQLServer.exe is incorrect when AWE is enabled.

Also, with AWE enabled, SQL Server acquires all the memory it can at startup (or up to the *max server memory* value if set), and holds those pages until the server is shut down. It does not dynamically manage that memory. It also does not page out that memory. So if you do have other applications that need memory on the system, you might want to limit SQL Server's memory usage by setting *max server memory.*

Lightweight Pooling

The *lightweight pooling* option is used to configure SQL Server to use lightweight threads, or fibers. The use of fibers can reduce context switches by allowing SQL Server to handle scheduling rather than using the Windows 2000 scheduler. If your application is running on a multiple-processor system and you are seeing a large number of context switches, you might want to try setting the *lightweight pooling* option to 1, which enables lightweight pooling, then monitoring the number of context switches again to verify that they have been reduced. This is most needed on systems with more than four processors. The default value is 0, which disables the use of fibers.

The *lightweight pooling* option is an advanced option that you can set with *sp_configure* when *show advanced options* is set to 1, or configure through Enterprise Manager. On the Processor tab of the SQL Server Properties dialog box, in the Processor Control section, select the Use Windows NT Fibers check box to enable the option, or clear the box to disable the option. Click OK, then stop and restart SQL Server to have the change take effect.

Locks

SQL Server 2000 dynamically configures the number of locks used in the system. You can use the *locks* option to set the maximum number of available locks, thus limiting the memory SQL Server uses for locks. The default setting is 0, which allows SQL Server to allocate and deallocate locks dynamically based on changing system requirements. The maximum amount of memory that SQL Server ever allows for locks is 40 percent of its total memory. We recommend that you leave the locks option at the default value of 0 and allow SQL Server to allocate locks as necessary.

The *locks* option is an advanced option that you can only set by using *sp_configure*. The new setting takes effect after you stop and restart SQL Server.

Max Server Memory

SQL Server 2000 dynamically allocates memory on an as-needed basis. To specify the maximum amount of memory, in MB, that SQL Server allocates to the memory pool, you can set the *max server memory* option. SQL Server takes some time to release memory; therefore, if you have other applications that periodically need memory, you can set the *max server memory* option so that SQL Server leaves some memory free for the other applications.

The default value is 2,147,483,647, which means that SQL Server acquires as much memory as it can from the system, while dynamically allocating and deallocating memory as other applications need it. Dynamic configuration is the recommended setting. If you plan to change this setting, calculate the greatest possible amount of memory you can give to SQL Server by subtracting the sum of the memory needed for Windows 2000 plus memory needed for any non–SQL Server uses from the total physical memory.

The *max server memory* option is an advanced option, so the *show advanced options* setting must be 1 in order to configure this option using *sp_configure*. You can set it on the Memory tab of the SQL Server Properties dialog box in Enterprise Manager by adjusting the slider under Maximum (MB) while the Dynamically Configure SQL Server Memory option is selected. This option takes effect immediately, without having to stop and restart SQL Server. (If you select the Use a Fixed Memory Size option, then you can force SQL Server to allocate the amount you set; SQL Server does not release that memory after it has been allocated—thus it is a fixed size. See the "Set Working Set Size" section later in this chapter.)

Min Server Memory

The *min server memory* option specifies the minimum memory, in MB, to be allocated to the SQL Server memory pool. The default value is 0, which allows SQL Server to dynamically allocate and deallocate memory. This is the recommended setting. This option is useful in systems in which SQL Server might leave too much memory free for other applications to use. For example, in an environment in which the server is used for print and file services as well as for database services, SQL Server might relinquish too much memory to these other applications. In such a case, you might want to change the value of the *min server memory* option so that SQL Server maintains at least that much memory.

The *min server memory* option is an advanced option you can also configure using *sp_configure* or Enterprise Manager. In Enterprise Manager, on the Memory tab of the SQL Server Properties dialog box, adjust the slider under Minimum (MB) while the Dynamically Configure SQL Server Memory option is selected. This option takes effect immediately without having to stop and restart SQL Server.

Set Working Set Size

The *set working set size* option specifies that the memory that SQL Server has allocated cannot be paged out for another application's use. When this option is set to 1 (enabled), the memory that SQL Server allocates is physical memory and cannot be swapped out even if it can be more effectively used by another process. You should not enable the *set working set size* option when you're allowing SQL Server to allocate memory dynamically. Only enable it in conjunction with setting *min server memory* and *max server memory* to the same value. In this way SQL Server allocates a static amount of memory as nonpageable.

This option is an advanced option that you can set with *sp_configure* or with Enterprise Manager. In Enterprise Manager, on the Memory tab of the SQL Server Properties dialog box, click Use a Fixed Memory Size, and set a fixed amount to be allocated. You must restart SQL Server for this setting to take effect.

Recovery Interval

The *recovery interval* option defines the maximum time, in minutes, that it will take the system to recover in the event of a failure. You set this option to tell SQL Server that you want to wait only *recovery interval* minutes for the system to recover from a crash. SQL Server then uses this setting and a special built-in algorithm to determine how often to perform automatic checkpoints so that recovery takes only the specified amount of time. SQL Server determines the time to allow between running checkpoints according to how much work is happening in the system. If a lot of work is being done, checkpoints are issued more often than if the system is not doing much work, because the less work you perform, the less time it takes to recover from a crash. Also, the longer the recovery interval, the more time is allowed between checkpoints.

Increasing the recovery interval might improve performance by reducing the number of checkpoints (checkpoints cause intense writes to disk, which might slow down user transactions for a few seconds), but with the side effect of increasing the time it takes for recovery. The default value is 0, which specifies that SQL Server will determine the interval for you—about a 1-minute recovery time. Increase the *recovery interval* option at your own risk. A value of 5 to 10 minutes is not unusual. The acceptable setting depends entirely on whether you can risk waiting 5 to 10 minutes for your database to recover in case of a system crash. The reason you might want to increase *recovery interval* is for the simple fact that we stated earlier—you will reduce the frequency of the disk I/O that each checkpoint entails, allowing users more freedom in the I/O subsystem to perform their transactions without interruption.

The *recovery interval* option is an advanced option you can configure using *sp_configure* or Enterprise Manager. In Enterprise Manager, on the Database Settings tab of the SQL Server Properties dialog box, enter the number in minutes in the Recovery Interval (min) box. A change to this option takes effect immediately, without having to stop and restart SQL Server.

User Connections

You don't need to set the number of user connections to SQL Server with a configuration option—SQL Server can dynamically allocate connections as needed. Although user connections are dynamically configured by default, you can set a maximum value with the *user connections* option. Use this option to specify the maximum number of simultaneous user connections allowed to SQL Server. You might want to set a maximum to avoid having too many connections to your system. The actual number of user connections allowed also depends on the limits of your application and the hardware in your system. SQL Server allows a maximum of 32,767 user connections, which is also the maximum value for the option. In most cases, you should not need to change the value for this option. It works well when left dynamically configurable by SQL Server.

User connections is an advanced option you can configure using *sp_configure* or Enterprise Manager. In Enterprise Manager, on the Connections tab of the SQL Server Properties dialog box, enter the value you want in the Maximum Concurrent User Connections box.

Summary

This chapter has discussed what performance is and how to measure it, and examined several important areas for tuning your SQL Server system, including tuning processors, the disk subsystem, and memory; optimizing database layout; and adjusting SQL Server configuration options. But these areas of tuning are only the beginning. The rest of this book offers more ways to optimize your database server's performance. The next chapter shows you the new features of SQL Server 2000 that provide better performance and more administration options than previous versions.

Chapter 5
New Features and Performance Enhancements

The new features in Microsoft SQL Server 2000 extend the ease-of-use, performance, manageability, and reliability of SQL Server 7.0. They also make SQL Server 2000 an excellent database platform not only for small-scale online transaction processing (OLTP) applications, but also for very large-scale OLTP, data warehousing, and e-commerce applications. If you are upgrading directly from SQL Server 6.5 to SQL Server 2000, (bypassing version 7.0), and you are not familiar with SQL Server 7.0, it would be helpful for you to read *Microsoft SQL Server 7.0 Administrator's Companion* (John Fronckowiak, Marcilina Garcia, and Edward Whalen, Microsoft Press, 1999), and *Microsoft SQL Server 7.0 Performance Tuning Technical Reference* (Steve Adrien DeLuca, Marcilina Garcia, Jamie A. Reding, and Edward Whalen, Microsoft Press, 2000). Enormous architectural changes were implemented in SQL Server 7.0. These changes remain in place in SQL Server 2000, but are not spelled out in this book, which focuses on features new to SQL Server 2000 since SQL Server 7.0.

Extended Memory Support

SQL Server 2000 Enterprise Edition can use the Microsoft Windows 2000 Address Windowing Extensions (AWE) API to support large address spaces. SQL Server supports 8 GB on Windows 2000 Advanced Server, and 64 GB on Windows 2000 Datacenter Server. AWE is supported only on these two operating systems—it is not supported by Windows 2000 Professional or Server editions. SQL Server also includes *awe enabled*, a new configuration option that lets SQL Server use AWE. (This option is defined in Chapter 4, "System Tuning.") To enable SQL Server to use the extended memory space, set *awe enabled* to 1. See "Memory Sizes Supported" in Chapter 2, "SQL Server 2000 Architecture Fundamentals," for information on AWE.

Named Instances of SQL Server

You can run multiple instances of SQL Server 2000, specifically called default and named instances, on the same computer, so you can group common application tasks to be served by a specific SQL Server instance. To identify a default instance, the network name of the computer alone is used. To identify a named instance, the computer name plus an instance name is used, in the form *computer_name\instance_name*. Each instance of SQL Server 2000 has its own folder location for its copy of program files and for its data files. You can have at most one default instance (having no default but only a named instance is an option). You also can have multiple SQL Server 2000 named instances, with or without a default instance. A default instance can be SQL Server 6.5, 7.0, or 2000 (any instance of SQL Server 6.5 or 7.0 is called the default instance, and named instances of these previous versions is not allowed). Only SQL Server 2000 allows named instances. If you run SQL Server 6.5 as the default instance and a SQL Server 2000 named instance, you can only switch between the two versions, not run them at the same time. With a SQL Server 7.0 default instance and a SQL Server 2000 named instance, both can run at the same time, without having to switch between the two. Applications can connect to multiple instances on one computer in the same way they would connect to an instance of SQL Server running on a different computer. You must simply identify the appropriate instance in the application.

When multiple instances of SQL Server are running, each instance competes for system resources, such as CPU and memory, and each instance yields resources only to the operating system, not to other instances. So if you have two instances running, for example, and each has its memory options set to default such that memory allocation is dynamic, then one instance can take most of the memory, leaving little for the second instance. You should set the memory option *max server memory* to a specific value for each instance to avoid letting one instance take all of the memory. For example you might give the one instance 60 percent of the memory and the other instance 40 percent. Note that multiple instances running on the same computer will generally not perform as well as if each instance was running on its own computer, because all instances compete for CPU, memory, and disk resources.

You create an instance using the SQL Server installation CD. You can choose to install a default instance or a named instance. To install a named instance, simply choose the Create A New Instance Of SQL Server option when installing and specify the name of the instance.

Federated Servers with Distributed Partitioned Views

In SQL Server 2000, you can spread databases across multiple servers, called *federated servers*, which make up *a federation*, for greater processing scalability. If your system provides services for large database systems or large Web sites, you might need the processing power of multiple servers to support the transaction load. Distributing processing over multiple servers is called *scaling out*, (as opposed to *scaling up*, which refers to upgrading to a single, more powerful computer). The servers in a federation are called *member servers.* Figure 5-1 shows a federation of three member servers.

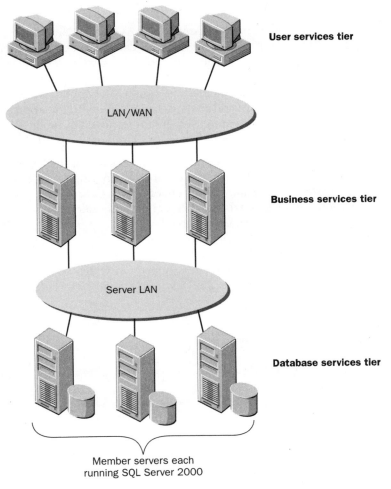

User services tier

Business services tier

Database services tier

Member servers each
running SQL Server 2000

Figure 5-1. *Federated servers.*

You create federated servers by spreading database tables across a group of servers, which you do by creating distributed partitioned views. This involves horizontally partitioning a table into smaller tables, each of which holds a subset of the complete table data. The subset tables are called *member tables,* and they reside on the member servers. The member tables have the same schema on each of the member servers. The data ranges for member tables are defined by CHECK constraints on the partitioning column. After you create the member tables on the member servers, you create a distributed partitioned view with the same view name on each of the member servers—this view consists of a union of all the member tables. Each view makes it appear that each server has a full copy of the original table. Applications can reference the view rather than a specific member table; they don't need to know which specific member server holds the requested data. You can make both SELECT and data modifications through the view.

Here's an example of a distributed partitioned view across three federated servers, Server1, Server2, and Server3. We can split up a table with sales data into three smaller tables based on the three possible values in the partitioning column, *Region_ID*. The users on the system typically access data in only one of the three regions at a time, so we can split the data for this table and other related tables by region. The application can determine which region the user is referencing and route the user's query to the appropriate member server. If all the data is on that member server, it is retrieved or modified without the application having to access any of the other member servers.

In our example we create three member tables, one on each of the federated servers, and distribute the data for those three member tables according to *Region_ID*. Specifically, we create a *WesternRegionSales* table on Server1, a *CentralRegionSales* table on Server2, and an *EasternRegionSales* table on Server3. Rows of sales data with a *Region_ID* of 1 go into the *WesternRegionSales* table, with a *Region_ID* of 2 into the *CentralRegionSales* table, with a *Region_ID* of 3 into the *EasternRegionSales* table. Next, we create a distributed partitioned view that encompasses all the member tables, so that applications can access data without having to specify in which of the three tables the data resides. The statement that creates the view on Server1 looks like this:

```
CREATE VIEW SALES_BY_REGION
AS
SELECT * FROM WesternRegionSales
UNION ALL
SELECT * FROM Server2.SalesDB.dbo.CentralRegionSales
UNION ALL
SELECT * FROM Server3.SalesDB.dbo.EasternRegionSales
GO
```

On Server2 the view is created as follows:

```
CREATE VIEW SALES_BY_REGION
AS
SELECT * FROM CentralRegionSales
UNION ALL
SELECT * FROM Server1.SalesDB.dbo.WesternRegionSales
UNION ALL
SELECT * FROM Server3.SalesDB.dbo.EasternRegionSales
GO
```

And on Server3 the view is created as follows:

```
CREATE VIEW SALES_BY_REGION
AS
SELECT * FROM EasternRegionSales
UNION ALL
SELECT * FROM Server1.SalesDB.dbo.WesternRegionSales
UNION ALL
SELECT * FROM Server2.SalesDB.dbo.CentralRegionSales
GO
```

If an application executes a SQL statement that references the *Sales_By_Region* view, and the application identifies the user as a region 1 user, it routes the request to Server1, although the user cannot tell where the data is located. If all the data requested by the user is found on Server1, there is no need to access Server2 or Server3—the ideal and most efficient model for federated servers. If, on the other hand, the requested data resides in member tables on more than one of the member servers, the SQL Server instance on Server1 generates a distributed query that pulls the result rows in from the other servers. This requires more overhead and processing power, and causes more contention on the tables.

Each member table requires a CHECK constraint, which you can define when you create the table, or alter later. When a SELECT statement is executed that references the partitioned view and contains the partitioning column in the search condition, SQL Server uses the CHECK constraints to determine which member servers contain the resulting rows, and searches only those servers. The CHECK constraint also allows only appropriate data to be inserted or updated in each member table. Without CHECK constraints, SQL Server still retrieves the data, but it must search each member table on each member server, causing unnecessary processing, and the application must be coded to check any modifications to ensure that they go to the appropriate server. This example of a CHECK constraint on Server1 indicates and ensures that only rows with *Region_ID* of 1 reside on that member server:

```
ALTER TABLE WesternRegionSales ADD CONSTRAINT Region_Check
CHECK (Region_ID = 1)
```

On Server2 the constraint looks like this:

```
ALTER TABLE CentralRegionSales ADD CONSTRAINT Region_Check
CHECK (Region_ID = 2)
```

And on Server3:

```
ALTER TABLE EasternRegionSales ADD CONSTRAINT Region_Check
CHECK (Region_ID = 3)
```

Partitioned views existed in SQL Server 7.0, but you could not update them, so you could use them only for read-only data. You can update views in SQL Server 2000, which means that when you update, insert, or delete data through the partitioned view, the data is modified on the appropriate member server automatically without the user having to know on which server the data lies. Also, SQL Server 2000 has an improved query optimizer that minimizes the amount of data transferred for distributed queries.

> **Note** For a detailed description of the rules concerning member tables and partitioning columns, and requirements concerning inserting, updating, and deleting with partitioned views, see "Creating a Partitioned View" in SQL Server Books Online, the online documentation provided with Microsoft SQL Server 2000. We recommend that you read these rules before designing your member tables.

We've talked about partitioning one table of a database, but what about the other tables? Ideally you partition as many tables as possible to maximize parallel processing across the federation of servers, and you locate related data on each member server to avoid distributed queries. In our example, related tables would include any more tables with data that could be partitioned by region ID, so that any data requested for a particular region would be found on the same server.

But there will probably be some tables that all users need full access to. These tables will not be part of a partitioned view. Instead, you can place full copies of these tables on each of the member servers, where they are accessed by their table name rather than a view name. You ensure that each member server gets any modifications to the data in these tables by creating INSTEAD OF triggers on each member server that perform a distributed query to update the data on other member servers. For example, say a table called *Products* stores the products for sale in all regions. This table exists in its entirety on each of the member servers. To update this table and keep data consistent across the member servers, you could create a trigger as follows on Server1, Server2, and Server3:

```
CREATE TRIGGER trig_products ON Products
INSTEAD OF UPDATE, INSERT, DELETE AS
BEGIN
DELETE Prod FROM Server1.SalesDB.dbo.Products Prod, DELETED D
WHERE Prod.Product_ID = D.Product_ID
INSERT Server1.SalesDB.dbo.Products SELECT * FROM INSERTED

DELETE Prod FROM Server2.SalesDB.dbo.Products Prod, DELETED D
WHERE Prod.Product_ID = D.Product_ID
INSERT Server2.SalesDB.dbo.Products SELECT * FROM INSERTED

DELETE Prod FROM Server3.SalesDB.dbo.Products Prod, DELETED D
WHERE Prod.Product_ID = D.Product_ID
INSERT Server3.SalesDB.dbo.Products SELECT * FROM INSERTED
END
```

As you can see, this trigger causes distributed processing to occur in order to complete the data modification on all of the member servers. To repeat, to get optimal performance with a federation, you should minimize the amount of distributed processing. The more data transfer between the federated servers, the slower the federation performance. It is best to distribute data between the member tables in the federation such that users only need to read or modify data from the one member server they access directly.

For federated servers to be an option for your system, your databases must have certain characteristics. If your databases are somewhat complex, it can be quite difficult to re-design them to be distributed in a way that fits the federated servers model. If you are designing your databases from the starting point, it might be an easier task because you can plan your table schemas for distribution ahead of time. If implementing federated servers is not an option for you, another option might be to offload certain tasks to another server which has a copy of the entire database, and use replication between servers to keep data synchronized. This is commonly done when separating OLTP tasks from re-porting tasks.

SQL Server 2000 Failover Clustering

SQL Server 2000 is a cluster-aware application that can be configured to provide failover capabilities. You must first install Microsoft Cluster Server (MSCS), which comes with the Windows 2000 Advanced Server and Datacenter Server operating systems only. Also, you must have SQL Server 2000 Enterprise Edition to support failover clustering. With *failover clustering*, if one system fails, SQL Server fails, or the system is taken offline, SQL Server processing switches to a second, clustered system—this switch is known as a failover. The goal of failover is to minimize system downtime. After a failover, you can restore the failed system and resume processing by switching back to the restored system—this is called *failback*.

Each system that is part of a cluster is called a *node*. Cluster Server with Windows 2000 Advanced Server supports up to two nodes in a cluster, and with Windows 2000 Datacenter Server it supports up to four nodes in a cluster. The nodes in a cluster share a common set of cluster resources, such as disk drives. Each node is connected to a common network and can communicate with all other nodes. The nodes send each other network messages called heartbeat messages. If the MSCS software detects the loss of a heartbeat from one of the nodes in the cluster, failover occurs for that node.

SQL Server 7.0 also supported failover clustering, but the administration of failover clus-tering is greatly improved in SQL Server 2000. SQL Server failover setup is no longer performed by running the Failover Cluster wizard, instead it is part of the SQL Server Setup program. First you must have installed the Microsoft Cluster Server service and config-ured it with the Cluster Service Configuration wizard on Windows 2000 Advanced Server or Datacenter Server. Before you start the SQL Server installation, create the same path on each node for the location where you want to install SQL Server program files. Then you can install SQL Server with the Setup program. At the start of the SQL Server instal-lation, the Setup program asks several questions regarding the cluster configuration. Then the regular SQL Server installation continues. After you've entered all the information, the Setup program copies SQL Server binaries (SQL program files) to all of the server nodes in the cluster, onto the local drive of each node in the path you specified during installation. This is why it's important to create the same path on each node before you start the installation. With this design, when a failover occurs with SQL Server 2000, only the databases are failed over, not the SQL Server binaries. (In SQL Server 7.0 the binaries were failed over also.)

The new administration tasks you can perform with failover clustering include:

- Administer failover clustering from any node in the cluster through Cluster Administrator
- Allow one cluster node to fail over to any other node in the cluster (assuming you have a three or four-node cluster with Windows 2000 Datacenter Server)
- Reinstall or rebuild a cluster instance on any node in the cluster without affecting the other cluster node instances
- Specify multiple IP addresses for a virtual server
- Add or remove nodes from the failover cluster by using SQL Server Setup
- Fail over or fail back to or from any node in the cluster

For more information on using Microsoft Cluster Server and steps for installing SQL Server for failover, see SQL Server Books Online.

XML Support

Extensible Markup Language (XML) is a World Wide Web Consortium (W3C) standard for representing information in a structured document form, which can be used to transport data between heterogeneous systems. New features in SQL Server 2000 support XML functionality. You can now use XML to access SQL Server through Hypertext Transport Protocol (HTTP) via a Uniform Resource Locator (URL). Other new features that support XML include:

- A FOR XML clause that can be used in SELECT statements to support retrieval of data in the form of an XML document instead of in the standard rowset output
- New system stored procedures to help manage XML data
- XML update grams that allow you to insert, update, and delete data in the database
- Functionality with which to run queries and stored procedures directly through a URL using HTTP
- Functionality with which to use templates and files in a URL to run multiple SQL statements
- The OLE DB Provider allows XML documents to be set as command text and return result sets as a stream

For more information on how to use XML with SQL Server, see "XML and Internet Support" in SQL Server Books Online and the XML Developer Center on MSDN on the Microsoft Web site (*http://msdn.microsoft.com/xml/*).

Database Maintenance Operations

Enhancements in SQL Server 2000 improve the performance and ease of some of the database maintenance operations that the administrator performs. These enhancements include faster differential backups, parallel database consistency checker (DBCC) operations, and parallel scanning with DBCC. For differential backups, the time it takes to perform the backup is proportional to the amount of data modified since the last full database backup. DBCC takes advantage of systems that have multiple CPUs by running in parallel on the CPUs, increasing DBCC performance. You can also now run DBCC without taking a shared table lock when scanning a table, so that updates can occur on the table simultaneously with the DBCC task.

Referential Integrity Enhancements

With two new clauses you can specify the behavior of SQL Server when it modifies a column in a table that is referenced by a foreign key constraint in another table. You can use the clauses ON UPDATE and ON DELETE in the CREATE TABLE and ALTER TABLE statements to specify the behavior. The options for these clauses are *cascading* or *no action*. Use *cascading* with ON DELETE so that when you delete a row from a parent table that is referenced by a foreign key, that delete cascades to the foreign key table, deleting the row from the foreign key table as well. *Cascading* with ON UPDATE is similar—an update to the referenced column data in the parent table cascades so that the foreign key table is updated the same way. If you use the *no action* option with ON DELETE or with ON UPDATE, SQL Server displays an error message if you delete a referenced row or update a referenced column in the parent table respectively, and the delete or update will be rolled back. See "CREATE TABLE" or "ALTER TABLE" in SQL Server Books Online for more information on these clauses.

Full-Text Search

Two new features in SQL Server 2000 improve full-text searching—change tracking and image filtering. Change tracking keeps a log of all the changes made to full-text indexed data, so that you can update the index with these changes. You can perform the update manually by flushing the log on a periodic basis, or you can configure updates to occur to the index when they occur to the data by using the background update index option. With image filtering you can index and query documents stored in image columns by extracting textual information from the image data. See "Microsoft Search Service" in SQL Server Books Online for more information on full-text searching.

New Data Types

SQL Server 2000 includes three new data types that provide greater programming flexibility:

- **bigint**—an 8-byte integer type (the largest integer data type)
- **sql_variant**—allows storage of values of different data types
- **table**—allows applications to temporarily store results for later use

Index Enhancements

Indexing enhancements in SQL Server 2000 provide more flexibility with indexes and allow you to:

- Create indexes on computed columns
- Specify the order indexes are created in, ascending or descending
- Specify whether the index should be created using parallel scanning and sorting

See "Table Indexes" and "Parallel Operations Creating Indexes" in SQL Server Books Online for information about these enhancements. For information on using indexes for performance tuning, see Chapter 18, "Using and Tuning Indexes."

Administration Enhancements

SQL Server 2000 administration enhancements will come in handy and make the administrator's job a little easier.

Log Shipping

Log shipping allows you to constantly dump and copy transaction log backups from a source server to a destination server or servers, and then load those logs onto the destination servers automatically. This provides you with a warm standby of the database and/or a separate read-only system to perform queries, such as business reports, to remove this processing from the source server. You can configure the schedule for each step, including configuring delays between copies and loads of log backups. See "Log Shipping" in SQL Server Books Online for more information.

SQL Profiler

Microsoft SQL Profiler includes more administration enhancements. There are two new ways you can limit a trace—by time and by size of the trace file. You can also trace several new events. To find these, open SQL Profiler and create or edit a trace file. On the Events tab in the Trace Properties dialog box, in Available Event Classes, expand Database, as shown in Figure 5-2. You will find four new events: Data File Auto Growth, Data

File Auto Shrink, Log File Auto Grow, and Log File Auto Shrink. Expand Performance to find three new events: Show Plan All, Show Plan Statistics, and Show Plan Text. SQL Profiler also includes enhancements for auditing SQL Server activities, so that the auditing meets the requirements of the C2 level of security defined by the United States government. For more information see Chapter 7, "Using SQL Profiler."

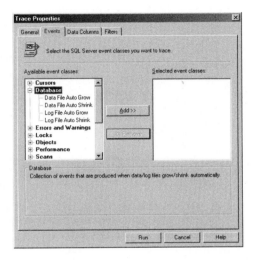

Figure 5-2. *SQL Profiler Trace Properties dialog box.*

SQL Query Analyzer

Microsoft SQL Query Analyzer now includes an Object Browser with which you can navigate and view database objects. To see this browser, open SQL Query Analyzer, click Tools, point to Object Browser, and click Show/Hide. The Object Browser appears on the left side of the SQL Query Analyzer window, as shown in Figure 5-3 on the following page. There are also three other new options in the Tools menu: Object Search, Manage Indexes, and Manage Statistics. With Object Search you can search for specific objects in a database by object type, such as views, stored procedures, user tables, and so on. With Manage Indexes and Manage Statistics you can manage indexes and statistics using a graphical interface similar to that of Enterprise Manager. There are also two new options on the Query menu: Show Server Trace and Show Client Statistics. For more information, see Chapter 16, "Using SQL Query Analyzer."

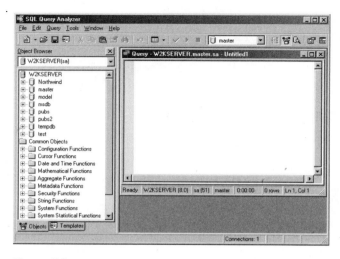

Figure 5-3. *SQL Query Analyzer with the Object Browser pane visible.*

Replication Enhancements

SQL Server 2000 provides several enhancements to replication. One is a new alternative to the immediate-updating subscriber option, queued updates. Queued updates are specific to snapshot and transactional replication. You enable queued updating to allow a subscriber to modify published data at the subscriber even while the publisher is not connected to the subscriber. The transactions that perform the data modifications queue up to be sent to the publisher and replayed asynchronously when the publisher does make a network connection with the subscriber. Loopback detection prevents the transactions from getting replicated back to the originating subscriber. See "Queued Updating" in SQL Server Books Online for more information.

An enhancement for all types of replication is support for replication schema changes. You can now add or drop columns from published tables and have those changes propagated to the subscribers.

Merge replication includes the following new enhancements:

- New conflict resolvers
- An option to resolve conflicts interactively
- Vertical filtering of merge publications
- Use of user-defined functions in dynamic filters
- Automated management of identity ranges at the subscriber
- Support for timestamp columns in published tables
- Use of alternate publishers when synchronizing data

For more information, see Chapter 14, "Tuning Replicated Systems."

Additional Enhancements

The above enhancements are by no means an exhaustive list of the new features in SQL Server 2000. There are also many improvements in the areas of Data Transformation Services (DTS), Analysis Services, Meta Data Services, and English Query. These are very specific and are not described in detail in this book. For information on these topics, see the following titles in SQL Server Books Online:

- Data Transformation Service Enhancements
- What's New in Analysis Services
- What's New in Meta Data Services
- What's New in English Query

Summary

This chapter introduced many new features in SQL Server 2000, some of which provide enhancements in performance. The following chapter discusses using System Monitor in the Windows 2000 Performance console to monitor the performance of your database system.

Chapter 6
Monitoring Performance with System Monitor

The Microsoft Windows 2000 operating system provides the graphical performance-monitoring tool, which is a Microsoft Management Console snap-in called System Monitor—"Performance Monitor" in previous versions of Windows NT. The Performance console assists in monitoring the performance of your database system, from hardware performance to Microsoft SQL Server specific performance. The console includes two parts—System Monitor and Performance Logs and Alerts—for monitoring your system in real-time, or in logging modes. This chapter discusses how to use the console, what to monitor, and how to interpret the output. We refer to the entire tool as System Monitor (instead of the Performance tool) because this is the common term.

System Monitor

The entities you monitor are called *counters*. They are grouped into categories called objects. In some cases, counters have instances, as well. For example, the % Processor Time counter is found under the Processor object, and there is a total processors instance as well as instances for each individual processor.

A default set of System Monitor objects and counters are installed with Windows 2000. The SQL Server installation provides SQL Server specific objects and counters that you can use in System Monitor. System Monitor uses remote procedure calls to collect information from SQL Server. The integration of these counters allows you to monitor system information, disk information, and SQL Server information simultaneously.

System Monitor consumes a small amount of CPU and disk resources on the system it is monitoring. On very busy systems, this overhead might be unacceptable, but generally it is not a problem.

In addition to monitoring performance counters, System Monitor allows you to

- View selected system performance objects and counters in real time.
- Log performance counter information for later analysis.
- Monitor multiple Windows 2000 systems from one System Monitor.

- Create alerts to notify you when certain performance conditions occur—for example, when the processor time goes above 90 percent. You can configure the alert to log an entry in the Event Viewer, send a network message, start a performance data log file, run a program when the condition occurs, or all of these.
- Trace events to record data about when certain activities occur for processes, threads, disk I/O, network, file details, and page faults. Trace logs require a parsing tool to interpret the output. You can create such a tool using APIs provided on the Microsoft Web site. Tracing is used rarely, except by Microsoft support providers.

This chapter looks at the first two methods more closely, because they are the methods for monitoring detailed performance information. See the Windows 2000 Help topic "Performance Logs and Alerts Overview" and the Microsoft Developer's Network online library at *http://msdn.microsoft.com/library/default.asp* for more information about creating alerts and tracing events.

Viewing Performance Data in Real-Time Mode

In real-time mode, you can view performance data in three different formats: chart, report, or histogram. Here are some examples of the three real-time mode views. First, start System Monitor: click Start, point to Programs, then to Administrative Tools, and then click Performance. The Performance console that contains System Monitor opens. Select System Monitor in the console tree on the left to view System Monitor in the right pane. If the monitor is not in chart view, click the View Chart button at the top of the right pane to switch to chart view. Use chart view (see Figure 6-1) to identify trends in the data over time. Click the View Report button to see the report view, as shown in Figure 6-2. Report view is extremely useful for objects and counters dealing with logical and physical disk I/O, because if you have multiple disks, you might need to view many counters at once, and they can be difficult to distinguish in chart view. Click the View Histogram button to see histogram view (see Figure 6-3), which is not commonly used, but can be useful for comparing multiple instances of a counter, such as % Processor Time, because the results for each instance are on the same scale and so easier to compare.

Logging Performance Data

One of System Monitor's most valuable features is its logging capability. Regularly logging system performance data is a good idea. When you change the system hardware or the application, you will have before and after log data you can use to compare the effect of the changes. (Always note dates and times when you make changes so you can relate them to the log files.) Also, you can use logs to identify trends in system performance relating to changes, such as more users running transactions and database growth. These logs can help you plan for future growth as well.

You can capture System Monitor data for a period of time and then analyze and compare log files later. Logging the information also lets you view the system behavior over time, which can reveal trends in system usage that you might not see by looking at real-time data. For example, in your log files you might find that disk utilization is typically high from

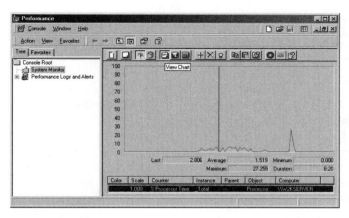

Figure 6-1. *The System Monitor chart view.*

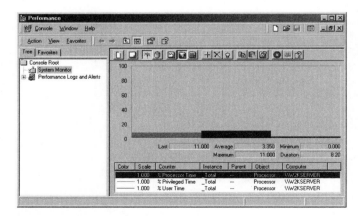

Figure 6-2. *The System Monitor report view.*

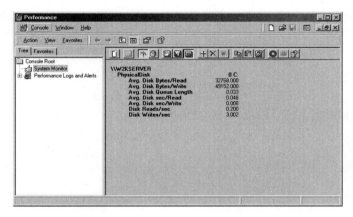

Figure 6-3. *The System Monitor histogram view.*

8 A.M. to 10 A.M., and lower for the rest of the day. You might be able to relate this trend to heavy data entry or a database backup that occurs between 8 A.M. and 10 A.M.

Be careful with the log file size when you are capturing data to a log—it can quickly get very large. If this happens, consider increasing the sampling interval when logging performance data. Generally, a 30- to 60-second interval is adequate to track all the counters and ensure that the data reflects the actual system state. If your sampling interval is too long, you might miss peaks and valleys in the data, which might mislead you in your tuning efforts. The longer period of time you want to collect data for, the longer you should make the sampling interval. For instance, if you want to collect data for only 30 minutes, and you want a detailed view of what the system is doing, you can use a smaller interval, such as 10 to 15 seconds. If you want to collect data for an entire 24-hour period, then 60 seconds would be an appropriate interval to keep the log file from getting huge.

> **Note** When you use System Monitor to log data, don't log the data over a network connection. It is much more efficient to start the log locally on the server you want the data from. You can access the log file later from a remote system if you need to. If you must log over the network, reduce the number of objects and counters to the most critical.

To start logging information on Windows 2000 using System Monitor, follow these steps:

1. Click Start, point to Programs, Administrative Tools, and then click Performance.

2. Expand Performance Logs And Alerts in the left pane of the Performance window.

3. Select Counter Logs in the console tree. (See Figure 6-4.)

Figure 6-4. *The counter logs in the Performance console.*

4. In the right pane, right-click the blank space and select New Log Settings on the shortcut menu.

5. Enter a name to identify the log settings in the New Log Settings dialog box, then click OK. (See Figure 6-5.) We chose CPU Log for the name of this log setting.

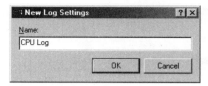

Figure 6-5. *The New Log Settings dialog box.*

6. In the CPU Log dialog box (the name you chose will appear as the title of this window instead of CPU Log), click the Add button to open the Select Counters dialog box.

7. Add the counters that you want saved to the log file by highlighting them and clicking the Add button. When finished adding counters, click Close in the Select Counters dialog box. On the General tab of the CPU Log dialog box, you can also set the interval for sampling data, as shown in Figure 6-6.

Figure 6-6. *Use the CPU Log dialog box to specify the counters and sample interval.*

8. Click the Log Files tab to set log file specific information, such as location, file name, file type, and maximum file size limit.

9. Click the Schedule tab to set the schedule for logging. If you do not enter a time for the logging to stop, it will continue until you stop it manually.

10. After you have finished, click OK. The log file name should appear in the right pane. The green icon next to the log name shows logging has started. The icon will be red if logging is stopped. (See Figure 6-7 on the following page.)

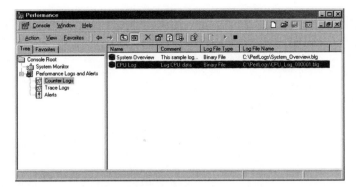

Figure 6-7. *The logging status is shown in the right pane of the Performance console.*

11. You can start and stop logging manually in this window by right-clicking the name of the log setting and selecting Start or Stop from the shortcut menu.

After you have collected the information and stopped the logging process, use the following steps to load logged data into the System Monitor and view it:

1. Click System Monitor in the left pane to open System Monitor in the right pane.

2. Click the View Log File Data button at the top of the right pane to open the Select Log File dialog box. (See Figure 6-8.) Navigate to the folder and select the log file you want to view and then click Open.

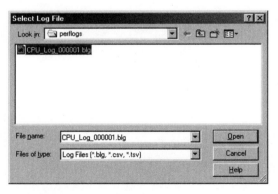

Figure 6-8. *Use the Select Log File dialog box to specify which log file you want to view.*

3. Click the Add button to add the counters you want to view from the selected log file. When you close the Add Counters dialog box you will see the selected counters in System Monitor. (See Figure 6-9.) Of course, only the counters that were actually logged to the file will be available for viewing.

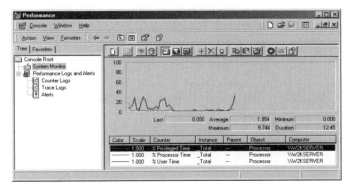

Figure 6-9. *The selected counters are displayed in System Monitor.*

Occasionally you might want to view the data in the log file from a particular time rather than looking at the entire file. For example, if you started your log file before users logged in to perform transactions, you might want to view only the data collected after all users were logged in, to keep from skewing the averages with data collected when no users were active. This is easy to do in System Monitor as follows:

1. After you have loaded your log file into System Monitor, click the Properties button at the top of the right pane.

2. In the System Monitor Properties dialog box, click the Source tab.

3. Near the bottom of the Source tab, slide the bars from both ends of the slide window to include the times that you want to view in the View Range. (See Figure 6-10.)

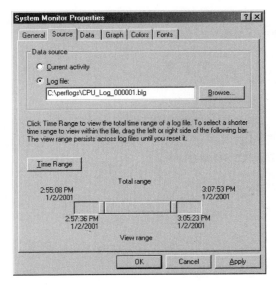

Figure 6-10. *Use the Source tab of the System Monitor Properties dialog box to specify the view range.*

4. (Optional) Use the other tabs in the System Monitor Properties dialog box to change different characteristics of the output.

5. Click OK to return to System Monitor and view the selected range of data.

System Monitor Objects, Counters, and Instances

This section covers the System Monitor's most interesting, useful, and commonly monitored objects, including SQL Server specific objects that become available by default when you install SQL Server. We explain what the counters mean, how to interpret the values, and how to tune and manage your system to ensure optimum performance.

Processor Object

The most obvious component to monitor and analyze is CPU utilization. The general processor information is contained in the Processor object. Your goal is to make sure that the processors don't cause a system bottleneck. A general rule is to avoid pushing CPU utilization over 80 percent for each processor you monitor. Peaks over 80 percent are acceptable, but an average utilization over 80 percent indicates that your processors might be causing a bottleneck. To fix a processor bottleneck, you must exchange your current processors for faster ones, add more processors to the system, or optimize your application to use less processing time.

For a system with multiple processors, System Monitor lists both an instance for each processor in the instance list in the Add Counters dialog box and a total instance, which displays the average value of all processors, as shown in Figure 6-11. In a single processor system, System Monitor lists the total and one processor instance—both refer to the single processor.

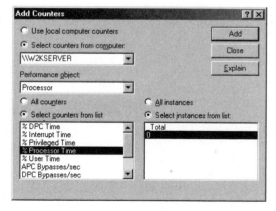

Figure 6-11. *Select which processor to monitor in the Add Counters dialog box.*

The counters that you should monitor for the Processor object are as follows:

- **% Processor Time** The percentage of time that the processor was executing a non-idle thread. This value is calculated by subtracting the amount of time the processor was idle from 100 percent. It is an excellent indicator of overall system CPU utilization.

- **% Privileged Time** The percentage of time that the processor spent working in the privileged mode (that is, performing operating system functions and running drivers, such as I/O). This includes time during which the CPU (or CPUs) was servicing interrupts and deferred procedure calls (DPCs). When the percentage of privileged time is high on your system, your system is probably experiencing a high number of system interrupts for I/O processing. You can confirm this condition by looking at the Interrupts/sec counter for the processors.

- **% User Time** The percentage of time the processor spent working in user mode. This type of work is generated by applications. Generally, you want to maximize the % User Time value and minimize % Privileged Time.

- **% Interrupt Time** The percentage of time the processor spent servicing hardware interrupts. Many hardware components of a system, such as the mouse, network interface cards, or disk controllers, can issue processor interrupts. Interrupts occur as part of normal Windows 2000 operation.

- **Interrupts/sec** The number of hardware interrupts per second that the processor received and processed. It does not include the system DPCs, which are counted separately. When you see excessive interrupts, examine the PhysicalDisk object counters. Generally, you can reduce excessive interrupts by making sure you have the latest disk controller driver and/or by adding I/O bandwidth. See Chapter 3, "Understanding the I/O Subsystem and RAID," for more information on I/O performance and tuning.

System Object

The System object and its associated counters measure aggregate data for threads running on the processor. They provide valuable insights into your overall system performance. The most important System counters are as follows:

- **Processor Queue Length** This counter indicates the number of threads waiting in the processor queue for an available processor. In other words, it counts the threads waiting to run. There is a single queue for all threads waiting for processor time even if your system has multiple processors. The counter tallies only the threads that are ready to execute but are still waiting, not those that are currently running. The Processor Queue Length counter of the System object should be monitored in conjunction with the Processor object data. When the Processor Queue Length value is greater than two per processor (the number of processors in the system multiplied by 2), you might have a CPU bottleneck. You can alleviate this condition by adding more processors, installing faster processors, or reducing the workload on the system. Tuning your queries or improving your index strategy can accomplish this workload reduction. These approaches are discussed in Chapter 17, "Tuning SQL Statements and Stored Procedures," and Chapter 18, "Using and Tuning Indexes."

- **Context Switches/sec** A context switch occurs when the operating system or application is forced to change from executing one thread on a processor to executing another thread on the processor—known as a context switch. Context switches occur when a running thread voluntarily relinquishes the processor, when a thread is pre-empted by a higher-priority ready thread, or when the processor switches between user mode and privileged (kernel) mode to run an executive or subsystem service. This counter is the sum of all instances of the object Thread: Context Switches/sec, which gives context switches per thread. You will always see some context switching on a multiprocessor system running multithreaded applications, but you should be concerned when you see more than 10,000 context switches per second.

An easy way to reduce the number of context switches is to enable fiber-based scheduling in SQL Server by setting the *lightweight pooling* configuration option to 1. (You can change this scheduling option using the *sp_configure* stored procedure or Enterprise Manager. See the "Lightweight Pooling" section in Chapter 4, "System Tuning," for details.) When you enable lightweight pooling, SQL Server schedules its own units of work within the Windows 2000 thread system and greatly reduces the number of context switches required. If after you set *lightweight pooling* your system is still experiencing excessive context switches, you can generally alleviate this condition by adding I/O bandwidth in the form of additional physical disks or disk controllers. Chapter 3 contains additional information on I/O bandwidth and throughput.

SQLServer: Buffer Manager Object

The Buffer Manager counters provide information about the memory buffers that SQL Server uses for data cache. These counters are as follows:

- **Buffer Cache Hit Ratio** The percentage of requests that reference a page currently located in the buffer cache. When a page is already in memory (in the buffer cache), SQL Server does not have to request a physical I/O to read that page from the disk subsystem. Since accessing memory is relatively inexpensive compared with a physical I/O, a high buffer cache hit ratio relates to increased system performance and throughput. A well-tuned system has a ratio of 90 percent or higher. If your buffer cache hit ratio is lower, allocate more memory to SQL Server. If all the existing memory is allocated to SQL Server, you should increase the amount of physical memory on your system.

- **Procedure Cache Pages** The number of pages used by SQL Server for storing compiled queries and stored procedures. This number multiplied by 8 KB yields the amount of kilobytes in use.

- **Free Pages** The number of free SQL Server memory buffers (in 8-KB pages). A consistently low, or zero, Free Pages counter value indicates low memory on your server. You should add memory to your system to alleviate this condition.

- **Page Reads/sec** The number of physical database page read requests issued by SQL Server per second. If you are monitoring the Page Reads/sec counter, you will see high values until your system reaches a steady-state condition. As more pages are read into memory and then re-accessed as cache hits, the number of page reads will decrease. If this value stays high, you might need to increase SQL Server's memory allocation, increase the physical memory on the system, or tune your queries.

- **Stolen Pages** This counter shows you how many 8-KB pages are being removed from the SQL Server data cache to satisfy the requirements of other applications on the system. Windows 2000 reallocates this memory to satisfy the requirements of other system components. To alleviate the impact of the lost pages on SQL Server, you can set the *sp_configure* option *min server memory* to some value other than the default of 0. This instructs SQL Server to initially request memory in the amount of the *min server memory* value and not to relinquish it to other applications. Be aware that this setting will probably slow the other applications on your system. When they attempt to allocate memory, they might not get all they request or require. This could cause Windows 2000 to page, which should be avoided. The only remedy for this latter condition is to add physical memory to your system.

- **Page Writes/sec** The number of physical database page writes per second issued by SQL Server.

Generally, if your system is dedicated to SQL Server, that is, if you are not running any other applications on the system, you should set the SQL Server *max server memory* configuration option to the default of 2,147,483,647. This value instructs SQL Server to allocate the maximum amount of memory that Windows 2000 will allow. If your buffer cache hit ratio is still low, you should add physical memory. If you have the *max server memory* parameter set to the default value and you add physical memory to the system, SQL Server will consume it as needed without any other configuration changes.

If your system is not dedicated to SQL Server, you have to balance the memory requirements of all running applications. You might need to limit the amount of memory that SQL Server can use to allow memory for other applications. You can do this by setting the *maximum server memory* to the amount you want. See more details on setting these parameters in the "Tuning Memory" section of Chapter 4.

SQLServer: Databases Object

The counters for the Databases object provide information about the SQL Server databases, including the amount of free log space available and the number of active transactions in the database. There is one instance of each counter for each SQL Server database on the system, so be sure when you monitor these counters that you have the database that you want to view selected in the instances window, as shown in Figure 6-12 on the following page. The interesting counters include those listed on the next page.

- **Log Flush Waits/sec** The number of database commits that are waiting for a log flush before they can continue. A log flush occurs when the data in the log buffer is flushed to the physical log file. To maintain the data integrity of a database page, the modified data page cannot be written to the data file disk until the log buffer is flushed to disk first. After the log buffer has been flushed to the log file, the transaction can commit and the dirty database page can be written to the data disk. When commits are waiting for log flushes, the log device is usually the bottleneck. You can remedy this condition easily by adding I/O bandwidth to your log devices. For example, you can try enabling the write cache on the controller used for the log file (only if you have a battery backup on the controller), or increasing the speed of the disk drives where the log file resides.

- **Percent Log Used** The percentage of the currently defined log space that SQL Server is using. A chart of this counter shows how fast your log file is growing, and when the file is truncated (probably as a result of a log backup command, which also truncates the log when it finishes backing it up).

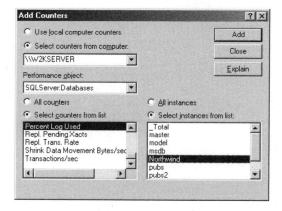

Figure 6-12. *Selecting the Percent Log Used counter for the Northwind database.*

SQLServer: General Statistics Object

The General Statistics object contains information about user connection activity. The most interesting counter is User Connections.

- **User Connections** The current number of user connections into SQL Server. Monitoring this counter on a regular basis can help you find trends in user activity and determine at what rate the number of users connected is increasing (if it is) as your business grows.

SQLServer: Latches Object

This object's counters provide information about the latches in effect on the internal SQL Server resources. A *latch* is a lightweight, short-term synchronization object that protects an action that does not need to be locked for the life of a transaction. When the relational engine is processing a query, it requests the storage engine to return a row each time a row is needed from a base table or index. While the storage engine is transferring the row to the relational engine, the storage engine must ensure that no other task modifies either the contents of the row or certain page structures, such as the page offset table entry that locates the row being read. It does this by acquiring a latch, transferring the row in memory to the relational engine, and then releasing the latch.

When you have a high number of latch waits per second or a long average latch wait time, the system probably has a low cache hit ratio and is having to perform physical I/Os. This ripples into an I/O bottleneck. The best way to alleviate this condition is to increase the physical memory on the system. If you cannot increase memory, you should increase the I/O bandwidth of your system. The counters are as follows:

- **Average Latch Wait Time (ms)** The average time, in milliseconds, that a latch request had to wait before it was serviced
- **Latch Waits/sec** The number of latch requests that could not be serviced immediately and were forced to wait for the resource to free up

SQLServer: Locks Object

The Locks object provides data about the individual lock requests made by SQL Server, such as lock timeouts and deadlocks. You will have multiple instances of these counters on your system. The counters are as follows:

- **Average Wait Time (ms)** The average amount of time, in milliseconds, that each lock request was forced to wait
- **Lock Timeouts/sec** The number of lock requests that timed out while waiting to acquire a lock
- **Lock Waits/sec** The number of lock requests that could not be satisfied immediately and required the calling thread to wait before being granted the lock
- **Number of Deadlocks/sec** The number of requests that resulted in a deadlock condition

SQL Server's data-locking mechanisms ensure data integrity for all queries and data accesses. Locks can be acquired at the data row level, page level, table level, or database level. The Locks object provides data about how applications and queries behave and coexist. The most critical counter to monitor here is Number of Deadlocks/sec. A *deadlock* is a condition in which two users or processes have locks on separate objects and each user or process is trying to acquire a lock on the object that the other user or process holds. SQL Server ends a deadlock by choosing a user whose transaction will be cancelled to break the deadlock; this user is called the *deadlock victim*. SQL Server rolls back the deadlock victim's transaction, notifies the user's application with error message 1205, cancels the user's current request, and then allows the transactions of the other users to continue. This user will have to resubmit the request.

Do not confuse deadlocking with normal blocking. When one transaction has a lock on a resource that another transaction requires, the second transaction waits for the lock to be released. Since, by default, SQL Server transactions do not time out, the second transaction is blocked, but not necessarily deadlocked. When your system experiences a deadlock, you need to examine what each user is attempting to do. Tools such as SQL Profiler and SQL Query Analyzer, discussed in Chapter 7, "Using SQL Profiler" and Chapter 16, "Using SQL Query Analyzer" will aid you in determining how to restructure your queries to minimize deadlocking. Several methods for avoiding deadlocks are outlined here:

- **Access objects in the same order.** If all transactions execute concurrently, you should strive to access the different database objects in the same order. Though not always possible, this technique makes deadlocks less likely to occur. For example, if two concurrent transactions obtain a lock on the *Supplier* table, and then the *Part* table, one of the two transactions will be blocked while waiting on the *Supplier* table lock, until the other transaction finishes. After the first transaction commits or rolls back, the second continues. No deadlock occurs. Using stored procedures for all data modifications can standardize the access order.

- **Avoid user interaction in transactions.** You should avoid writing transactions that include user interaction because users tend to be slow in responding to requests for feedback, such as a prompt for a parameter requested by an application. For example, if a transaction is waiting for user input and the user goes to lunch, or even home for the weekend, the user holds up the transaction, preventing its completion. This degrades system throughput because any locks held by the transaction are released only when the transaction is committed or rolled back. Even if a deadlock situation does not arise, other transactions accessing the same resources are blocked, waiting for the transaction to finish.

- **Keep transactions short and in one batch.** Deadlocking typically occurs when several long-running transactions execute concurrently in the same database. The longer the transaction, the longer the exclusive or update locks are held, blocking other activity and leading to possible deadlock situations. Keeping your transactions in one batch minimizes network round-trips during a transaction and reduces delays in completing the transaction and releasing locks. Optimizing your queries so they complete faster will reduce both blocking and deadlocking.

- **Use as low an isolation level as possible.** Though it is sometimes difficult, you should determine if your transaction can run at a lower isolation level, for example, read committed (the SQL Server default level) rather than serializable. A transaction implementing the read committed level will hold share locks while data is being read, then release the locks after the data is read even though the entire transaction might not be finished. Therefore if the same read is performed a second time in the same transaction, you might not get the same results, because another transaction could have updated that data. Using a lower isolation level, such as read committed, holds shared locks for a shorter duration than a higher isolation level, such as serializable, reducing locking contention.

You should always monitor the counters for average wait time and the number of lock waits per second, although these events are not as important as deadlocks. You will always encounter locking on your system; the secret is to minimize the number of lock waits and the amount of time spent waiting, thus reducing blocking and the amount of time a transaction will wait when blocked by another. By following the preceding recommendations for deadlocking, you can also minimize the number and duration of locks.

SQLServer: Memory Manager Object

The Memory Manager object provides useful data about how SQL Server is managing its allocated memory. As each process executes on the database, it requests and is granted memory resources. By monitoring the Memory Grants Pending counter you can determine how many users or processes are waiting for memory grants. When SQL Server is starved for memory, the Memory Grants Pending value increases, because more users or processes are waiting for memory. You can alleviate this condition by increasing the amount of memory allocated to SQL Server or by increasing the amount of physical memory on your system. The most useful counters under this object are as follows:

- **Memory Grants Pending** The current number of processes waiting for a workspace memory grant
- **Target Server Memory (KB)** The total amount of memory that SQL Server can consume
- **Total Server Memory (KB)** The total amount of memory that SQL Server is using

SQLServer: SQL Statistics Object

The SQL Statistics object provides valuable insight into how your queries and transactions are behaving. The Batch Requests/sec counter shows you how many SQL batches the server is receiving. A SQL *batch* is a group of one or more SQL statements that are sent to the server at one time. Passing several SQL statements to the server at one time improves performance. When you submit statements in a batch, SQL Server can compile them into a single execution unit, which allows SQL Server to process the statements more efficiently. The following are the most interesting counters for the SQL Statistics object are listed on the following page.

- **Batch Requests/sec** The number of SQL batch requests that the server is receiving
- **SQL Compilations/sec** The number of SQL statement compilations that SQL Server is performing per second
- **SQL Re-Compilations/sec** The number of SQL statement recompilations that SQL Server is performing per second

LogicalDisk and PhysicalDisk Object

Since the counters for the LogicalDisk and PhysicalDisk objects are similar, we cover them together. Depending on your I/O system configuration, you will want to monitor either the logical or physical disk counters. If you are using a RAID I/O disk subsystem, the physical disk counters might provide more meaningful data. In other cases, the logical disk counters will suffice. Basically, logical disk counters provide information by disk driver letter such as C:, D:, E:, while physical disk counters are by Windows 2000 disk number, such as Disk 0, Disk 1, Disk 2, etc. By default, with Windows 2000 the physical disk counters are enabled. To enable logical disk counters, you must run the DISKPERF command with the appropriate parameter. For details on running Diskperf, see the "Monitoring Disk I/O" section in Chapter 4.

The LogicalDisk and PhysicalDisk objects provide the same counters which give disk I/O information according to either the logical or physical disk perspective. These object have the following counters:

- **% Disk Read Time** The percentage of elapsed time that the selected disk is busy servicing read requests
- **% Disk Write Time** The percentage of elapsed time that the selected disk is busy servicing write requests
- **% Disk Time** The percentage of elapsed time that the selected disk is busy servicing read or write requests, computed as the sum of % Disk Write Time and % Disk Read Time
- **% Idle Time** The percentage of time during the sample interval that the disk was idle
- **Avg. Disk Queue Length** The average number of both read and write requests that were queued for the selected disk during the sample interval
- **Avg. Disk Read Queue Length** The average number of read requests that were queued for the selected disk during the sample interval
- **Avg. Disk Write Queue Length** The average number of write requests that were queued for the selected disk during the sample interval
- **Avg. Disk sec/Read** The average time, in seconds, of a read of data from the disk
- **Avg. Disk sec/Write** The average time, in seconds, of a write of data to the disk
- **Avg. Disk sec/Transfer** The time, in seconds, of the average transfer (average of both reads and writes) from a disk
- **Disk Reads/sec** The rate of read operations on the disk

- **Disk Writes/sec** The rate of write operations on the disk
- **Disk Transfers/sec** The rate of read and write operations on the disk

You can gain much insight from the volume of data in the disk counters. We'll look at some of these counters in more detail. The first counter to investigate is Avg. Disk Queue Length, which monitors the average number of both reads and writes queued for a particular disk. If you are running a RAID subsystem with multiple hard drives in a single volume, this number is the total for all drives in that volume. For example, if you have seven drives in a volume, and there are on average nine queued requests, approximately 1.28 (9/7) requests are queued to each drive. A general rule is to keep the average number of queued requests at two or fewer per disk. When this counter's value exceeds two per disk, your system will be in an I/O bound state. You can alleviate this by adding more disks for the data or by increasing the relative speed of the disks.

Another important set of counters are Avg. Disk sec/Read, Avg. Disk sec/Write, and Avg. Disk sec/Transfer. The average disk seconds per transfer is an average of the aggregate of the seconds per read and the seconds per write. The seconds per read, write, or transfer are also referred to as the *disk latency* and are an indication of how long the disk is taking to complete requests. Latency is covered in more detail in Chapter 3. You generally want a value for Avg. Disk sec/Write of 12 msec or less. If you have a disk controller that has write caching enabled, you generally will see times at or below 4 msec per write. If your disk seconds per write are consistently above this range, you should increase the number of disks holding the data or use faster hard disks.

The same general rules apply to the average disk seconds per read. Read times of 11 to 15 msec or below are adequate for most systems. If your SQL statements tend to access the data sequentially, you should investigate the use of a disk controller that provides a read cache along with the write cache. This will allow the system to read additional rows for each read requested by the server. If the next read request is for this additional data, it will be serviced from the cache rather than from the relatively slower physical disk. If your data access is not sequential, read caching is not usually beneficial and in fact can degrade the overall system performance.

Memory

Memory is a very valuable resource in any system. Windows 2000 not only allows but encourages the over commitment of memory. Windows 2000 provides a transparent mechanism that allows applications to "believe" that they have more memory than is physically available on the system. As Windows 2000 processes applications, it pages (swaps) unused memory pages to a paging file on disk. Some minimal paging is normal in most systems, but excessive paging can impair overall system performance.

Windows 2000 attempts to maximize memory utilization based on the demands applications place on it. As more is demanded of the memory subsystem, Windows 2000 starts paging. Paging occurs in one of two forms: soft or hard. *Hard paging* (also called *hard page faults*) means that Windows 2000 uses the page file on disk to resolve memory references. Hard paging is expensive because it involves both disk and CPU resources.

Soft paging is slightly different. It means that a user or process in an application has requested memory pages that are physically in memory, but are not part of the application's working set. Most processors today can handle a large amount of soft paging. Hard paging, however, causes significant delays.

Hard paging is easily detected using the System Monitor counters. The best indicator of hard paging is the Pages/sec counter for the Memory object. When this value is consistently greater than zero, your system is hard paging. (You will occasionally see some paging even on a well-tuned system because Windows 2000 performs general housekeeping and memory optimization.) If you are allowing SQL Server to dynamically adjust memory, you can add memory to the system or remove other applications that are competing with SQL Server for memory to reduce the hard paging. If you have set the *max server memory* parameter manually, you might need to lower that value, add memory to the system, or remove other applications competing for memory resources.

Soft paging is a little more difficult to monitor. Because there is no specific counter for soft page faults, you have to calculate this value. The number of soft page faults per second is derived by subtracting the counter value for Pages/sec from the value for Page Faults/sec. Soft page faults frequently occur when SQL Server first accesses its data pages. These should not be any concern for overall system performance.

The following Memory object counters allow you to monitor system paging:

- **Page Faults/sec** The overall number of faulted pages handled by the processor per second. A *page fault* occurs when a process requires code or data that is not in its working set (its space in physical memory). This counter includes both hard page faults (those that require disk access) and soft page faults (where the faulted page is found elsewhere in physical memory).

- **Page Reads/sec** The number of times the disk was read to resolve hard page faults. (Hard page faults occur when a process requires code or data that is not in its working set or elsewhere in physical memory and must be retrieved from disk.) This counter includes reads to satisfy faults in the file system cache (usually requested by applications) and in noncached mapped memory files.

- **Page Writes/sec** The number of times pages were written to disk to free up space in physical memory. Pages are written to disk only if they are changed while in physical memory, so they are likely to hold data, not code.

- **Pages/sec** The number of pages read from or written to disk to resolve hard page faults. It is a sum of the Page Reads/sec and Page Writes/sec counters.

Summary

This chapter discussed how to use System Monitor to assist you in your tuning efforts. System Monitor contains a wealth of performance data that you can use to monitor and tune your system. We have explored which objects and counters in System Monitor are most useful, what the data means, and what you can modify on your system to ensure the best use of all components. The next chapter looks at another useful tool for tuning: SQL Profiler.

Chapter 7
Using SQL Profiler

Debugging a performance problem starts with locating the roots of the problem—which, in many cases, are ineffective SQL statements. If you know or suspect that inefficient SQL is at fault, SQL Profiler can help you determine which statements are to blame. This chapter explains how to determine which SQL statements might be using excessive resources or performing poorly. It also shows how to decompose SQL statements to determine which resources are being used—information with which you can more effectively tune your system.

When you look for SQL statements to tune, start with the ones that use the most resources, take the longest to run, or are executed most often. Tuning a SQL statement that runs occasionally and for a short time does not affect the overall performance of the system, whereas tuning a SQL statement that uses many system resources has a noticeable effect on system performance. By narrowing down the candidate SQL statements to the 10 or 20 that are most likely to affect the system, you can make better use of your time.

You can use the SQL Profiler to trace events within SQL Server and order these events to provide information that assists in determining application and query problems. By tracing activity within SQL Server you can tell which applications, stored procedures, and SQL statements take the most time. You can also tell which SQL statements are run most often. The information the profiler provides varies with how you have configured it and with the type of event you choose to monitor. Statistics it can provide include data on event execution duration, CPU time used, number of reads and writes, and more. This information is invaluable for determining where to concentrate your tuning efforts. This chapter introduces the profiler's features, explains how to use it, and how to analyze the information it provides.

We begin with an overview of the profiler's functions and capabilities, then cover how to open and use the profiler, including how to use the built-in filters and how to create your own filters. Then we discuss how to analyze profiler data and present scenarios that show how you can use the profiler to debug performance problems. The chapter ends with a brief explanation of how to use the profiler to capture, replay, and debug SQL statements.

SQL Profiler Overview

The SQL Profiler graphical tool, which comes with Microsoft SQL Server, provides a mechanism for database administrators (DBAs) to monitor SQL Server *engine events*, that is, events that occur within the SQL Server engine itself. These events include the following:

- Cursor events
- Database growth or shrinkage
- Errors and warning messages
- Locks acquired or released on SQL Server objects
- Login events, such as connects, disconnects, and failed attempts
- Remote procedure call (RPC) batch status
- SQL execution parallelism
- Start or end of a stored procedure
- Start or end of a SQL statement within a stored procedure
- Start or end of a SQL batch
- Table scans
- Transact-SQL SELECT, INSERT, UPDATE, and DELETE statements

SQL Profiler works by setting up *traces* (also called *trace filters*). A trace, or trace filter, is a set of stored events to be profiled. The profiler comes with several predefined trace templates; you can also create your own, as we discuss later in this chapter in the "Creating Trace Templates" section.

The predefined trace templates provided with the profiler are well organized and work well under many different cases. You can modify these trace templates for your specific needs, and then save them as new trace templates, saving yourself a lot of work. The trace templates are as follows:

- **Standard (SQLServerProfilerStandard.tdf)** Provides detailed information on the Transact-SQL statements that have been issued and SQL batches that have been completed. This trace template also includes information on sessions, logins, and logouts.

- **Stored Procedure Counts (SQLServerProfilerSP_Counts.tdf)** Collects data on the stored procedure name that has started. The results are grouped by the event class, the server name, the database ID and the object ID that has been accessed.

- **TSQL (SQLServerProfilerTSQL.tdf)** Collects Transact-SQL statements in the order in which they were submitted. The result is a list of Transact-SQL statements and the time each was issued.

- **TSQL By Duration (SQLServerProfilerTSQL_Duration.tdf)** Displays the Transact-SQL statements that have been issued as well as the time it takes for those Transact-SQL statements to execute. The time is displayed in milliseconds.

- **TSQL For Replay (SQLServerProfilerTSQL_Replay.tdf)** Provides detailed information on the Transact-SQL statements that have been issued. The intent of this trace template is to provide data that can be used to replay Transact-SQL statements in SQL Query Analyzer.
- **TSQL Grouped (SQLServerProfilerTSQL_Grouped.tdf)** Collects data similar to that gathered by the preceding TSQL trace, but the resulting data is grouped by the application name, the Windows NT user name, the Login name, and the process ID under which the Transact-SQL statement was submitted.
- **TSQL Stored Procedures (SQLServerProfilerTSQL_SPs.tdf)** Displays the stored procedure as well as the Transact-SQL commands within that stored procedure. The results are ordered by time.
- **Tuning (SQLServerProfilerTuning.tdf)** Provides detailed information on the Transact-SQL statements that have been issued and SQL batches that have been completed.

These predefined trace templates are very useful. For example, the TSQL By Duration (SQLServerProfiler_Duration.tdf) trace template can help you determine which SQL statements take the most time to execute. This gives you a place to start looking for problem queries.

Caution The profiler can use significant system resources, causing a performance problem itself. The more events you trace, the more overhead you use.

In addition to tracing SQL Server engine events, you can use SQL Profiler to debug SQL statements. The profiler can single-step through SQL statements, and capture and replay SQL statements submitted by any user in the relational database management system (RDBMS).

Using SQL Profiler

Start SQL Profiler by clicking Start, then pointing to Programs, then to Microsoft SQL Server, and then clicking Profiler. The profiler opens, but does not begin until you define the events that you want to profile. The initial screen is blank. SQL Profiler contains the following menus:

- **File** Use to create, open, close, and modify the properties of trace filters or SQL scripts.
- **Edit** Use to clear trace windows, find text strings, and copy data.
- **View** Use to control the profiler environment, for example, show or hide toolbars.
- **Replay** Use to manipulate SQL statements when running in SQL debug mode. Statements can be started, single-stepped, paused, and manipulated from here.
- **Tools** Use to open SQL Server tools such as the Create Trace wizard as well as external tools such as Enterprise Manager and the Query Analyzer.

- **Window** Use to control the tool's windowing environment.
- **Help** Use to open Help on the profiler and Transact-SQL.

The profiler also has a number of convenient toolbar buttons that you can use to perform functions such as trace manipulation, windowing, and tool invocation.

Setting Trace Options

You can modify the SQL Profiler trace options by selecting Options from the Tools menu to display the General tab of the Trace Options dialog box, as shown in Figure 7-1.

Figure 7-1. *The General tab of the Trace Options dialog box.*

On this screen you can set the default trace template name and the default trace template file name. These options save you a few seconds by choosing the trace template name for you. Of course, when you open the profiler you can change the current trace template. In addition to choosing the default trace templates, you can also select the Start Tracing Immediately After Making A Connection check box to have tracing begin immediately after the connection to the database is made. Tracing commences using the default trace template selected in the Template Name drop-down list. On the Display tab you can specify the font name and font size that the profiler uses.

Click OK when you've completed setting the default trace options. The next section shows how to run the predefined traces; later we'll discuss how to modify those traces and create your own trace filters.

Running Traces

To start profiling you must base a trace on an existing trace template or create a new trace from scratch. To create a new trace, click File, point to New, and then click Trace to open the Connect to SQL Server dialog box, as shown in Figure 7-2. From this dialog box you can select a trace template, run it directly, or modify it and then run it.

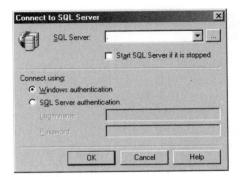

Figure 7-2. *In the Connect to SQL Server dialog box you can specify the connection settings when you create a new trace.*

Specify the server name and the connection settings for SQL Server in the Connect to SQL Server dialog box and click OK. The value "." represents the local server as chosen in the example. Once you have connected to the SQL Server you want to monitor, you will see the General tab of the Trace Properties dialog box. This initial screen includes a trace template to use as a starting point. You can modify these trace templates, and because you don't have to start from scratch they help get you started.

Trace Templates

This section walks through the predefined trace templates to provide some general information on what SQL Profiler monitors.

TSQL

The TSQL trace collects Transact-SQL statements in the order in which they have been submitted—information you can use to view the activity on the system. Then you can correlate this activity with other events on the system, such as deadlocks or other system problems.

Start the TSQL trace by selecting TSQL from the Run Traces menu, clicking File, then pointing to Open and clicking Trace Template. Then select SQLServerProfilerTSQL.tdf from the Open menu, as shown in Figure 7-3.

The first screen to appear contains two panes: in the upper half is the summary pane, and in the lower half is the details pane. (See Figure 7-4.) You may want to maximize this screen, unless you are running several traces at once. If your system is busy you will immediately see information in the profiler, as shown in Figure 7-4.

The data collected and displayed by the TSQL trace includes the Event Class (type of event), the SQL statement text, the server process ID (SPID), and the time the statement began execution. You can select each line in the summary pane to display the SQL text in the details pane.

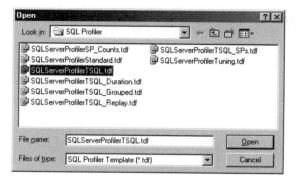

Figure 7-3. *Selecting the TSQL predefined trace template.*

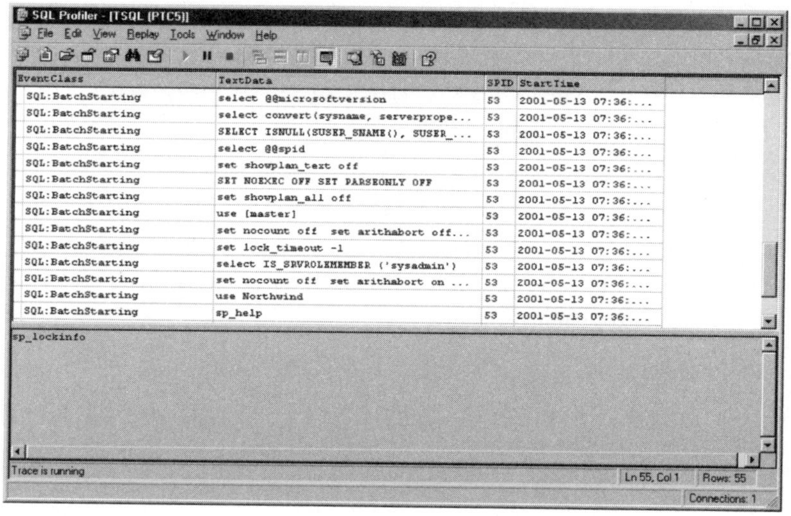

Figure 7-4. *The TSQL trace.*

This trace is good for monitoring system activity. Because it saves only a small amount of data, you can save space and still collect a few days' worth of traces (depending on how active your system is). You can use this data to find problem SQL statements and to provide a record of what SQL statements were run.

TSQL (Grouped)

The TSQL (Grouped) trace collects data similar to that gathered by the TSQL trace, but groups the resulting data by the application name, the Windows NT user name, the login name of the user who has submitted the SQL statements, and the client process ID (unless you change the grouping). This information is useful when you are looking for a problem that specific users have reported, such as a few users who are experiencing deadlocks.

This trace displays a screen like the one in the previous example. Again, after you open the trace it immediately begins collecting data, as shown in Figure 7-5. The output of the event pane is grouped as it would be by a GROUP BY statement. All of the events that have the same ApplicationName, NTUserName, LoginName, and ClientProcessID are adjacent to each other.

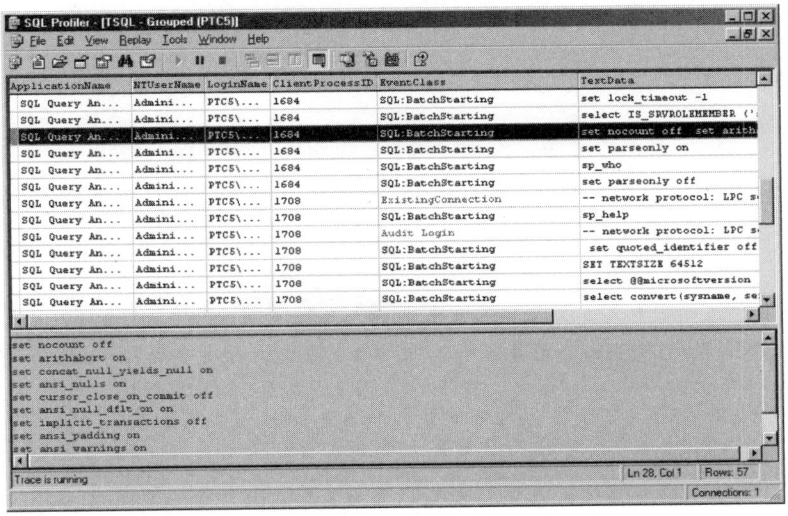

Figure 7-5. *The TSQL (Grouped) trace.*

The TSQL (Grouped) trace is useful when you want to debug a set of SQL statements invoked by a single user running a third-party application. By filtering the events in this manner, you can view both the order and the syntax of the SQL statements that an application has used. Furthermore, by checking the timestamps for when the SQL batches started, you can get a fairly good idea of how long each step in the application is taking. Keep in mind that delays may be caused by the application as well as by slow-running SQL statements.

To more accurately measure the time it takes to run each SQL batch, you can modify the trace by adding the SQL:BatchCompleted event and then selecting the Duration data column. The Duration column does not show any data on the SQL:BatchStarting event, because no end is captured. The value of the duration is in milliseconds, as shown in Figure 7-6.

If your goal is to find long-running SQL statements within a specific application, this method can be extremely useful. By capturing the beginning and ending times of the SQL statements, you can easily browse through the data to find the SQL statements that take the longest time to run. This gives you a good starting point for tuning the application.

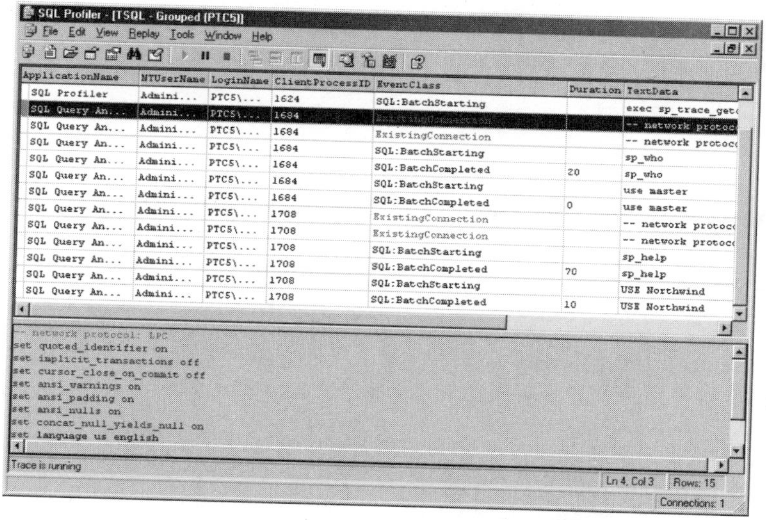

Figure 7-6. *The TSQL (Grouped) trace with the SQL:BatchCompleted event and Duration column added.*

Stored Procedure Counts

The Stored Procedure Counts trace keeps track of stored procedures and how often they have been run. The results are grouped by EventClass, ServerName, DatabaseID and ObjectID. The last column displayed is the SPID. This is a very simple trace, as shown in Figure 7-7. Knowing the number of times that various stored procedures run can be useful in determining which stored procedures are good candidates for tuning. Since you may not have time to analyze and tune all stored procedures, focusing on the most heavily used stored procedures is a good strategy. The event captured is SP:Starting. If you want to add Duration, you must also capture SP:Completed.

When tuning an application, we usually look for SQL statements that run for a very long time. It is also good to look for SQL statements or stored procedures that are run repeatedly. The frequency with which a stored procedure is run is a major consideration for the total amount of resources that it is using. An inefficient stored procedure that is constantly run is a good candidate for tuning. It is a good idea to add SP:Completed and Duration to this trace.

TSQL Stored Procedures

The TSQL Stored Procedure Steps trace displays a stored procedure as well as the SQL commands within that stored procedure. The results are ordered by the time the event started. (See Figure 7-8.) This trace is similar to the TSQL trace, but includes an additional column that shows which stored procedure calls each SQL statement. This information can be very useful when debugging stored procedures, especially those that call other stored procedures.

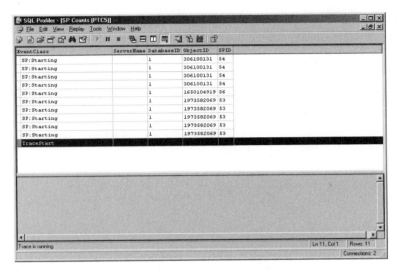

Figure 7-7. *The Stored Procedure Counts trace.*

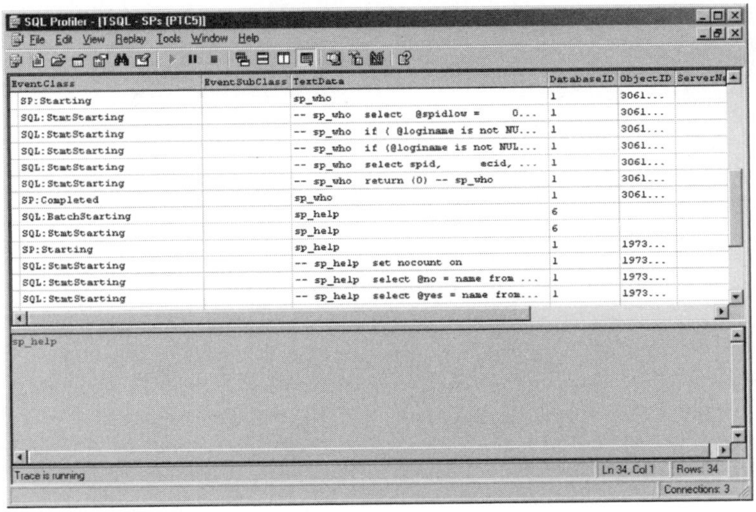

Figure 7-8. *The TSQL Stored Procedure Steps trace.*

Before SQL Profiler was available it was difficult, sometimes impossible, to determine which SQL statements were using excessive resources. In SQL Server 6.5, the SQL Trace facility displayed only the SQL statement itself. But by using the TSQL Stored Procedure Steps trace you can easily track the problem SQL statements once you know from which stored procedure they are being run. Identifying these problem SQL statements is much more manageable than before.

TSQL By Duration

The TSQL By Duration trace displays the Transact-SQL statements that have been issued, as well as the time (in milliseconds) that it takes for those Transact-SQL statements to execute. Figure 7-9 shows a sample screen generated by running this trace. This trace allows you to identify specific SQL statements that take an excessive amount of time so that you can focus your tuning efforts on them.

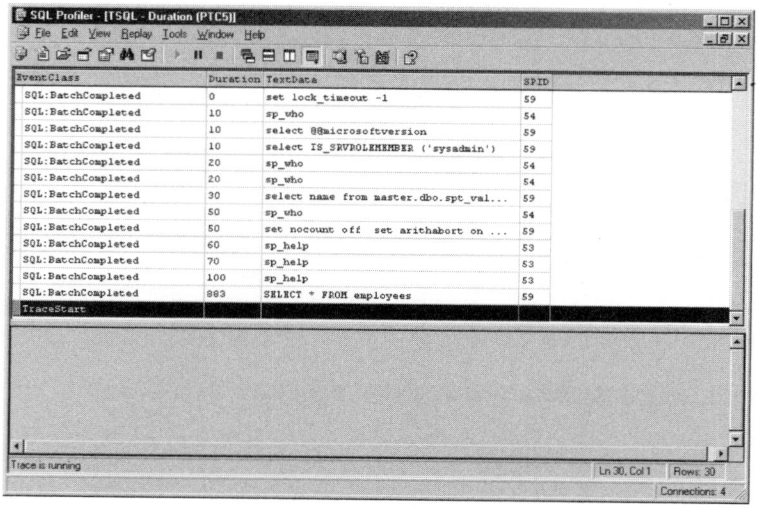

Figure 7-9. *The TSQL By Duration trace.*

This trace is sorted first by EventClass and then by duration, so the longest running events are the lowest events within each class. The EventClass and duration are followed by the data of the SQL statement that had been executed, as well as the SPID.

TSQL For Replay

The TSQL For Replay trace provides detailed information on the Transact-SQL statements that have been issued, as shown in Figure 7-10. This trace provides data that can be used to replay SQL statements that have been run on the server. These SQL statements can be rerun on this or another server.

This trace is useful for capturing a set of SQL commands for replay. If more than one user is connecting to this server, however, the SQL commands are intermingled when captured. This may or may not be what you want. To correct this situation, you can change the filter properties to trace only the single user ID you want. How to modify filters is described in the next section, "Modifying Trace Properties."

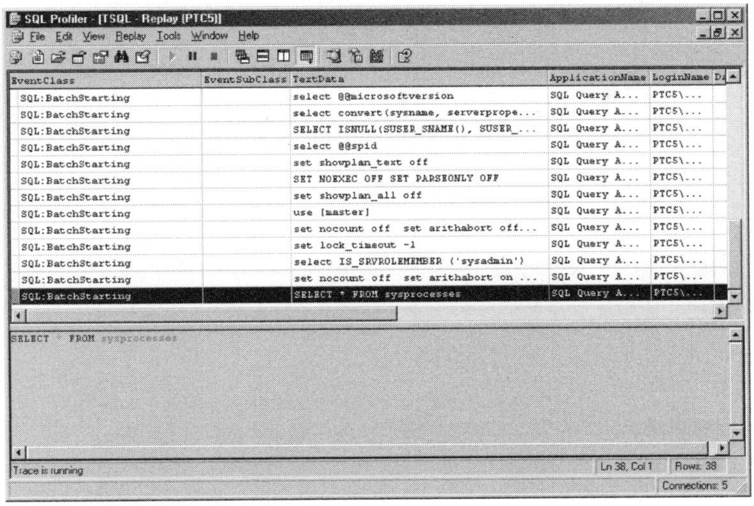

Figure 7-10. *The TSQL For Replay trace.*

Tuning

The Tuning trace simply provides detailed information on the Transact-SQL statements and stored procedure calls that have been issued, as shown in Figure 7-11. This trace provides execution information and the duration of these executions, which can be useful when you tune the system.

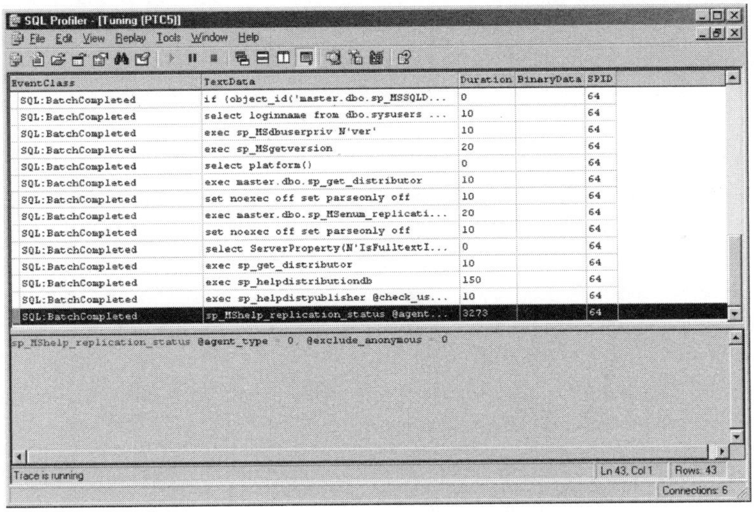

Figure 7-11. *The Tuning trace.*

This trace is useful for quickly tracking down long-running or frequently run SQL statements or stored procedures.

Standard

The Standard trace collects a multitude of data on system logins and logouts, stored procedures, and Transact-SQL execution completions, as shown in Figure 7-12. It displays this data in many different columns.

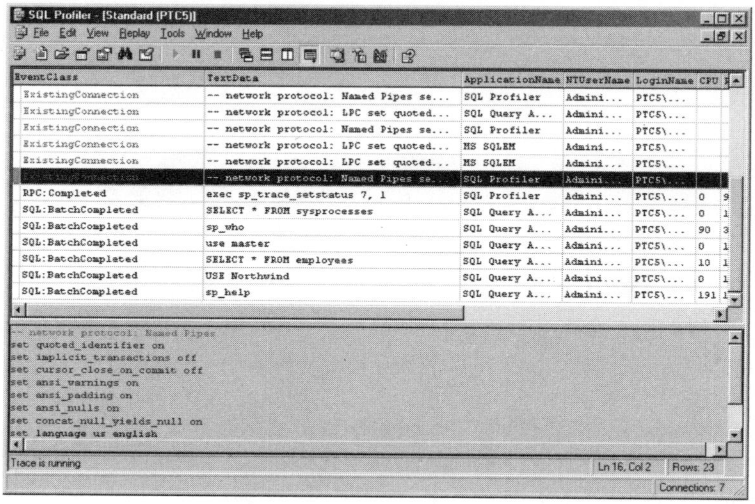

Figure 7-12. *The Standard trace.*

You can use this trace as a system auditing device or for tuning SQL statements and stored procedures.

Modifying Trace Properties

After you have selected a trace, you can modify the trace properties (events, data columns and filters) by first stopping the trace and then selecting Properties from the File menu. The Trace Properties dialog box appears and displays the General tab, as shown in Figure 7-13.

On the General tab you have the following settings:

- **Trace Name** The name that the trace will be saved under.
- **Template Name** The current trace template you are using. You select a different trace template from the template directory.
- **Template File Name** The name of the trace template file that you want to use. This option is used for selecting trace templates that do not exist in the trace template directory.
- **Save To File** Select this check box to open the Save As dialog box to specify a trace file to save the trace data to.

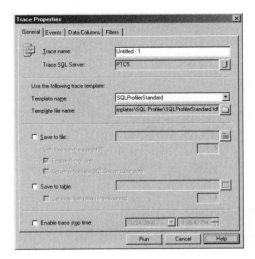

Figure 7-13. *The General tab of the Trace Properties dialog box.*

- **Save To Table** Select this check box to specify a database and table to save trace data to.
- **Enable Trace Stop Time** Select this check box and specify a time when the trace collection should end.

Saving Trace Data

When running traces it is often useful to save the trace data for later analysis. You can save trace data to a file or to a table within SQL Server itself. To save profile data to a file, select the Save To File check box. Use the Save As dialog box to navigate to the desired folder and specify the file name. By saving profile data to a file, you can either view the trace in SQL Profiler again or replay the trace. By saving the trace to a trace table you can use complex SQL Statements to perform analysis on the trace data itself. This is discussed later in this chapter in the "Using SQL Statements to Analyze Trace Data" section.

To save profile data in a SQL Server table, select the Save To Table check box. In the Connect To SQL Server dialog box, specify the server for the table and click OK. In the Destination Table dialog box specify the database, and table name and click OK.

Trace data saved to a table can be either viewed in the profiler again or replayed. Capturing the data to a table keeps it secure within SQL Server for easy recovery as well as allowing for complex analysis. For long-term traces this is probably the better option. For example, if you want to continuously run a trace that logs unsuccessful login attempts, it would be a good idea to save this data in a SQL Server table. The data is managed under SQL Server and can be viewed and manipulated with SQL commands.

Adding or Deleting Events in an Existing Trace Filter

The Events tab in the Trace Properties dialog box (see Figure 7-14) is the core of SQL Profiler. On this tab you can add or delete events in a trace filter. The set of events being monitored is what provides you with useful trace information. The Events tab is made up of two lists. The left list, Available Event Classes, is a list of events you can monitor but have not selected. The list on the right, Selected Event Classes, is a list of events you have selected for monitoring. Double-click an event in the Available Event Classes list to select that event for monitoring and move it to the Selected Event Classes list. Double-click an event in the Selected Event Classes list to remove it from the list of monitored events and place it in the Available Event Classes list. You can also use the Add and Remove buttons to move events from one list to another.

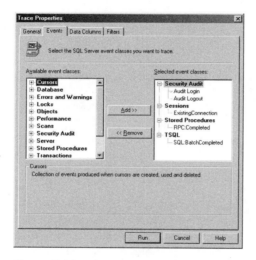

Figure 7-14. *The Events tab of the Trace Properties dialog box.*

The events you can monitor are categorized by their general application within SQL Server. These categories are as follows:

- **Cursors** These trace events are related to cursor processing, such as CursorOpen, CursorClose, CursorExecute, CursorPrepare, and CursorUnprepare. If you are interested in who is using what cursor and when, these events will tell you.

- **Database** These trace events are related to data file and log file size changes.

- **Errors And Warnings** These trace events display error and warning messages. Some, such as ErrorLog and EventLog, display messages that are being written to their respective logs. Other events, such as Missing Column Statistics and Missing Join Predicate, are messages typically given to the user running the SQL statement. Also included are OLE DB errors.

- **Locks** These trace events display information about lock problems that are occasionally experienced in SQL Server. They include lock acquisition and release events as well as escalations and other lock-related events including deadlock chains. If you have ever tried to debug deadlocks, you will really appreciate these trace events.

- **Objects** These trace events allow you to monitor which database objects are being accessed, and by whom. This trace category is made up of object creation, deletion, open, close, and autostat events.

- **Performance** This category includes events on the degree of parallelism of executions, execution plans, and statistics.

- **Scans** This category consists of the scan started and ended event, which gives information on table scans.

- **Security Audit** This category consists of the events related to the addition and modification of users and roles, as well as session information such as logins and logouts.

- **Server** This category consists of the ServerMemoryChange event.

- **Sessions** This category consists of the ExistingConnection event.

- **Stored Procedures** The Stored Procedures category provides information on the use of stored procedures such as starting, ending, input parameters cache hits and misses, and other events such as stored procedure recompiles.

- **Transactions** This category allows you to collect transactional information.

- **TSQL** This category contains traces related to Transact-SQL execution. It is made up of statement and batch execution events as well as preparation events.

- **User Configurable** This category is made up of the user configurable events that you can also use with System Monitor as explained in Chapter 6, "Monitoring Performance with Windows 2000 System Monitor."

By selecting the best traces and collecting the most relevant information for your particular needs, you can tune your system quickly and effectively. To effectively tune your system you must first determine the root cause of the problem. The profiler is the ideal tool for this, if used properly. Too little information will leave you without enough data to solve the problem. Too much information will overwhelm you and take too much time to sift through.

Modifying the Data Columns

On the Data Columns tab of the Trace Properties dialog box, you can add or delete columns in a trace filter, as shown in Figure 7-15. The data columns you select specify what data is collected each time an event occurs. If you do not select the correct data columns, the information that you get from SQL Profiler might not meet your needs.

Note Not every event has every data column associated with it. For example, the duration, CPU, and I/O columns contain only useful data at the end of a Transact-SQL statement or SQL Batch. No data is displayed in those data columns on SQL:BatchStarting and similar events.

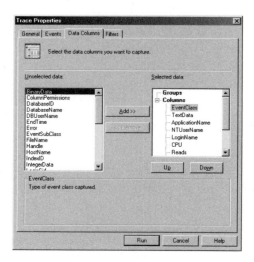

Figure 7-15. *The Data Columns tab of the Trace Properties dialog box.*

The left side of this tab contains the Unselected Data list, and the right side contains the Selected Data list. By double-clicking or by using the Add and Remove buttons, you can move columns from one list to the other to select or deselect those columns.

You can use the options on this tab not only to select which columns are displayed for each event, but also how that data is sorted and grouped. The Selected Data list has two main branches into which data can be placed: Groups and Columns. The Groups branch is used to hold columns that you want to group together. The Columns branch specifies the order of the selected columns. You can move a column up and down within a branch and between the Groups and Columns branches by selecting its name and clicking the Up or Down buttons.

Grouping is useful for separating specific data, such as NT User Name and SQL User Name. Such a separation occurs in the TSQL (Grouped) predefined trace. Separating the data into groups can remove a lot of confusion. If you have ever used the SQL Server 6.5 Trace utility you will really appreciate this feature.

Once the data has been grouped, it will then appear in columns in the order specified by the names in the Columns branch. This order can be modified to suit your own tastes. By creating a trace filter that is exactly what you need; additional analysis work can be minimized.

Selecting the proper data columns is very important. Here are the columns and the values you can select for them:

- **ApplicationName**   This column shows the application name that has been set for the current session if set by the application.
- **BinaryData**   Some events allow binary data to be captured. This column represents that data.
- **ClientProcessID**   The ID of the process on the client.
- **ColumnPermissions**   This is displayed if a column permission has been set.
- **CPU**   The number of milliseconds used by the event.
- **DatabaseID**   The ID for the current database.
- **DatabaseName**   The name of the current database.
- **DBUserName**   The SQL Server user name of the client.
- **Duration**   The number of milliseconds used by the event.
- **EndTime**   The timestamp of the completion of the event. This is valid only for end events.
- **Error**   The error number of a given event.
- **EventClass**   This is the classification of the event used by SQL Profiler and is the name of the event that you have selected. This event cannot be removed from the trace.
- **EventSubClass**   The type of event subclass.
- **FileName**   The logical name of the file that is being modified by the event.
- **Handle**   The ODBC, OLE DB, or DB-Library handle used by the process that has caused the event.
- **HostName**   The Client computer name.
- **IndexID**   The ID of the index being affected by the event.
- **IntegerData**   Where applicable, the integer value of data captured in the event.
- **LoginName**   The login used by the user who has caused the event.
- **LoginSid**   The security ID (SID) of the user who has caused the event.
- **Mode**   Some events use the mode value to keep track of the state of the event.
- **NestLevel**   The level of nest within a nested operation.
- **NTDomainName**   The domain in which the user belongs.
- **NTUserName**   The Windows NT user name of the connected user.
- **ObjectID**   The ID of the object being accessed by the event.
- **ObjectName**   The name of the object being accessed by the event.
- **ObjectType**   The type of object being accessed by the event.
- **OwnerName**   The database user name of the owner of the object accessed by the event.

- **Permissions** An integer representation of a bitmap of the type of permissions that had to be checked by the execution of the event.

- **Reads** The number of logical disk reads performed by the server on behalf of the event.

- **RoleName** The name of the application role that was enabled during the execution of the event.

- **ServerName** The name of the SQL Server instance being traced.

- **Severity** The severity level of an exception.

- **SPID** This is the server process ID. Each connection into SQL Server has a unique SPID. This event cannot be removed from the trace.

- **StartTime** The start time of the event.

- **State** The error state code.

- **Success** A bit representing whether the event was successful (1) or not (0).

- **TargetLoginName** The login name that was targeted by the event, such as a create login, etc.

- **TargetLoginSid** The SID that was targeted by the event, such as a create login, etc.

- **TargetUserName** The user name that was targeted by the event, such as a permission grant.

- **TextData** This column is important because it shows you the text of the SQL statement, stored procedure, or SQL batch being executed.

- **TransactionID** The ID that the system has assigned to the transaction.

- **Writes** The number of physical disk writes that have been performed by the server on behalf of the event.

Further Filtering Trace Data

On the Filters tab in the Trace Properties dialog box you can add filtering criteria to your event tracing, as shown in Figure 7-16. This is useful when you want to include or exclude events of specific types.

Items you can add to a filter include the following:

- **ApplicationName** Specify which application to include or exclude from the trace. This is great if you want to include the profiler itself (excluded by default in most of the trace templates), or if you want to exclude the events generated by the SQL Server Agent.

- **ClientProcessID** Specify a specific client process that you want to trace. You can hone in on a specific job.

- **CPU** Specify the minimum and maximum amounts of time (in milliseconds) that a job must run in order to be logged in the profiler.

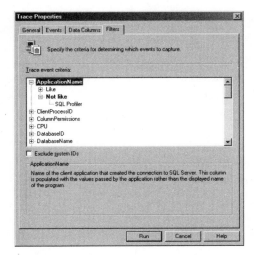

Figure 7-16. *The Filters tab of the Trace Properties dialog box.*

- **ColumnPermissions** When you're tracing as a security audit, this can filter events where a column permission was set.

- **DatabaseID** Specify the ID of the database that you want to monitor.

- **DatabaseName** Specify the name of the database that you want to monitor.

- **DBUserName** Specify a specific user to include or exclude. This can be very useful in tracking down a specific problem or tracing a specific stored procedure.

- **Duration** Specify the minimum and maximum amounts of elapsed time (in milliseconds) that the job must run to be considered a valid event. This is useful if you are searching for long-running jobs.

- **EndTime** Specify the time you want to collect the data. Use in conjunction with StartTime to set up a time window.

- **Error** The error number of a given event.

- **FileName** The logical name of the file being modified by the event.

- **Handle** The ODBC, OLE DB or DB-Library handle that the event is using.

- **HostName** The name of the computer that has generated the event.

- **IndexID** The integer ID of the index that was accessed by the event.

- **LoginName** The login name of the user who has executed the event.

- **Mode** The integer used to represent the state of the process that has executed the event.

- **NTDomainName** The domain of the client that has generated the event.

- **NTUserName** Specify a Windows NT user name to trace, or to exclude from tracing.

- **ObjectID** Specify the object (by ID) to monitor or exclude.
- **ObjectName** Specify the object (by name) to monitor or exclude.
- **ObjectType** Specify the type of object to monitor or exclude.
- **OwnerName** Specify a specific object (by owner name) to monitor or exclude.
- **Permissions** Include or exclude an event based on the permissions checked. (We do not find this filter very useful.)
- **Reads** Specify a minimum and maximum number of logical reads that an event must have in order to be included in the trace. This option is useful for finding resource-consuming jobs.
- **RoleName** Include or exclude an event based on the application role being enabled.
- **Severity** Include or exclude an event based on a range of error severity levels.
- **SPID** Include or exclude an event based on the SPID of the user who has caused the event.
- **StartTime** Specify a time when you want to collect the data. Use this filter in conjunction with EndTime to set up a time window.
- **State** Same as Error. The error number of a given event.
- **Success** Include or exclude events based on whether they have succeeded (1) or failed (0).
- **TargetLoginName** Valid only for operations that target a login name, such as adding a new login.
- **TargetUserName** Valid only for operations that target a login name, such as adding a new login.
- **TextData** Include or exclude events that contain a particular piece of text. This can be useful for choosing a specific table; or including a command, such as INSERT, UPDATE, or DELETE. Multiple entries should be separated by a ; (semicolon) and wildcards are designated by the % (percent sign).
- **Writes** Specify a minimum and maximum number of logical writes that an event must have in order to be included in the trace. This option is useful for finding those resource-consuming jobs.

As you can see, you can apply a great deal of additional filtering to your traces. By adding filtering criteria, you can configure traces to find the specific events that you are looking for. Later in this chapter you will see how to generate trace filters based on specific tasks.

Creating Trace Templates

Creating your own trace template is fairly straightforward. To create a new trace template, on the File menu, point to New, and then click Trace Template, or point to Open, and then click Trace Template. Following the second method you will be prompted to open an existing trace template first. You will see the General tab of the Trace Template Properties screen, as shown in Figure 7-17. On the General tab, click Save As. The Save As dialog box opens so you can give the new trace template a name. Enter a name in the File Name box and click Save.

Figure 7-17. *The General tab of the Trace Template Properties dialog box.*

Modify the Events, Data Columns, and Filters as described in the previous sections. Then you are ready to use this trace template to start profiling.

Analyzing Profile Data

Analyzing profile data involves reading page after page of saved data. This data can be quite voluminous, so we recommend that you use SQL Profiler's filtering capabilities to help reduce that data.

The basics of analyzing and interpreting profile data involve understanding the data that your trace saved. Regardless of which event you trace, the information includes a set of data as specified in the Data Columns tab of the Trace Properties dialog box. This data contains information such as the following on connections, transactions, SQL statements, and stored procedures:

- **Type of event** What types of events occurred. Examples of events are the beginning or completion of SQL batches, and the establishment or termination of connections.
- **Connection information** Which user was connected, where that user was connected from, and details about the user connection.
- **Object information** What object was accessed during this operation.
- **SQL text** Which SQL statement was executed.
- **Resource information** How long the event took and how many resources were used during the event. This is the key information gathered by the profiler.

Interpreting the data gathered by the profiler is very important. Let's look at a list of the data that is gathered and what this information means. You can modify the properties of the trace and add or remove data columns depending on whether you want to view specific data. Some of these data columns are selected by default for all event classes. These default columns are highlighted in italics in the following list.

- ***ApplicationName*** The name of the client application used to run this specific event. Every connection to SQL Server must be via some sort of application. This information can help you track down an application that is using excessive resources.

- **BinaryData** The binary data is specific to the event class that is being monitored. With some events this data further specifies the event; for example, the binary data for Locks:Acquired displays the lock ID. In other cases the BinaryData column does not hold any information.

- ***ConnectionID*** The ID that SQL Server has assigned to the connection. This number is assigned when the connection is established, and is released when the connection is dropped. Sometimes events are triggered by system processes. In that case a connection ID might not be present.

- ***CPU*** The amount of CPU time, in milliseconds, that was used by the event. This data could be either valuable or useless, depending on the event. Events such as ExistingConnection and Disconnect will sometimes show very high CPU values; but this data will not help you find resource consumers because this value represents a cumulative CPU count for the connection rather than an individual measure of resource consumption by a particular SQL statement. In other cases, the CPU counter can be valuable.

- ***DatabaseID*** The ID of the database currently in use.

- ***Duration*** The amount of elapsed time, in milliseconds, for the event. This is useful for a high-level overview of system performance, because it represents the response time of the users (such as a user clicking a button).

- ***EndTime*** The time that the event ended.

- ***EventClass*** The type of event that is being shown.

- **EventSubClass** The subtype of event that is being shown.

- **HostName** The name of the SQL Server that is being traced.

- **IntegerData** Like the binary data, integer data is also specific to the event class that is being monitored. With some events this data further specifies the event. In other cases the Integer Data column does not hold any information.

- **LoginName** The SQL Server user name of the connection that has caused the event.

- ***NTUserName*** The Windows NT or Windows 2000 user name.

- **ObjectID** The ID of the object that has been accessed via this event.

- **Reads** The number of logical reads that have been performed by this event. This value does not represent the number of physical reads. The number of physical reads cannot be determined within the profiler.

- **SPID** The server process ID of the process that has caused the event.
- **StartTime** The start time of the event. This column can be useful if you are tracing a certain event or set of events that caused performance degradation within a specific time frame. The Start Time and End Time columns can be used to locate specific events.
- **Text** The text value of the event (if applicable). This is the text of a SQL statement.
- **TransactionID** The system-assigned transaction ID of the transaction that has initiated the event.
- **Writes** The number of logical writes that have been performed by this event. This value does not represent the number of physical writes. The number of physical writes cannot be determined within SQL Profiler.

Analyzing the profile data involves extracting the data relevant for the type of work that you are doing from these columns. Selecting the best grouping for the columns can enhance your ability to interpret the data. You will start to get a better feel for using SQL Profiler in the next section, which presents a few different scenarios and analyzes the resulting data.

Using SQL Statements to Analyze Trace Data

One benefit of saving trace data to a table is that you can analyze the trace data using SQL statements. SQL statements can be very powerful tools. Using SQL statements you can pull out such data as:

- Number of times a stored procedure has been run
- Minimum duration
- Average duration
- Maximum duration
- Minimum CPU time
- Average CPU time
- Maximum CPU time

Depending on the available data, you can use the SQL aggregate functions to find a number of valuable statistics. An example of such a SQL statement is shown here. This SQL statement is designed to work with stored procedures only.

```
SELECT SUBSTRING(TextData, 1, 20) AS 'Name',
COUNT(*) 'Count',
AVG(duration) AS 'Avg Duration', SUM(cpu) AS 'Avg CPU',
AVG(reads) AS 'Avg reads', AVG(writes) AS 'Avg writes'
FROM trace
WHERE EventClass=12
GROUP BY SUBSTRING(TextData, 1, 20)
```

Note Because TextData is **text** data type, you must use the SUBSTRING function to convert it to a character data type before you can use it in a GROUP BY clause. EventClass 12 represents SQL:BatchCompleted.

The following is sample output from this query:

Name	Count	Avg Duration	Avg CPU	Avg reads	Avg writes
sp_help	1	1043	451	5414	8
sp_helpdb	1	690	290	1993	0
sp_helptable	1	60	0	7	0
sp_lock	5	36	80	86	0
sp_who	6	43	90	50	0
sp_who2 active	1	60	30	517	2
sp_who2	1	570	160	1399	16

The type of query to use varies depending on the type of events that you are looking for. If you are looking at stored procedures you need to create a specific query that filters out stored procedure calls. Using SQL you have a lot of flexibility.

Sample Scenarios

This section provides some examples of how SQL Profiler can help you debug performance problems on your system or simply act as a SQL Server monitor. We hope that these scenarios give you a better idea of how to use this tool and give you some ideas for creating your own traces.

Looking for Long-Running SQL Statements

Long-running queries can indicate a poorly tuned system, a poorly written application, or simply a job that does a lot of work. In any case, finding and tuning these long-running SQL statements will improve the performance of that job, and perhaps the performance of the system in general, by relieving some of the processing load from the server.

Recommended Trace Event

The best way to find long-running queries is to use the following counter and to group by the Duration column.

- **TSQL, SQL:BatchCompleted** How long the execution of the SQL batch took to complete. This indicates the latency of the transaction step.

Grouping by the Duration column orders the output of the trace based on how long each statement took to run. Scroll down to the end of the trace data window to see the longest running statements listed. This would be a good place to start tuning.

Looking for Resource Consumers

A trace that looks for applications or users that consume excessive resources can be a useful tool for a DBA. This type of trace should look at SQL statements that consume both CPU and I/O resources. Which one you are most concerned with is determined by how your system is running.

Recommended Trace Events

The best way to find the excessive resource users is to select the following events to monitor, and group by CPU, Reads, or Writes, depending on whether you are most concerned with I/O or CPU usage.

- **Sessions, ExistingConnection** This is useful for displaying connections that already exist when SQL Profiler is started.
- **TSQL, SQL:BatchCompleted** This event shows how long the SQL batch has taken to complete. The CPU, Reads, and Writes data columns will indicate the resources used by this event.

This type of trace can help identify the heavy resource consumers and give you a starting point for tuning the applications.

Using SQL Profiler to Detect Deadlocks

Depending on what your users are doing, deadlocks might or might not be a problem in your system. Many deadlocks can be a severe problem, in which case identifying their cause can be essential to improving performance.

Recommended Trace Events

When you use SQL Profiler to look for the cause of deadlocks, include the following events, grouped by Event Class, in the trace definition:

- **TSQL, SQL:BatchStarting** The SQL batch that is running
- **Locks, Lock:Deadlock** The event of the deadlock itself
- **Locks, Lock:Deadlock Chain** The sequence of events leading up to the deadlock

By identifying the cause of the deadlocks you can better solve the problem. By selecting these events you can trace back to the cause of a deadlock. However, profiling these events can be quite resource intensive and you should do so at your own risk.

Using the Profiler as a System Log

In addition to using SQL Profiler as a debug tool for solving specific problems, you can use it to monitor and record general SQL Server usage. When you use the profiler as a system log, it is often better to save the data to a database table than to a file. By saving the data to a database table, you can create stored procedures or SQL statements that query the data more effectively.

To set up the profiler to act as a system monitor you must think about which events you want to monitor. These events will provide information that you can later use to determine system activity.

Recommended Trace Events

When you use SQL Profiler as a system monitor, include the following events in the trace definition:

- **Sessions, ExistingConnection** This is useful for displaying those connections that already exist when the profiler is started.
- **Errors and Warnings, ErrorLog** It is always a good idea when using the profiler as a system monitor to include messages that go into the error log.
- **Errors and Warnings, EventLog** It is also a good idea to include messages that go into the event log.
- **Security Audit, Audit Login Failed** This event logs in attempts that did not succeed. This can be very useful in finding intruders.

Under normal conditions this type of trace does not consume excessive system resources and is safe to run continuously.

Looking for Performance Problems

The SQL Profiler can be especially useful in finding performance or functional problems within SQL Server. One frequently overlooked problem is stored procedure recompilation. There are a number of documented reasons why a stored procedure might recompile. When this occurs, mild to severe performance problems can result.

The best way to determine if stored procedure recompiles are occurring is to enable the Stored Procedures event SP:Recompile. This event triggers on the SQL statement that caused the recompile to occur. Whenever this event occurs, the entire stored procedure is recompiled, which can be quite time consuming. You should enable this event occasionally, and if you see large numbers of recompiles, take action, such as rewriting the stored procedure.

Debugging SQL Statements

In addition to tracing events within SQL Server, SQL Profiler can debug transactions or stored procedures by capturing and replaying SQL statements. You can replay SQL statements in single steps, as within a debugger, and analyze the individual steps. The function of the profiler is similar to that of other Microsoft development tools. This section provides a brief overview of how to capture and replay SQL statements and how to single-step through those statements.

Capture and Replay

If you have access to the stored procedure or application source code that you want to debug, it is not really necessary to capture the SQL statements. However, it is often difficult to determine exactly what variables are being passed to the stored procedure or which path is being taken within a stored procedure. In these cases, as well as when the application in question is proprietary and source code is not available, it is necessary to capture the SQL statements within SQL Profiler.

To capture SQL statements for replay, select the SQLServerProfilerTSQL_Replay trace template. This trace template provides all the events that you need to trace TSQL statements. After you select the trace template, it is a good idea to filter the amount of data collected to a single user or system, depending on your preferences.

After running the trace for the length of time you want, save the trace to a file or to a database table. When you are ready to replay the SQL script, select that trace data as shown in the next section.

Single-Stepping

Once you have captured a SQL script (or you have a SQL script that has been written for your application), it is a simple matter to run it. On the File menu, point to Open and then either click Trace File or Trace Table (depending on how you saved the trace). When you open the trace, the controls available within SQL Profiler change; icons and controls for running the SQL statements become visible, as shown in Figure 7-18.

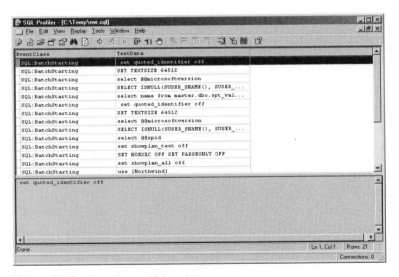

Figure 7-18. *Running a SQL script.*

Initially, the profiler displays two panes. The top pane contains the event and text, and the lower pane contains the SQL statements. Once you start running the SQL statements, a third pane containing the results of the steps appears, as shown in Figure 7-19.

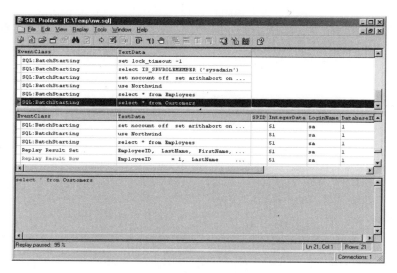

Figure 7-19. *Single-stepping through a SQL script.*

From here it is easy to single-step through the stored procedure or SQL statements by clicking the Execute One Step toolbar button. If you use conditionals, you can view the path taken and see the values assigned to variables. This allows you to easily debug complex SQL statements and stored procedures by seeing what is happening while they are running.

In addition to single-stepping through the stored procedure, you can set breakpoints within profiler. With breakpoints you can use the Run To Cursor toolbar button to run a number of SQL statements. Thus, the profiler allows you to perform the following actions with SQL scripts or stored procedures:

- **Pause execution** You can momentarily pause execution of SQL statements (by clicking the Pause Selected Trace toolbar button) and then resume as needed.

- **Run** You can run the entire SQL script (by clicking the Start Selected Trace toolbar button).

- **Run to breakpoint** By setting breakpoints in certain areas you can avoid having to single-step through the entire file.

- **Run to cursor** By simply clicking on an event, you can run to where the cursor is currently pointing (by clicking the Run To Cursor toolbar button or pressing Ctrl+F10).

- **Single-stepping** You can run SQL statements one at a time (by clicking the Execute One Step toolbar button or pressing F10).
- **Stop execution** You can stop execution at any time and resume at a later time (by clicking the Stop Selected Trace toolbar button).

SQL Profiler provides many of the same features you will find in a SQL debugger or in the SQL Query Analyzer. These features allow you a lot of flexibility and ease of use in debugging problem stored procedures or SQL statements.

Summary

This chapter provided an overview of SQL Profiler, one tool that can be used to help determine what the performance problem is, which is a task that can be as difficult—or more difficult—than actually solving the problem. SQL Profiler is a powerful tool for this task and can be used in conjunction with other tools and methods that you will learn about in this book.

To become proficient at using the profiler you should take the time to experiment with it. Create your own traces using the predefined trace templates and see how they work. Then analyze the trace data and see what types of information it provides. With practice you will become more comfortable with the profiler and your skills will improve.

Part II
Sizing and Capacity Planning

Chapter 8
Modeling for Sizing and Capacity Planning

A *model* is a mathematical construct you can use to understand a physical system. This chapter examines the principles and variables involved in modeling system capacity. First, however, we provide some background on capacity planning itself.

Introduction to Sizing and Capacity Planning

The discipline of capacity planning has two forms: preconfiguration capacity planning and postconfiguration capacity planning.

Preconfiguration Capacity Planning

Preconfiguration capacity planning, or *sizing,* involves anticipating how much hardware you'll require to process your workload within a specified time, as spelled out in the service level agreements (SLAs) or elsewhere.

SLAs are the most common way to establish the conditions of operation agreed upon by all organizations involved in the operation and performance of the system. The SLAs are outlined as a result of meetings among these groups to ensure performance and smooth operation of the system. For example, an SLA might specify that the workload item or transaction in question should execute within a certain response time, say, five seconds. An SLA might specify that no more than 85 percent of memory will ever be used, ensuring 15 percent free space at any time so that page faulting won't get out of hand. Such specifications are agreed on by the users, the operations group, the applications analysts, and the performance group (and also who ever is responsible for capacity planning, if there is no separate capacity planning group) to ensure that satisfactory operating conditions are always met. If a violation is recorded, it usually indicates a failure or overloaded resource somewhere in the system.

In preconfiguration capacity planning, there is usually no real performance data to work with because the system hasn't been designed, so you must use whatever other information is available. Results will vary depending on the accuracy of this information.

Postconfiguration Capacity Planning

Postconfiguration capacity planning is a complex and ongoing performance study of hardware and software resource consumption on a system that is already set up and processing. You perform postconfiguration capacity planning so that your organization can adequately prepare for workload growth in relation to system resources. These studies are primarily established to provide capacity data to the system manager, DBA, and operations manager about their system's growth. They use this data to justify system alterations designed to maintain the level of system performance defined in the SLAs.

Capacity planning studies offer other highly useful features, including the ability to perform predictive analysis on the historic data to project where the system's capacity is heading. The capacity planner can also project "what if" scenarios (predictive analysis) on workloads. In a common postconfiguration capacity planning study scenario, you perform the analysis using historical performance data stored in a database. Through this analysis, you can project trends in the normal growth of CPU utilization (the time a CPU is busy during an observation period), disk usage, memory usage, and network usage. You can also project sudden rises in CPU, disk, and memory utilization caused by adding new users onto the system. These studies can be extremely detailed and can involve profiling the activities of specific users or types of users (such as accounts payable personnel) to predict exactly what kind of resource consumption would take place if you added these users and workload. This predictive analysis gives the system manager time to obtain the necessary hardware before the new users are added to the system, averting any degradation of system performance or response time.

You can also obtain tuning information through postconfiguration capacity planning studies. For example, adding users will result in more database table accesses. You can monitor and track the number of tables that users access and how often they access them. This information can help you determine whether relocating some of these tables to different disk drive arrays will prevent a potential bottleneck in the disk subsystem. In this and the following three chapters, we look at how to perform both types of capacity planning functions, and examine their similarities and differences.

History of Capacity Planning, Benchmarking, and Simulations

In the early years of multiple-user computers, capacity planning and performance were not well understood or developed and were mostly the province of consulting firms who specialized in the field. By the early 1970s, a sizing project for such a firm consisted of finding customers who were running an application that "ran like" the target customer application. Finding these customers was difficult, and matching companies or organizations and their application use was even more challenging.

Emergence of System Simulation and Benchmarking

In the mid-1970s, customers and application suppliers developed an analysis methodology that consisted of running a specific benchmark or workload to guess at the optimal initial size of a machine. This process involved building an application similar to that of the customer in question and running it on similar hardware to gather performance statistics. These statistics were then used to determine the best size machine to meet the customer's needs. This process also enabled "what if" scenarios to be run with the benchmark to determine what size machine would be required if more users, application processes, or data were added to the system. The one drawback to this process was its expense. The early benchmarks, originally developed to simulate customers' usage patterns, began to be used mostly by system vendors as marketing tools to sell systems and to compare the relative performance of competing hardware offerings.

During this period, analysts were developing methods of predicting usage of resources on an existing system. On the surface, this process seemed less challenging than pre-configuration capacity planning, but it proved to be just as difficult because tested methodologies did not exist, nor were tools available to collect the necessary data. Scientists such as Dr. Jeffrey Buzen, a pioneer in capacity planning, were still developing theories on usage and determining how to perform calculations to model usage.

Evolution of Benchmarking Standards

By the 1980s, the early benchmark simulations had evolved into standard benchmark loads, such as the ST1 benchmark, the TP1 benchmark, and the Debit/Credit benchmark, but the emphasis was on finding the fastest-performing hardware for promotional use instead of on developing a standard application workload that could be used to size and maintain systems. Customers still could not use these benchmark offerings for system hardware comparisons because their situations were different. Customer demand led to the formation of a computer industry consortium, the Transaction Processing Performance Council. The council specified standardized transaction loads for more than 45 hardware and software manufacturers. These benchmarks could often show the relative capabilities of hardware and database software; unfortunately, they were not useful for sizing an application workload.

At the same time, client/server computing and the use of relational database technology was maturing, and the need to predict the initial size of a system and its capacity maintenance requirements was growing. Most modern applications are now written based on client/server architecture. Servers are typically used as central data storage devices, and the user interface is primarily run locally on a desktop machine, or on a remote Web site. This cost-effective strategy for using expensive server processing power takes advantage of the graphical user interfaces (GUIs) to which customers are accustomed. Because servers running database applications are heavily utilized, these servers are now the focus for most sizing projects and capacity planning studies.

Sizing and Capacity Planning for Small- to Average-Size Systems

To date, the application simulation benchmark remains the most common method for sizing servers, and the collection of historical performance data and the use of capacity planning techniques on this data are still the most accurate ways of predicting the future use of a machine. Although the process is expensive and time-consuming, organizations can achieve a fairly significant degree of accuracy if they simulate the exact usage of the server. Because large projects may require a multimillion-dollar investment on the part of the organization or the system vendor, however, only the largest organizations can afford systems for this kind of testing. So how to perform in-depth, accurate system sizing and capacity planning for small- to average-size systems? A few easy calculations and a general knowledge of system use are all you need to size and predict the usage of a system to within 10 percent accuracy. The method and calculations for the procedure are in this chapter and in Chapter 9, "Sizing the Database and Application Servers," Chapter 10, "Methods for Sizing a System," and Chapter 11, "Capacity Planning."

Modeling Principles for Sizing and Capacity Planning

Like any structured science, capacity planning has rules you must adhere to. In this section we look at the rules that govern the maximum allowable values of some parameters, such as CPU utilization and queue length, that affect the performance of a system. We use the knee of the curve principle to model these parameters.

Queuing Theory and the Knee of the Curve

Queuing theory states that utilization has a direct effect on queues, and because queues are directly related to response time (in fact, queue length is part of the response time equation), utilization thus has a direct effect on response time.

Consider the following analogy. Suppose you go to the supermarket at 3:00 A.M. You pick up the items you require and then go to the cashier for checkout. At this time in the morning there is no one in front of you, so the utilization of that cashier is 0 percent and the queue length (objects, or in this case people, in front of you) is also zero. Your response time for completing the shopping transaction will be equal to your service time because there is no one in front of you. This means that your service time (in this case the time it takes you to complete the transaction of being checked out and paying for the groceries) is all the time it will take you to complete this task.

Now consider this scenario at 5:00 P.M., a much busier time for a supermarket. You come to that same cashier, but now eight people are in front of you. Your response time for completing the shopping transaction now is equal to the sum of individual service times of all the people in front of you (some people have three items to check out; others many more) plus your own service time. In the second case the use (or utilization) of the cashier was much higher, which had a direct effect on queues and therefore on your overall wait or response time.

When we look at computer systems, we find that a CPU whose utilization in a steady state is above 75 percent has drawbacks. Queues grow exponentially in such a state. From the performance perspective, *linear growth*—the even, incremental growth of utilization—is preferable, as shown in Figure 8-1.

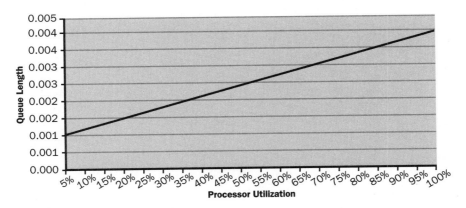

Figure 8-1. *Graph of linear utilization growth.*

Even, incremental growth does not take place in CPUs with utilization factors over 75 percent. In such a system, a point is reached at which the growth becomes *exponential*, rising geometrically and straight up to infinity. This point is known as the *asymptotic* point or the *knee of the curve*. Figure 8-2 depicts this type of growth. Notice that at about 75 percent utilization the curve that indicates the growth of the queue length goes from linear to asymptotic growth (or growth that appears to go straight up).

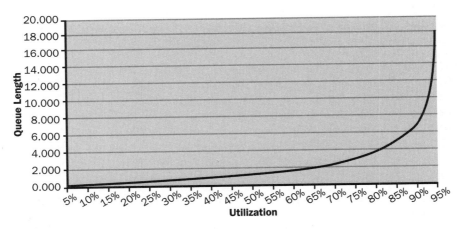

Figure 8-2. *Graph of exponential queue length vs. utilization growth.*

Figure 8-3 illustrates that utilization has a direct effect on the response time. Notice that the curve in this graph is the same as that in the queue length graph. This is why you never want to run your CPUs in a steady state of over 75 percent utilization. This is not to say that you can never run your CPUs above 75 percent utilization for short periods of time, but the longer you do, the more negative impact you will see in terms of queue lengths and response time. The relationship among utilization, queuing length, and response time is one of the most important in sizing and one you should consider when you select the number and speed of CPUs for your system.

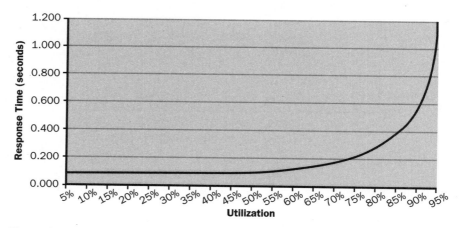

Figure 8-3. *Graph of response time vs. utilization growth.*

For example, say you are sizing a system. You calculate that your system will produce anticipated total processor utilization factors of 180 percent. It would be better to buy three CPUs that will run at about 60 percent, keeping the utilization 15 percent under the knee of the curve, than to have two CPUs running at about 90 percent, which would make the utilization 15 percent over the knee of the curve.

The knee of the curve principle also applies to other facets of your system, such as disks, although these components do not have the same knee of the curve as processors. The knee of the curve for disks tends to be at 85 percent utilization, as opposed to 75 percent for processors. This utilization figure applies to the size and I/O capability of the disk drive in question. For example, a 9-GB disk should not store more than 7.6 GB of data at any given time. Observing this limit allows for growth and, more importantly, helps keep down response times. A disk at full capacity will have longer seek times, adding to your overall response time.

By the same principle, if a disk drive has an I/O capability of 70 I/Os per second, you would not want to have a constant I/O arrival rate of more than 60 I/Os per second in a steady state of operation. By following this principle you can minimize your overall response times because you will not use your processors or disks at maximum utilization. You will get the most out of your system and have a reserve capacity for peak utilization periods.

Atomic Demand Modeling and Queue Modeling

A model of a computer system is simply a group of equations that calculate the utilization of certain parts of the system (CPU or disk) and other statistics. These equations yield information that is useful for maintaining a well-running system. *Atomic demand modeling* is the technique of identifying elements of a system and performing calculations on those components to produce statistics, such as CPU utilization, that show the demand on each resource in a workload. It is called *atomic* demand because it separates each part of the workload to find each component's statistics. Each part or component has a separate set of equations that produces statistics for that component.

When you group resources together to perform certain functions, you form a service chain. Modeling a service chain is known as *queue modeling*. Consider that a transaction involves not only a database, but also many different machines such as a client, network, and other servers, all of which have components such as CPUs, memory, and disks that the transaction might use. All these resources can be broken down to their respective components and then modeled.

Service Chains

A *service chain* is a collection of resources that are used in the processing of a transaction or service. The total response time is the sum of all the service times in the service chain. Indeed, SLAs cannot exist without identifying and observing the service chain. When a transaction is requested, and the response time of that transaction exceeds the time agreed to in an SLA, it is important to subject all resources involved in processing the transaction to close scrutiny and performance observation. Doing so will allow the system management staff advance notification of any failures that will result in violation of an SLA.

The first thing a system manager must do is identify the components of the service chain. Figure 8-4 illustrates a typical service chain. In this example, the workload flow starts at the client, then proceeds through the network, then through a network router to the server (which could be an application server), then to the database server, where the desired information is retrieved; finally, the information is sent back to the client via the reverse path. The complete response time for this transaction is the sum of all the service times of the individual components of the service chain during the round-trip.

After identifying these components, you can arrange to have them monitored by System Monitor in the Performance console and collect historic performance data to produce capacity planning reports on their activities. This way you can stay aware of any increases in activity that may violate certain SLAs. You can also use the historic performance data to predict growth trends and thus stay alert as to when the system will need additional resources to maintain the SLAs.

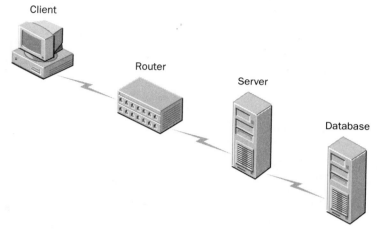

Figure 8-4. *A typical service chain.*

Mathematics for Modeling

You will begin to understand a system's workload when you can see what kinds of events take place during execution. The statistics that you gather on the various components will reveal the effects of execution. These statistics are the results of calculations that are performed by the System Monitor's report generator or by a spreadsheet that a performance analyst uses to track capacity. This section discusses the types of statistics that are gathered and how to interpret them.

Understanding the Basic Model Set

You begin the job of modeling system capacity by gathering certain information on the system in the form of independent variables. *Independent variables* are inputs to equations that calculate system statistics such as CPU utilization or CPU queue length. These inputs are not usually calculated. Instead, they are either directly selected by the user or returned to the user by a reporting mechanism such as the System Monitor.

The three independent variables for the basic model of system capacity are observation time (*T*), busy time (*B*), and completions (*C*). *Observation time* (the amount of time the system is observed) is selected by the analyst performing the study. *Busy time* (the time the system was active during the observation period) is returned to the user by the monitoring mechanism. *Completions* (the number of transactions that were completed during the observation period) is a value returned to the analyst by a transaction monitor.

With just these three independent variables, you can calculate the six different dependent variables of the basic model. A *dependent variable* is the result of a calculation that is either directly or indirectly dependent on the independent variables.

Given the values of the three independent variables, you can calculate the following information:

The utilization of the CPU	$U = B / T$
The transaction throughput of the system	$X = C / T$
The average resource service time	$S = B / C$
The transaction capacity of the system	$Cp = 1 / S$
The average resource queue length	$Q = U / (1 - U)$
The average resource response time	$R = (Q * S) + S$

Now that you understand the equations, let's look at the vital statistics you can gather using the three independent variables. Figure 8-5 provides an example of such data. The independent variables in this example are as follows: we observed the system for 43 seconds (T), during which there were 96 completed transactions (C), and the system was actually busy processing the workload for 31 seconds (B). From this information we can calculate that the utilization (U) was at 72.09 percent, and the average transaction throughput (X) was 2.23 per second. The average service time for these transactions (S) was 0.32 second, and the average system queue length (Q) was 2.58. Transactions were completed in an average time of 1.15 seconds (R), and the system capacity (Cp) was 3.125 transactions per second. A quick analysis of these values would indicate that the CPU utilization was just under the recommended maximum value based on the knee of the curve model.

```
T = 43 Seconds

C = 96 Seconds

B = 31 Seconds

U = 31/43 = 72.09% util
X = 96/43 = 2.23 trans per sec
S = 31/96 = .32 sec
Q = .7209/.2791 = avg q 2.58
R = (2.58 * .32) + .32 = 1.15 sec
Cp = 1/.32 = 3.125 trans per sec
```

Figure 8-5. *An example of calculating system statistics.*

The Utilization Law

There are two ways to calculate the percentage of utilization. We saw the first method earlier, namely, the equation $U = B / T$. Because not all performance monitors return the time in seconds that a CPU was busy, there is another way to determine utilization. We can derive this law algebraically, as follows:

*Utilization = Throughput * Service*

This equation is known as the *utilization law*.

If we apply the utilization law and use the values calculated in Figure 8-5, we can derive the value for utilization as follows:

$$U = X * S$$

$$B / T = (C / T) * (B / C)$$

$$31/43 = (96/43) * (31/96)$$

$$0.72093 = 2.23256 * 0.32292$$

$$0.72093 = 0.72093$$

$$72.09\% = 72.09\%$$

As you can see, the derivation $B / T = (C / T) * (B / C)$ is depicted, proving that the utilization law calculation $U = X * S$ produces the same results as the utilization equation $U = B / T$. Plugging in the values from Figure 8-5, this derivation is as follows:

$U = B / T$, or 31 busy seconds / 43 observed seconds

$X = C / T$, or 96 transactions completed / 43 observed seconds

$S = B / C$, or 31 busy seconds / 96 transactions completed

Both sides of the equation yield the same result: 72.09 percent utilization.

Arrival Rates and Queues

The arrival rate (Ar) is another independent variable that an analyst might find useful. This value can reveal queue sites within a system or service chain. Let the variable A equal the number of arrivals per second at a resource site. Then the equation for arrival rate is as follows:

$Ar = A / T$

Suppose that we have 96 transactions arriving at a resource site per second, a 43-second observation period, and a throughput of 2.23. We calculate the arrival rate as follows:

$Ar = 96 / 43 = 2.23$ *arrivals per second*

We thus find that the arrivals are equal to the throughput of 2.23 per second. Figure 8-6 shows the arrival rate vs. throughput rate for this system. Because the arrival rate for this system is the same as the throughput, queues will not accumulate at this site.

On the other hand, if transactions were delivered in batches at the arrival rate of 125 arrivals per second (and the original completion value of 96 was maintained), the model would give us these results:

$Ar = 125 / 43$, or *2.91 per second*

$X = 96 / 43$, or *2.23 per second*

$Ar - X = 2.91 - 2.23 = 0.68$

Arrivals ────────→ **Resource Site** ├───→ Throughput
Ar = A/T   X = C/T
Ar = 96/43   X = 96/43
Ar = 2.23   X = 2.23

Figure 8-6. *Arrival rate and throughput rate for an example system.*

In this example there is a queue buildup of 0.68 transaction overlap per second. This simple study mathematically reveals a queue site so that you can take proper action.

End-to-End Response Time

So far we have discussed the model of an individual system's resources. We can now begin to assemble a larger, multitier model. When we consider response time, we do not think in terms of the single site's response time but of all the resources that make up the service chain for that transaction. So the first step in determining end-to-end response time is identifying the components that make up the service chain.

One way to determine this would be to list or draw the service chain to find all the resource sites of a transaction. For example, assume that there is a client machine, a network, an application server, and a database server. You could designate these components as follows: Transaction = new transaction, Client = client machine, Network1 = the network over which this load is traveling to the application server, ApServ = application server, Network2 = the network over which this load is traveling to the database server, and DbServ = database server. Figure 8-7 illustrates this service chain.

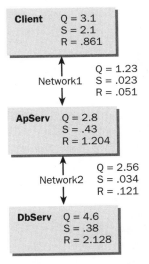

Figure 8-7. *A service chain and the computation of the end-to-end response time.*

After you identify the service chain, you execute a performance measurement in order to retrieve the values of the independent variables. When this is done you can determine the end-to-end response time for the transaction. The complete response equation is as follows (the Σ symbol indicates summation):

$$R = \Sigma\, Ri = \Sigma\, [(Q_i * S_i) + S_i]$$

Figure 8-7, on the previous page, depicts the conceptual path that the data in our hypothetical service chain takes to complete a transaction. The transaction starts off at the client machine, which is running a 0.861-second response time. The execution path travels through Network1, to the application server, then through Network2 until it reaches the database server. The request is not yet satisfied. After the data is retrieved, it must travel back through Network2 to the application server for further processing and formatting, through Network1, and finally back to the client machine.

Now you can calculate the end-to-end response time for this transaction:

$$R_{Client} = (3.1 * 0.21) + 0.21 = 0.861$$

$$R_{Network1} = (1.23 * 0.023) + 0.023 = 0.051$$

$$R_{ApServ} = (2.8 * 0.43) + 0.43 = 1.634$$

$$R_{Network2} = (2.56 * 0.034) + 0.034 = 0.121$$

$$R_{DbServ} = (4.6 * 0.38) + 0.38 = 2.128$$

$$Ri = R_{Client} + R_{Network1} + R_{ApServ} + R_{Network2} + R_{DbServ} + R_{Network2} + R_{ApServ} + R_{Network1} = 6.599$$

The total end-to-end response time is thus 6.599 seconds. If this transaction were under an SLA, the SLA should be set at eight seconds, giving the management team a 1.4-second margin of safety.

The next thing you do is establish the model with the above numbers, knowing at that point that the response time will be 6.599 seconds for the service chain. After this is done, you need to identify a performance monitoring configuration to measure the service chain and to set alert thresholds at the various model values (for example, Client queue length greater than 3.1, or ApServ service time greater than 0.43). If these values are exceeded, you will know that an SLA has been violated and where the problem is located.

Developing a Conceptual Model

We are now ready to develop a basic conceptual model of a service chain for a transaction. Remember that not all transactions or workloads need to be profiled in this manner, but certainly the transactions that are under SLAs should. If you intend to use this information to determine the capacity of critical systems, these workloads should also be profiled. An example of this conceptual model report is shown in Figure 8-8.

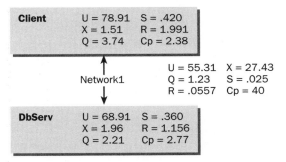

Figure 8-8. *The conceptual service chain model.*

In this figure you can see how a conceptual model of a service chain is developed. The information derived from it is valuable for understanding the present usage and for forecasting future usage. The statistics in Figure 8-8 tell us that the client machine is over-utilized and has high queue lengths. There is not much room for future growth on this machine. At $U = 68.91$, the database server has some room for growth in CPU utilization; however, the queue length is 2.21, which is over the limit and may indicate performance problems. Network1 has a sufficient reserve capacity. At this point you must decide whether the queue length on the database server will cause unacceptable response times for users or violate SLAs.

Remember that this is a conceptual view of a record for a service chain within a performance database. We recommend that you collect this data on a regular basis, at an interval of one record per day. With this data you can report on how the individual system or service chain is growing, and can predict how the machine will be performing in the future. You can even perform "what if" sizing scenarios on this data to see what will happen to the system if you add more transaction completions to each segment in order to model the effects that additional users would have on the system.

Summary

This chapter covered the basic concepts and techniques of system modeling. With this information, you can perform capacity planning for systems within a service chain. Understanding the basic model is essential for preconfiguration capacity planning. The principles presented in this chapter, such as the knee of the curve principle, govern the sizing process. In the next chapter, we discuss how these principles affect the number of CPUs, the number of disks, and the amount of memory you need to process your workload in an acceptable time frame while allowing for additional growth and maintaining SLAs.

Chapter 9
Sizing the Database and Application Servers

Preconfiguration capacity planning is the most important phase of any system's development. Many systems turn into maintenance nightmares because the sizing phase of development was overlooked or haphazardly performed. All the tuning in the world won't solve your problems if the hardware is inadequate to perform the task. This chapter discusses factors to consider when you size your system so that you can avoid this fate.

Preconfiguration Capacity Planning

Preconfiguration capacity planning has many facets. Memory, disks, and CPUs are usually the focal points, but there is more to consider. How will the system be configured for disk fault tolerance? Will a database reside on this system? Will the application reside on this system, or on another system?

Any sizing scenario must address this basic question: how will the system be used? There are many types of workloads. For example, many information systems retrieve data but don't allow writing data to the database interactively. These systems update the database in a batch mode. Some systems that are interactive, on the other hand, might perform as many writes as reads to the database. What a system will be doing results in vastly different configurations based on the expected workload. This section covers the factors you should consider in any basic preconfiguration capacity planning.

Transaction Processing Types

One of the first things to decide is what type of system you will need based on the workload type, which usually depends on what type of transaction is being processed. For example, for a server that performs only database functions; we need only to consider reads and writes to estimate its workload. In fact, any transaction can be broken down into database or file reads and writes. When a SELECT or UPDATE statement is executed, the database server interprets the statement as a series of read and write operations. Broken down to this atomic level, a database server mostly processes I/Os. You thus should select a system that can handle both the type and volume of transactions you expect, and the I/Os those transactions will generate. In contrast, if a system will perform application functions such as accounts payable, it's less concerned with the retrieval of the basic information than with what it does with the data once it gets it.

These two systems would have different configuration requirements for carrying out their respective tasks. The database server would have a large data farm in which to store the data and carry out I/O functions; the application server, on the other hand, would not need this data storage capacity.

In either case, the sizing question to answer is what type of transaction will be processed. The two main transaction types are online transaction processing and decision support.

Online Transaction Processing (OLTP)

The OLTP transaction is a workload unit that usually runs in a short period of time because it deals with the database in real time or in online mode. In other words, many of these transactions update the database constantly, based on the most current information available, so that the next user can rely on that information being up to date. For example, in an order entry system, all the information pertaining to inventory is kept in tables spread across a disk system, and the database is online. Any user has access to the database information. Database tables, such as *Item* or *Stock_Level*, need to have the most current information on the types and quantity of the items that are sold. When you receive an order for a certain quantity of a specific item, you can access the database tables to see if it's available, and how much of it is in stock, to prevent overselling it.

Decision Support System (DSS)

The second type of transaction is decision support. Such a transaction is usually complex and read intensive. Little writing to the database occurs. A decision support system usually provides information to management staff to help them make business decisions—for example, decisions about business growth, levels of stock on hand, and so on. The U.S. Air Force uses a DSS to inform high-level personnel about the current status, location, and weaponry of its jet fighters, bombers, and personnel. A system such as this needs certain characteristics, such as massive processor power and usually a large database capacity.

Unlike an OLTP system, a DSS limits the time spent processing requests rather than limiting the utilization of the processor. Indeed, most DSS queries utilize a processor at 100 percent until query completion. In an OLTP system, throughput of transactions is commonly measured in transactions per second (TPS) or transactions per minute (TPM), but in DSS processing, throughput is usually measured in queries per hour (QPH). Decision support stresses completing as many whole queries as possible, whereas OLTP stresses completing as many transactions as possible—without regard to how many queries are actually completed. The same principles of configuration apply to both OLTP and DSS processing: You don't want to overload the system in terms of size or I/O.

Peak Utilization vs. Steady-State Processing

A major consideration of sizing is the time frame for processing requests. During a typical sizing session, the analyst will eventually come across the time frame or duration of processing, which is not to be confused with the response times of individual transactions. Rather, it is the amount of time during the day, week, or even the year that processing times are the slowest. Peak utilization is when use of the machine and its various components is at the maximum.

As an example, let's walk through a sizing scenario of an automatic teller machine (ATM) system. For the planning session, the most important information is how many transactions will be processed, what these transactions consist of in terms of reads and writes, and how long the system is processing them. Figure 9-1 shows the arrival rate of transactions at a popular bank's ATM, graphed over a 24-hour period. Notice the uneven arrival rates, which are indicative of OLTP transactions. In this case let's say that a total of 250,000 transactions will be completed during a working day (which is 24 hours), and 150,000 of them will take place during the hours of 11:00 A.M. and 2:00 P.M. (lunch time), representing the peak utilization period for that day.

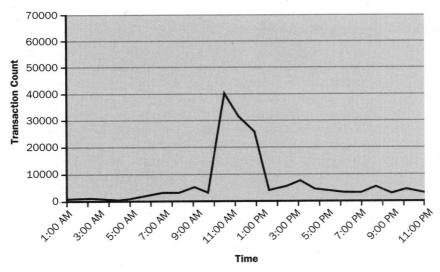

Figure 9-1. *The utilization for transactions at an ATM.*

In Chapter 8, "Modeling for Sizing and Capacity Planning" we defined the equation for arriving at throughput as Throughput = Completions/Time. In this scenario, we have identified the peak utilization period as between 11:00 A.M. and 2:00 P.M. (or 10,800 seconds), and the transactions to be completed during this interval as 150,000. Thus, the throughput rate during this time is 150,000/10,800, or 13.89 transactions per second. The system in question must therefore be capable of at least 13.89 transactions per second. By building a system that can handle this peak period load, we can handle the worst part of the processing day. During the rest of the day, the system should experience satisfactory processing utilization and response times.

When you cannot define the peak utilization period, you can do precapacity planning by estimating the transaction activity expected during steady-state processing. You know the maximum number of transactions you expect to complete in a processing day, and you know the length of your processing day, so you can calculate the average transactions per unit time.

In our scenario, suppose we know that a total of 250,000 transactions will be completed during a working day, which is 24 hours, but we don't know the arrival rate of these transactions. We can use the same equation to determine the throughput: Throughput = 250,000/24 hours (86,400 seconds). The throughput is thus equal to 2.89 transactions per second. Because we don't know the actual arrival rate for these transactions, however, we should size the system with a built-in reserve capacity. *Reserve capacity* refers to a certain portion of system processing power left in reserve to accommodate the more stressed workload periods.

Single-Tier vs. Multitier Systems

A *single-tier system* is one in which all components reside on the local machine. This architecture is basically a stand-alone system. The configuration is usually a large mainframe type, with the user interfaces, database, and applications all working on the single system. This type of system usually needs more attention from system administrators, particularly in performance tuning and capacity planning, because there is a greater possibility that the various components will contend for the same resources. A stand-alone system can have severe performance problems because of the queuing factor. These systems are also more complicated to maintain than their multitier counterparts. However, they are still popular because of their sheer processing power.

A *multitier system* is two or more systems linked together to perform workload processing. These configurations are less expensive than their single-tier counterparts because they can be composed of an inexpensive desktop system, a smaller server-type system (such as one of the popular multiprocessor Intel solutions) for the database, and possibly another server for the applications (although most of the popular applications reside on the user interface system or the desktop system), all connected by a network.

This solution, also known as a *client/server* solution, is probably the most frequently selected because of its ease of use and low cost per transaction. These solutions are relatively inexpensive in comparison with the much larger mainframes, are extremely space efficient, and do not require housing in a special computer room. The multitier system is also much less expensive to maintain than the mainframe counterpart. Currently, the most users select these systems rather than single-tier systems because they are user friendly and productive when configured correctly.

Page Faulting

To help size memory, we use the principle of *page faulting*. Page faults are normal system occurrences that are used to retrieve data from the disk. If a system needs a certain code page and it is in memory, a *logical I/O* event occurs: The data is read from memory and the transaction that needed the data is processed. If the code page or data page is not in memory, however, the system must perform a *physical I/O* to read the needed page from the disk. This is accomplished through page faulting.

A system issues a page fault interrupt when a needed code page is not in its working set in main memory. The page fault causes another part of the system to perform a physical I/O and retrieve the data from the physical disk. A page fault does not cause the page to be retrieved from disk if that page is on the standby list, and hence already in main memory, or if it is in use by another process with which the page is shared.

There are two types of physical I/Os: user and system. A *user physical I/O* occurs when a user transaction asks to read data that is not found in memory. A simple data transfer from the disk to memory occurs. This transfer is usually handled by some sort of data flow manager combined with disk controller functions. A *system physical I/O* occurs when the system requires a code page for a process it is running and the code page is not in memory. The system issues a page fault interrupt, which prevents processing until the required data has been retrieved from disk. After this retrieval, processing continues. Both physical I/O conditions prolong response time because the retrieval time for data found in memory takes several microseconds (millionths of seconds) whereas physical I/Os can take up to several milliseconds (thousandths of seconds). Because page fault activities cause physical I/Os, and physical I/Os prolong response time, you can achieve better system performance by minimizing page faults.

Three types of page faults can occur in a system:

- **Code address faults** If the system is executing operating system code and the next code address is not in memory, the system issues a page fault interrupt to retrieve the next code address from the disk. The transfer of the code data from the disk to memory requires a single physical I/O.

- **Code page faults** If the system is executing any other code and the next code page is not in memory, the system issues a page fault interrupt to retrieve the next code page from the disk. Again, the transfer of the code data from the disk to memory requires a single physical I/O.

- **Page fault swap** In the case of a data page that has been modified (known as a *dirty* page), a two-step page fault known as a *page fault swap* is used, causing the system not only to retrieve the new data from disk but also to write the current data in memory to the disk. This two-step page fault requires two physical I/Os. If swapping occurs often enough, it can be the single most damaging factor for response time.

When you estimate the minimum memory requirement for a new system, always try to anticipate the total memory that you will need to process the workload by finding the memory specifications of all processes (including the operating system and database engines) that will run on your system. And don't forget about page faults. To maintain a system's memory, you should collect information about page fault activity and store it as part of the performance database. You should perform predictive analysis (covered in Chapter 11, "Capacity Planning") on this data to project when in the future you will require additional memory. You should maintain a comfortable margin of available memory (at least 10 percent, if not more) for peak utilization.

Disk Requirements of the Database Server

When you size a database server, you must consider everything that the server is going to do. As in every type of sizing, you must consider the functionality, the number of users, and the transactions that will result because of your workload. You should consider the load on memory, CPUs, the disk farm, and the network in order to design an adequate system with a space for growth. This section concentrates on the database itself to determine the adequate amount of disk drives required to support a workload. The next chapter covers how to determine adequate CPU, memory, and network resources, as well as how to calculate the processing performance of these elements.

RAID Fault Tolerance

Most computer companies today provide fault tolerance through the support of RAID technology. (See Chapter 3, "Understanding the I/O Subsystem and RAID," for a discussion of RAID.) Remember that the most commonly used RAID levels are as follows:

- **RAID 0** Single disk drive
- **RAID 1** Mirrored disk drive
- **RAID 5** Multiple disk drives, data striping

Because RAID 0 requires a single disk or set of disks, it has a single point of failure—in other words, if the disk drive fails, you will lose the data on that disk drive and therefore the entire database. Figure 9-2 depicts two RAID 0 configurations. The first, a single-disk configuration, shows the single point of failure, which is the primary disk. A RAID 0 configuration can also be made up of multiple disks, all of which are potential single points of failure. When the disk controller sets up this kind of RAID 0 configuration, there is no redundancy of the data stripe and therefore no data fault tolerance.

RAID 1 provides a mirror image of the database disk drive. If a disk drive fails, you have a backup data drive complete with all the data that was on the failed disk drive. If you specify RAID 1, users get the added benefit of *split seeks* (discussed in Chapter 3), which enable the system to search both drives simultaneously, greatly accelerating search speed and reducing transaction response time.

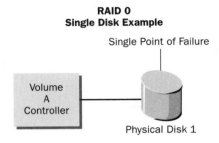

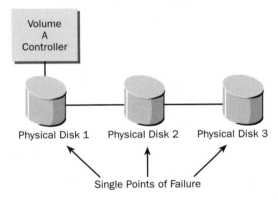

Figure 9-2. *RAID 0 single-disk and multiple-disk configurations.*

The choice of RAID level directly affects the number of disk I/Os because different RAID levels alter the number of writes to the disk. For example, RAID 1 requires twice as many writes as RAID 0. If the user describes a transaction as having 50 reads and 10 writes and wants to use RAID 1, the number of writes increases to 20.

Figure 9-3 on the following page shows two different RAID 1 configurations using single and multiple disks. In any RAID 1 configuration there are twice the number of disk drives as in a RAID 0 array. The benefit of the RAID 1 configuration is that it offers the fastest possible recovery from a physical disk failure.

If a RAID 0 configuration has two designated disk drives, a comparable RAID 5 configuration would have three disk drives. A RAID 5 configuration includes a parity stripe that contains information about the data on the other two drives, which can be used to rebuild a failed disk's data. This database protection scheme comes with a performance cost as well as a dollar cost. Each write under RAID 5 adds twice the number of reads and twice the number of writes for each transaction processed because each transaction must be written to two disks, and the parity stripe must be read, altered to incorporate the new data, then written. This redundancy lengthens the transaction response time slightly.

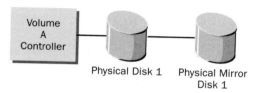

RAID 1
Single Mirrored Disk Example

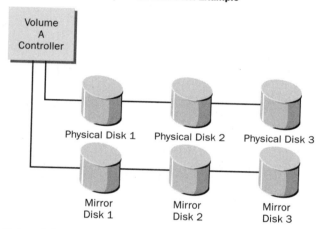

Multiple Mirrored Disk Example

Figure 9-3. *Single and multiple RAID 1 disk configurations.*

Figure 9-4 depicts a typical RAID 5 configuration before and after a disk failure. After a failure the parity is used to rebuild the failed disk's data. In this example, physical disk 2 has failed. The system recovers by rebuilding physical disk 2's data on the online spare disk.

Rules for Database Disk Drives

Many people are surprised at how many disk drives they need for their database because they think in terms of the database size only and do not take into account the amount of I/Os that the workload will cause. In addition, the I/Os caused by the use of RAID arrays are often forgotten or overlooked.

A positive feature of having additional disk drives is that this setup provides more access points to the data, so you are less likely to encounter the bottlenecks that might occur had you used fewer drives. For example, suppose you have a 10-GB database system that generates 140 I/Os per second. Using the 85 percent rule for disk space utilization discussed in Chapter 8, you would need one 12-GB drive to accommodate the size of the database.

RAID 5

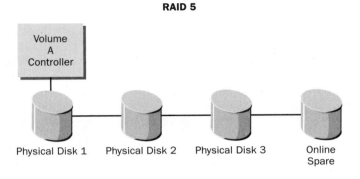

Recovery After a Failure

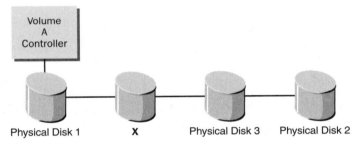

Figure 9-4. *RAID 5 disk configuration.*

Now look at the drive requirement from an I/O point of view. If the disk drives were rated at 70 I/Os per second, the utilization rule would yield 59.5 I/Os per second. At this rate it would take three disk drives to accommodate the number of I/Os per second based on using only 85 percent of the I/O capacity of each drive. Therefore, because I/O capacity analysis yields the greatest result, which is three disk drives, we should use three 4-GB drives (a total of 12 GB, as we calculated earlier), each rated at 70 I/Os per second. This will give us a capacity of 180 I/Os per second; at 140 I/Os per second, we will be using 78 percent of that capacity.

Note   When you size a disk subsystem, always apply the 85 percent utilization rule to both the size of the database and the number of I/Os per second that users will generate. Use whichever criterion results in the larger number of drives. Remember that too many I/Os per second on the disk drives cause bottlenecks and therefore prolonged response times.

File Structures, Queries, and the Resulting I/Os

To size a database, you must anticipate the number of I/Os that will be generated based on the number and type of transactions that will be processed. This information is necessary not only to size the database in terms of number of disks, but also to calculate the CPU utilization and other necessary statistics. So where do you begin? The first stage of any sizing is to determine the questions to ask and whom to ask. For this information, you should enlist the help of the database administrator and the person writing the application queries or transactions. Figure 9-5 shows the most basic block diagram of a record in a table called *Customer*. This information will help in analyzing the transaction I/Os.

Customer Row

| Num | Name | OrderNum | Info |

Figure 9-5. *Block diagram of a table layout.*

After you've created the diagrams, you can start to think about the transactions that will be used in this workload system. There are a few issues that you must take into account before you proceed. If you are creating the queries, remember that certain techniques are more efficient than others. When issuing a query to find a customer record, for instance, it is better to structure the query to request the customer record by a unique key such as the customer number. For example, you might want to use a query similar to this one:

```
SELECT Num, Name FROM Customer
WHERE Num = "12345"
```

This strategy will reduce the amount of reads necessary to retrieve the required record.

Another thing to take into account is the number of table joins created by the query. The more joins created, the more reads are necessary to gather the data you want. Figure 9-6 depicts a typical table join. In this case the customer table is joined to the order table; the actual link is at the "O.N.," or order number. The type of query shown in Figure 9-6 will return the existing customer record and all order records for that customer. So if there were 25 past orders for that customer, 26 records will be returned.

```
SELECT C.Name, O.Item
FROM Customer C, Order O
WHERE C.OrderNum = O.Num
AND C.Num = "12345"
```

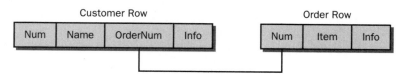

Customer Row

| Num | Name | OrderNum | Info |

Order Row

| Num | Item | Info |

Figure 9-6. *A example of a table join.*

Figure 9-7 shows a typical table join and the expected returned records. In this case the query resulted in a return of five records: one customer record and four order file records. You might be saying to yourself, this is too easy; there must be something hidden in all this, and you would be correct. In the previous case the number of reads is not simply five, since additional reads take place just to find this information. You find the true number of reads and writes that will occur by using values known as *index factors*. These take into account the hidden, or behind-the-scenes, reads and writes that take place as a result of executing a query involving joins.

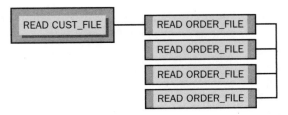

Figure 9-7. *The results of a table join: the returned records.*

Figure 9-8 depicts the index values you should use for calculating the total number of reads and writes associated with a transaction. When we calculate the number of reads on a random-type query, such as OLTP, we use a higher value because the likelihood of the record being in the cache is not as good as when performing sequential reads and writes.

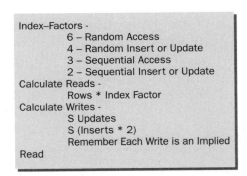

Figure 9-8. *Using index factors to calculate the number of reads and writes generated by a query.*

Let's use the index factors to calculate the average number of reads and writes for a simple transaction. Assume that the example system is an order entry system. Let's see how we can ascertain the average number of reads and writes for a transaction of inserting a new order. The new order transaction consists of the following elements:

Phase 1: Two random row selections with data retrieval

Phase 2: One random row selection with retrieval and update

Phase 3: Two row insertions

We can now apply the index factors and calculate the number of disk accesses. The results are shown in Table 9-1.

Table 9-1. Average Number of Reads and Writes for a New Order Transaction

	Number of Rows	Index Factor	Total Reads	Total Writes
Phase 1	2	6	12	0
Phase 2	1	6	6	1
Phase 3	2	4	8	4

The total number of I/Os for our sample transaction is 26 reads and 5 writes (assuming a RAID 0 configuration). Last, you figure out the RAID differential for this transaction. In this case using RAID 5 would result in 36 reads and 10 writes (see the equation in the "RAID Fault Tolerance" section which appears previously in this chapter). You must perform these calculations for each transaction in the workload.

Sizing the Database Disk Farm

When you size the database disk farm, or find the required total number of data disks (disks that contain only database files, not system or database log files), you must have certain information, which you gather during the interview process. One of the most important pieces of information is the estimated size of the database. This in itself can determine the size of the disk farm: If this value is larger than the total number of I/Os that are expected per second, then it will be the size of the disk farm (see "Rules for Database Disk Drives" earlier in this chapter). In our sample sizing, suppose that the expected total size of the database is 38 GB. The 85 percent rule of disk usage means that we will need twelve (rounded to the next whole value) 4-GB drives to store a database of this size.

We'll apply all the information we have so far to a simulated sizing situation. The system in question is an order entry system composed of the transactions in Table 9-2. In this example, we use a RAID 0 configuration.

Table 9-2. Transactions and I/Os for a Sample Order Entry System

Transaction Name	Reads*	Writes*	Transaction Count
New Order	77	36	865
Repeat Order	84	41	325
Order Status	56	0	255
Shipping	204	0	205
Items	1200	0	865

The values for reads and writes are for a single transaction in a RAID 0 configuration.

The next piece of information you need is the time factor for processing the workload. In this case the working day is defined as 6 hours (21,600 seconds). With this piece of information we can begin to figure out what the disk farm should look like. First we must calculate the total I/Os that are generated by this workload, as shown in Table 9-3.

Table 9-3. Total I/Os for the Sample System's Workload Using RAID 0

Transaction Name	Total Reads	Total Writes
New Order	66,605	31,140
Repeat Order	27,300	13,325
Order Status	14,280	0
Shipping	41,820	0
Items	1,038,000	0
Total	1,188,005	44,465

So far, we assumed a RAID 0 configuration. In reality, you need to find out what the actual RAID level for a database will be. The most frequently used RAID configuration for the database disk drives is RAID 5, so let's now use that type here. We will calculate the effect the RAID factor has on the totals. In this case the total number of reads will increase to 1,276,935 and the total number of writes will increase to 88,930. This yields a total transaction I/O count of 1,365,865.

To find out how many I/Os per second this total count gives, we will assume the 6-hour processing time (21,600 seconds). In this simulation the I/Os per second turn out to be 63.234 or, rounded to a whole value, 63 I/Os per second. We can now calculate that the total number of disk drives required to process the I/O load is one 4-GB drive. A typical 4-GB drive has an I/O capacity of 70 I/Os per second. When compared with the required amount of disk drives for space (twelve 4-GB drives), we find we need more disk drives to accommodate the size than we would based solely on the I/O activity. Thus, the disk farm for this system should be twelve 4-GB drives.

Sizing the Application Server

Sizing the application server is somewhat easier than sizing the database server. In this case you have to choose the processing model. There are three possibilities: the single-tier model; the client/server multitier model; and the client/server, application server, and database server multitier model.

Single-Tier Model

In a single-tier model the application resides on the same system as the database. In this case the first thing to determine is how you will lay out the configuration. In some single-tier systems you can segregate the database from the application. In most cases this will be necessary because the database activity would interfere with the application activity. For example, if an application request screen runs on the same processor as a database disk process, they interfere with each other's operation. While the request is being processed, the request screen freezes because the database disk process is running, taking up the CPU time until the request is processed. If the database disk process runs on another processor, the request screen can go on to another user request while the database is retrieving the first request. As you can see, configuration has a lot to do with the sizing of the single-tier system. If you size your system correctly but configure the processors incorrectly, you could find yourself overloading some processors, while others do very little work.

Multitier Model

In the multitier configuration, usually a single user has an application running on the client machine, and in this case the only thing to be concerned about is the size of the application and the utilization factors. Most of the popular Microsoft applications make this information available. Because this configuration has single-user clients, you don't have to worry about queuing on the client machines. Queuing occurs when you have multiple requests going through the system at once. In this case the queuing takes place on the database server or the network, not the client machine.

Another use of the multitier system is the application server. In this configuration there is a client, but this client does not run the application, only the interface to the system. A separate application server processes the application code and the requests. This can cause queuing on the application server when multiple requests come in. The number of threads created to process the requests from different users of the application can also cause high CPU utilization factors and high memory usage. The memory can be over-used because of the number of code and data pages these additional threads entail.

Another factor to consider is the number of users who will connect to this machine. Each user will have an interface process which will increase CPU and memory usage. This interface process runs in the background and connects the user to the system. Multitier application servers are usually deployed as a part of a security system in which the administrators do not want users to have copies of the application on the individual client machines. A well-known user of this configuration is the military.

Summary

This chapter explained the factors that you must take into account to size a system correctly. These factors include the types of transactions being processed, the amount of time the system spends processing, the RAID level being used, and the number of I/Os generated by typical transactions. Using this information, you can size a system correctly.

The next chapter uses these principles to show the application of this method of sizing. It demonstrates not only how to determine the amount of hardware and software required to process your workload, but also how to calculate and obtain the statistics for the processing characteristics of the proposed system.

Chapter 10
Methods for Sizing a System

Preconfiguration capacity planning can seem complicated on the surface, but it follows logical rules. Most analysts who perform this task have their own methods. The most accurate method is to establish a reliable benchmark: to run the actual workload on a system and gather performance statistics to produce an accurate picture of the workload's effect. This method allows you to not only accurately estimate the hardware you need to carry out the processing, but also to use "what if" scenarios to predict sudden elevated levels of utilization caused by increasing the number of users on the system, and to predict where those elevations will occur. This method presupposes that the application workload is written and functional and that the database is, or can be, built to carry out the testing. When these criteria are met, the only task left is to load and run the tests.

Although the benchmark method is the most accurate for building a system, its use is limited by several factors. An obvious problem for benchmark sizing is that the expense is usually far beyond what a small business is prepared or able to pay. Benchmark sizing exercises are usually confined to large organizations that can fund this function. Another problem is that you must develop the workload and database to the point that you can place them on a system and do the processing.

Fortunately, there's another sizing method you can use to estimate the hardware requirements for processing a workload. This method, which we call *statistical hardware estimation*, relies on having a complete application and database design schema and uses the following conditions for the target system:

- The steady-state CPU utilization is less than 75 percent.
- The cache hit ratio is at least 90 percent.
- No disk drive exceeds 85 percent utilization of space or I/O activity.
- The server is a dedicated database server.
- The distribution of disk I/Os is even across all drives.
- The number of disk controllers is sufficient to meet the demand of the workload.

The logic behind these conditions was covered in depth in the previous two chapters. In this chapter we assume these conditions hold for the target system and use them to figure out the capacity for the CPU.

Sizing the Processor

Let's focus on sizing a database server. Predicting the capacity of a CPU on a database server is not as complicated as you might think. Remember that a database server is processing only transactions. The application is running on a client machine, so application sizing does not enter into the equation. The server will process requests in the form of read and write operations—that is, it will process I/Os. So the task at hand is to determine how many I/Os will be generated by the transactions and how fast they need to be completed. You need to know how many transactions the system will be required to process and the definition of either the working day (in hours) for this system or the peak utilization period. As we saw in Chapter 9, "Sizing the Database and Application Servers," it's always preferable to size for the peak utilization period because it represents the worst-case scenario. Unfortunately, in most cases this information is not available.

For a deep understanding of the transactions a system will process, you need access to the transaction anatomy (profile), which will help you determine the numbers of reads and writes (I/Os) that the transaction will generate, and enable you to calculate the anticipated CPU utilization. The techniques for anticipating the number of I/Os caused by a transaction are covered in Chapter 9.

The single most important phase of sizing is getting information about the workload and the environment in which it will be processed. You gather this information from interviews with the database designer, application designer, management, and the system administrator.

The Interview Process

The interview process can yield the bulk of the information you need for sizing the CPU. The essential data you require concerns the I/Os for a database server: what type of transactions, how many of each transaction, and how many I/Os these transactions will cause. The application designer can provide pertinent information about the nature of the transactions. The database designer can provide information pertaining to the tables and the indexes that will be affected by these transactions. Other factors you must consider are the time these transactions will take to be processed and the fault tolerance of the database disk drives.

Let's look at an example of an interview. A company is developing an order entry system for sales that they want to deploy in a few months. The company has limited funds for a system to process the online and telephone orders to be placed. They want an accurate estimation of the hardware requirements for processing this workload within certain time limitations. At a meeting with the database administrator you learn that the database size will be 30 GB. This estimation includes the index tables and the temporary files the database will use. The database administrator also provides the database schema and the number of tables it will use. There will be five main tables, the largest of which will be 3 GB.

The application developer determines that this order entry system will consist of five main transactions and calculates that the number of reads and writes (at RAID 0) are as given in Table 10-1. The application developer and the system administrator determine that they require fault tolerance, but they would like to be economical. This requirement is best fulfilled by a RAID 5 selection for fault tolerance. You must also consider additional I/Os generated by fault tolerance equipment when you size the CPU. (See Chapter 3, "Understanding the I/O Subsystem and RAID" and Chapter 9, "Sizing the Database and Application Servers.")

Table 10-1. Transaction I/Os for Sample Order Entry System with RAID 0

Transaction Name	Reads*	Writes*	Transaction Count
New Order	93	29	1100
Repeat Order	72	33	431
Order Status	63	1	250
Shipping	66	1	250
Items	1800	1800	1100

*The values for reads and writes represent a single transaction.

The only thing left to find out is the working day for this workload. Management provides this information: the working day is eight hours. At this point you can begin to determine the CPU requirement for this particular workload.

Note   For an existing system, you can profile transactions by running each of the transactions separately and using System Monitor in the Performance console to track the number of I/Os generated. This information can be used to adjust the speed, type, and number of CPUs in use.

Calculating CPU Utilization

After you determine the total number of reads and writes caused by transactions and add the I/Os caused by the RAID level you have selected, you have all the information you need to calculate the CPU utilization. Use the following formula to determine the CPU utilization of a proposed system:

*CPU Utilization = Throughput * Service Time*

where Throughput is the number of I/Os, and Service Time is the amount of CPU time per I/O. This formula simply states that utilization is the total number of I/Os the system processes (throughput) multiplied by the time it takes to perform each task (service utilization).

To determine the capacity of a specific processor, perform the following steps to account for every transaction that will be processed as part of this workload set:

1. Use the following formula to calculate the total number of reads that will go through the system:

   *Total Reads = $\sum$ (Reads per Transaction with RAID * Transaction Count)*

   From the interview information (see Table 10-1) and the number of I/O increases with RAID 5 (see the "Disk Calculations" section in Chapter 3), you can calculate the total number of reads for each transaction. These results are summarized in Table 10-2. Plugging these values into the formula yields the following:

   *Total Reads = $\sum$ (Reads per Transaction with RAID 5 * Transaction Count)*

   = 166,100 + 59,478 + 16,250 + 17,000 + 5,940,000

   = 6,198,828

   Table 10-2. Total Number of Reads for Sample Order Entry System with RAID 5

Transaction Name	Reads	Transaction Count	Reads per Transaction
New Order	151	1100	166,100
Repeat Order	138	431	59,478
Order Status	65	250	16,250
Shipping	68	250	17,000
Items	5400	1100	5,940,000
Total			6,198,828

2. Use the following formulas to determine how many of these reads will be physical I/Os and how many will be logical I/Os (memory reads):

   *Total Logical Reads = Total Reads * Cache Hit Ratio*

   Total Physical Reads = Total Reads – Total Logical Reads

   We have calculated the total number of reads to be 6,198,828 under RAID 5. Using these equations and the criterion of a 90 percent cache hit ratio gives us the following figures: the logical read count is 5,578,945 (rounded), and the physical read count is 619,883 (rounded).

3. Use the following formulas to convert the total number of each read type to reads per second:

   Logical Reads per Second = [(Total Logical Reads / Work Period) / 60] / 60

   Physical Reads per Second = [(Total Physical Reads / Work Period) / 60] / 60

From the interview process you know that the work period is set at 8 hours, so you can determine the logical read rate:

Logical Reads per Second = [(5,578,945 / 8 hours) / 60] / 60

$$= 5,578,945 / 28,800 \text{ seconds}$$

$$= 193.71$$

Determine the physical read rate the same way:

Physical Reads per Second = [(619,883 / 8 hours) / 60] / 60

$$= 619,883 / 28,800 \text{ seconds}$$

$$= 21.52$$

4.   Use the following formulas to calculate the amount of CPU utilization for each of the read functions:

*Logical Read Utilization = Logical Reads per Second * Logical Read CPU Time*

*Physical Read Utilization = Physical Reads per Second * Physical Read CPU Time*

With these formulas you can calculate the cumulative service times for each of the read functions. The calculation for the logical read utilization is as follows:

*Logical Read Utilization = 193.71 * Logical Read CPU Time*

$$= 193.71 * 0.0001$$

$$= 0.0194$$

$$= 1.94\%$$

The calculation for physical read utilization is as follows:

*Physical Read Utilization = 21.52 * Physical Read CPU Time*

$$= 21.52 * 0.002$$

$$= 0.043$$

$$= 4.3\%$$

The total read utilization for this proposed system would be 6.24 percent CPU utilization.

Note   The formulas here use 0.0001 second for the logical read CPU time (service time) and 0.002 second for the physical read CPU time, which are the values for a 200-MHz Pentium processor. The service times will vary depending on the type and speed of the target CPU.

5. Use the following formulas to calculate the total number of writes that will go through the system:

*Total Writes = $\sum$ (Writes per Transaction with RAID * Transaction Count)*

Using this formula and the number of I/Os increase with RAID 5, we can derive the information in Table 10-3 regarding the write activity. Plugging these values into the equation for total writes gives us the following:

Total Writes = 63,800 + 28,446 + 500 + 500 + 3,960,000

= 4,053,246

Table 10-3. Total Number of Writes for Sample Order Entry System with RAID 5

Transaction Name	Writes	Transaction Count	Writes per Transaction
New Order	58	1100	63,800
Repeat Order	66	431	28,446
Order Status	2	250	500
Shipping	2	250	500
Items	3600	1100	3,960,000
Total			4,053,246

6. Now find the number of writes per second that will pass through the system by performing the following calculation:

Writes per Second = [(Total Writes / Work Period) / 60] / 60

For the sample system, you can calculate the writes per second as follows:

Writes per Second = [(4,053,246 / 8 hours) / 60] / 60

= 4,053,246 / 28,800 seconds

= 140.74

7. Use the following formula to determine the total CPU utilization involved in processing the writes:

*CPU Write Utilization = Writes per Second * Write CPU Time*

Use the previously calculated yields for CPU write utilization:

*CPU Write Utilization = 104.74 * Write CPU Time*

*= 104.74 * 0.001*

= 0.1047

= 10.47 %

Note This formula uses 0.001 second for the CPU write time. For these calculations a 200-MHz Pentium processor was used. The actual service times will vary depending on the type and speed of the target CPU.

8. Use the following formula to calculate the total CPU utilization for the transactions:

    Total Utilization = Logical Read Utilization + Physical Read Utilization + Write Utilization

    The CPU utilization is calculated as follows:

    Total Utilization = 1.94% + 4.3% + 10.47%

    = 16.71%

    This value represents steady-state utilization.

9. Finally, use the following formula to calculate the total number of processors required for this workload:

    Total CPUs = CPU Utilization / Number of CPUs

    where Number of CPUs brings the total utilization below 75 percent. In the sample system, the processor count would be set to one CPU because the utilization is already below 75 percent.

Calculating System Statistics

You can use your calculations pertaining to CPU utilization to determine more information about the system. Recall from Chapter 8, "Modeling for Sizing and Capacity Planning," that knowing utilization allows you to calculate such statistics as the system's throughput, capacity, and average queue lengths and response times. This section provides examples of these calculations.

I/O Throughput

Calculate the I/O throughput with the following formula:

I/O Throughput = Total I/Os / Work Period

If we apply this formula to the previous values for the example system, we find the following:

I/O Throughput = 10,252,074 / Work Period

= 10,252,074 / 28,800 seconds

= 356 (rounded)

The I/O throughput is 356 I/Os per second.

System Capacity

Calculate the capacity of the system with the following formula:

System Capacity = 1 / Average Service Time

where

Average Service Time = Work Period / Completions

In the sample system the average service time would be calculated as follows:

Average Service Time = Work Period / Completions

$$= 28,800 / 10,252,074$$

$$= 0.00281$$

Given this value, system capacity is calculated as follows:

System Capacity = 1 / Average Service Time

$$= 1 / 0.00281$$

$$= 355.9 \ per \ second$$

Note The system capacity is usually calculated as Capacity = 1 / S (where S is service time), and the service time is calculated as S = Busy / Completions. The calculation above uses the work period as the busy time. This calculated capacity is the minimum capacity of this system. The actual system would probably have a higher throughput capacity. This example is meant to give you an idea of the way capacity calculations work.

Queue Length and I/O Response Time

Use the following formula to calculate the queue length of the system:

$$Q = U / (1 - U)$$

where Q is queue length and U is CPU utilization.

For the example we will use the estimated figure of 16.71 percent utilization for the single CPU.

$$Q = U / (1 - U)$$

$$= 0.1671 / (1 - 0.1671)$$

$$= 0.2$$

The response time per I/O if a single-processor system were used for the sample order entry system would be calculated as follows:

*Response Time = (Queue Length * Service Time) + Service Time*

$$= (0.2 * 0.00281) + 0.00281$$

$$= 0.003372 \ second$$

Note Remember that the expected service time is the average time per I/O without any queuing at all. Response time is the service time and the queue time combined.

Transaction Response Times

The last thing to calculate is the expected transaction flow (not I/O flow) in terms of the expected response times for each transaction. For the sample system we will use the figures compiled in the previous transaction tables, which are summarized in Table 10-4.

Table 10-4. Summary of Transactions in the Sample Order Entry System with RAID 5

Transaction Name	Reads	Writes	Transaction Count
New Order	151	58	1100
Repeat Order	138	66	431
Order Status	65	2	250
Shipping	68	2	250
Items	5400	3600	1100

You can use the steps that follow to derive a transaction's response time.

1. Calculate the number of physical reads and logical reads for the transaction:

   *Logical Reads = Transaction Reads * Cache Hit Ratio*

   Physical Reads = Transaction Reads – Logical Reads

   In our example, we can calculate the following for the New Order transaction:

   *Logical Reads = 151 * 0.90*

   = 136

   Physical Reads = 151 – 136

   = 15

2. Calculate the service time for the reads of the transaction:

   Read Service Time = Total Logical Read Service Time + Total Physical Read Service Time

   where

   *Total Logical Read Service Time = Logical Read Service Time * Logical Reads*

   and

   *Total Physical Read Service Time = Physical Read Service Time * Physical Reads*

   In our example of the New Order transaction, the calculation would be as follows:

   *Read Service Time = (0.0001 * 136) + (0.002 * 15)*

   = 0.0136 + 0.03

   = 0.0436

3. Calculate the service time for the writes of the transaction:

   *Write Service Time = Transaction Writes * Service Time*

   In the case of the New Order transaction, this would be the following:

   *Write Service Time = 58 * 0.001*

   $$= 0.058$$

4. Calculate the total transaction service time:

   Transaction Service Time = Read Service Time + Write Service Time

   In our example of the New Order transaction, this calculation would be as follows:

   Transaction Service Time = 0.0436 + 0.058

   $$= 0.1016$$

5. Calculate the response time for the single-processor system you decided was to be used for this workload:

   *Response Time = (Queue Length * Service Time) + Service Time*

   In our example of the New Order transaction, this would be as follows:

   *Response Time = (0.2 * 0.11016) + 0.1016*

   $$= 0.12192 \ second$$

Note You must perform this procedure for each transaction in the workload system. The sum of the transaction response times is the transaction flow for the system.

Sizing Memory

When you perform capacity planning for memory, you need certain pieces of information, including the number of concurrent users who will be on the system, the type of transaction workload, and, of course, the operating system. You must also take into account the optimal cache hit ratio and page faulting. You would typically start the sizing process by interviewing the database designer, the DBA, and management personnel. In our example, you are sizing a database server, so information pertaining to the memory usage of client applications does not affect database server size.

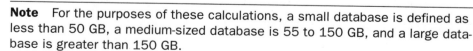

Note For the purposes of these calculations, a small database is defined as less than 50 GB, a medium-sized database is 55 to 150 GB, and a large database is greater than 150 GB.

Let's consider the sample system. The first piece of information you need is the number of concurrent users. For the example, you learn that on average, 200 concurrent users will be on the system at any given time. You will thus need 100 MB of memory just for the users.

Note   As mentioned in "Sizing the Application Server" in Chapter 9, each user will have an interface process which will increase CPU and memory usage. Generally, you should allow 500 KB of memory for each user to accommodate this process.

Next you need to know the operating system that will be used. In this case, the operating system is Windows NT, which uses about 20 MB of memory. (Windows 2000 uses about 64 MB.) This brings your total memory use up to 120 MB so far. The next piece of information you need is the size of the database executable that you are going to use—in this case, Microsoft SQL Server, which is 5.5 MB. The total memory required is now 125.5 MB.

The final piece of information you need is the size of the database processing area. This area consists of two elements: the log area and the database cache. The log area holds the information about write activity that is taking place. This area, sometimes called the *audit trail*, is extremely important because if a system failure occurs during the processing of a transaction, the data stored here will be used to restore the "before" image of the database, that is, the database state as it was before the failure occurred. Thus audit trails enable you to roll back partially complete transactions caused by a disk failure.

Note   A good rule for sizing the log is to use 500 MB for a small database, 1 GB for a medium-sized database, and 2 GB for a large database.

The other element in the database processing area is the database cache. All the data your system processes will pass through it. The larger the database cache, the greater your cache hit ratio. Obviously, you want the highest cache hit ratio you can achieve. A cache area that is too small will cause physical I/Os because the system must access the disk to retrieve data not present in the cache. These physical I/Os increase the response time of the transaction.

To calculate the required cache size, use the following formula:

*DB Cache Size = DB Cache Block Size * DB Block Elements*

where DB Cache Block Size is the block size for SQL Server (which is 8192), and DB Block Elements is the number of blocks placed in cache.

Note   No set cache size guarantees a 90 percent or better cache hit ratio. A good rule is to use a database cache size of about 300 MB for a small system, 750 MB for a medium-sized system, and 1 GB for a large system. Systems with very large databases (around 300 GB) can require as much as 3 GB of cache to achieve the optimal cache hit ratio.

From the information you've collected so far, you can calculate the minimum amount of memory you need. The following formula is commonly used for calculating minimum memory:

$$Minimum\ Memory = System + User\ Memory + DB\ Process\ Area$$

where

$$System = Operating\ System + SQL\ Server\ Database$$
$$User\ Memory = Concurrent\ User\ Count * Memory\ per\ User$$
$$DB\ Process\ Area = Log\ Area + DB\ Cache\ Size$$
$$DB\ Cache\ Size = DB\ Cache\ Block\ Size * DB\ Block\ Elements$$

You can use the equations above to calculate the minimum memory required for normal operation of online transaction processing (OLTP) applications. For example, consider a system that uses 300 MB for the database cache, 500 MB for logs, 20 MB for the operating system, and 5.5 MB for SQL Server. Let's further assume that there are five users, each requiring 20 MB. Using the equations above, we can arrive at the minimum memory requirements as follows:

$$System = Operating\ System + SQL\ Server\ Database$$
$$= 20\ MB + 5.5\ MB$$
$$= 25.5\ MB$$

$$User\ Memory = Concurrent\ User\ Count * Memory\ per\ User$$
$$= 5 * 20\ MB$$
$$= 100\ MB$$

$$Minimum\ Memory = System + User\ Memory + DB\ Process\ Area$$
$$= 25.5\ MB + 100\ MB + 800\ MB$$
$$= 925.5\ MB$$

$$DB\ Cache\ Size = 300\ MB$$

$$DB\ Process\ Area = Log\ Area + DB\ Cache\ Size$$
$$= 500\ MB + 300\ MB$$
$$= 800\ MB$$

In an OLTP application system, you should check the cache hit ratio when the system is installed. A high cache hit ratio will help ensure that your system has excellent response time and performance.

Note The target cache hit ratio for your system should be as close to 100 percent as possible, and not less than 90 percent.

Sizing the Disk I/O Subsystem

Now that you have sized the memory and the processor, it's time to size the disk I/O subsystem. This part of the system is easy because you have already calculated most of the required parameters. First you need the total number of I/Os that the system will process. You already have this information from the processor sizing. Next, you need the size of the database. The database designer can provide this information; in our sample system, the database is 30 GB. When you size the disk subsystem, it is important to realize that you are sizing for either the size of the database or the number of I/Os per second, whichever yields the greater number of disk drives. (See the "Rules for Database Disk Drives" section in Chapter 9.)

We'll take an in-depth look at how to calculate the proper number of disk drives for your system. You need to store four major components: Windows NT, SQL Server, log files, and the database itself. To determine the total number of drives your system requires, calculate the number of drives you need for each component, then add the numbers together.

Operating System Disks

First you need to calculate the number of disk drives needed to support the Windows NT operating system and the SQL Server database. Usually, you will want these disk drives to be a separate volume using a RAID 1 configuration (mirrored disk drives) for the fastest possible recovery. The number of disk drives might vary depending on size, but usually the Windows NT operating system and the SQL Server database system can fit on a single disk. Our simple calculation would look like this:

*Operating System Disks = Operating System DB Disks * RAID Factor*

where Operating System DB Disks is the number of disk drives for the Windows NT operating system and SQL Server, and RAID Factor is the number of RAID drives.

In this case, the result would be two for mirrored disk drives. (Windows NT and SQL Server are on one disk, and that disk is mirrored in a RAID 1 volume.) We do not recommend setting the operating system volume to RAID 5 or RAID 0. You must have at least two initial disk drives to use RAID 5, so you wouldn't be saving any disk space, and you will want the fastest possible recovery for the operating system and the database executable.

Log File Disks

Next you should calculate the number of disk drives you need to support your system's log files. This depends largely on the total number of writes per second your transactions will cause, which you calculated when you sized the processor. For example, consider a workload that resulted in 1,500,000 writes using a RAID 0 volume. This would result in 52.08 I/Os per second, and would require only one disk drive at RAID 0. If we now switch to the recommended RAID 1 level, we're looking at 3,000,000 writes over an 8-hour period, or 104.17 writes per second (remember that using RAID 1 results in twice as many writes per transaction as RAID 0), but they are going to twice as many disk drives.

To calculate the number of drives needed, use the following formula:

Log Disk = (Writes per Second / Max Disk I/O) + RAID Factor

where

Writes per Second = [(Total Writes / Work Period) / 60] / 60

*Max Disk I/O = Maximum I/Os per Disk * 85%*

RAID Factor is the number of extra disk drives needed to support the fault tolerance you want. If we use the ceiling of 85 percent utilization for the number of writes allowed on a disk drive that has a capacity of 70 I/Os per second, we get the following calculation for the workload described above:

Log Disk = (Writes per Second at RAID 0 / Max Disk I/O) + RAID Factor

= 52.08 / 59.5

= 0.88 (without RAID consideration)

You should round up the Log Disk value to the next whole integer: this system would need one disk drive for the logs at RAID 0. Because we want to use RAID 1, that number should be doubled (the drives will be mirrored). Thus, at RAID 1 this system requires two disk drives for the logs.

Database Disks

The final step is calculating the number of disk drives the database will require. Remember to calculate the number of drives required based on both the size of the database and the number of I/Os per second, and to use the larger of the two numbers of drives.

Size Criterion

To determine the number of disk drives required to accommodate the database size, use the following formula:

*Disks for Size = [DB Size / (Max Disk Size * 85%)] + RAID Factor*

where DB Size is the database size in bytes, Max Disk Size is the maximum disk size in bytes, and RAID Factor is the number of extra disk drives needed to support the desired fault tolerance. For example, you would calculate the number of 12-GB disks needed for a 30-GB database using RAID 1 as follows:

*Disks for Size = [30 GB / (12 GB * 0.85)] + RAID Factor*

= (30 / 10.2) + RAID Factor

= 2.9 (rounded up to 3 disks, without RAID)

The drives must be mirrored for RAID 1, so you would need six 12-GB drives to accommodate this database. If this example were for RAID 5, you would require only three disk drives to accommodate the database (plus one drive as an online spare if necessary).

Note   A RAID 5 level is recommended for database drives.

I/O Criterion

The number of disk drives required to accommodate I/Os can differ drastically from the number of drives required to accommodate the database, as we saw in an earlier example in Chapter 9. The I/O requirement might cause you to revise your recommendation concerning the size of the disk subsystem. To calculate this value, follow these steps:

1. Calculate the total number of read I/Os that will go through the system by using the following formula:

   *Total Reads = $\sum$ (Reads per Transaction with RAID * Transaction Count)*

2. Determine how many of these read I/Os will be physical reads and how many will be logical reads by using the following formulas:

   *Total Logical Reads = Total Reads * Cache Hit Ratio*

   Total Physical Reads = Total Reads – Logical Reads

3. Convert the total number of physical reads to reads per second by using the following formula:

   Physical Reads per Second = [(Total Physical Reads / Work Period) / 60] / 60

4. Calculate the total number of write I/Os that will go through the system by using the following formula:

   *Total Writes = $\sum$ (Writes per Transaction with RAID * Transaction Count)*

5. Calculate the total number of physical I/Os per second by using the following formula:

   Total Physical I/Os per Second = (Total Physical Reads + Total Writes) / Work Period (in seconds)

6. Calculate the total number of database disk drives by using the following formula:

   *Num DB Disks = [Total Physical I/Os per Second / (Max Disk Capacity * 85%)] + RAID Factor*

   where Max Disk Capacity is the maximum disk I/O capacity per second and RAID Factor is the number of extra disk drives needed to support the desired fault tolerance.

Sizing Example

You now have the information you need to calculate the number of disk drives required to process the workload in the example. In the case of the operating system, you would calculate the following:

*Operating System Disks = Operating System DB Disk * RAID Factor*

Considering that the disk space requirements are small for the operating system (Windows NT) and the SQL Server database engine, two 2-GB disk drives would be enough for this load.

For the log file space, you can use the following calculation. Remember to round up to the next integer value:

Log Disks = (Writes per Second / Max Disk I/O) + RAID Factor

In the example, the equation would look as follows:

Log Disks = (70.37 RAID 0 Writes per Second) / 59.5) + RAID Factor

= 1.18 (without RAID consideration)

Round up to get two disks before you consider the RAID level. For the example, you would need four 4-GB disk drives because of the number of writes associated with this workload and the selection of RAID 1.

The final piece of information you need about the I/O subsystem to handle the order entry workload is the number of database disk drives. Use the following equation:

*Disks for Size = [DB Size / (Max Disk Size * 85%)] + RAID Factor*

= 30 GB / 10.2 GB

= 2.9 disks (without RAID consideration)

For the example (a 30-GB database using RAID 5), you need four 12-GB disk drives to support the database: three for the database, and one for the online spare. Most new servers are equipped with the hot pluggable feature that allows for dispensing with the online spare disk drive. The database can easily fit on a single disk array. Not taking the I/Os involved in the order entry system into account, its size would require a comparatively small amount of disks.

Now you must calculate the number of disk drives required to support the number of I/Os required to process this workload:

*Num DB Disks = [Total Physical I/Os per Second / (Max Disk Capacity * 85%)] + RAID Factor*

= (162.26 RAID 5 Physical I/Os / 59.5)

= 3 disk drives for I/O capacity (without RAID consideration)

To factor in the RAID disks for RAID 5, you must decide how many disks will make up the arrays and how many controllers will be used. You can get information on array disk maximums and controller capacity from the various hardware vendors.

The final number of disk drives for the order entry system would be as follows:

- Three 12-GB disk drives for I/O capacity without additional RAID disk consideration
- Four 4-GB disk drives for the log activity
- Two 4-GB disk drives for the operating system and SQL Server database system

The final estimated system configuration is as follows:

- One CPU (at least 200 MHz).
- Six 4-GB disk drives.
- Three 12-GB disk drives without online spare.
- About 750 MB for the cache area and 125.5 MB for the users, the operating system, and database, or 900.5 MB total minimum memory (using the rule from the "Sizing Memory" section of this chapter). In this exercise it would be wise to round the memory to 1 GB.

The difference between sizing a database server and an application server is that in the latter case you must take into account how many applications (or copies of an application) will be running simultaneously and make sure that there is enough memory for them. The application server will generally require more memory and fewer disk drives than the database server.

Summary

Sizing a server, be it a database server or an application server, is a lengthy process, but if you use the calculations in this chapter it is not a complicated one. Remember that the process in this chapter not only gives you information pertaining to the amount of equipment required to process your proposed workload but also offers statistics about the system you are creating. If the information you get from the interview process is essentially correct, this method should result in a rewarding sizing experience and a system that is within a reasonable percentage of its optimal size. Remember to account for initial growth of the workload, database, and memory. This will buy you time to start a stringent capacity planning and data collection process so that you can predict and plan for future growth.

The next chapter covers the postconfiguration capacity planning process of data collection and analysis in detail. This process, diligently followed, gives users, administrators, and management information about the current capacity of their system and about how to plan for additional capacity.

Chapter 11
Capacity Planning

Capacity planning involves performing complex, continuing performance studies on an existing system. These studies measure the consumption of hardware and software resources to ensure that the criteria established by any service level agreements (SLAs) for the system are met, and to ensure that the system's performance is stable. SLAs (discussed in Chapter 8, "Modeling for Sizing and Capacity Planning") are set up to ensure that the system keeps enough reserve capacity available to maintain the specified response times of critical activities under peak load conditions.

You can also use capacity planning studies to perform "what if" scenarios on workloads. In a typical capacity planning study, the analyst uses historic performance data stored in a database to project trends in the following areas:

- CPU utilization
- Disk usage
- Memory usage

The analyst can also project sudden rises in CPU, disk, and memory utilization caused by the addition of new users to the system.

In the past, capacity planning studies were mostly performed on large mainframes, because the process and hardware required were so expensive. Analysts commanded high wages for their expertise. Over the years, more people have become acquainted with this discipline, and there is a growing demand for capacity planning on the smaller servers that are so prevalent in today's market. Smaller businesses, which make up a significant portion of today's computer industry, want to plan for the growth of their systems and avoid seeing increased use of computer resources lead to lengthened response times for workload completions.

In most cases, capacity planning studies involve profiling the activities of specific types of users so that you can perform "what if" scenarios, in which you add simulated users (such as people who perform general ledger functions) to the system to predict exactly what kind of resources they will use. This gives a system manager enough information to obtain the necessary hardware before the actual new users are added to the system, averting any degradation of the system's performance or response time.

This chapter explains the practice of capacity planning and shows how to use it to your advantage, to see the future of your system's resource consumption.

Performance Tuning vs. Capacity Planning

The differences between capacity planning analysis and performance tuning analysis are also the differences between what information is collected and how often. Different System Monitor counters are useful for each type of analysis. When you tune a system, you look for anomalies that cause your system to perform unacceptably. Generally, you concentrate on one area of the system at a time, such as the disk subsystem or CPU, and collect short-term data concerning that area. In a capacity study, you analyze trends in resource consumption for workloads on your system. You therefore collect a sampling of data that is representative of your entire system's processing over a long period of time.

For example, suppose you want to tune your system's disk subsystem. The goal is clear: you want to distribute I/Os to the disk drives equally to avert bottlenecks that might hamper performance. First, you measure the disk subsystem to find out which disk or disks bear the majority of the I/O workload. You set up the measurement by defining the counters that you want the System Monitor to collect. The set of counters you select for monitoring is known as a *measurement configuration*. In this case, you would collect physical disk statistics such as I/O and disk utilization counters.

After you collect the data, you typically graph the activity to visually review the resource consumption of the various disk drives. Figure 11-1 displays the collected data in a graph that shows the I/O distribution among the disk drives. In this case, Disk F is doing most of the work. Next you move one or two of the more frequently used tables to a lesser-used disk, such as disk G, to even out the distribution. When you tune performance, it's best to change one thing at a time and then measure the results of that change. That way you can easily back out the change and revert to the original system configuration.

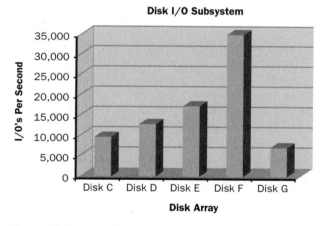

Figure 11-1. *A performance graph of an untuned I/O subsystem.*

Figure 11-2 illustrates the change in I/O distribution caused by relocating some tables. The objective of this tuning exercise is to get the graph as flat as possible by distributing the load among all the disks, so this change was beneficial. Systematic table relocation will eventually result in a tuned I/O subsystem.

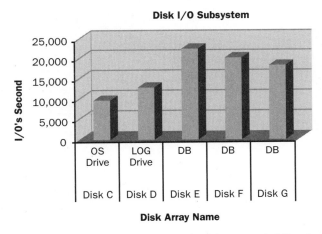

Figure 11-2. *A performance graph of the example I/O subsystem after relocating some tables.*

In a capacity study, the objective is clear: you want to study trends in workload resource consumption on your system. The method is also clear: collect a representative sampling of data over a long period of time to track these trends. What is unclear is how to make use of your results: what hardware will you need to add to address the trends you see? For example, suppose you have had a study in progress for five months. You are tracking the I/O usage of your system after you have tuned it as in the performance tuning example just described. You produce a graph that shows the monthly average growth of I/O usage on disk F, as shown by the solid line in Figure 11-3 on the following page.

In October, when the study began, disk F had a usage of 21,897 I/Os per second. This has grown to 29,132 I/Os per second in February 2001. You can now project when the I/O usage of disk F will exceed its maximum of 40,000 I/Os per second. The dotted line in Figure 11-3 indicates the projected growth from February through August 2001, when the disk will reach its maximum I/O capacity.

Capacity planning studies differ from performance tuning studies in terms of their length and the concentration of data collection. When you tune the system for performance, as in the earlier example, you concentrate on one area of the system at a time—in this case, the disk I/O subsystem. In a capacity study, you collect data that is representative of the entire system. The counters that you select to analyze will also differ. Some counters are clearly for tuning purposes, such as the Cache Size counter of the SQL Server: Buffer Manager object, which is used to adjust cache size to obtain a particular cache hit ratio. You generally would not collect this data for capacity planning purposes, because once you set this counter, the value doesn't change unless you change it manually. In contrast, counters such as Processor: % Processor Time change as the use of your system increases or decreases. For capacity planning, you should select counters that reflect system usage.

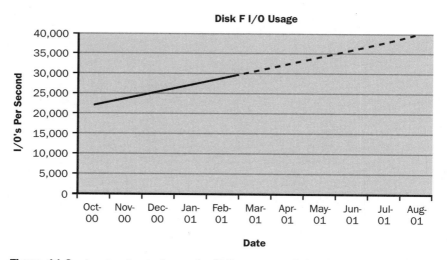

Figure 11-3. *A capacity study graph of I/O usage on disk F (solid line = actual usage; dotted line = projected usage).*

Now that you have a little background as to what capacity planning is and how these studies can help you in planning for your system's growth, we can proceed with how to perform these studies. The first rule of capacity planning is that you should perform the study on a well-tuned system. If you perform a capacity study on a system that is not tuned, you will not get a clear picture of the resource growth because the resources might be used unevenly. Some resources will have reached their capacity while others still have room for growth. You should run system components at close to the same level as others in their group. For example, all disks should be similar in terms of use, free space, and I/O traffic; otherwise, you will have to upgrade one disk array at one point in time and then another possibly not long after that. If you balance the components to begin with, they will all need upgrades at around the same time, so you can avoid multiple downtimes.

Data Collection

Microsoft has an excellent performance monitoring and data collection tool called System Monitor which you can use for either performance tuning or capacity planning. Remember that the differences between the two types of studies are what counters you select and how long you measure them. Another difference is the length of the interval over which the counter values are averaged. You can see the average disk reads per second over an hour's usage at a time by selecting an interval of one hour for the Physical Disk: Disk Reads/sec counter, or over the last three hours if you select that interval length. A good collection interval for a capacity planning study is eight hours. You can store this interval easily in daily averages that represent usage for workloads. Some people prefer an interval of one hour, but whatever interval you choose should be averaged for daily usage. When you collect more data, you should average it into weekly snapshots, which are preferable to monthly segments since monthly data tends to flatten spikes that could indicate peak utilization periods. For more information on System Monitor, see Chapter 6, "Monitoring Performance with Windows 2000 System Monitor."

The first step in a capacity planning study is to select the relevant counters. The combination of counters is important for painting an accurate picture of the system's usage. For example, on a database server you will want to collect information that pertains to the whole system, but concentrates on the database activity and physical disk activity. A very basic measurement configuration for a database server is shown in Figure 11-4.

Basic Database Server Measurement Configuration

Memory	Available Bytes
Memory	Page Faults/sec
Network Interface	Bytes Total/sec
Network interface	Current Bandwidth
Network Interface	Bytes Sent/sec
Network interface	Bytes Rec/sec
Physical Disk	% Disk Time
Physical Disk	Avg. Disk sec/Read
Physical Disk	Avg. Disk sec/Write
Physical Disk	Current Disk Queue length
Physical Disk	Disk Reads/sec
Physical Disk	Disk Writes/sec
Processor	% Processor Time
Processor	Processor Queue length
Server	Server Sessions
SQL Server: Cache Manager	Cache Hit Ratio
SQL Server: Databases	Transactions/sec
SQL Server: General Statistics	User Connections
System	File Read Operations/sec
System	File Write Operations/sec
System	Processor Queue length

Figure 11-4. *A basic measurement configuration for a database server.*

The counters in this configuration give a good statistical picture of this server's resource use; they cover all the major resource areas (memory, disks, and CPU) while concentrating on the disk I/O subsystem. Notice the physical disk information that is being collected. The Avg. Disk sec/Read and Avg. Disk sec/Write counters indicate how long an average read or write takes—information that is used in sizing. See Chapter 10, "Methods for Sizing a System" for more about sizing. The % Disk Time counter indicates the utilization of the disk drives that make up the drive array. The SQL Server counters give information on the current cache hit ratio, how many transactions per second the database is processing, and how many users are currently connected to the database.

It is better to collect more counters than you need than not enough. Most people start off with a more elaborate measurement configuration than the example shown in Figure 11-4 and pare it down as they learn from experience what information they do not need. The following lists describe counters that are useful for capacity planning, categorized by the type of machine being analyzed and the area of analysis. Usually, you should select more than one counter from each category to get a complete capacity planning view of the systems you want to analyze.

Counters for All Machines

The counters in this section are useful for capacity planning on all types of machines: clients, database servers, or application servers. The counters are categorized by the type of data they return.

CPU data (Processor object)

- **% Privileged Time** The percentage of time the operating system was busy.
- **% Processor Time** The percentage of time the processor was busy, using the equation B/T. (See Chapter 8 for more on this and other equations used for sizing and capacity planning.) If the observation period was one hour (T) and the processor was busy 30 minutes (B), then the CPU was busy 50 percent of the time. Remember to measure all CPUs in the system.

Memory data (Memory object)

- **Available Bytes** The amount of free space in memory. This value is a snapshot, not an average; it will need to be averaged for a day's usage.
- **Page Faults/sec** The number of page faults per second for code pages and data pages, averaged over the interval period.
- **Pages/sec** The number of actual pages being moved from disk to memory or back to disk. Only data pages are written back to disk when they are modified. Code pages do not get modified.

Network data (Network Interface object)

- **Bytes Received/sec** The number of bytes received by this system per second, averaged over the interval period.
- **Bytes Sent/sec** The number of bytes sent by this system per second, averaged over the interval period.
- **Bytes Total/sec** The total number of bytes sent and received by the system per second, averaged over the interval period. This counter's value is the sum of the Bytes Received/sec and Bytes Sent/sec counters.
- **Current Bandwidth** The current size of the line.

User activity (Server object)

- **Server Sessions** The number of user sessions currently going on within the server.

Disk I/O subsystem data (PhysicalDisk object)

Note   To use Physical Disk counters, you must be logged on as *Administrator*.

- **% Disk Read Time** The percentage of time that the disk was busy performing a read function. This counter is useful if you want to know how much of the overall disk time is spent reading. You can consider this counter optional if you are measuring % Disk Time.

- **% Disk Write Time** The percentage of time that the disk was busy performing a write function. This counter is useful if you want to know how much of the overall disk time is spent writing.

- **% Disk Time** The percentage of time that the disk was busy performing read or write functions. This counter is necessary for capacity planning studies and should be collected for every disk array within the system. The % Disk Time value is the sum of the % Disk Read Time and the % Disk Write Time counters.

- **Avg. Disk Queue Length** The actual disk queue for read and write operations. This counter is necessary for capacity planning studies. A disk queue of two is the maximum recommended value for this counter.

- **Avg. Disk sec/Read** The average time (in milliseconds) a read operation takes. This time is important because prolonged read and write operations indicate an overutilized disk.

- **Avg. Disk sec/Write** The average time (in milliseconds) a write operation takes. This time is important because prolonged read and write operations indicate an overutilized disk.

Counters for Database Servers

There are a number of specialty counters for dedicated servers. Some of the more important counters for database servers are listed here.

- **Cache Hit Ratio (SQLServer: Cache Manager object)** The percentage of time that a record was found in cache. The recommended cache hit ratio is 90 percent or more.

- **User Connections (SQLServer: General Statistics object)** The number of users connected to this database.

- **Transactions/sec (SQLServer: Databases object)** The number of transactions started for the database. These transactions come in the form of requests from client machines that are serviced by the database.

- **Data File(s) Size (KB) (SQLServer: Databases object)** The cumulative size of the data files that reside on a disk array. This counter is useful for tracking disk usage growth for capacity planning studies.

- **Percent Log Used (SQLServer: Databases object)** The percentage of the log that is used. This counter is helpful for tracking log growth in capacity planning studies.

To find the complete list of SQL Server counters, open the Performance console, click System Monitor in the left pane, and click the Add button on the toolbar in the right pane to open the Add Counters dialog box, as shown in Figure 11-5. To access a specific set of counters, select the appropriate object from the Performance Object drop-down list. The various counters associated with the object (in this case, SQLServer:Databases) are displayed in the left list at the bottom of the Add Counters dialog box.

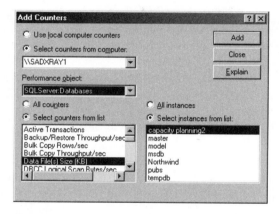

Figure 11-5. *The System Monitor's Add Counters dialog box.*

Click the Explain button to open the Explain Text window and then select a counter from the list to display a definition for that counter in the window. System Monitor also tells you what kind of counter the selected entity is. The counter selected in this example is Data File(s) Size (KB). Notice that capacity planning2 is highlighted on the right to indicate the name of this database.

Counters for Web Servers

You can find the Web server specialty counters under the Web Service object.

- **Anonymous Users/sec** The connection activity for the Web service per second, averaged over the interval period.
- **Current Connections** The number of current active connections to the Web server. This counter is useful for tracking user activity on the server.
- **Connection Attempts/sec** An activity counter that shows the number of attempts to connect to this server.
- **Total Anonymous Users** The total count of users that established a connection with this Web service since the service was started. This counter combined with the Anonymous Users/sec counter is useful for seeing trends in user activity.

Counters for Application Servers

You can find the counters that are particularly useful for performing capacity planning on application servers under the Process object.

- **% Processor Time** The percentage of processor time that the process selected for monitoring (the instance) has used in the system.
- **Elapsed Time** The time, in seconds, that the process instance has been running. This counter is useful for tracking activity trends over long periods of time. It is also useful for "what if" scenarios, to see what will happen to CPU utilization if you add more application users.
- **I/O Data Operations** The number of read and write operations generated by the process instance. This counter is useful for keeping track of I/O activity for application types, as well as for analyzing "what if" scenarios concerning user-generated I/O activity.

Service Chains

Service chain monitoring is similar to single-node monitoring, except that you collect data on several machines. For example, suppose you want to track the complete workload for a general ledger system. You will need to collect data from the client machine, the application machine (the process will either be on the client machine or on the application server), the network, and the database server. This data collection process encompasses three, and possibly four, different elements and a variety of counters. The data that this collection of counters supplies is useful in "what if" scenarios. Monitoring service chains also allows you to compile utilization data on these chains that you can use for maintaining SLAs and predicting future growth of the services.

Data Analysis

The aim of performing capacity planning studies is to maintain the performance you achieved when you tuned the system's performance. To do this, you must first build a capacity planning database by taking repetitive measurements each day at the same time for a period of weeks or months. Then you must create reports that use the historic capacity planning data to see what the current performance is and to determine how to maintain the same performance in the months to come. This process is known as *predictive analysis*. When you perform predictive analysis, the more data points you have, the more accurate the prediction will be. If you want to project usage of a CPU for three months, make sure you have at least that much historic data.

For ease of analysis, export the performance data into a Microsoft Excel spreadsheet or SQL Server database. We will look at the data within an Excel spreadsheet. Suppose that you have collected several counters for capacity analysis of a database server named System1. Figure 11-6 shows a simple format for storing the counter data in Excel that lends itself to sorting by any of the counters and to producing graphs. Any format that you use should include the configuration of the system as a reference.

Configuration: Machine Name: System1 — Network: 100 Mbits/Sec — CPU: Pentium III, 4 X 533 MHz — Disk Controllers: 2, 2 Channel — Memory: 1 GB — Disk C: 2 X 2 GB, RAID 0 — Disk E: 7 X 2 GB, RAID 5 — Disk F: 7 X 2 GB, RAID 5

Machine Name	Avg. Weekly Work Ending	Processor (4) Avg. All CPU's %Processor Time	Processor Avg. All CPU's Avg. Q Length	Memory %Free Space	Memory Page Faults/Sec	Physical Disk %Disk Time Disk E:	Physical Disk Disk Queue Disk E:	Physical Disk %Disk Time Disk F:	Physical Disk Disk Queue Disk F:	SQL Server Cache Manager Cache Hit Ratio
system1	1/1/1999	35.50%	0.55	36.23%	0.23	19.30%	0.24	13.23%	0.15	91.34%
system1	1/8/1999	33.98%	0.51	36.13%	0.22	19.78%	0.25	12.98%	0.15	91.21%
system1	1/15/1999	36.45%	0.57	35.87%	0.31	20.13%	0.25	13.56%	0.16	91.34%
system1	1/22/1999	36.47%	0.57	35.13%	0.32	20.67%	0.26	14.03%	0.16	90.78%
system1	1/29/1999	37.96%	0.61	34.12%	0.31	21.12%	0.27	13.93%	0.16	90.78%
system1	2/5/1999	38.65%	0.63	33.93%	0.35	21.56%	0.27	14.39%	0.17	90.62%
system1	2/12/1999	39.23%	0.65	33.41%	0.35	22.01%	0.28	14.60%	0.17	90.45%
system1	2/19/1999	38.56%	0.63	32.89%	0.36	22.47%	0.29	14.86%	0.17	90.29%
system1	2/26/1999	42.65%	0.74	32.36%	0.40	22.92%	0.30	15.12%	0.18	90.12%
system1	3/5/1999	45.76%	0.84	31.84%	0.42	23.37%	0.30	15.38%	0.18	89.96%
system1	3/12/1999	47.32%	0.90	31.32%	0.44	23.82%	0.31	15.64%	0.19	89.79%
system1	3/19/1999	46.98%	0.89	30.80%	0.46	24.28%	0.32	15.90%	0.19	89.63%
system1	3/26/1999	49.34%	0.97	30.28%	0.48	24.73%	0.33	16.16%	0.19	89.46%
system1	4/2/1999	51.45%	1.06	29.75%	0.50	25.18%	0.34	16.42%	0.20	89.30%
system1	4/9/1999	50.35%	1.01	29.23%	0.52	25.64%	0.34	16.68%	0.20	89.13%
system1	4/16/1999	52.63%	1.11	28.71%	0.53	26.09%	0.35	16.94%	0.20	88.97%
system1	4/23/1999	59.35%	1.46	28.19%	0.55	26.54%	0.36	17.20%	0.21	88.80%
system1	4/30/1999	60.85%	1.55	27.67%	0.57	27.00%	0.37	17.46%	0.21	88.64%
system1	5/7/1999	63.45%	1.74	27.14%	0.59	27.45%	0.38	17.73%	0.22	88.47%
system1	5/14/1999	62.56%	1.67	26.62%	0.61	27.90%	0.39	17.99%	0.22	88.31%
system1	5/21/1999	63.05%	1.71	26.10%	0.63	28.35%	0.40	18.25%	0.22	88.14%
system1	5/28/1999	64.63%	1.82	25.58%	0.65	28.81%	0.40	18.51%	0.23	87.98%
system1	6/4/1999	66.20%	1.96	25.06%	0.67	29.26%	0.41	18.77%	0.23	87.81%
system1	6/11/1999	67.76%	2.10	24.53%	0.69	29.71%	0.42	19.03%	0.24	87.65%
system1	6/18/1999	69.36%	2.26	24.01%	0.71	30.17%	0.43	19.29%	0.24	87.48%
system1	6/25/1999	70.94%	2.44	23.49%	0.73	30.62%	0.44	19.55%	0.24	87.32%
system1	7/2/1999	72.52%	2.64	22.97%	0.75	31.07%	0.45	19.81%	0.25	87.15%

Figure 11-6. *A Microsoft Excel spreadsheet with sample capacity data ready for analysis.*

Historic Data Reporting

Historic data reporting is exactly what it sounds like—reporting on the past activity of the system. In the preliminary analysis of such a report, you look for trends such as growth (or lack of growth) associated with a system component, such as a gradual or radical increase in CPU use, I/Os per second, file size, number of transactions, memory use, or number of users. At this point you look for components that need more analysis, such as predictive analysis or *correlative analysis* (performing "what if" scenarios on the data to see how changes in one variable affect another). A good place to start the preliminary analysis is with the utilization counters, which show the overall usage of the system. If you see a growth trend in system utilization, it usually (but not always) indicates that the entire machine is in a growth trend.

The first report you produce for System1 is CPU (processor) utilization. First you produce a graph tracking the utilization of the processors for the last six months. Figure 11-7 shows the historic data collected from January 1, 2001, through July 2, 2001. Note that the values on the Percent Utilization axis of this graph range from 0 to 75 percent, not 100 percent. This is because the 75 percent knee of the curve is the maximum steady-state utilization. (See "Queuing Theory and the Knee of the Curve" in Chapter 8.) If you look at the graph itself, you can see that a growth trend has been taking place since the beginning of the data collection period. Use is growing on an almost weekly basis.

Note If you are collecting information on individual processors in a multiprocessor system, you should have a column in your data format for averages of the individual entities. This will give you a system average of CPU utilization so you can look at the system as one utilization value (which represents all CPUs in the system). This perspective makes analysis much easier.

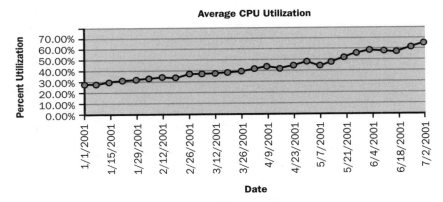

Figure 11-7. *CPU utilization graph for a six-month period.*

When you notice such a growth trend, the next step is to find other counters that are on the rise. One of the most damaging problems in system performance is a long CPU queue, which is tracked by the Processor Queue Length counter, so it's a good idea to produce a graph for this counter. If you see a Processor Queue Length value of two or more, you must adjust the system (either by removing processes or adding CPUs) to shorten this queue length. Figure 11-8 shows the graph produced for this counter. As with the processor use, there is a growth trend since the date of the first collection in January. This comes as no surprise—you will almost always see a growth trend in the CPU queue length when there is a growth trend in CPU use.

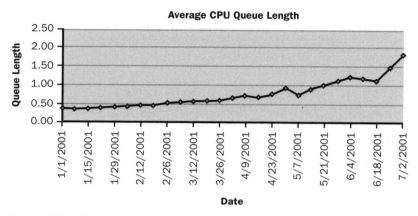

Figure 11-8. *The graph of the Processor Queue Length counter for a six-month period.*

You should then proceed to graph all the counters that you selected for collection. After producing these graphs, you should perform predictive analysis for this system because of the growth trends you noticed in this phase of the capacity planning analysis.

Predictive Analysis

When you see consistent growth trends, it is logical to want to know when your system will hit the maximum values so that you have time to order equipment if necessary or perform fine tuning to the system before SLAs are violated. Microsoft Excel makes this kind of analysis easy to perform. You have already produced graphs such as Figures 11-7 and 11-8 for the historic counter data. The next step is to project the data into the future.

In the case of CPU use, you want to know when the maximum steady-state utilization of 75 percent will be attained. The steps are the same as for any projection in Excel:

1. Open the worksheet that contains the chart on which you wish to perform predictive analysis.

2. Right-click the line on the chart and select Add Trendline on the shortcut menu. The Add Trendline dialog box appears, as shown in Figure 11-9.

3. In the Add Trendline dialog box, select the Linear trendline type. This type of trend is useful for seeing how long it will take for an event to happen.

4. On the Options tab, set the appropriate options. As you can see in Figure 11-10, the Options tab allows you to select forecasting and to specify how many units into the future you would like to project (in this case units equates to days). For our analysis, we selected 130 days.

5. Click the OK button. The graph will be completed, the dates adjusted, and you will see exactly when you will exceed the selected boundary.

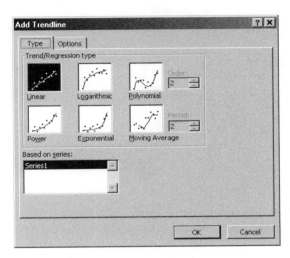

Figure 11-9. *Selecting the trendline type in Microsoft Excel to produce a graph of projected growth in CPU utilization.*

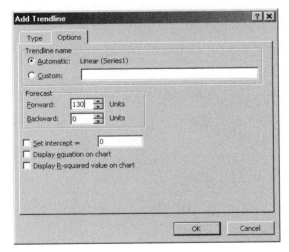

Figure 11-10. *The Options tab in the Add Trendline dialog box.*

The graph in Figure 11-11 clearly shows that the CPU utilization will reach the maximum steady-state utilization of 75 percent sometime in the middle of September. This information will give you plenty of time to avert any sudden violations of service level agreements.

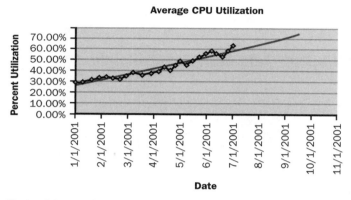

Figure 11-11. *The completed trendline graph for CPU utilization (squares = actual data points; solid line = projected use).*

Next you want to determine when response times will start to noticeably reflect this utilization increase. Usually response times start to show sudden rises long before the utilization hits its maximum projected increase; you can see this trend by considering the rise in queue lengths. Figure 11-12 shows the same actual data points as Figure 11-11 but with a logarithmic trendline that takes the queue lengths into consideration. As you can see, before the processors reach their projected mid-September milestone of 75 percent utilization (as we expected based on a linear rise in utilization), there is an exponential rise in queue length in the beginning of August. Thus users will see the effects of the rise in CPU utilization at that earlier point. All counters that show a growth trend should be graphed using linear and exponential trendlines so you can prepare for the increases.

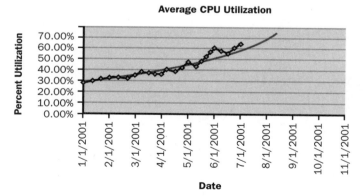

Figure 11-12. *Predicted logarithmic increases in queues.*

Correlative Analysis

Correlative analysis is used to perform "what if" scenarios on the data to see how changes in one variable affect another. Taking the previous example of CPU use, one option for this system is to move some of the utilization from its CPUs to another machine. If you kept track of processes that were running on this system, you can predict what rate of growth these processes will have and what effect removing some of them will have.

Figure 11-13 depicts the system CPU utilization broken down by process. Here three processes—process 1, process 2, and process 3—make up the total utilization of System1. You can see that process 2 rose in utilization around April 23, 2001 and has been increasing from that point on. Moving this process to another machine should reduce the total utilization of System1.

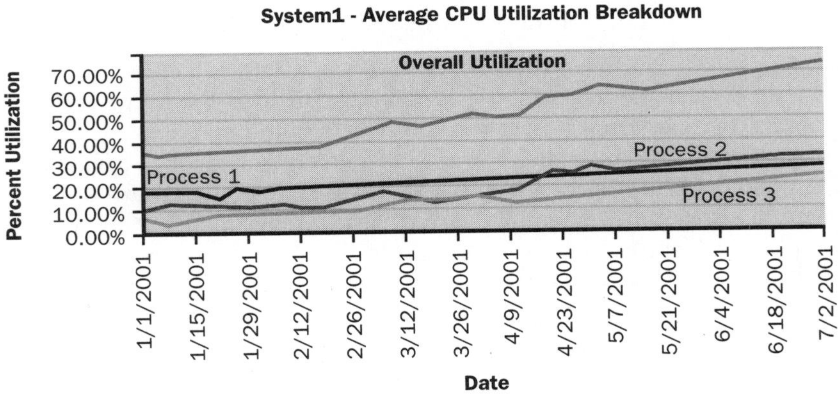

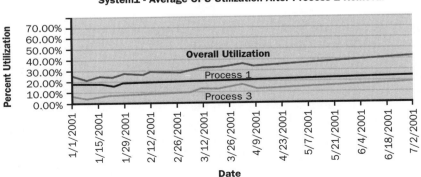

Figure 11-13. *Average utilization broken down by process.*

Figure 11-14 shows the reduction of utilization in System1 after removing process 2 from the running processes. You can see that this reduction extends the amount of time before the system reaches the maximum use. At this point you can produce another graph showing this time extension more precisely.

Figure 11-14. *Average utilization after removal of process 2.*

Service Chain Reporting

Service chain reporting can show the cost that workloads have on systems in terms of utilization and resource consumption. Service chain measurements and analysis span more than one system and involve multiple machines, such as a client machine, a database server, and sometimes a Web server. When you analyze a service chain, it is important to remember that you can look at the information in two ways: as an average utilization spread over a couple of machines or as a series of individual utilizations.

For example, if you view the workload utilizations spread out across three machines as being 12 percent on the client machine, 18 percent on the application server, and 22 percent on the database server, then the service chain has an average 17.33 percent utilization. This calculation can give a misleading view of the situation. In this case it would be wiser to view the information as three separate entities rather than as a whole, especially if you are trying to determine what effect adding a certain number of more specific types of users to a system will have.

For example, suppose the data just described represents the usage for a general ledger workload. There are presently four users. This would imply that each user places three percent utilization on the client machine, 4.5 percent utilization on the application server, and 5.5 percent utilization on the database server. If you were to add two more users engaged in performing general ledger activities, you would be adding six percent utilization to the client machine, nine percent to the application server, and 11 percent utilization to the database server. The final effect of all six users on the various systems would be as follows:

- Final client machine utilization 18%
- Final application server utilization 27%
- Final database server utilization 33%

When you perform "what if" scenarios on service chains, remember that the workload is usually spread out across multiple machines, so you must measure all aspects of the workload on the various machines, including processes and user activity.

Summary

Capacity planning can open up a new world of knowledge concerning the systems that you use and for which you are responsible. This information can truly make you the master of this domain in terms of understanding the workload and being able to avert overutilization and violation of SLAs. Through historic data analysis and predictive analysis, you can foresee the future growth of a system due to normal usage. Correlative analysis allows you to manipulate processes and users within systems for tuning purposes and see the results of these adjustments without actually performing the changes.

Part III
Configuring and Tuning the System

Chapter 12
Online Transaction Processing Systems

Online transaction processing systems, or OLTP systems, are the traditional backbone of database processing. OLTP-style systems can be everything from small single-machine systems that process a few transactions per minute to massive clustered systems that process more than 500,000 transactions per minute. Across this spectrum, however, the concepts involved in OLTP-system design are the same.

This chapter looks at the characteristics of an OLTP system as well as the different components of the system. We look at two-tiered and three-tiered OLTP systems. In addition, we explore database design for OLTP systems and provide other tuning hints for OLTP.

What is an OLTP System?

The industry defines an OLTP system as a system that represents the state of a particular business function at a specific point in time. An online transaction processing database typically supports large numbers of concurrent users who perform transactions that change data in real time. A transaction is simply a series of operations that are performed as one logical unit of work. Although individual user requests for data tend to reference few records and complete quickly, many of these requests are made at the same time. Common examples of these types of databases are airline ticketing systems, retail order-processing systems, and banking transaction systems. Maintaining data integrity is the primary concern in this type of application. Here are some characteristics of OLTP systems:

- Multiple concurrent users running multiple simultaneous transactions
- Short transactions that perform a specific business function
- Databases with many tables that have varying attributes, sizes, and relationships
- Contention on the databases during data access and data modification
- Randomness of data access
- Significant I/O (reads and writes) to the databases
- Databases are defined with referential integrity
- Transaction integrity—ACID properties are met

Next we'll take a closer look at the characteristics of a transaction. A transaction must meet four specific requirements to qualify as a valid transaction and to maintain data integrity—these requirements are known as the *ACID properties*. SQL Server provides mechanisms to help ensure that a transaction meets each of these properties. ACID is an acronym that stands for the following:

- **Atomicity** SQL Server ensures that all data modifications in a transaction are completed as a group if the transaction is successful, or that none of the modifications occur if the transaction is not successful—in other words, SQL Server ensures the *atomicity* of your transactions. The transaction must be performed as an atomic unit—thus the term "atomicity." For a transaction to be successful, every step (or statement) in the transaction must succeed. If one of the steps fails, the entire transaction fails, and any modifications made since the transaction started are undone. SQL Server provides transaction management that determines whether a transaction has succeeded or failed and undoes any data modifications as necessary in the case of a failure. For example, a banking transaction to transfer money from one account to another might involve two steps: taking funds out of your checking account, and placing them into your savings account. If the step that removes the funds from your checking account succeeds, you want to make sure that the funds are placed into your savings account before the transaction finishes. You can code these two steps into one transaction to have SQL Server ensure the atomicity property so that either both or none of the steps occurs.

- **Consistency** *Consistency* means that all data remains in a consistent state— that the integrity of the data is preserved—after a transaction finishes, regardless of whether the transaction completed successfully or failed. Before a transaction begins, the database must be in a consistent state, which means that the integrity of the data is upheld and that internal structures, such as B-tree indexes and doubly-linked lists, are correct. After a transaction occurs, the database must also be in a consistent state—a new state if the transaction succeeded, or, if the transaction failed, the same consistent state it was in before the transaction started. The actions of the transaction, taken as a group, should not violate any of the integrity constraints imposed by the database platform. If your data is consistent and your transactions maintain logical consistency and integrity of data, SQL Server ensures the consistency of the data after a transaction. In our banking transaction example, when you move funds from your checking account to your savings account, the account balances should be consistent and reflect the transaction's effect on your checking balance and your savings balance.

- **Isolation** Modifications made by concurrent transactions must be isolated from the modifications made by any other transactions. There are varying levels of isolation. A transaction sees data in the state it was in before another concurrent transaction modified it, after a concurrent transaction has completed, or in an intermediate state. The isolation level you should choose depends on your business needs. For example, if you ask an airline ticket agent to reserve the last available seat on a flight and the agent begins reserving the seat in your name, another agent should not be able to tell another passenger that the seat is available. SQL Server provides varying levels of transaction isolation. See SQL Server Books Online for details on isolation levels.

- **Durability** *Durability* means that once a transaction is committed, its effects are permanent in the database, even in the event of a system failure. The SQL Server transaction log and your own database backups provide durability. If a component of the server machine fails, if the operating system fails, or if SQL Server fails, SQL Server recovers the database when it is restarted. SQL Server uses the transaction log to replay the committed transactions and to roll back any uncommitted transactions that were affected by the system crash. If a data drive fails and data is lost or corrupted, you can recover the database using database backups and transaction log backups. If you plan your backups well, you should always be able to recover from a system failure. Unfortunately, if you have not planned your backup strategy well, you might not be able to recover your database to a specific point in time, as you might need. You should always practice recovering from backups before a real situation occurs where you will have to do it. See Chapter 15, "High-Performance Backup and Recovery" for more information on performing backup and restore operations.

A good illustration of the ACID properties of an OLTP system is a cash withdrawal from an ATM system. The ATM withdrawal transaction is considered atomic if it updates your account information when it dispenses the cash. It is considered consistent if the amount of money disbursed by the ATM machine is the same as the debit made to your account. The withdrawal adheres to the isolation property if the ATM program is unaffected by other programs concurrently reading and writing your account information. Finally, the ATM transaction is considered durable if once the transaction is complete, or committed, your account balance accurately reflects the withdrawal even if the ATM machine or communication lines fail.

System Configuration Options for OLTP Systems

Whether an application is a spreadsheet program running on a desktop computer (such as Microsoft Excel), or a financials application running on a big server or mainframe system, the application must have these three components:

- **Presentation** Presents the graphical user interface (GUI) and interacts with the user
- **Application logic** Performs calculations and determines the flow of the application to support the business logic
- **Data** Manages the underlying data that must be accessed through the application

There are differing architectural configuration and implementation options for these three components, which balance application- and load-dependent factors like cost, scalability, and component reusability. These options include two-tier and three-tier architectures, which are described in the following sections.

Two-Tiered Architecture

A two-tiered system includes two physical computers—the client machine and the database server. There are two basic types of two-tiered systems, and where the application components reside determines a system's type. With the first type, the presentation and application logic components both reside on the client machines, which access the data from the database server via network connections, as shown in Figure 12-1. Clients read data from the database, perform business logic, and update data back to the database when necessary. This two-tiered model is best used with a small number of users (generally fewer than 100), accessing a single database that runs on a fast, secure network.

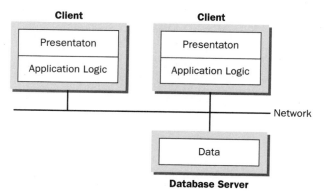

Figure 12-1. *Two-tiered architecture.*

To improve network performance, you can reduce the amount of network traffic by using SQL Server stored procedures to perform more of the application logic on the database server side, as shown in Figure 12-2. This is the second type of two-tiered system. Stored procedures provide a method for users to execute groups of SQL statements together remotely on the database server. The application calls stored procedures by name, passes in any necessary parameters, and retrieves any results from the procedure. Because the server does more of the processing, rather than passing separate SQL statements one at a time with the client performing intermediate logic, the amount of traffic between the client and the server is reduced. Stored procedures also increase reusability because they can be called by multiple presentation components. They also provide a central management capability. If you want to change a stored procedure, you simply alter it once in the database and all users will use the new code, without having to copy new application code to the clients. We recommend using stored procedures whenever possible. It is not unusual for applications to use stored procedures 95 to 100 percent of the time.

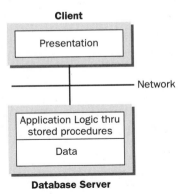

Figure 12-2. *Two-tiered architecture with stored procedures.*

If you have a large number of users, need to access multiple database systems, or have non-secure network environments, then the two-tiered models might present the following limitations:

- Each active client must maintain a connection to the database. Each database connection uses system resources such as memory, so as more users connect, the performance of the database server degrades.

- A large number of database connections also leads to high contention for resources such as locks. Clients might have to wait for other clients to release locks before they can continue their work.

- Security focuses on granting or denying user permissions to data in the database. This does not work well outside of trusted LAN environments.

- Applications are tightly bound to a specific database system and specific data formats, making it difficult to reuse the application logic for other applications.

- Using stored procedures limits reuse of code, because the procedures are not compatible with other database vendors.

- Stored procedures also lack features such as multiple interface support, externalized security, and transaction properties.

Two-tiered models work best for single applications that do not require broad reuse. If, on the other hand, your application supports a large number of users (or has the potential to in the future); needs more and higher levels of security; requires broad reusability of application components; or must access multiple database systems and mainframe applications, then you should consider the three-tiered architecture described next. Also note that a two-tiered system could also include a third computer (in addition to the database server and the client machine), which serves as a terminal for the end user to view the application GUI. It does not perform any functionality other than sending keystroke and mouse commands from the user to the client machine, and receiving the display.

Three-Tiered Architecture

In a three-tiered architecture, each of the three database application components is divided into distinct units. In this three-tiered model, presentation components make requests for application services to a middle-tier server. The middle-tier server performs business logic and make requests to the database server (or mainframe applications) to access data. Thus, the presentation component resides on the client, the application logic component resides on the middle-tier, or application server, and the data component resides on the database server, as shown in Figure 12-3.

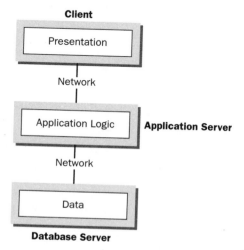

Figure 12-3. *Three-tiered architecture.*

Splitting the application logic component off from presentation and data gives you the following benefits:

- Application components can be replicated onto several application server machines so that they run in parallel. Client loads are spread across the multiple application servers, providing scalability, reliability, and performance.

- Developers can use powerful tools such as Microsoft Visual Basic and Visual J++ to develop reusable application components, instead of depending on the limited stored procedure languages.

- Application components can share database connections through connection pooling, so that each client does not make a connection to the database. Instead, the middle tier manages client connections through a pool of available connections. So 1000 clients don't generate 1000 connections to SQL Server, which would use up a lot of the memory from the system and degrade performance. Instead, maybe only 200 connections are configured for the pool, and the 1000 users through the application component share those 200 connections.

- Access to middle-tier components can be granted or denied on a component-by-component basis.

Guidelines for Designing OLTP Systems

You should keep several guidelines in mind when you design your OLTP systems. Though the following concepts might seem basic, you can greatly improve system performance by adhering to them.

OLTP and Decision Support Workloads

Often you'll need to support both OLTP business requirements and some decision support (reporting) or data mining requirements. Each of these workload types has different needs, and they often conflict with one another. For example, a typical OLTP system performs lots of fairly short transactions that access data in a random fashion, while the decision support system (DSS) performs more complex queries that can take longer to complete and can access data sequentially. These long report queries can hinder the response time of the OLTP transactions. If this happens on your system, the easy solution is to move the DSS onto a separate computer, to maximize the performance of each workload. If your system is not very busy, you might not have a problem performing the DSS queries on the same system as the OLTP database, provided you have enough CPU and I/O capacity to support both workloads without degrading performance. Or, if possible, you might run reports during the night while no OLTP transactions are occurring, so that each workload runs at different times to avoid conflicts. But generally, when OLTP workloads run simultaneously with DSS, running your DSS reports on their own system is a big win for performance.

Separating the databases brings up some issues. You need some type of mechanism to keep both databases in sync. If you do not require real-time data in the DSS database and the data will be read-only, you can back up the OLTP database regularly and then restore it to the DSS database, or use Data Transformation Services (DTS). This process introduces some lag into the currency of the data on the system. If you require real-time data for your DSS database, then you should explore the replication features of SQL Server 2000, which we cover in detail in Chapter 14, "Tuning Replicated Systems." Replication works well in this scenario.

Data Placement and Filegroups

One of the biggest concerns in an OLTP system is maintaining good I/O performance. Because OLTP systems generally have many users accessing and modifying data in a random pattern, balancing I/O across disks is critical. You should spread your data across as many physical disk drives as possible to eliminate potential I/O bottlenecks. The easiest way to spread data in SQL Server 2000 is to place your files in filegroups.

Placing data in multiple files and filegroups improves database performance by allowing you to create a database across multiple disks, multiple disk controllers, or RAID disk arrays. For example, if your computer has four RAID disk arrays (in addition to your C: drive), you can create a database that comprises three data files and one log file, with one file on each disk array. You can group the three data files in one filegroup so that the data is spread across the three corresponding disk arrays. This allows for more parallel data access since the data is spread across more physical disks. The following code provides an example of this:

```
CREATE DATABASE SALES
ON PRIMARY
(       NAME          = SALES_ROOT,
        FILENAME      = 'C:\SALES_ROOT.MDF',
        SIZE          = 8MB,
        FILEGROWTH    = 0),
FILEGROUP REGIONAL_DATA_FG
(       NAME          = REGIONAL_DATA_1,
        FILENAME      = 'E:\REGIONAL_DATA_1.MDF',
        SIZE          = 400MB,
        FILEGROWTH    = 0),
(       NAME          = REGIONAL_DATA_2,
        FILENAME      = 'F:\REGIONAL_DATA_2.MDF',
        SIZE          = 400MB,
    FILEGROWTH        = 0),
(       NAME          = REGIONAL_DATA_3,
        FILENAME      = 'G:\REGIONAL_DATA_3.MDF',
        SIZE          = 400MB,
        FILEGROWTH    = 0),
LOG ON
(       NAME          = SALES_LOG,
        FILENAME      = 'L:\SALES_LOG.LDF',
        SIZE          = 1000MB,
        FILEGROWTH    = 0)
```

You can place data where you want by creating tables on specific filegroups. Doing so improves performance because all I/Os for a specific table can be directed at a specific disk. For example, a heavily used table can be placed in one file in a particular filegroup located on one disk, and other, less heavily accessed tables can be placed in files in another filegroup located on a second disk. The following code shows sample SQL statements for allocating a table to a single file and filegroup:

```
CREATE DATABASE SALES
ON PRIMARY
(       NAME          = SALES_ROOT,
        FILENAME      = 'C:\SALES_ROOT.MDF',
        SIZE          = 8MB,
        FILEGROWTH    = 0),
FILEGROUP CUSTOMER_DATA_FG
(       NAME          = CUSTOMER_DATA,
        FILENAME      = 'E:\CUSTOMER_DATA.MDF',
        SIZE          = 200MB,
        FILEGROWTH    = 0),
```

```
FILEGROUP PRODUCT_DATA_FG
(      NAME          = PRODUCT_DATA,
       FILENAME      = 'F:\PRODUCT _DATA.MDF',
       SIZE          = 150MB,
       FILEGROWTH    = 0)
LOG ON
(      NAME          = SALES_LOG,
       FILENAME      = 'L:\SALES_LOG.LDF',
       SIZE          = 800MB,
       FILEGROWTH    = 0)
GO
CREATE TABLE CUSTOMER
(
    .
    .
    .
) ON CUSTOMER_DATA_FG
GO
CREATE TABLE SPORTING_GOODS
(
    .
    .
    .
) ON PRODUCT_DATA_FG
GO
CREATE TABLE CLOTHING
(
    .
    .
    .
) ON PRODUCT _DATA_FG
) GO
```

SQL Server 2000 writes data to filegroups using a proportional fill strategy across all the files defined in a filegroup. (See "Filegroups and File Placement" in Chapter 2, "SQL Server 2000 Architecture Fundamentals.") If you have enabled the automatic growth option for the database, SQL Server expands one file at a time in a round-robin fashion to accommodate more data as soon as all the files in a filegroup are full. For example, suppose that a filegroup comprises three files, all set to grow automatically. When space in all files in the filegroup is exhausted, only the first file is expanded. When the first file is full again and no more data can be written to the filegroup, the second file is expanded. When the second file is full again and no more data can be written to the filegroup, the third file is expanded. If the third file becomes full again and no more data can be written to the filegroup, the first file is expanded again, and so on, such that each file grows proportionally.

The following code shows two different techniques for specifying file growth:

```
CREATE DATABASE SALES
ON PRIMARY
(       NAME        = SALES_ROOT,
        FILENAME    = 'C:\SALES_ROOT.MDF',
        SIZE        = 8MB,
        FILEGROWTH  = 0),
FILEGROUP CUSTOMER_DATA_FG
(       NAME        = CUSTOMER_DATA,
        FILENAME    = 'E:\CUSTOMER_DATA',
        SIZE        = 200MB,
        FILEGROWTH  = 50MB,
FILEGROUP PRODUCT_DATA_FG
(       NAME        = PRODUCT_DATA_FG,
        FILENAME    = 'F:\PRODUCT_DATA',
        SIZE        = 200MB,
        FILEGROWTH  = 20%)
LOG ON
(       NAME        = SALES_LOG,
        FILENAME    = 'L:\SALES_LOG.LDF',
        SIZE        = 500MB,
        FILEGROWTH  = 0)
```

The first technique is to specify the file growth size as a specific value. In this example, the CUSTOMER_DATA file will grow 50 MBs at a time, provided there is adequate space on the E: drive. The alternative technique is to specify file growth as a percentage of the current file size. In the example, the PRODUCT_DATA file will grow by 20 percent of the current file size, provided there is adequate space on the F: drive. Setting file growth equal to 0 indicates that automatic file growth is not enabled, so the file will not grow.

Here are some things to keep in mind when you use files and filegroups:

- Almost every small database (3 GB or less) will work just fine with a single data file and a single transaction log file. For performance reasons, you should not put the transaction log file on the same physical disk or disks as your data files. This will isolate the transaction log I/Os from those accessing your data drives.

- For larger databases you might want to create multiple files and filegroups. Using multiple files gives you parallel data access across files. For example, when you perform a backup, each file can be read from simultaneously.

- If you choose to use multiple files, you should create an additional filegroup and use it as the default filegroup for your data files. This allows you to reserve the primary file for system tables and objects only.

- To maximize your system's performance, create your files or filegroups on as many available local physical disks as possible to spread the data and achieve more parallel I/O.

Tuning OLTP Transactions

A good strategy for OLTP systems is to strive to make your transactions as short as possible. This minimizes the duration of locks and improves overall data concurrency and performance. We cover this concept in more detail in Chapter 17, "Tuning SQL Statements and Stored Procedures."

You should also avoid free-form user input fields in your transactions. If your transactions take input that is in an unpredictable form, it will be difficult, if not impossible, to predict the span and amount of data the query will access. Limiting user input to a finite set of well-defined values will aid in your tuning efforts.

Another technique you should use in your OLTP transactions is to attempt to execute a single stored procedure for the entire transaction. This minimizes the system context switches and allows you to process as much data as possible in a single context. See Chapter 17 for more discussion about stored procedures.

One often overlooked technique for OLTP transactions is to place all the references to frequently accessed tables at or near the end of a transaction. This allows you to minimize the duration of the locks held on these popular tables. This technique is often not possible to use, but it is something you should attempt to do.

Also, call stored procedures from your application as much as possible, rather than sending dynamic or ad-hoc SQL statements. Using stored procedures reduces the amount of information sent across the network between client and server, thus improving network performance.

Controlling Data Content

Several strategies regarding data can improve performance of your OLTP system. For example, you should limit the amount of redundant data in your database. Reducing the redundancy of your data speeds up the data updates that your transactions perform. This in turn improves overall system concurrency and throughput.

> **Note**   Redundant data is advisable in some instances, such as when you are trying to limit the impact of joins on your queries. Such instances tend to be rare. See Chapter 19, "Using SQL Query Analyzer" for more information on joins.

Generally, OLTP systems require little or no historical or aggregate data in their online tables. You should archive data that is rarely referenced in separate databases or move it out of the heavily updated tables and into tables that contain only historical data. In some cases old data might not be needed at all, so you might consider creating a SQL Server job that purges the old data once a week, once a month, or as needed. In most cases you should put this historical data onto a separate server, to perform data analysis and reporting. For example, if users need to access data only from a *Transaction_Record* table that is less than one year old, you could copy data greater than one year old out of the table into another table (using INSERT INTO, replication, or DTS for example). Then you could delete the old records from the *Transaction_Record* table. This strategy keeps tables and indexes as small as possible, so there is less data for OLTP queries to sift through, improving response times. If you do want to access the historical data to perform analysis and reports, see Chapter 13, "Data Warehouses" for details about data warehousing and methods of transforming data for analysis.

Database Backup

The nature of an OLTP system is one of continuous operations. This generally means that the system must be available twenty-four hours a day, seven days a week. Downtime might be tolerated, but it must be kept to an absolute minimum. Database and transaction log backups are a must! With this in mind, SQL Server 2000 allows you to back up your databases even while they are being used. Doing so consumes system resources, so you should still schedule the full database backups to occur when your system has the lowest use to minimize the impact on your end users. Transaction log backups should be scheduled more often, such as every half hour or less, which will reduce the amount of log data to be backed up each time and will help the log backups to finish faster.

Your decisions about the redundancy of the data in your database can also affect backup duration and performance. If you can reduce the amount of redundant information in your tables, you will probably get a performance boost for your queries and reduce the time required to back up the databases. This also applies to the historical and aggregate data that you move out of the online database.

Also, using more than one data file for your database can be beneficial when you are performing backups and restores, as well as when you're accessing data. For a backup or restore, SQL Server assigns one backup thread to each data file, so if you have multiple files, they can be backed up in parallel. See Chapter 15 for more information on backup and recovery.

Indexes

One of the most common misconceptions concerning OLTP systems is that more indexes are better. Actually, you should avoid over-indexing tables. Each index you create must be updated each time a new row is added or deleted, or an indexed column is modified. When you define too many unnecessary indexes, the system can start to thrash as it updates a large amount of index data.

If the number of indexes on a table grows to a large number or many composite indexes are created with multiple columns, you will generally see some performance degradation. When you insert a single row into the database, the system performs one data page write and one or more index page writes for each index on that table. For example, if you were to define six nonclustered indexes on a table, the system would perform a minimum of seven writes to the database just to insert one row. If you do an update-in-place, the overhead is even higher. With those same six nonclustered indexes, this procedure generates up to 13 writes to the database, because an update-in-place is actually a delete operation immediately followed by an insert operation.

You can improve performance in some cases by locating nonclustered indexes on separate physical disks from the data tables themselves—especially for heavily used indexes on large tables. This is because the index data can be accessed in parallel with the table data pages, so that while the index is accessed by one transaction, another transaction can be accessing the data pages simultaneously. See Chapter 18, "Using and Tuning Indexes" for more on index tuning.

OLTP System Tuning

Tuning an OLTP system is like juggling several chainsaws blindfolded. You can do it, but you must be aware of everything going on in your system. It is generally advisable to begin your attack on one area that you suspect is a bottleneck. Make a change and gauge its effects, then change something else, and so on, until you are satisfied with the system's performance. Typically, once you alleviate the initial problem, you might notice another bottleneck that had been masked by the impact of the first bottleneck. Depending on the state of your system, the tuning process can involve several iterations through bottlenecks. Keep attacking them one at a time and you can bring your server to a fully tuned state. In this section, we examine the most common areas where OLTP performance tuning can help prevent and eliminate bottlenecks.

Processor Subsystem

The idea behind tuning processors is very simple—make sure your processor power is sufficient to support the amount of work requested in a timely manner. This topic is covered in detail in Chapter 4, "System Tuning," and Chapter 10, "Methods for Sizing a System." If you have already optimized your application (or if you cannot spend time optimizing code and need performance results immediately), then you are ready to determine whether you need more or faster CPUs. One of the most important things to remember is that multiple processors provide much better overall performance, even for a few users. This is because one thread can run per processor, so that work can be done in parallel across processors. Never have a database server with a single processor unless only one or a few users are accessing it. Use the rule from Chapter 4 which states that if you detect steady CPU use at 80 percent or higher, then your system would benefit from more or faster processors.

Memory Subsystem

In any environment, not just OLTP, optimizing memory utilization can go a long way toward improving system performance. Memory configuration also affects the behavior of other components of your system. For example, a small data cache that holds only a small percentage of the database data pages forces SQL Server to access the physical disks more frequently to retrieve data, which might produce an I/O bottleneck if your disk subsystem can't support the amount of I/O occurring. A good, simple rule is to throw as much memory at the problem as you can afford. If the physical memory in your system is as large as your data and indexes, then your entire database can be cached. This will give you the best data access speed possible. This is not a common practice, though, because balancing memory and physical disk accesses can provide excellent performance as well, and you don't have to spend an excessive amount of money on memory. If you have enough disks in the I/O subsystem, you can achieve low I/O latencies (quick I/O response times), providing quick data access. And disks are less expensive than memory.

If you add physical memory to your system, and you have SQL Server memory parameters set to the defaults, then SQL Server will expand its data cache to consume as much of the additional memory as it can. Chapter 4, "System Tuning," and Chapter 6, "Monitoring Performance with Windows 2000 System Monitor," contain more information on monitoring memory and data cache use.

Pinning Tables in Memory

SQL Server provides a technique called pinning a table to guarantee that once a table's data is read into the data cache, it remains there until the SQL Server is restarted. After data from the specified table is read into the data cache, SQL Server will not flush those pages from the cache. This does not mean that the entire table will be cached and remain in cache, only that the pages that are read into cache will not be flushed out. The rows in the table are not pinned until after the first access. In other words, they are not pre-read from disk and stored in memory. If you have small, frequently accessed tables, these might be good candidates for pinning. The following code provides examples of the SQL statements used to pin tables in memory:

```
SP_TABLEOPTION "STORE", "PINTABLE", TRUE
GO
SP_TABLEOPTION "REGION", "PINTABLE", TRUE
GO
```

Pinning tables is a powerful method for holding frequently accessed data in the data cache, but it comes with a cost. The data cache consumed by the pinned table(s) cannot be used for any other data. That memory is effectively off limits for reuse. If you were to pin a large table, you could consume excessive amounts (or even all) of the data cache and severely degrade performance. Use this option with caution.

Page-Level and Row-Level Locking

SQL Server 2000 allows you to specify the level of locking to use on your indexes. By default, SQL Server 2000 implements row-level locking. If a row-level lock cannot be acquired, SQL Server will attempt a page-level lock, and finally a table-level lock. The more locks acquired on an index or table, the more overhead incurred to manage those locks. Therefore, if many rows are being accessed on a page, having one page lock would incur less overhead than having many row locks. SQL Server converts many row locks or many page locks to a table lock if necessary to reduce lock management overhead, but row locks never escalate to a page lock. Depending on your application and stored procedures, you might want to have particular indexes that never allow page-level locks to be acquired, but instead acquire row-level locks. Note that with clustered indexes, the index locking level also affects the data pages, because they are the leaf nodes of the index. You can override SQL Server's default lock escalation behavior by disallowing row or page locks, or both, through the *sp_indexoption* stored procedure. You should only adjust locking behavior using *sp_indexoption* if you are certain that a particular type of lock is better for a certain index. For example, if there is a table with a clustered index whose data is usually accessed by one or a few rows at a time, then you can choose to disallow page-level locking, telling SQL Server to always use row-level locking. On the other hand, if many rows are accessed from the table that might be on the same page or pages, then it might be better to disallow row-level locking so SQL Server will first try page-level and then table-level locking.

With SQL Server 7.0 the only options for index locking were *AllowPageLocks* and *AllowRowLocks*. Those are still available in SQL Server 2000, but two others have been added—*DisAllowPageLocks* and *DisAllowRowLocks*—to make the logic a little clearer on what your value for the option is doing. The following code shows some examples of specifying lock escalation:

```
SP_INDEXOPTION "CUSTOMER_INDX", "DisAllowPageLocks", TRUE
GO
SP_INDEXOPTION "PRODUCT_INDX", "AllowRowLocks", TRUE
GO
```

The first example sets *DisAllowPageLocks* to TRUE for the index CUSTOMER_INDX, which instructs SQL Server not to attempt a page-level lock on that index. Thus, the order of lock escalation is row, then table level. The next example sets *AllowRowLocks* to TRUE for the index PRODUCT_INDX. (This is the default, so you would need to run this command only if you previously disallowed row locks for this index.) Thus, the lock escalation is row, page, then table-level locks. Again, use this option with caution.

I/O Subsystem

After the memory subsystem (or data cache), probably the most critical component of an OLTP system is the disk or I/O subsystem. Chapter 3, "Understanding the I/O Subsystem and RAID," discusses many concepts regarding I/O subsystem performance. For OLTP performance, the critical concepts are use of caching controllers and ensuring sufficient I/O capacity on the physical disk drives to support the amount of I/O requests made by your application.

One major area of concern is the I/O capacity of your physical drives. Different disk drives service I/O requests at different rates. An average disk drive can handle roughly 85 to 100 random reads and writes (or I/Os) per second. Your disk drives might be slower or faster. You can improve disk access by putting multiple physical drives in a RAID array. You should use System Monitor in the Performance console to determine the number of physical reads and writes your application is generating. Chapter 6 contains details and examples of how to capture this information.

Summary

In this chapter, we took a look at what makes up an OLTP system. All OLTP systems share general characteristics, and they are the most common type of system in use today. We also explored two-tiered and three-tiered OLTP architectures and design philosophies that will assist you in developing your OLTP environment. In addition, we looked at the major areas of concern in OLTP performance. The next chapter discusses tuning issues that arise with data warehouse systems.

Chapter 13
Data Warehouses

Data warehouses, which typically contain selected historical business data of an organization, are designed specifically to assist decision support systems and online analytical processing (OLAP) applications. This chapter compares data warehouses with online transaction processing (OLTP) systems, introduces OLAP concepts and Microsoft Analysis Services for data warehousing, and provides the foundation you need to begin planning your own data warehouse. It discusses designing a data warehouse, importing data from an OLTP system, and finally, techniques for tuning your system for the type of analytical queries that you run on these databases.

Comparing OLTP and Data Warehouse Systems

Data warehouse systems differ from OLTP systems in their goals and design. This section reviews the purposes and drawbacks of OLTP systems and then introduces the key elements and implementation challenges associated with data warehouses.

OLTP

OLTP systems focus on minimizing the work and duration of the individual transaction. An OLTP database is a complex schema of two-dimensional table structures and relationship rules that are unknown to end users and can challenge the architect. The data in an OLTP database is modified regularly, so successive OLTP queries for the same item might not return the same value. These characteristics—complex data structures and result sets that defy repetition—mean that reporting tools generate large, complex rules and requests that bring servers to a crawl due to the design of the relational database management system (RDBMS).

OLTP systems are not well-equipped to generate reports that can support timely decision-making based on business trends. For example, suppose someone in Marketing requires a report on total sales by region for May. The worker sends a request to IT, where it is added to a list of requests from other departments with dissimilar business requirements. Next, this simple English language request results in complex SQL queries that are difficult to understand and debug, and devour CPU and I/O system resources. Finally, because the OLTP database uses a locking mechanism to isolate transactions, the report and associated queries prevent accesses and updates to large quantities of data during the run, degrading the performance of other OLTP transactions. In short, generating complex reports from an OLTP database schema can prove difficult and slow.

Data Warehouses

Data warehouse systems were developed in response to the core problem of reporting against OLTP systems. A data warehouse typically contains selected historical business data of an organization. Unlike data in an OLTP system, data in the data warehouse is not modified or deleted. Instead it is drawn from the source OLTP system, transformed and summarized, then appended to the data warehouse as necessary. Because there are no data updates or deletes, reports return consistent values. Because its data is historical, and not constantly updated, the data warehouse can generate massive record counts very quickly.

Data warehouses do have their drawbacks. Obviously, a database with insert-only properties can grow far beyond its source OLTP in size. The growth of the core data is further exaggerated by the pre-aggregation of certain data according to specific reporting needs. (For example, where it is common to request the daily sum of transactions for a specific product in a particular town, you can dramatically improve system performance by pre-aggregating the number of transactions per product by town.) Storing the aggregations can result in nearly exponential growth over the original data—known as *data explosion*. The actual growth rate is a function of the number of dimensions, the number of levels in the hierarchies, and the total number of parent-to-child relationships.

Another challenge in building a data warehouse arises from the necessary duplication of data from the source database, and the resulting strain on hardware budgets to provide the storage space. Additional problems involve poor indexing support from the primary vendors—a traditional binary tree implementation is typically very inefficient in a dimensional system.

Because of the vast amounts of data, heavy CPU requirements for aggregation, and unpredictable query plans involved, implementing a data warehouse presents a challenge to nearly every component of the traditional RDBMS, from the hardware and software to the IT staff who manage it. Nevertheless, a well-designed data warehouse can greatly improve the reporting and analysis capabilities of your business, providing you with data to make better decisions for future growth.

Analyzing Data Warehouse Data

Data stored in data warehouses is typically analyzed using OLAP applications, which are specifically designed to analyze and generate reports on historical data.

OLAP

The term online analytical processing, or OLAP, was coined in 1993 by Dr. E. F. Codd to describe a system to integrate the otherwise distinctly different functions of OLTP and decision support systems (DSS). An OLAP server takes advantage of the multi-dimensional and read-only nature of historical data and uses a specialized bitmapped index to locate data faster. Where an OLTP system consists of many small, concurrent transactions, an OLAP system consists of only one updating transaction per period, during which new rows are appended to the database. Because the single transaction is inserting data, not updating, the transformation process is transparent to the end user and has little or no effect on concurrency.

The OLAP server takes advantage of the multi-dimensional design of the data in that, when it is queried, its result set is not a series of rows and columns, as in an RDBMS, but a collection of attributes and measures aligned on a series of axes. This can be represented graphically as a three-dimensional cube. Three primary storage mechanisms are associated with these cubes: relational OLAP (ROLAP), hybrid OLAP (HOLAP) and multidimensional OLAP (MOLAP). For information on how to choose which storage mechanism is right for your organization, see the "Storage Design Issues" section later in this chapter.

Data Warehousing Tools

To support the data warehousing industry, Microsoft offers the Data Warehousing Framework, a wide range of tools that encompasses Data Transformation Services (DTS), the Microsoft Repository, and Analysis Services (formerly known as OLAP Services). Most of the Data Warehousing Framework is included with the SQL Server RDBMS with no extra cost or licensing requirements. One of the framework's most important features is that the use of HOLAP, ROLAP, or MOLAP is completely transparent to the end user. This unrivaled ease of use feature allows the administrator to provide the solutions that best fit the business needs and budget.

Designing a Data Warehouse

The basic components of a data warehouse are fact tables and dimension tables. These components can be used in different designs, such as the star schema and snowflake schema. This section provides examples of each.

Tables and Schemas

Fact tables are a central table that hold business data measures, and dimension tables are satellite tables that define the dimensional properties of that data. Along with the table and schema design, you'll need to make decisions about your OLAP storage mechanism and the design of your cubes.

Fact Tables

Fact tables are tables in a data warehouse that define business data *measures*. Facts contain value information for a specific event, or transaction, such as a bank deposit, a product sale, or an order. A fact table typically holds numeric rather than character data. For example, it might contain such fields as RegionID, SalespersonID, ItemID, and CustomerID. A fact table has many foreign keys that correspond to the dimension tables, described in the next section. Figure 13-1 shows a fact table for an example customer and sales data warehouse.

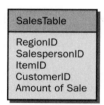

Figure 13-1. *A sample fact table.*

The fact tables hold the majority of important information in the data warehouse. Therefore, they make up the bulk of the database in terms of both size and activity. As you might imagine, a typical fact table could consist of millions, or even billions, of records and consume over a terabyte of disk space.

Dimension Tables

Dimension tables are used to refine the data contained in the fact table, or to describe it in more detail. The data is typically character data. Where a fact table has such fields as RegionID, SalespersonID, ItemID, and CustomerID, the dimension tables hold information such as the region name, salesperson name, the item description, and customer names and addresses. An example of a dimension table that stores detailed customer information is shown in Figure 13-2. Each dimension table stores rows of data with character information that describes the corresponding fields in the fact table in more detail.

Figure 13-2. *A sample dimension table.*

The relationship of the two tables necessitates foreign key constraints from the fact tables on the dimension tables. For example, you would not want a customer ID to be allowed into the fact table if there were no corresponding row for that customer (with the customer name, address, phone number, etc.) in a dimension table. A foreign key constraint in this case ensures that no customer ID values exist in the fact table but not in the dimension table.

By separating detailed information from the fact tables, you reduce the amount of data that must be scanned in the fact table, thus improving query performance. Unlike data in fact tables, the data in dimension tables might need to be updated at times, such as when a customer address changes; but it will have to be changed in only one place—the dimension table—rather than in the many rows of the fact table where that customer ID might exist. An additional benefit of segregating descriptive information from fact information is that more fact records can exist in a single data page, reducing I/O requirements overall.

Dimension tables are smaller and have fewer rows of data relative to the fact table—usually a few hundred or even a few thousand members, as compared with millions of facts. A dimension table holds only one row of data per customer, for example, where the fact table might have many rows of data that record various transactions for that same customer ID. Now let's take a look at the two most efficient database schemas for data warehouses and see how the fact and dimension tables are related in each one.

Star Schema

The *star schema* is the most popular design technique for data warehouses. This schema consists of a single fact table surrounded by multiple dimension tables that hold denormalized data describing the facts in the fact table. Each of the dimension tables has a field that corresponds to a field in the fact table. Figure 13-3 on the following page shows a sample star schema for a sales scenario. The CustomerID field in the *SalesTable* fact table has a corresponding customer ID field in the *CustomerTable* dimension table. Similar corresponding field relationships exist for the RegionID, SalespersonID, and ItemID fields in the fact and dimension tables. Fields in the fact table that link to a dimension table are referred to as *dimensional keys*. If you imagine a fact table surrounded by dimension tables, as in this figure, you can see how it resembles a star.

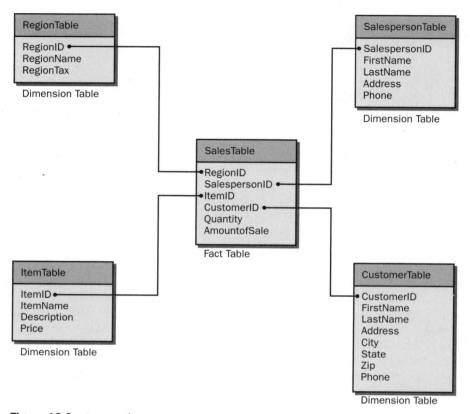

Figure 13-3. *A star schema.*

Snowflake Schema

A *snowflake schema* is a variation of the star schema. It involves dimension tables that join to other dimension tables before being joined to the fact table. The schema thus resembles a snowflake, as shown in Figure 13-4. This schema could involve more than one layer of dimension table joins before joining to the fact table. Snowflake schemas are often the result of normalization attempts. In general, practice has shown that snowflaking provides little performance improvement and can complicate the conceptual data design, hiding potential problem areas. The type of schema implemented, star or snowflake, is usually a function of the architect's style and familiarity with the source data. In cases where the person designing the OLAP database was also the one who designed the OLTP database, it might be difficult to visualize a flattened design.

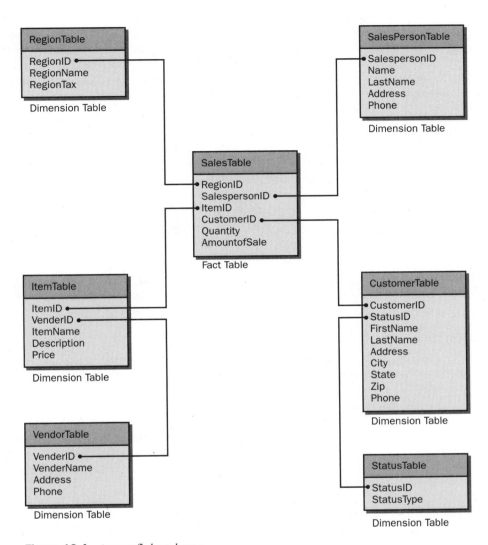

Figure 13-4. *A snowflake schema.*

Table Design Issues

The following discussion of complex table design issues includes information on features specific to Analysis Services, the Data Warehousing Framework component that you can use to access data in your data warehouse.

Ragged or Unbalanced Hierarchies

SQL Server 2000's Analysis Services is the first version to allow ragged and unbalanced hierarchies. A ragged hierarchy is generated when the logical parent member of at least one member is not in the level immediately above the member. This can cause branches of the hierarchy to descend to different levels. For example, consider a region dimension defined by the levels Country, State, City, and Zip. Data from the United States fits nicely into this model because there are states in the country, cities in the states, and zip codes in the cities. Many European countries, however, do not have states. Because there are no state entities for the parent country, we have generated a ragged hierarchy.

An unbalanced hierarchy is generated when a member might or might not have children, based solely on its value. This often results from merging business requirements to satisfy the entire enterprise. For example, consider an organization chart in individual business units, where the business units have different numbers of management levels. While one unit has four levels of management, another might have twelve. The result can be very difficult to model in a star schema.

Ragged and unbalanced hierarchies challenge system performance, data load times, and data accuracy. Although SQL Server 2000 Analysis Services allows them, you might still want to consider eliminating them whenever possible. One simple solution to a ragged hierarchy is to repeat the parent member in the child. That is, in the region example above, reuse the country name in the state. You then have at least one child member per parent, which dramatically reduces the complexity of the system.

Sparse Data

SQL Server 2000's Analysis Services offers a way to handle sparse data. For example, suppose your company sells heaters, has several offices including one in Arizona, and sells products in all offices throughout the year. It is unlikely that your Arizona office will sell many heaters in Arizona in August. Now imagine a physical representation of a cube. Even if there is no value in a given coordinate, the coordinate does still exist. SQL Server is unique in the market in that it will not store any data at that coordinate. In fact, the missing coordinates are assumed to have a 0 value for aggregation purposes, and the next valued coordinate is referenced. This dramatically reduces the amount of disk space SQL Server consumes, compared to competing products.

Semi-Additive Measures

In modeling, we assume constants in the world. Data warehouse design must take into account *semi-additive measures*—that is, cases when specific attributes of a measure do not aggregate evenly across the other attributes. This is most common when a measure is a count based on a time snapshot.

For example, imagine a fact table summarizing orders. Our target application might not require detailed transactional data, but instead looks only for the quantity of items sold each hour, the number of customers involved in the sales, and the associated revenue markers. In this case, the customer count is semi-additive—it does not sum across all products for the same period. During hour x, five units of item A were sold to three customers. During the same period, 10 units of item B were sold to eight customers. A summed aggregation for all products during that period would mislead you into thinking there were 11 customers during that period, when in fact, of the eight customers that purchased item B, three also purchased item A. This example shows how a key trend indicator can be completely misrepresented.

In such a situation, the most obvious and robust solution is to lower the granularity of the fact. That is, instead of designing a fact table using summary snapshots of a point in time, consider breaking the fact down to the transactional level and aggregating across the transactions. Now, when you want to know how many customers are involved in a sale of a given product over a given period, and the quantity sold, you can derive accurate information that illustrates the important trend that item A is only selling to customers who bought item B. This might even expose the cause for certain trends, such as a particular marketing effort.

Calculated Measures

When you design your data warehouse, you might want to take advantage of Analysis Services' support for calculated measures. A common use of a calculated measure is to determine the gross profit of a given sale. When that calculated measure is defined in the cube, it is available to clients as if it had been populated in the fact table directly.

A calculated measure can have a profound impact on the server, however, particularly in terms of the cube-building process. The calculated measure is itself not stored with the fact data. This can be a big I/O saving feature, particularly in ROLAP- and HOLAP-based solutions. In ROLAP and HOLAP implementations where I/O is an issue, calculated measures can mean the difference between success and failure. (Generally speaking, MOLAP solutions do not share these concerns, because MOLAP can compress data.) See the "Storage Design Issues" section later in this chapter for more information on MOLAP, ROLAP, and HOLAP.

Note that the aggregation of the calculated measure *might* be stored. If Analysis Services determines a need to store the aggregation, the server must calculate each possible value for each fact record during the build process. In a ROLAP solution, Analysis Services inserts the aggregated values in a table on the target RDBMS. The HOLAP solution stores the aggregations in the compressed data store, dramatically reducing final disk space consumption. The biggest danger lies in processing extremely large cubes because build windows might quickly be threatened. In a fact table with 10,000,000 records, for example, calculating the distinct values for each record and the accompanying explosion of possible aggregations would challenge any server.

If you are using MOLAP, you might want to provide for the physical storage whenever possible. One solution would be to use a calculated column in the star schema on the relational database. When it builds the fact definition in the cube, Analysis Services interprets the referenced column as a physical value and stores it as such. Because the cube data is compressed, the storage of the value does not generate a significant impact on the final disk consumption. At the same time, the use of a calculated column that is not indexed in SQL Server will not consume any RDBMS disk space, as the values are not stored. So you avoid all but the most extreme disk consumption concerns while reducing window requirements for the cube build process.

Storage Design Issues

As discussed earlier, an OLAP server's result set is a collection of attributes and measures aligned on a series of axes, and there are primary storage mechanisms associated with the resulting cubes: ROLAP, HOLAP and MOLAP. This section presents the advantages and disadvantages of each of these mechanisms to help you determine which would be most appropriate to your organization's requirements.

MOLAP

MOLAP, or Multi-dimensional Online Analytical Processing, is the most common OLAP storage mechanism. It consists of a data store in which the fact data and associated aggregations reside in a multi-dimensional file. New indexing strategies, including bitmap indexes, provide additional support for querying the multi-dimensional data. To reduce disk consumption, the resulting data is stored in a compressed form. Because the data is read only, compression does not negatively affect queries. Conversely, the compression might often speed query response times, as fewer read I/O requests are needed. The major disadvantages of MOLAP are that it is not well understood, and that historically it lacked broad reporting support.

ROLAP

ROLAP, or Relational Online Analytical Processing, does not use a separate multi-dimensional data store, but uses the relational database to store a two-dimensional representation of the multi-dimensional data. ROLAP defines additional tables outside the star schema in which the pre-aggregations are stored to assist in reducing query efforts. The relational data store allows users who are already familiar with the concepts to use any number of reporting tools against it. The disadvantages of ROLAP are that the relational data store either lacks many of the necessary mechanisms for providing high speed data access, or has inefficient versions of those mechanisms.

HOLAP

HOLAP, or Hybrid Online Analytical Processing, attempts to remedy the inherent inefficiencies of ROLAP while addressing the tool concerns associated with MOLAP. A HOLAP solution uses both the relational and the multi-dimensional data store. The star schema is stored in the RDBMS, but the pre-aggregated values are stored in the multi-dimensional data store. This allows the user to determine how the system is queried. With the multi-dimensional store, any requests that are not satisfied by the materialized aggregates are passed on to the RDBMS. The primary disadvantage here is that the query response times can differ significantly, based on the location from which the HOLAP system must retrieve the values.

Cube Design Issues

As discussed earlier, the result set from a query of an OLAP server is a collection of attributes and measures aligned on a series of axes that can be represented graphically as a three-dimensional cube.

Aggregation Design

An important consideration for cube design is the impact of the number of aggregations you select. The first impulse of nearly every new OLAP designer is to request 100 percent of aggregations, based on the assumption that all possible combinations of intersections have been pre-calculated, resulting in the highest possible client performance. While the logic is not completely flawed, problems arise as the cube definition begins to grow. Consider a fact with one measure and two dimensions, product and time, each consisting of a single level. The result is a possible eight aggregations. Adding just one measure causes the aggregation count to jump from eight to sixteen.

You can specify the number of aggregations Analysis Services should prepare, and they can be enforced based on total count or disk consumption. One source of confusion is determining which aggregations are stored. For example, if you requested 50 percent of aggregations, you would have no means of accurately predicting which aggregations would be stored.

But you do know that in a large system, it is unlikely that you will frequently require all possible aggregations. Probably you will need only a small percentage of aggregations at any given time. In fact, you might find that certain required aggregations are sensitive to specific periods. That is, some aggregations might be needed only once a year. During that period when they are needed, however, the frequency of requests might indicate that you should include them in your storage for that period.

Further, you might find that the typical end user can tolerate a 20-second response time. The company president, however, cannot tolerate greater than sub-second responses and the vice presidents are willing only to tolerate 5-second response times. Analysis Services stores a history of queries against the cube in the query log, which is a Microsoft Access database on the local server. Within the query log detail is the OLAP database, user name, time requested, time completed, and a numeric representation of the dimensional coordinates used to satisfy the query. After the OLAP database has seen some use, the log can provide valuable information regarding usage patterns.

Cube Partitions

Every cube consists of at least one partition, and in the Enterprise Edition of Analysis Services, each cube might have multiple partitions. Partitioning is based on the existence of distinct data requirements that are easily constrained. This is very similar to the concept of the partitioned view in SQL Server.

Additional partitions provide many benefits, including new opportunities for performance improvements. You can realize these by defining partitions on distinct logical drives, the definition of remote partitions which reside on other Analysis Services servers. Also you can specify aggregation designs that differ for each partition based upon data content, access patterns and available I/O.

Here's an example based on regional sales, or rather all sales for all agents in a given region. As Figure 13-5 shows, a company with four regions defines a cube based on four partitions. The east region might have distinct, unique access paths from those of the north, south, and west regions. By segregating the partition data, you can design each partition's aggregations for that region's usage patterns. While the north region seems to share similar access patterns with the south, the north might exhibit sharply lower tolerances for query response times than the south. Furthermore, the south and west regions use Oracle to store the source data for the cubes, the north region uses SQL Server, and the east region uses DB/2. You can easily address all these conditions using partitions.

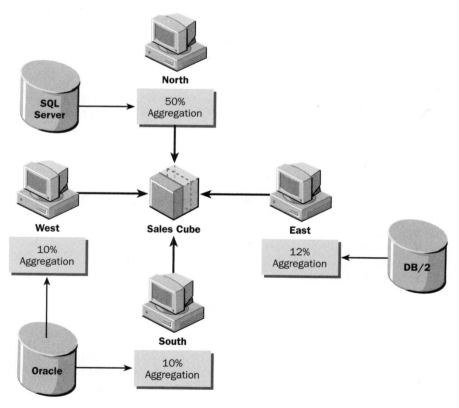

Figure 13-5. *Partitioned sales data.*

Because you can define a cube with partitions on multiple servers, you can use readily available commodity servers that meet business requirements of the day, rather than defining a single server to meet the requirements of a future two years away. This is a common theme in SQL Server 2000, and benefits you and your company because a project is easier to sell to management when you don't have to start the conversation with a request for a new $2 million server.

Configuring a Data Warehouse for Performance

This section looks at several areas that can affect the performance of your data warehouse system: the amount and type of hardware in the system, the choice of RAID levels, and the physical layout of your database. Chapter 3, "Understanding the I/O Subsystem and RAID," and Chapter 4, "System Tuning" discuss RAID levels and CPU, disk, and memory tuning in general. Here we focus on tuning issues specific to the data warehouse, based on the fact that a data warehouse consists of read-only data. We also look at issues specific to Analysis Services.

Hardware

In general, you must be sure that you have enough hardware for your data warehouse system so that it will run efficiently. Specifically, you need enough CPUs, disk drives, and memory. See Chapter 4 for details on how to tune an existing system for hardware. For details on sizing and capacity planning for a new system, see Part II, "Sizing and Capacity Planning."

Processors

In most cases, using multiple CPUs is preferable to having multiple servers composing the data warehouse system. While the data warehouse nearly always will benefit from the addition of CPUs, Analysis Services might not. In many cases, other server resource constraints (such as memory and disk drives) often severely tax an OLAP system long before the CPU is saturated. In a server where build times are excessive, multiple processors might help, but consider using remote partitions instead. Scaling the server out rather than up provides performance benefits to the users and the build process, increasing total system resources such as bus bandwidth.

While they do not always benefit Analysis Services, servers with multiple CPUs are particularly valuable for the data warehouse. The data warehouse might also benefit from SQL Server's parallel query feature, which allows a single query to be processed by more than one thread in parallel. IQP was introduced with SQL Server 7.0 specifically with the data warehouse in mind, and is substantially improved in SQL Server 2000. The additional support of index intersection capabilities blends well with IQP, because each processor can build a list of matching rows for each dimension member. After the list is complete, SQL Server simply performs a hash join to locate the common elements, using the result to perform the bookmark lookup.

Where SQL Server 2000 and Analysis Services reside on the same physical server, processor counts quickly become gating factors for system speed. During the build process, the server attempts to handle both user and build queries against SQL Server. When the query is fulfilled, Analysis Services attempts to process any calculations needed for aggregation. When the build process completes, Analysis Services compresses the data being stored. We don't recommend running both SQL Server and Analysis Services on a single physical machine if both server processes are being actively queried, or in a ROLAP or HOLAP solution. In a MOLAP solution, however, it's completely acceptable to use a local SQL Server database as a temporary data store for the star schema. If you do use SQL Server as a temporary storage mechanism, you might want to shut down the SQL Server service after the build process is complete, freeing valuable system resources.

Disks

The number of disk drives in a data warehouse system should be determined by I/O capacity. You need to have enough drives to spread the data across so that each disk drive is performing a low number of reads—much fewer than the I/O capacity for that disk. This allows your disks to perform quickly and provides room for growth. As your database grows, and more data must be read to complete queries, you should continually monitor your disk I/O rates and I/O latencies to determine at what point you might need to add disk drives to the system. If the disk drives exceed their I/O capacity, thus causing I/O requests to wait a long time in the I/O queue, you will see a decrease in performance.

Analysis Services has different disk requirements than the data warehouse. First, consider the location of the Analysis Services temporary file folder. In general, fault tolerance is not a concern here, so you might want to use RAID 0 to allow for the greatest write speed. The final data has no write requirements, however, with the exceptions of the write table for what-if analysis and during the build process, so you might consider using RAID 5 for the Data folder. The low cost of RAID 5 and read efficiency make it an excellent fit in most situations.

Memory

For system memory, the general rule is the more the better. In Analysis Services, memory is probably the single most important item. In a data warehouse, memory falls behind disk I/O in priority. However, the more memory you have to allocate to the SQL Server data cache, the better chance you have of finding needed pages in the cache. The cache hit ratio will probably never get up to the ideal value of 98 to 99 percent, as found in OLTP systems. It might be as low as 10 percent because of the nature of OLAP. One query might run only once a day; making it unlikely that the data for that query will be found in the cache. Other queries that follow that particular query might require totally different data pages, and so might not find their pages in the cache for the same reason. The cache-hit ratio might thus be lower for an OLAP than an OLTP system.

Optimizing the Query Log

Analysis Services can use the query log to make informed decisions about which aggregations to store based upon query history and any user-provided parameters, such as aggregations from queries that took longer than 30 seconds during the given date range. If you are willing to invest a little time, you can develop very powerful aggregation design criteria using complex multi-step processes and simple Access SQL statements. The query log collects only one out of every 10 requests by default however, which results in a somewhat random sampling of data, so the queries in the log might not accurately represent user access patterns. You can increase the frequency of log inserts to increase the accuracy of the sampling, but in high-demand environments, logging can seriously affect total server performance. When you change the log frequency, try to balance the degree of accuracy required with the impact of the logging on the server.

Summary

We have covered some basic concepts of data warehouses and OLAP in this chapter. We described the most popular techniques used in designing data warehouses—the star schema and the snowflake schema—and offered tips on how to optimize different areas of your system for the data warehouse and your OLAP cubes. The next chapter discusses how to optimize your data replication systems.

Chapter 14
Tuning Replicated Systems

Replication in Microsoft SQL Server 2000 is greatly improved over SQL Server 7.0. To make best use of this replication system, you must configure, monitor, and tune the replication components as well as the underlying SQL Server system. This chapter discusses how to design a replication system with performance in mind. We talk about how to use the Windows 2000 Performance console's System Monitor counters to monitor the SQL Server replication components, and explain what can be tuned and how to tune a system for replication.

Replication Overview

Microsoft SQL Server replication is based on the publish and subscribe metaphor. This metaphor uses the concept of publishers, distributors, and subscribers. A *publisher* is a database that makes data available for replication. A *distributor* is the server that contains the distribution database. The distribution database is used to store replication data. A *subscriber* is a server that receives replicated data and stores the replicated database.

The publisher distributes a *publication*, which is a collection of one or more articles. An *article* is data to be replicated; it can be an entire table, certain columns, or certain rows. The distribution can be either a push distribution or a pull distribution. A *push distribution* is one in which the data is pushed from the publisher regardless of whether a subscriber asks for it. A *pull distribution* is one in which the subscribers request data on a regular basis.

Types of Replication

SQL Server 2000 offers three different types of replication, which provide varying degrees of data consistency within the replicated database as well as different levels of overhead. The three types replication are snapshot, transactional, and merge.

Snapshot Replication

Snapshot replication is the simplest and most straightforward of the replication types and involves taking a picture, or snapshot, of the database and propagating it to the subscribers. The advantage of snapshot replication is that it does not involve continuous overhead on the publishers and subscribers. The disadvantage is that the database on the subscriber is current only to the point at which the snapshot was taken. In many cases this type of replication is sufficient and efficient, such as when the data in question is not modified and needs to be replicated only occasionally. You can easily handle applications such as phone lists, price lists, and item descriptions by snapshot replication because you can update these lists once per day during off hours.

Snapshot replication works through the Snapshot Agent, which takes a snapshot of the entire database. This snapshot is copied to the distributor and used later to create the subscribing database. This snapshot is usually used to create the initial database for transactional replication.

Transactional Replication

You can use transactional replication to replicate both tables and stored procedures. With *transactional replication* the changes made to articles are captured from the transaction log and propagated to the distributor, which later passes them on to the subscribers. Transactional replication makes it possible to keep the publisher and subscriber at almost exactly the same state and so is the best choice when it is important to keep all the replicated systems current.

Transactional replication works by reading the transaction log and replaying transactions that have been used to update, insert, or delete data from the database. Once a transaction has been logged in the transaction log, a log reader process copies the transaction into the distribution database. This log reader process either runs continually or on a regularly scheduled basis, depending on how you have configured transactional replication. Once the log reader has put the transactions into the distribution database, they are replayed on the subscribing systems; again, the frequency is based on how you have configured replication. Throughout this chapter we discuss how to configure replication for optimal performance.

Merge Replication

Merge replication is similar to transactional replication in that it keeps track of all the changes made to articles. Instead of propagating transaction changes, however, merge replication periodically transmits changes to the database. These changes can be batched and sent as necessary. Merge replication is designed to allow both the publisher and subscribers to make changes to the database. These changes eventually propagate to all subscribers to the merge replication; multiple systems can thus be kept synchronized.

Replication Tuning Basics

In general, tuning replication is the same as tuning any other type of SQL Server system, but replication systems do have some special performance attributes that you need to address. These attributes depend on the type of replication that you are doing and are addressed throughout this chapter. There are, however, some things you can do to improve replication systems in general.

- **Filter data to reduce the amount of published (replicated) data.** By reducing the replicated data, you can reduce network traffic and minimize the storage needed. The goal is to replicate the minimum amount of data necessary.

- **Separate log files.** Each database that is replicated should have its log files on a separate disk volume. This maximizes the performance of both the transaction log and replication. We address this topic in more detail in the "Tuning for Transactional Replication" section later in this chapter.

- **Run snapshots for snapshot and transactional replication at off-peak times.** Because snapshot replication uses many resources at once, careful scheduling is worthwhile to reduce its effect on the system.

- **Specify an optimal snapshot folder.** Depending on how often snapshots occur and how large they are, you might want to place the snapshot on a high performance I/O subsystem or store them on the publisher system.

- **Tune distribution based on need.** The distribution process should run as infrequently as possible. Distribution that is constantly running creates high overhead on the system.

These are just general guidelines for replication. As you will see later in this chapter, each replication type has its own specific tuning considerations.

The Distributor

Before getting into the various replication types, let's first look at the distributor. The distributor is a SQL Server that uses a database as a repository of replication data. This data is held in a SQL Server database for several reasons, among which are the following:

- **Performance** The job of the distributor is to acquire, hold, and then distribute data—a job description that fits SQL Server perfectly.

- **Reliability** SQL Server supports a high level of recoverability. By means of the transaction log, SQL Server can recover from system failures without losing any data.

- **Ease of use** SQL Server replication communicates directly with the distributor via SQL Server communications protocols; so setting up and configuring the distributor is easy with SQL Server Enterprise Manager.

Because the distributor uses a SQL Server database to process replication information, you must configure and tune the distribution database as you would any other SQL Server database. The default distribution configuration might work for smaller replication systems, but you probably want to configure the distributor manually based on the amount of work your specific system is doing.

In addition to the replication data that is stored in the distribution database, the distributor system might contain snapshot data. It is common to store the snapshot data on the distributor, but it is not a requirement. With SQL Server 2000, snapshot data can be stored on any network storage that can be accessed by the distributor.

Configuring the Distributor

The SQL Server Configure Publishing and Distribution Wizard does not place the SQL Server transaction log and data files optimally by default. We recommend that you do not choose the default location for the distribution database. Instead, manually configure the distribution database within the wizard. Depending on the frequency of modifications to your database, the amount of activity in the distributor can be quite high. Because the distributor uses a SQL Server database, all modifications to the distributor must be logged in its transaction log.

In addition, you can choose whether or not to place the snapshot folder on the distributor system. Although the distributor controls the snapshot, it is easy to set the snapshot location to another SQL Server. Configuring the snapshot location is covered in more detail in the next section.

Keeping these facts in mind, you should configure the distribution database and log to be large enough to perform the work required and fast enough to perform it efficiently. Here are a few guidelines for achieving these goals:

- Use a RAID controller on the distribution database system. If you use a hardware RAID controller, the fault-tolerance activities will be performed in hardware, which is more efficient than using software RAID.

- Configure the distribution database's transaction log on a RAID 1 volume. The transaction log should be isolated to allow for the higher performance that is achieved with sequential I/Os.

- Configure the transaction log to be large enough so that you don't have to constantly back it up. Depending on your needs, it might be possible to run all day without backing up the transaction log; you can then perform that task at night.

- Configure the distribution database on a RAID 1 or RAID 10 volume. RAID 5 is not appropriate because of the many writes to the distribution database.

- Configure the distribution database to be large enough to hold extra replication data. If a subscriber were to fail, you might have to hold several days' worth of replication data if you are using transactional or merge replication.

- Tune the distribution database as you would any other SQL Server database.

By correctly configuring the distribution database in the beginning you can avoid costly performance problems later.

Selecting the Snapshot Location

With SQL Server 2000 replication, you do not have to place the snapshot folder in any particular directory or even on the distributor. Typically the snapshot folder should be on the distributor, because that way the publisher has to make only one copy to the distributor, and then the distributor copies the snapshot to the subscribers. If snapshots are infrequent, however, and the subscribers are few, you might want to keep the snapshot on the publisher. This will reduce network traffic when the snapshot is created, but increase overhead on the publisher when multiple subscribers request the snapshot.

The snapshot will also run faster if you place it on the publisher. This will reduce the time that the locks are held on the database during the snapshot. If this is an issue, storing the snapshot locally might help. You are prompted to choose the snapshot location by the Configure Publishing and Distribution Wizard, as shown in Figure 14-1.

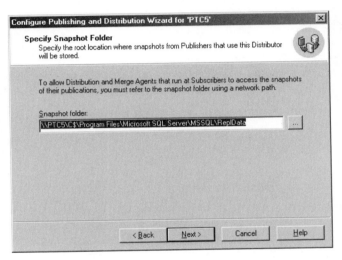

Figure 14-1. *The Specify Snapshot Folder page in the Configure Publishing and Distribution Wizard.*

Configuring the Distributor with Enterprise Manager

To configure the distributor using Enterprise Manager, use the Configure Publishing and Distribution Wizard to create publishing and distribution. On the Customize The Configuration page, click Yes so that you can set the distribution database name and location manually rather than accepting the defaults. You can enable publishing, create publications as well as subscribers, and specify where the distribution database resides on the Provide Distribution Database Information page, as shown in Figure 14-2 on the following page. By specifying this location you can configure the distribution database as recommended in the guidelines given earlier, which is the most important aspect for enhancing performance.

Unfortunately, you can set only the location of the distribution database, not its size, in the wizard. To modify the size of the distribution database, you must select that database in Enterprise Manager. If you prefer changing the location and size simultaneously, you can use the *sp_adddistributiondb* stored procedure.

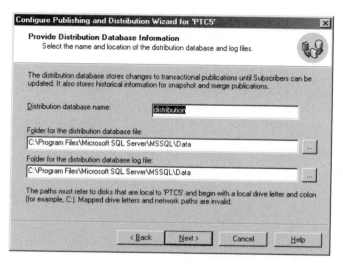

Figure 14-2. *Use the Provide Distribution Database Information page to set custom replication settings.*

Configuring the Distributor with *sp_adddistributiondb*

The system stored procedure *sp_adddistributiondb* allows you to create the distribution database by hand, which is useful when you want to specify the size and location of the database and its transaction log. Creating the distribution database via the stored procedure is also handy for reusability. Once you have created a script that creates the distribution database, you can use it on different systems or to recreate the distribution database in the event of a system reconfiguration.

> **Note** Before you can create the distribution database, you must create the distributor. You can do this using the system stored procedure *sp_adddistributor* with the distributor's system name as the parameter.

The syntax for the *sp_adddistributiondb* stored procedure is shown in SQL Server Books Online. The following example illustrates the process of creating a distribution database using stored procedures:

```
sp_adddistributor Dash
```

Executing this procedure initializes the system named Dash as a distributor. You can now create the distribution database and specify its properties as follows:

```
sp_adddistributiondb
@database=dist,
@data_folder='C:\SQLServer\Data',
@data_file='dist.mdf',
@data_file_size=10,
@log_folder='C:\SQLServer\Data',
@log_file='dist.ldf',
```

```
@log_file_size=2,
@min_distretention=0,
@max_distretention=72,
@history_retention=96,
@security_mode=0,
@login='sa',
@password='',
@createmode=0
```

This code creates the *dist* database, which uses the file C:\SQLServer\data\dist.mdf for the data file and C:\SQLServer\data\dist.ldf for the transaction log. The data file is 10 MB and the transaction log is 2 MB. The other parameters are self-explanatory. This method allows you to script creation of the distribution database and easily repeat the process as necessary.

Monitoring the Distributor

You monitor the distributor using System Monitor in the Windows 2000 Performance console. SQL Server adds a number of objects to the Performance console when SQL Server replication is present. These objects are discussed in subsequent sections on the specific types of replication.

The most important object to monitor in the case of the distributor is the SQLServer: Replication Dist. object. This object provides the following counters:

- **Dist: Delivered Cmds/sec** The number of commands per second delivered to the subscriber. This value gives you a good idea of how much replicated data is being sent to the subscriber.

- **Dist: Delivered Trans/sec** The number of transactions per second delivered to the subscriber—another value that indicates how much replicated data is being sent to the subscriber.

- **Dist: Delivery Latency** The average amount of time between when a transaction is delivered to the distributor and when it is applied to the subscriber. This value can give you some insight into how backed up the distributor is.

Although these counters give you some indication of how the distribution process itself is doing, tuning the distributor really comes down to tuning the SQL Server database. Things to look for on the distributor include the following:

- **High CPU usage** Are one or more CPUs running at high rates (greater than 75 percent) for long periods of time?

- **I/O bottlenecks** Are I/O rates too high? Look for I/Os per second and seconds per I/O in System Monitor, as described in Chapter 6, "Monitoring Performance with Windows 2000 System Monitor." Do not exceed recommended I/Os per disk drive and beware of I/O latencies that are too high.

- **SQL Server problems** Are SQL Server response times too high? You can determine this by running test queries against the distribution database and monitoring response times.

The distributor is a key component in the replication system and should be well tuned. The next section provides some tips on how to do this.

Tuning the Distributor

As mentioned earlier, you tune the distributor in basically the same manner as any other SQL Server system, for the most part. However, there are a few differences that you should keep in mind. When snapshot replication is running (including the initial snapshot for other replication types), a large number of I/Os will occur at one time. Because so much data is being written to the distributor, the I/O subsystem might become overloaded. This will increase the time it takes to perform the snapshot, so it is a good idea to monitor the system during the snapshot.

You can enhance performance of the distributor with proper sizing, although as you have seen in Chapters 8 through 11 of Part II, "Sizing and Capacity Planning," sizing is not always an easy task. It generally is a good idea to give the distributor a little extra capacity. The distributor is the link between the publishers and the subscribers; therefore, you should carefully configure it so that it is not a bottleneck. Here are some tips for tuning the distributor:

- Tune the I/O subsystem. The distributor requires sufficient I/O performance capacity, just as any other SQL Server system.

- CPU power is not usually a problem. In most cases the types of operations a distributor performs are not extremely CPU intensive. It is, however, advisable to use a multiprocessor system with at least two CPUs to allow concurrent operations to take place.

- Tune Windows 2000. Typically, not much Windows 2000 tuning is necessary. However, there are a few things you can do, such as to configure the Server service to maximize throughput for network applications. Doing so will set the memory system to favor applications over file services. (To configure the Server service, right-click the connection in the Network and Dial-up Connections dialog box, and choose Properties.) Also, remove any services that won't be used, such as Internet Information Services (IIS) and File Transfer Protocol (FTP) services.

- Tune SQL Server, using the techniques and guidelines given within this book.

By properly configuring and tuning the distributor, you can enhance replication.

Tuning for Snapshot Replication

Snapshot replication differs from the other replication methods in that the entire task of replication takes place at once. With transactional and merge replication, an initial snapshot is propagated to the subscribers and then replication is constantly applied to those systems. Snapshot replication is a full refresh of the database and is therefore much more straightforward. This section shows you how to configure and tune a snapshot replication system for excellent performance.

Attributes of Snapshot Replication

Because snapshot replication copies an existing database and propagates it to the distributor and then to the subscriber, the limiting performance factor is the system's ability to move large amounts of data. Factors that can limit this ability include the following:

- **I/O performance on the publisher** Because the database (either in whole or in part) is copied from the publisher, the performance of the I/O subsystem on the publisher can be a limiting factor. The snapshot task is more I/O intensive than CPU intensive; so CPU power is not usually a factor.

> **Note** If the I/O capacity is available, you might want to leave the database snapshot on the publisher itself. This will reduce the network overhead associated with copying the snapshot to the distributor. However, we recommend this only when there is sufficient I/O bandwidth such that the performance of the publisher is not adversely affected.

- **I/O performance on the distributor** The distributor receives large amounts of data at one time, and later distributes that data. A slow I/O subsystem here will bog down snapshot replication.

- **I/O performance on the subscriber** The distributor attempts to distribute a database or subset of a database to the subscriber in one shot. If the I/O subsystem is inadequate, replication performance will suffer.

- **The bandwidth of the network connecting the publisher, distributor, and subscriber** Because large amounts of data are transferred, the network can easily become a bottleneck. This is especially true if you perform replication over a WAN. If the network is a problem, your alternatives are to suffer the performance degradation or upgrade your network. Running snapshots only at off hours can minimize this problem.

Properly sizing and configuring the snapshot replication system can reduce the effect of these factors and improve performance. This involves properly configuring and sizing the publisher, the distributor, the snapshot location, and the subscriber(s).

Configuring for Snapshot Replication

As you have just seen, it is important to configure the publisher, distributor, and subscriber with sufficient I/O capacity to absorb the load of the replication. Because the snapshot is distributed as a data file rather than as commands that have been generated from within the database, it is not necessary to tune SQL Server on the distributor for snapshot replication. When the snapshot is generated, the data is extracted from the database and a snapshot file is created. This file is stored (either on the distributor or in the location you specified during configuration) as a normal Windows NT or Windows 2000 file external to the distribution database; the distributor is used only to keep track of the snapshot file, not to store it. Thus the overhead on the distribution database during snapshot replication is very low.

You can specify some configuration choices that make a great deal of difference to the performance of snapshot replication. Here are some guidelines for configuring snapshot replication:

- Configure sufficient I/O capacity on the publisher, distributor, and subscriber.
- Configure the distributor to keep the snapshot on the publisher system.
- Configure the distributor and publisher to reside on the same system.
- Increase the number of bulk copy program (BCP) threads.

Let's look at each of these configuration guidelines in more detail.

Configure Sufficient I/O

Because a large amount of data is copied at one time, a slow disk subsystem slows the entire replication process. Thus, you should enhance the performance of the I/O subsystem. As with any SQL Server system, the transaction log should be located on its own RAID 1 volume for data protection. The data files should be located on one or more RAID 10 or RAID 5 volumes. The RAID level that you use depends on whether you are configuring the publisher, the distributor, or the subscriber.

Configuring the I/O Subsystem on the Publisher

Whether you should use RAID 5 or RAID 10 for the data files on the publisher depends on the read and write ratio of that data volume. As mentioned in Chapter 3, "Understanding the I/O Subsystem and RAID," any disk volume that experiences more than 10 percent writes is not a good candidate for RAID 5 because of the excessive overhead associated with RAID 5 writes. Such a disk volume should use RAID 10 instead. To determine whether you can use RAID 5, monitor the system and track the number of writes versus reads. In either case, the I/O subsystem should be properly sized as outlined in Part II, "Sizing and Capacity Planning."

Configuring the I/O Subsystem on the Distributor

Because the snapshot actually stores a file on the distributor for snapshot replication rather than using the SQL Server database, you must make sure that the snapshot location has enough I/O capacity to absorb a large number of writes. Thus, the snapshot location is better suited for RAID 10 than for RAID 5. As you will see later in this section, in some cases locating the snapshot on the publisher might be more efficient.

Configuring the I/O Subsystem on the Subscriber

The subscriber experiences a large number of writes during snapshot replication. If the database is large, this can take a significant amount of time. You can enhance the performance of the snapshot by using a RAID 10 volume rather than RAID 5, because RAID 5 performs poorly for large numbers of writes.

Note When configuring the I/O subsystems for snapshot replication, consider the size of the database. A snapshot replication that replicates only a few hundred rows and takes only a few seconds can easily work on any RAID level.

Set the Snapshot Location

Because snapshot replication copies the entire article to the distributor and then copies it to the subscriber later, it is possible to remove the distribution system from the replication process. The distributor is still used, but you can configure it to store the snapshot on the publisher. This cuts down on network activity.

You can use the Configure Publishing and Distribution Wizard to set the snapshot location. This was shown previously in Figure 14-1. Once the publication has been created you can change the snapshot location on each publication within the Create and Manage Publications dialog box, as shown in Figure 14-3. First open the Create and Manage Publications dialog box by clicking Tools, pointing to Replication, and clicking Create and Manage Publications.

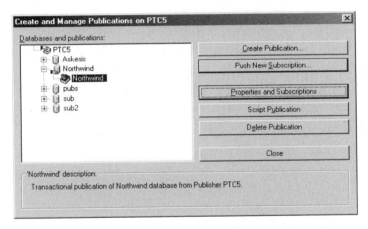

Figure 14-3. *The Create and Manage Publications dialog box.*

After you select the publication in the Databases and Publications tree, the Properties and Subscriptions button becomes available. Click the Properties and Subscriptions button to open the Publication Properties dialog box, as shown in Figure 14-4 on the following page.

Within the Publication Properties dialog box, click the Snapshot Location tab, as shown in Figure 14-5 on the following page. This tab allows you to select a new snapshot location for an existing publication. Unlike SQL Server 7.0, where all publications had to use the same snapshot location, SQL Server 2000 replication allows each publication to have a different snapshot location.

This setting allows you to tune each individual publication for optimal performance and flexibility. After you select the Generate Snapshots In The Following Location check box, you'll see a warning if you have set replication to accept SQL Server 7.0 systems. The ability to use a different snapshot location per publication is a SQL Server 2000 feature and is not compatible with SQL Server 7.0.

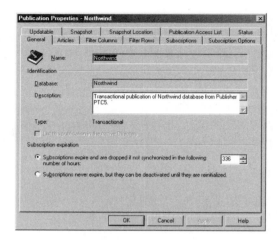

Figure 14-4. *The Publication Properties dialog box.*

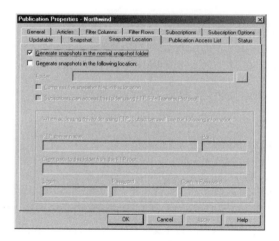

Figure 14-5. *Use the Publication Properties dialog box to change the snapshot location.*

Configure the Distributor and Publisher on the Same System

When all you are doing is snapshot replication, you can easily configure the publisher and distributor to be on the same system. This cuts down on network traffic because no extra network data needs to be sent to the distributor. If performance on the publisher is an issue, however, you are better off keeping the snapshot on a remote distributor and letting the distributor handle the distribution overhead.

Increase BCP Threads

You can also enhance performance by increasing the number of BCP threads that are used for the snapshot process. You can do this through Enterprise Manager. In the console tree under the server you want, expand the Replication Monitor folder, the Agents folder, and then select the Snapshot Agents folder. In the right-hand pane, right-click the publication you want and select Agent Profiles on the shortcut menu. This opens the Snapshot Agent Profiles dialog box, as shown in Figure 14-6.

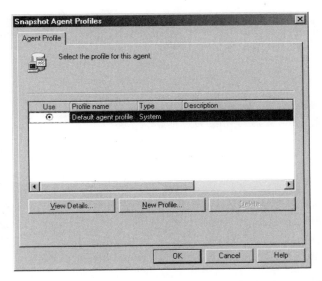

Figure 14-6. *The Snapshot Agent Profiles dialog box can be used to create a new profile.*

In the Snapshot Agent Profiles dialog box, click New Profile. This opens the Replication Agent Profile Details dialog box and creates a copy of the agent profile, which you can then modify. You can increase the value of the *MaxBcpThreads* parameter, as shown in Figure 14-7 on the following page. Once you have made your changes, name the profile and click OK. This saves the profile; you then select that profile in the Snapshot Agent Profiles dialog box for use in snapshot replication.

After you configure your system for snapshot replication, you can begin to monitor it, and further tune the system as necessary.

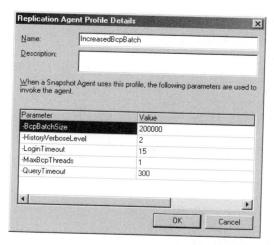

Figure 14-7. *The Replication Agent Profile Details dialog box.*

Monitoring the Snapshot System

You monitor the snapshot system using System Monitor, with the following performance objects and counters:

- **SQLServer:Replication Agents:Running** This object displays a count of each type of agent that is running.
- **SQLServer:Replication Snapshot** This object provides counters for the number of commands and the number of transactions per second delivered to the distributor.
- **PhysicalDisk** The counters under this object are very useful, because many performance problems with snapshot replication are I/O-related.
- **Processor** This object provides information on the system processors.
- **System** This object gives you a good overview of the entire system.

These performance objects and counters will give you a fairly good idea of how things are going, but snapshot replication can occur very quickly, so don't blink. Things to watch for include the following:

- **I/O bottlenecks** Are I/O rates too high? Look for I/Os per second and seconds per I/O. Follow the guidelines in Chapter 3 and throughout Part II, "Sizing and Capacity Planning," to determine what is too high.
- **Network bottlenecks** It is difficult to find a network bottleneck, but you might be able to determine if you have one by calculating the network throughput and comparing that with the snapshot replication time.

By looking for I/O and network problems and solving them if they exist you can improve the performance of snapshot replication.

Tuning the Snapshot System

Tuning the snapshot system usually just involves proper configuration. The critical things to look for during snapshot replication are I/O and network problems. To determine if you are network bound, you should look at the performance of the network and then determine if that network is sufficient for your replication needs. Here's an example.

Suppose you have a database that is 5 GB. In a 10BaseT network, there is a maximum bandwidth of 10 megabits per second, which is approximately 1 MB per second. Thus replicating this database will take the following amount of time:

*[5 GB * 1024 (MB/GB)] / 1 (MB/sec) = 5120 seconds, or 1.4 hours*

In contrast, a 100BaseT network can perform the same replication in 8.3 minutes. A Gigabit Ethernet network can do this same task in 51 seconds. The network comparison is summarized in Table 14-1.

Table 14-1. Comparison of Performance Times for Snapshot Replication with Various Network Speeds

Network Speed	Time (for 5-GB database)
10BaseT	5120 seconds (85.3 minutes, or 1.4 hours)
100BaseT	516 seconds (8.3 minutes)
Gigabit Ethernet	51 seconds

As you can see, the size of your network really does count. By performing calculations like this you can get a good idea of how fast the replication should be. If these tasks take much longer, you probably have a bottleneck somewhere else. How to find and solve these bottlenecks is covered in various chapters and sections throughout this book.

Tuning for Transactional Replication

Transactional replication differs from snapshot replication in that each transaction is replicated from the publisher to the distributor and then to the subscriber. The Log Reader Agent reads the transaction log, as described in the next section. Transactional replication is initially set up using a snapshot, as in snapshot replication; however, once this snapshot has been created, replication is continuous.

Attributes of Transactional Replication

Transactional replication starts with a snapshot that is copied to the distributor and then to the subscriber. Once the snapshot has been completed, the Log Reader Agent reads the transaction log of the publisher either on a continual basis or on a regular schedule, depending on how you configure the Log Reader Agent.

On the publisher the only additional overhead comes from the reads being performed on the transaction log. The Log Reader Agent itself runs on the distributor and connects to the publisher to read the transaction log. These transactions are then placed into the distribution database on the distributor and are eventually sent to the subscribers. Factors that can limit transactional replication include the following:

- **I/O performance on the publisher's transaction log** The transaction log on the publisher is read to determine what changes have been made to the database. Because the transaction log is now being read as well as being written, the sequential nature of the transaction log might be disrupted. This might cause a bottleneck if the I/O subsystem is not carefully configured.

- **Performance of the distributor** Depending on how much replication is being done and how many publishers are using the distributor, there might be a performance problem at the distributor. Earlier, in the "Configuring the Distributor" section, you learned how to configure and tune the distributor; that information applies here.

- **Performance of the subscriber** Depending on what is occurring on the subscriber, there might be a performance problem here. If this happens, you need to tune your SQL Server in the usual way.

Reducing the effect of these factors through proper sizing and configuration of the systems involved will improve performance.

Configuring for Transactional Replication

Tuning the publisher, distributor, and subscriber mainly involves proper configuration of these component's I/O subsystems. There are, however, some configuration choices that can make a great deal of difference for the performance of transactional replication. Here are some guidelines.

- Configure sufficient I/O capacity, following general I/O capacity guidelines. In addition, some specific I/O changes should be available on the publisher because of the added overhead it experiences.

- Tune the commit batch size on the distributor.

- Tune the Log Reader Agent.

Next we discuss each of these configuration guidelines.

Configure Sufficient I/O

You can enhance the performance of the entire replication process by configuring sufficient I/O capacity. As with any SQL Server system, the transaction log should be located on its own RAID 1 volume for data protection. The data files should be located on one or more RAID 10 volumes (it is rare that RAID 5 is appropriate). Unlike in snapshot replication, there are only minor I/O considerations for the publisher, distributor, and subscriber in transactional replication. Those considerations are described here.

Configuring the I/O Subsystem on the Publisher

In general the publisher should follow normal SQL Server configuration guidelines as described throughout this book. In addition, you might need to increase the I/O capacity of the transaction log. Normally we recommend that the transaction log be configured on a RAID 1 volume. If necessary, depending on how busy your system is, you might need to use more disk drives in a RAID 10 volume. RAID 5 is not appropriate for the transaction log.

Configuring the I/O Subsystem on the Distributor

The distributor should be configured so that the distribution database has its transaction log on a dedicated RAID 1 disk volume. This allows the distribution database to achieve maximum transaction log performance, improving the overall performance of the distributor.

Configuring the I/O Subsystem on the Subscriber

Transaction replication does not call for any special I/O configuration on the subscriber. Simply follow general sizing and configuration guidelines as described throughout this book.

Tune the Commit Batch Size on the Distributor

The commit batch size on the distributor determines how many replication transactions are committed in a single batch. While the distribution database is updated, locks are held on the distribution tables. Increasing the batch size allows more rows to be committed at a time, thus increasing the time that locks on those rows are held. Decreasing the batch size means fewer rows will be committed at a time, thus decreasing the time that the locks on those rows are held and giving other processes a chance to access the distribution database.

The commit batch size lets you make a trade-off. If you use a smaller batch size, locks are held for shorter times but occur more often. A larger commit batch size is more efficient because more rows are committed at a time, but the total lock time is increased. For example, if the batch size is small you might have to allocate 10 locks for 1 ms each. A much larger commit size might allow you to do the entire commit in 7 ms. The cumulative lock time is much longer, but the time that an individual lock is held is much shorter.

If there is a large amount of activity on the distribution database from several different sources (that is, the publisher and several subscribers), you might want to try reducing the batch size. If the Log Reader Agent is running on a periodic schedule and has a lot of transactions to insert into the distribution database, you might benefit from a larger batch size. There might actually be no need to change it, but if you do, compare the results of both increasing and decreasing the batch size to determine which is better.

You can configure the commit batch size through Enterprise Manager. Expand the Replication Monitor folder, then Agents, and then the Distribution Agents folder within the console tree in Enterprise Manager. Right-click the appropriate Distribution Agent and click Agent Profiles on the shortcut menu. This opens the Distribution Agent Profiles dialog box, as shown in Figure 14-8 on the following page.

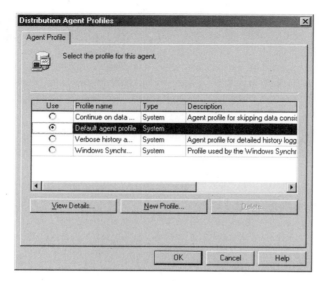

Figure 14-8. *The Distribution Agent Profiles dialog box is used to create a new profile.*

In this dialog box, select a profile and click New Profile. This opens the Replication Agent Profile Details dialog box and creates a new distribution agent profile, which you can modify. Before you can save this profile you must name it. Pick something descriptive so that you can easily remember why you created this profile. You can change the *CommitBatchSize* parameter in the dialog box, as shown in Figure 14-9. Once you have made your changes and named the profile, click OK. This saves the profile; you then select that profile from the Distribution Agent Profiles dialog box for use in transactional replication.

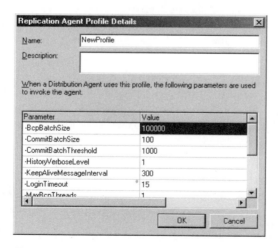

Figure 14-9. *The Replication Agent Profile Details dialog box.*

Tune the Log Reader

By configuring the log reader you might be able to reduce its effect on the publisher's transaction log, although the Log Reader Agent is rarely a performance problem. There are several ways to make the log reader process more efficient. One way is to use a caching controller for the log drive volume. Because the Log Reader Agent reads from the log drive, a cache on a controller allows the read from the cache, rather than causing a random I/O.

Another way to tune the log reader is to modify the frequency with which it runs. The log reader can run on a continuous basis or periodically. You configure the periodic frequency of the Log Reader Agent through the polling interval setting. On a system that is not experiencing a lot of update activity, you might want the log reader to run continuously; but on systems in which the transaction log is busy, configuring the log reader to run less frequently can improve performance of the publisher. This is so because reads from the transaction log tend to randomize the otherwise sequential I/Os. If the publisher does not read from the transaction log as frequently, the transaction log I/Os will be allowed to remain mostly sequential.

Yet another way to make the Log Reader Agent more efficient in heavily used systems is to increase the read batch size. This setting specifies how transactions are read from the transaction log and copied to the distributor. In addition, it might be useful to increase the batch size when increasing the polling interval. If you increase the read batch size for the Log Reader Agent, we recommend that you increase the commit batch size for the distributor to correspond to the new read batch size.

You can configure the Log Reader Agent through Enterprise Manager. Expand the Replication Monitor icon, then Agents, and then the Log Reader Agents folder within the console tree in Enterprise Manager. Right-click the appropriate Log Reader Agent and select Agent Profiles. This opens the Log Reader Agent Profiles dialog box, as shown in Figure 14-10 on the following page.

In this dialog box, highlight a profile and click New Profile. This opens the Replication Agent Profile Details dialog box and creates a copy of the selected agent profile, which you can then modify. You can change the *PollingInterval* parameter as well as the *ReadBatchSize* parameter in the dialog box, as shown in Figure 14-11 on the following page. Once you have made your changes and named the profile, click OK. This saves the profile; you then select that profile from the Log Reader Agent Profiles dialog box.

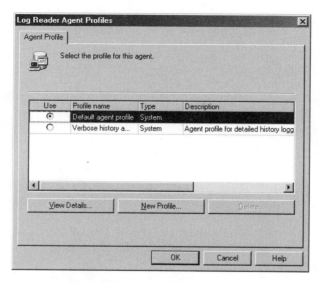

Figure 14-10. *The Log Reader Agent Profiles dialog box is used to create a new profile.*

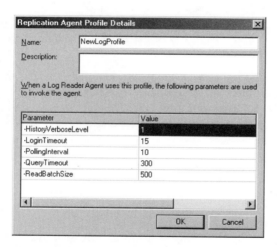

Figure 14-11. *The Replication Agent Profile Details dialog box.*

Monitoring the Transactional Replication System

As with the other replication types, monitoring transactional replication is done via System Monitor in the Performance console. Use the following objects:

- **SQLServer: Replication Agents**   Keeps track of the number of each type of agent that is running.
- **SQLServer: Replication Dist.**   Provides information on distribution latency. Long latencies can be a sign that the distributor is overloaded.
- **SQLServer: Replication Logreader**   Provides data on log reader activity and latency. Look for long latencies, which can indicate a problem reading the transaction log on the publisher. Also watch the number of delivered transactions per second. If this value is high, you might need to add more I/O capacity to the disk volumes that hold the transaction log.

By using System Monitor to watch these values, you can sometimes determine if there is a performance problem in the Log Reader Agent or in the distributor. This System Monitor data provides a lot of valuable information, but might not always identify problems.

Tuning the Transactional Replication System

The main task in tuning the transactional replication system is to properly configure the system and monitor it, as discussed in the previous section. In addition, after the system is in production and you can monitor it, you might need to modify the read batch size and the polling interval. The default value of 10 seconds is usually pretty good for the latter. Shortening the polling interval causes transactions to replicate faster, at the expense of more overhead on the transaction log. Lengthening the polling interval reduces the overhead on the transaction log, but leaves transactions in the log longer before they are replicated.

In update-intensive systems you might need to increase the read batch size. This allows the Log Reader Agent to read more transactions at a time from the transaction log. By increasing this value and leaving the polling interval at 10 seconds, you can replicate more transactions with less added overhead.

As with snapshot replication, it is necessary to monitor the capacity of the network and increase it if necessary. If your system appears to be performing well (that is, CPU and I/O usage are within their capacity limits) but the replication process seems to be taking too long, you might have a network problem. Unfortunately, network problems cannot easily be diagnosed with System Monitor; you will need to use a network monitor such as Microsoft System Management Server (SMS). Look for network usage near the capacity of the network card.

In addition to these tuning guidelines, remember that the publisher, distributor, and subscribers are SQL Server systems just like any other SQL Server system. Thus, follow the tuning guidelines given throughout this book when dealing with these components.

Tuning for Merge Replication

Unlike transactional replication and snapshot replication, merge replication is not a one-way replication. Modifications can be made on either the publisher or any number of subscribers. Another difference is that where transactional replication is external to the normal operations of SQL Server (it is performed by reading the transaction log), merge replication uses internal triggers that are created on the replicated tables in order to track changes to them.

Attributes of Merge Replication

As is the case for transactional replication, merge replication begins with a snapshot, but since the snapshot occurs only once it is not important to tune it. The merge system creates tables both on the publisher and distributor in order to perform replication. In addition a new column holding a unique row identifier is added to every replicated table so that the replication agent can effectively track changes. Since merge replication is bidirectional, this column is used to note that a row has been replicated. Without this column, an insert done for replication would be replicated back to the originator and would ping-pong back and forth (which is why transaction replication cannot function bidirectionally).

When a row is inserted or modified, the trigger marks that row as needing replication. When the Merge Agent runs, it collects all the marked rows and sends them to the distributor for replication. At the same time, the Merge Agent modifies any rows on the publisher that have been modified on the subscriber system or systems. In this way it performs two-way replication.

Configuring for Merge Replication

As with transactional replication and snapshot replication, the I/O subsystem and network are very important for merge replication. In addition to configuring sufficient I/O, you can improve merge replication by configuring the merge batch size. Increasing the batch size so that there are fewer, larger batches will make replication more efficient. In addition to the merge batch size, you might want to tune the initial snapshot. I/O configuration and the other considerations are described here.

Configure Sufficient I/O

You can enhance the performance of the entire replication process by configuring sufficient I/O capacity. As with any SQL Server system, the transaction log should be located on its own RAID 1 volume for data protection. The data files should be located on one or more RAID 10 volumes. As with most applications RAID 5 is rarely appropriate. As with transactional replication, merge replication causes only minor I/O considerations for the publisher, distributor, and subscriber.

Configuring the I/O Subsystem on the Publisher

In general the publisher should follow normal SQL Server configuration guidelines as shown throughout this book. Unlike transactional replication, no additional load is put on the transaction log, so just follow normal tuning guidelines.

Configuring the I/O Subsystem on the Distributor

You should configure the distributor so that the distribution database has its transaction log on a dedicated RAID 1 disk volume. This will allow the distribution database to achieve maximum transaction log performance, improving the overall performance of the distributor.

Configuring the I/O Subsystem on the Subscriber

Because merge replication is multidirectional, the subscriber and publisher are tuned similarly. Follow the general sizing and configuration guidelines as discussed throughout this book.

Configure the Merge Batch Size

In busy systems you can improve the performance of merge replication by configuring the merge batch size. The merge batch size determines how many changed rows are copied to the distributor at a time. When you increase the batch size, fewer and larger batches are sent, which might be more efficient.

You can configure the Merge Agent through Enterprise Manager. Expand the Replication Monitor folder, then Agents, and then the Merge Agents folder within the console tree in Enterprise Manager. Right-click the Merge Agent you want and select Agent Profiles on the shortcut menu. This opens the Merge Agent Profiles dialog box, as shown in Figure 14-12.

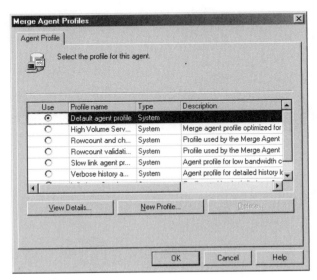

Figure 14-12. *The Merge Agent Profiles dialog box is used to create a new profile.*

Notice that the Merge Agent Profiles dialog box has many predefined profiles you can select. If possible, chose a profile that fits your needs from this list. If a predefined profile is not appropriate you can create your own.

In this dialog box, highlight a profile and click New Profile. This opens the Replication Agent Profile Details dialog box and creates a copy of the selected agent profile, which you can then modify. The Replication Agent Profile Details dialog box is shown in Figure 14-13. There are a number of parameters that you can configure, including the following:

- **BcpBatchSize** The number of rows to be sent. Increasing this parameter increases the number of rows that are copied in a single bulk copy operation. Depending on your network and I/O subsystem, this might increase performance or might not help at all. In some cases, decreasing the batch size might increase performance. Determining the best value for this parameter requires some trial-and-error testing.

- **DownloadGenerationsPerBatch** The size of the generation batch download. This is essentially the change information for merge replication. Increasing this parameter enhances performance for systems in which many rows are modified at a time or in which frequent updates are done.

- **UploadGenerationsPerBatch** The batch upload size. This is essentially the change information. As with the download batch size, increasing this parameter enhances performance for systems in which many rows are modified at a time or in which frequent updates are done.

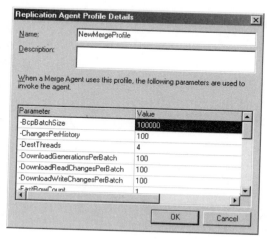

Figure 14-13. *The Replication Agent Profile Details dialog box is used to create the new profile.*

You should document your changes to these parameters and any performance improvements or degradation that result from these changes. This information will enhance further configuration and tuning.

Once you have made your changes and named the profile, click OK. This saves the profile; you then select that profile from the Merge Agent Profiles dialog box.

Monitoring the Merge Replication System

You monitor merge replication using System Monitor in the Windows 2000 Performance console, with the following objects:

- **SQLServer: Replication Agents** Stores the number of each type of agent that is running.
- **SQLServer: Replication Merge** Provides data on merge rates. This object provides information on conflicts per second, uploads per second, and downloads per second.

The SQL Sever merge replication counters are not extremely helpful for determining performance problems. The best way to tune a merge replication system is to simply tune the SQL Server system as usual and pay special attention to the network. As with the other replication types, tune the distributor.

Tuning the Merge Replication System

The main steps in tuning the merge replication system are to properly configure the system and monitor it as discussed in the previous section, with a special emphasis on I/O and network performance. Once you have put the system into production you can monitor it using System Monitor, but you will not find very useful merge data. Instead you must rely on other SQL Server counters and Windows 2000 counters to tune the system.

As mentioned in the "Configuring for Merge Replication" section, you might want to modify the BCP thread count and batch sizes if your system does a lot of updates. Increasing the BCP thread count increases the performance of the original snapshot. Increasing the batch sizes moves more changes at a time, which might be more efficient. By moving more changes at a time you affect the system less frequently; however, each time you do, you perform more work, causing a larger effect on the system.

In addition to these changes, you can change the polling interval, although the default polling interval usually works fine. Before tuning the polling interval, try changing the batch sizes instead. If you feel that you need merge replication to run more frequently or less frequently, then change the polling interval.

As with other replication types, you should monitor the network and increase its capacity if necessary. If your system appears to be performing well (that is, CPU and I/O usage are within their capacity limits) but the replication process seems to be taking too long, you might have a network problem. System Monitor does not provide sufficient information to determine SQL Server network problems. A network monitor such as SMS should be used. Look for network usage that is near the capacity of the network card. If you are near the capacity of your network, either purchase faster network cards or add a private network for the purposes of replication, backup and recovery, or both.

In addition to these tuning guidelines, remember that the publisher, distributor, and subscribers are SQL Server systems just like any other SQL Server system. Thus, you should follow the tuning guidelines given throughout this book.

Summary

SQL Server 2000 offers three types of replication: snapshot, transactional, and merge. Tuning replication depends on what type of replication you are running, although there are some general tuning guidelines for the distributor because it is involved in all replication types. Only a few specific things need to be tuned for replication. Most of the tuning involves properly configuring the I/O subsystems of the publisher, distributor, and subscribers for replication, and then monitoring and reconfiguring those components as necessary. The next chapter explains how to configure and tune a system for high-performance backup and recovery.

Chapter 15
High-Performance Backup and Recovery

Your company's most valuable asset might be the data in its databases. It's important to form a backup and recovery strategy and a disaster recovery plan. Without them you run the risk of losing data that might cost thousands or even millions of dollars.

As with any activity on the SQL Server system, backup and recovery comes at a cost. The backup process creates overhead on the system while it is running. It is to your advantage to minimize this cost by improving the performance of backup operations. This chapter explains how to improve the speed of backup operations and how to set up the best backup and recovery solutions for your business. It also presents a variety of guidelines and tips for improving your backup and recovery strategy and for setting up a disaster recovery plan.

Backup and Recovery Concepts

Backup and restore are related topics that have to do with saving data from the database for later use and copying that data back to the system. Recovery has to do with the ability of the relational database management system (RDBMS) to survive a system failure and replay transactions. Throughout this chapter the term recovery is used to describe restoring the database and then recovering transactions.

Backup and Restore

Database backup and restore operations are similar to the backup and restore operations you can do with the operating system. The backup operation involves copying data from the database to another location. This operation can be a *full backup*, in which the entire database is copied, or an *incremental backup*, in which only recent changes are copied. The transaction log is also backed up on a regular basis. You can use the transaction log backup to restore transactions that have occurred since the last full or incremental backup.

The restore operation involves copying the backup data to the database. This process should not be confused with recovery. These topics are separate and should be treated as such. The restore operation is essentially a reloading of the database from the backup files.

Recovery

Recovery is the ability of the database to replay (recover) transactions after a system failure. Because SQL Server does not write changes to the data files immediately to disk every time a change is made in the database, a system failure might leave the database in a corrupt state. To maintain the integrity of the database, SQL Server logs changes in the transaction log. Before a transaction can be committed, the change information must be written to the transaction log. In the event of a system failure, on restart SQL Server uses the transaction log to roll forward transactions that had been committed and roll back transactions that had not been committed at the time of the failure.

> **Caution** The transaction log is essential to the recovery of transactions in the event of a failure and is therefore essential to the integrity of the database. Because it is so important, the transaction log should always reside on a RAID 1 or RAID 10 (mirrored) volume.

When a transaction is rolled back by SQL Server, the transaction is nullified and all the data changed by this transaction is restored to its original values. This process is identical to concluding a transaction with the ROLLBACK command. When a transaction is rolled forward, the changes that it had made to the database are replayed to synchronize the data files with the current state of the database.

In the event of a system failure that requires you to restore the database using backup files, the transaction log and transaction log backups are used to recover the database to the point of failure. Thus, restore and recovery operations work together. In the event of a power failure or a spontaneous system reboot, only a recovery operation might be necessary.

Non-Logged Operations

The rules of logging and recovery do have some exceptions. SQL Server 2000 improves the performance of large I/O and log intensive functions by introducing non-logged operations, or BULK_LOGGED recovery mode.

Under certain conditions, SQL Server can perform operations that are not logged to the transaction log. Because they are not logged, they have to be redone in the event of a recovery. In addition, because these changes are not written to the transaction log they are not backed up during transaction log backups. It is important to know the effects of running in BULK_LOGGED recovery mode before you enable it. The operations that can be performed in BULK_LOGGED recovery mode are:

- SELECT INTO
- BULK COPY and BCP
- CREATE INDEX
- Some text operations

Restrictions on Non-Logged Operations

This section describes several restrictions that apply to non-logged operations.

SELECT INTO

The SELECT INTO statement is a good candidate for non-logged operations because it is used to create a new table in the database. Because the SELECT INTO statement cannot select into an existing object it cannot be used for updates, only creations of new data. This creation process can be repeated easily, so you can choose to perform this operation logged or not logged.

BULK COPY and BCP

Several restrictions apply to BULK COPY and BCP operations in order for them to be performed as non-logged. These restrictions are:

- The recovery mode must be set to BULK_LOGGED. This is done using the ALTER DATABASE command or the SQL Server Enterprise Manager.
- The database option *select into/bulkcopy* must be set to true on the database where you want to perform the non-logged operation. This option can be set using the sp_dboption stored procedure.
- The target table cannot have any indexes, or if the table has any indexes they must be empty when the bulk copy starts.
- The target table cannot be replicated, since transactional replication uses entries in the transaction log for its replication.
- The TABLOCK hint must be specified to force a table lock.

These restrictions allow the bulk copy operations to save space in the transaction log and to run faster. In the event of a restore from backup, however, these operations must be redone.

CREATE INDEX

The CREATE INDEX statement is also a good candidate for non-logged operations, because you can recreate the indexes as needed. Recreating the indexes is not difficult to manage, but if the tables are large it could be quite time- and resource-consuming.

Text Operations

Certain text operations such as WRITETEXT and UPDATETEXT can also be non-logged. There are no restrictions and whether or not they are logged is determined by the database option.

Setting the Recovery Mode

To enable non-logged bulk operations you must set the recovery options on the database itself. The recovery options can be set to FULL, BULK_LOGGED, and SIMPLE depending on your preferences. You set these options by using the ALTER DATABASE command as shown on the following page.

```
ALTER DATABASE Northwind
SET RECOVERY BULK_LOGGED
```

or

```
ALTER DATABASE Northwind
SET RECOVERY FULL
```

or

```
ALTER DATABASE Northwind
SET RECOVERY SIMPLE
```

In BULK_LOGGED recovery mode, bulk operations that meet the restrictions above are not logged, but all other operations are logged. In FULL recovery mode all operations are logged. In SIMPLE recovery mode data can be recovered only to the last backup.

Recovery Mode Concerns

Since the recovery mode defines the tolerance that your system has to failure, it should be used with caution. You will see performance improvements on non-logged bulk operations, but increased recovery time in the event of a failure.

Backup and Restore Ramifications

If you choose not to log these operations it will improve the performance of the transaction log backups by creating less data to be backed up, meaning faster backup times. Unfortunately this improved backup performance comes at the price of having to redo the bulk operations by hand in the event of a system recovery. This might be acceptable in the case of index creation, especially if you recreate indexes regularly. In the case of bulk inserts, however, you must replay these inserts and create and maintain a recovery plan.

Types of Backups

Several methods exist for performing backups. These methods differ by the type and amount of data being backed up. This section describes the different types of backups: full, file or filegroup, differential, and transaction log.

Full Backup

A full backup involves backing up the entire database. All the data files that are part of the database are backed up. In systems with multiple databases, all the databases should be backed up. Depending on how often the data is modified, these databases can be backed up on different schedules. With large databases this operation can be quite time-consuming. This chapter explains how you can minimize this time by tuning the backup system. You can also reduce the backup time by performing differential backups or filegroup backups rather than full backups.

File or Filegroup Backups

File or filegroup backups involve backing up a single file or the files that make up a filegroup. This operation is much faster than backing up the entire database, but protects only the backed up data. The entire backup is composed of individual file or filegroup backups from different times. In the event of a system failure that requires a restore, it might take much longer to restore the database from the collection of file or filegroup backups than from a full backup, because you must restore all the transaction log backups that occurred after the last backup was performed on the file or filegroup that failed. If the entire database has to be restored and the file or filegroup backups are from different times, the transaction log backups must be applied from the time of the oldest individual backup component.

Differential Backup

Differential backups allow you to back up only the information that has changed since the last backup. Differential backups are faster and consume less disk space than full backups because they back up only part of the data. The downside is that differential backups are more difficult and time-consuming to restore than full backups. A differential backup requires the restoration of the last full backup and the last differential backup before failure.

Transaction Log Backup

As changes are made to the database, all information about them is logged in the transaction log. The exception is the non-logged operations mentioned earlier in this chapter. Because writes to the data files are not immediate, it is important to log these changes to a durable medium (that is, one that is not subject to power failures) such as a disk drive. If the changes were not logged to durable media and power were to be lost or the system were to fail, it would be impossible to recover unrecorded transactions. SQL Server therefore logs all changes to the transaction log. A transaction is not considered committed until the commit record has been written to the transaction log. Because the transaction log stores a large amount of data, it is necessary to periodically clear it out to make room for more log records. SQL Server clears the transaction log as part of the transaction log backup.

Factors Affecting Performance of Backup and Recovery

A number of factors affect backup and recovery performance. It is impossible to say which performance factor is most important, since any number of components can cause a performance bottleneck. This section explores the most common sources of backup and recovery bottlenecks, which include the I/O subsystem, the network, and SQL Server itself. First let's look at how these components work together to perform a backup.

The Backup Process

A typical backup operation for SQL Server consists of the following steps:

1. The data is read from the SQL Server database or file to be backed up. Because SQL Server recognizes that backup I/Os are sequential, these I/Os are combined into an I/O that is larger than the normal 8 KB page size. During backup and recovery operations, 64-KB I/Os are performed.

2. The data that has been read is either written to tape or disk, or copied over the network to the network backup server. This backup thread will not read any more data until the copy has completed.

3. If a network backup server is being used, the data is copied to memory (the NTFS cache) on the backup server and then the backup data is copied to disk. If you're using NTFS, the copy is considered complete when it finishes writing into the NTFS cache. Until this operation begins taking place there is no additional I/O activity on the SQL Server system because the backup thread is waiting on the copy to complete.

4. The control of the backup operation is returned to the backup process on the SQL Server system once the copy has completed. This process is replayed until all of the required data has been backed up.

One problem with this process is that it is sequential. Parts of the system (either the SQL Server system or the backup server) are periodically idle while other components of the system are busy. By performing these operations in parallel, you can keep all components busy at the same time. If you configure your database and backup process properly, multiple threads can perform this operation in parallel. This is discussed in more detail in the "SQL Server" section later in this chapter.

I/O Subsystem

The I/O subsystem can frequently be a cause of a backup and recovery bottleneck. The I/O bottleneck can occur either on the SQL Server system or on the backup medium itself. On the SQL Server system, I/Os for backups occur in the same manner as with any other disk operation. However, since the goal of the operation is to copy data from the database as quickly as possible, the I/O subsystem might often be overdriven. Because you are copying data from the database to a backup medium, this medium (disk or tape) might also be a bottleneck.

I/O on the SQL Server System

To configure your system for maximum backup performance, monitor it during backup operations as well as during normal day-to-day operations. When monitoring the I/O subsystem during a backup operation, look for the number of I/Os per second as well as the seconds per I/O. If disk latencies (seconds per I/O) exceed 25 ms, you are probably experiencing an I/O bottleneck on the SQL Server system.

I/O on the Backup System

Your goal should be to minimize the time that a backup takes because running a backup creates overhead on the SQL Server system. As long as this overhead exists on the SQL Server system, the user community experiences degraded performance. The I/O capacity of the backup medium is often a bottleneck because the backup system might be underconfigured or misconfigured.

Backing Up to Tape

To determine if your backup performance is adversely affected by the performance of the tape device to which you are backing up, calculate the maximum throughput of the tape device and compare it with your backup times. If this comparison indicates that your backups are occurring at tape speed, then the tape device is a limiting factor.

For example, if you are using a tape drive that can write data at 1 GB per hour, and it takes two hours to back up 2 GB, then you are probably being limited by the speed of the tape device. Conversely, if you are backing up to a tape device that can write data at 1 GB per hour and it is taking three hours to back up 2 GB, your problem probably lies elsewhere.

You can improve backup performance by taking any of the following actions:

- **Replace the tape device.** You can replace the tape device with a faster device if your current device is too slow. The fastest tape devices claim backup performance of up to 3.5 TB per hour.
- **Add tape devices.** You can back up to multiple devices simultaneously, which increases the throughput of the backup by striping the data and by writing it in parallel.
- **Back up to disk as a first stage.** You can first back up all files to disk, either locally or over the network, and then copy those backup files to tape. This increases the performance of the crucial stage of the backup during which SQL Server is involved. This method is known as *staging* the backup, and the area on disk that is used as the intermediary area is known as the *staging area*.

As you can see, there are several methods of increasing performance of a backup to tape. You can combine these methods to provide for better backup performance, as discussed later in this chapter.

Backing Up to Disk

Backing up to disk is a common way to perform SQL Server backups. To optimize the performance of these backups, you should configure the I/O subsystem on the backup system to be able to handle large numbers of write I/Os. Since SQL Server will write to the backup system as fast as possible, you should make sure that the I/O subsystem is not a bottleneck.

To determine if the backup system is a bottleneck, use the System Monitor in the Windows 2000 Performance console and *diskperf* as described in Chapter 4, "System Tuning." Look at the number of I/Os per second as well as the seconds per I/O. If disk latencies are greater than 25 ms, you are experiencing degraded performance. Increasing the performance of the I/O subsystem will increase backup performance.

I/Os to the backup system are 100 percent writes, so RAID 5 is inappropriate for back-ups because it has a high write overhead. RAID 10 is the recommended configuration (unless you are severely budget limited) because it offers a high degree of fault toler-ance and incurs only one additional physical I/O for each write I/O.

Network

When you perform SQL Server backups over the network, the network itself can be a bottleneck. It might surprise you to know that the network is often the cause of backup performance problems. Let's look at a few examples of how this can occur.

A typical 10BaseT network has a throughput of 10 megabits per second, which is approxi-mately 1.25 MB per second. This network can back up approximately 4,500 MB per hour, or 4.4 GB per hour. It can take a significant amount of time to back up your database at this rate. In contrast, a 100BaseT network can achieve 44 GB per hour, and a Gigabit Ethernet network can back up 440 GB per hour. If you use a Gigabit Ethernet network and a fast I/O subsystem on the SQL Server system, you must ensure that the backup system can support the resulting I/O rates.

> **Note**   These performance ratings are theoretical maximums. Depending on the packet size, network traffic, and the individual components in your net-work, you might find that your actual throughput is less.

SQL Server

In addition to providing sufficient I/O and network capacity, you can also improve backup performance by providing sufficient SQL Server resources. You can do so through SQL Server configuration parameters and through the design of the database itself.

Backup Threads

When backups are run to more than one backup device, the backup operations are done in parallel, improving the performance of the backup. Each backup operation requires a SQL Server thread in order to run. If the *max worker threads* option is not set high enough or if the system is so busy that all the worker threads are in use, the backup operation must wait for another backup thread to finish before it can acquire a thread. Thus, it is important to make sure that the *max worker threads* parameter has a sufficiently high value. The default setting of 255 is usually sufficient to provide enough threads to achieve adequate parallelism on backups; if you have decreased this value for other tuning purposes, you might experience backup and recovery performance problems.

Multiple Backup Devices

When you use multiple backup devices, the backup operation proceeds in parallel, improving performance. By keeping enough backup threads active concurrently you can keep the SQL Server system and the backup server active at the same time. In addition, RAID controllers thrive on concurrent I/Os. Since a disk array is made up of many disk drives, more concurrent I/Os mean that all the disk drives can be active at once, increasing performance.

Configuring the System for Maximum Backup and Recovery Performance

To achieve optimal performance on backup and recovery operations, you need to properly configure the system so that there is enough I/O and network capacity to run the backup as quickly as possible. This section discusses methods for determining the capacity of the I/O subsystem and network and ways of configuring these devices to achieve better performance.

Analyzing Performance Needs of a Backup

It is always a good idea to start by analyzing the performance needs of your backup, then determine if your hardware can meet these needs. This analysis provides a goal to shoot for as well as to measure your success against. In addition, it provides valuable information that you can present to management if it is necessary to purchase additional hardware.

Determine the Goals

Determining a throughput goal is a fairly easy task. In fact, this goal might already be defined in a service level agreement (SLA). To determine the required throughput, simply determine the size of the backup set and divide by the allotted backup time window. This will tell you exactly what throughput you must achieve.

For example, if you have a database that is 250 GB and you are allotted a 4-hour time window for backups, the required throughput is 250 GB divided by 4 hours, or 62.5 GB per hour. You might or might not be able to achieve this capacity with your current hardware configuration, as we will determine in the next section.

Calculate the Capacity

To calculate the throughput or capacity of the backup system, you must examine each component. You will probably find that the throughput of the entire system is limited by a single component. Charting the throughput of each link in the chain can determine which is the weakest link.

For example, consider a system that is backing up the large SQL Server system described earlier (a 250-GB database) to a backup system over a 100BaseT network. The database system is configured with 20 disk drives running RAID 10. The backup system has a disk subsystem configured with seven disk drives running RAID 5. To analyze this system, you should look at the capacity of each of the components.

The system that is running SQL Server (the system that is being backed up) is configured with 20 disk drives running RAID 10. Using the rule of 85 I/Os per second per disk drive yields the following read capacity (remember that SQL Server backups use 64-KB I/Os):

85 I/Os per second per disk * 20 disks * 64 KB per I/O = 108,800 KB/sec = 373.5 GB/hr

As you have already seen in the "Network" section, a 100BaseT network has a theoretical maximum of 44 GB/hr.

The backup system is configured as RAID 5, so each write causes four physical I/Os. Thus the capacity of the seven-disk RAID 5 disk subsystem is

(85 I/Os per second per disk * 7 disks * 64 KB per I/O) / 4 I/Os per write = 9520 KB/sec = 32.6 GB/hr

Write caching can help improve this performance. However, the RAID 5 write performance will be improved only slightly by adding the cache.

The I/O subsystem on the backup server and the network could both be limiting factors in this scenario, as you can see from the values in the following table:

Component	Performance
I/O subsystem on the SQL Server system	373.5 GB/hr
100BaseT network	44 GB/hr (theoretical maximum)
I/O subsystem on the backup system	32.6 GB/hr

Note The figures in this example are simplifications of the actual performance of these components in order to illustrate the importance of each component. The actual performance depends on many different factors, such as block size, write caches, and controller performance. In other words, your mileage might vary.

Compare the Results

After you have calculated the performance of the components that are available for performing the backup, you will have a good idea of how the system will behave. Comparing the values you obtain with your desired goals might also give you a clue as to how you can improve the system. In the example, the required throughput of 62.5 GB/hr cannot be achieved because of the I/O limitation of 32.6 GB/hr on the backup system as well as the limitation of the network. Clearly a configuration change is necessary.

Configuring the Network

As you have seen, you must first determine your performance needs and then configure your system so that it can sustain the performance to meet those needs. In the case of the network, several configuration options are available.

One way to achieve high performance is to use the fastest network hardware available. Hardware such as the Gigabit network performs well but can be quite expensive. If your budget allows for it, a high-performance network is an effective solution.

Another way to improve backup performance is to configure a dedicated network for backup and recovery operations. This alternative allows the entire bandwidth of the network hardware to be used for backups, speeding up performance. Ensuring that the overhead on the SQL Server system is not prolonged due to network problems is especially important for transaction log backups, as mentioned earlier.

If a dedicated network is not enough, you can improve backup performance by configuring multiple network cards in your system and creating multiple networks. You can use these additional networks specifically for backup and recovery. To configure multiple networks, create new subnets, each with its own IP subnet address. The backup system and the SQL Server system should each have an address on these new subnets. When configuring the backup devices, give them the IP address of the backup system. Assign each backup device an address on a different subnet, as shown in Figure 15-1.

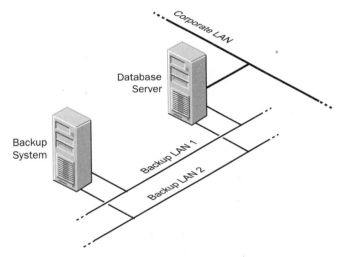

Figure 15-1. *Using multiple subnets for backup and recovery operations.*

You can configure the backup devices on the individual subnets within SQL Server Enterprise Manager. Select the database you are going to back up, then select Backup Database from the Tools menu. On the General tab of the SQL Server Backup dialog box, click the Add button to add a new backup device. In the Select Backup Destination dialog box, click File Name and enter a filename using the Universal Naming Convention (UNC). To specify exactly which network device to use, specify the IP address as the server name, as shown in Figure 15-2 on the following page.

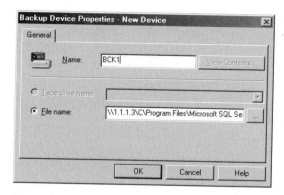

Figure 15-2. *Specifying the UNC name in the Backup Device Properties - New Device dialog box.*

If you need multiple network segments, create multiple backup devices that each use a different segment. In this manner, you can increase network bandwidth by adding more and more networks.

Configuring the I/O Subsystem

The configuration of the I/O subsystem on the SQL Server system is usually dictated by normal performance tuning activities. If your system operates under a heavy workload, you have probably already configured the I/O subsystem on your server. However, if your backup is experiencing a performance problem on the SQL Server system, you can monitor the I/O subsystem and add more disk drives if necessary.

Configuring the I/O subsystem on the backup server is a fairly straightforward activity. Once you know what performance is required, you can follow the guidelines given throughout this chapter to determine how many disk drives are needed and how they should be configured. Since the I/Os to the backup system's disk drive are 100 percent writes during the backup operation, you must consider the additional I/Os generated by RAID 5. Table 15-1 shows approximately how much throughput you can achieve when writing to disk subsystems using various RAID configurations.

Table 15-1. Throughput Comparisons for Different RAID Configurations (100% Writes)

Configuration	Throughput Capacity per Disk Drive
RAID 0 at 64 KB per I/O	27 GB/hr
RAID 1 or RAID 10 at 64 KB per I/O	13.5 GB/hr
RAID 5 at 64 KB per I/O	6.75 GB/hr

Although the figures in Table 15-1 are rough estimations of throughput using the fastest disk drives on the market today, this information can help you calculate the number of disk drives necessary to achieve the desired backup performance. It is important to remember that if you exceed the recommended throughput as shown in the table, the I/O latency will increase, degrading I/O performance. Degraded I/O performance will degrade backup and recovery performance.

Backup Scenarios

This section suggests some methods for performing backup and recovery operations and discusses how you can optimize them. The examples in this section will give you ideas on how you can best configure your backup and recovery system for performance while customizing it based on your individual needs and budget.

Local Backups

Local backups are probably the most common type of configuration for small to medium installations. Here the backup device or devices are connected directly to the system where SQL Server is running, and the backup goes directly from SQL Server onto the tape drive or disk:

Advantages

Because the backup medium is local, there is no need to transfer data across the network, eliminating the network as a potential bottleneck. This can be a big advantage on systems that share a busy network. You also have the option to back up from SQL Server to disk and then copy the backup file to tape. This can reduce the time during which SQL Server performance is degraded. Local backups are the best choice for very large systems in order to avoid sending large amounts of data over a network.

Disadvantages

The major disadvantage of the local backup is that the backup files are local. If something were to happen to the system, such as a fire, the backup medium would be destroyed along with the database. In addition, if the server were disabled it would be necessary to recover the backup files before a new system could replace the problem system. Furthermore, for many systems a local backup is not feasible because of the number of SQL Server resources involved.

Configuration

If you are backing up directly to tape, you need to ensure that your tape system can perform the desired backup in the desired time frame. This might involve purchasing faster tape hardware or striping the backup over several tape devices.

If you are backing up to disk, you should configure the disk drives in a RAID 10 array. RAID 5 cannot absorb all of the required write I/Os without causing high latencies. This array should be separate from the transaction log and data arrays so that it does not interfere with their performance. Follow the procedures outlined earlier in the "Configuring the I/O Subsystem" section to configure sufficient I/O capacity.

Network Backups

Network backups are very common. They can range from a server supporting one or more SQL Server systems on a network with a shared disk or tape system up to a full-blown Enterprise backup server (which is the same thing on a larger scale). By using a network, you can share resources that might be relatively unused for much of the time among several servers.

The most common scenario is a network backup server that stores the most recent full backups on disk, as well as storing the transaction log backups that have occurred since those full backups. Either on a regular schedule or triggered by an event, these backup files are then written to tape and archived in a safe storage facility. As needed, older backup files are removed from the disk subsystem after they have been archived to tape. In the event of a system failure, the latest full backup is on disk and can be easily and quickly restored, along with the latest transaction log backups.

Advantages

The main advantage of the network backup server is that the resources can be shared among multiple SQL Server systems. Instead of having several systems that back up to an array of two or three disk drives, you can combine the disks into a larger array. This larger array can perform the backup much faster because the I/O capacity is greater.

Disadvantages

The disadvantage of the network backup server is that the backup runs over the network, which can very easily become a performance bottleneck. More complex configuration and backup coordination might be needed to overcome this problem.

Configuration

You need to follow some tuning and configuration guidelines to effectively use a network backup server. These include the following:

- Configure the number of disk drives and the RAID level based on performance needs. Don't configure only for the amount of space needed, because this might leave you with an I/O bottleneck.
- Carefully schedule backups. If you are sharing the disk subsystem among several SQL Server systems, spread out the load. Alternate times so that only one system is backing up at a time.
- Regularly monitor the backup system and make sure that the network, the I/O subsystem, or both are not becoming bottlenecks. If a problem arises, you need to reconfigure.
- Keep at least two full backups online so that you can restore the older one if the new one is corrupted. If you delete the old backup before you do a new one and the system fails during the backup, you might be left with no alternative but to go offsite for your archived backup files.
- The files being restored will be loaded in bursts; so be sure to monitor all the peak times. This is when problems are most likely to show up.

Storage Area Networks

Other backup configurations include new hardware and software products such as the storage area network (SAN). A SAN allows you to share components of the I/O subsystem, such as disk and tape arrays, among several servers. This can provide a high-performance solution that is fairly cost-effective because the shared resources need not be duplicated. These alternatives are new and will no doubt evolve and improve over time.

Backup Tips and Recommendations

In this section we provide a number of miscellaneous suggestions on how to make the backup and recovery process more efficient. These suggestions are categorized by the component to which they apply.

SQL Server System

The best way to tune the SQL Server system for backup is to simply tune the system in general. If you follow the guidelines and tips given throughout this book for configuring your system for excellent performance, you will find that backup and recovery are also well tuned. You can do a few additional things specifically for backup and recovery, as follows:

- **Configure multiple files.** SQL Server assigns backup threads to each file that is being backed up. A database with a single file will be allocated only one backup thread, whereas a database with multiple files will be allocated multiple threads during the backup process. Multiple threads allow for parallel operations, which increase performance.

- **Increase the size of network packets.** If backup performance is crucial, you can increase the size of network packets. Since backup and recovery use 64-KB pages, by increasing the network packet size you should see higher network performance. However, this is not generally recommended because it can degrade performance for other applications accessing SQL Server.

- **Use non-logged operations where appropriate.** This will make transaction log backups quicker, but at a high maintenance cost. Do this at your own risk.

As you can see, there is not much that needs to be done on the SQL Server system besides normal tuning exercises.

Network

When performing network backups, you should be careful that the network itself does not become a bottleneck. The network is a fixed-bandwidth component that might or might not be busy when you want to perform your backup. Knowing what kind of network you have allows you to determine the maximum throughput, but you must keep in mind that other users and applications might be using some of that bandwidth. If possible, monitor the network and make changes as necessary. Some tips for increasing network performance are listed on the following page.

- **Use the fastest network available.** Doing so increases the bandwidth and might eliminate a bottleneck; however, this could be an expensive solution because the latest and fastest hardware is usually also the most expensive.
- **Use multiple networks.** Use several network segments for the backup operation. This allows you to increase the throughput to that of multiple network segments.
- **Use a dedicated network.** By dedicating a network to backups, you can ensure that not only will the backup performance be improved, but also the user community will not experience performance slowdowns due to the network being used for other purposes.

Network components can easily cause a backup and recovery bottleneck. Carefully plan and implement the network with backup performance in mind.

Network Backup Server

The network backup server is a frequent source of backup and recovery bottlenecks. It is not uncommon for multiple backups to the server and a tape backup of the server to happen simultaneously. This can cause a tremendous load on the I/O subsystem. By properly configuring for these peak loads, you might be able to avoid this bottleneck. Some tips and guidelines to help in your configuration include the following:

- **Configure sufficient disk drives.** A disk drive can handle only so much I/O. You can overcome this limitation by adding multiple disk drives in a RAID array. Configure a sufficient number of disk drives to achieve the desired performance.
- **Use RAID 10.** A fault-tolerant RAID array is a must to protect your data. Because of the excessive overhead incurred by RAID 5 during write operations, RAID 5 is not a good candidate for this application.
- **Configure the Server service to maximize performance for file services.** This configuration will optimize the file system buffer cache for file service operations.

As with the other components, the network backup server should be carefully monitored. The I/O subsystem in particular should be carefully watched.

General Tips and Guidelines

Here are some tips that can be helpful in determining the best backup schedule for your system.

- **Plan full backups for off hours.** If your company does not run in a 24 x 7 environment, the off hours are the best time to do backups. This will both improve the performance of the backup and reduce the effect of the backup on the user community.
- **Schedule a full backup over several days.** If your database is very large and you cannot perform a full backup in the allotted time, split it up. You can do a file or filegroup backup on a piece of the database. Over a period of several days you can back up all the data in this manner.

- **Use differential backups.** If you cannot afford the time to do a full backup every night, you can do a differential backup during the week and a full backup over the weekend.

- **Use multiple backup devices.** Using multiple backup devices allows SQL Server to make some of the backup operations parallel. SQL Server creates a number of threads based on the number of data files and number of backup devices. Making operations parallel improves both backup and recovery performance.

- **Use multiple data files.** By using several data files rather than one large one, SQL Server can better make the backup parallel and improve both backup and recovery performance.

- **Stage the backup.** You can do the backup as a disk backup initially, and then copy the disk backup files to tape. This method has the benefit of allowing faster backup performance as well as keeping the latest few backups available on disk, which improves the restore performance for those backup files.

- **Create a reasonable backup schedule.** One of the best ways to improve the performance on the system being backed up is to avoid unnecessary backups. You must determine what the most effective backup schedule is based on your needs. Don't back up more than you need to, but don't sacrifice the security of your data for performance. Based on your needs, create a backup plan that is best for you.

- **Keep the most recent backups on disk.** In the event that a restore is necessary, a restore from a disk that is available on the network can be started immediately. A restore from tape might involve getting the tape from storage, loading the tape, and then restoring the backup from that tape.

As you can see, there are many different things you can do to improve backup and recovery performance. However, don't take chances with your backups: don't sacrifice the security of your data for performance.

Review of Component Capacities

Table 15-2 on the following page summarizes the various throughput capacities given throughout this chapter. The disk I/O throughputs are based on 125 I/Os per second (for random I/O). Exceeding this I/O rate will cause latencies in excess of 25 ms, which can increase exponentially as the throughput is increased. These ratings are based on theoretical maximums that are usually unachievable in practice; your mileage might vary.

Table 15-2. Component Capacities

I/O Components (64 KB per I/O)	Capacity (100% Writes)
1 disk drive, RAID 0	27 GB/hr
1 disk drive, RAID 1 or RAID 10	13.5 GB/hr
1 disk drive, RAID 5	6.75 GB/hr

Network Components	Capacity
10BaseT	4.4 GB/hr
100BaseT	44 GB/hr
Gigabit Ethernet	440 GB/hr

Summary

Backup and recovery are very important to the stability of your system. The data in your database might be one of the most valuable assets that your company has; its loss could be devastating to your business. It is therefore essential that this data be protected from permanent loss. This chapter presented a review of backup and recovery techniques and provided a number of guidelines and tips for improving those techniques.

Since the backup operation incurs a significant amount of overhead, tuning this operation is essential. By improving the performance of backup operations, you minimize the overall performance impact on the system. In this chapter you learned how to improve the speed of backup operations and how to configure your system for maximum efficiency. This information should help you to protect your data while minimizing the overhead on the system.

The next chapter begins Part IV, "Tuning SQL Statements." This part of the book discusses how to make SQL statements more efficient, as well as how to use hints and stored procedures to improve performance. The next chapter introduces SQL Query Analyzer and how you can use it to help tune SQL statements.

Part IV
Tuning SQL Statements

Chapter 16
Using SQL Query Analyzer

Microsoft SQL Server 2000 SQL Query Analyzer is a tool that allows the user to run ad hoc queries against a SQL Server database. In addition, the SQL Query Analyzer provides information on the resources that a query consumes; which aids in analyzing and tuning the performance of your system. SQL Query Analyzer has a graphical user interface for designing and testing SQL statements, batches, and scripts interactively. You can open SQL Query Analyzer from the Start menu, from the command line, or from the Tools menu in SQL Server Enterprise Manager.

This chapter begins by exploring the features in SQL Query Analyzer. It then looks at how to run queries and interpret the results, using sample SQL code to walk through the process. It also discusses how to use the Index Tuning Wizard and how to manage table statistics.

SQL Query Analyzer Features

SQL Query Analyzer offers the following features:

- **Free-form text editor** You enter and edit SQL statements in the editor. The free-form design gives you the flexibility to develop your own coding style. You can also modify and debug the SQL statements in the same window.

- **Color coding of SQL syntax** Color coding improves the readability of complex statements. SQL Query Analyzer uses color coding to indicate SQL keywords, such as SELECT and UPDATE, and to indicate strings in quotes. This latter feature assists you to debug SQL statements by highlighting unclosed quotation marks.

- **Customizable display mode** Results can be presented in either a grid or a free-form text window. Also, you can save query results directly to a file.

- **Object Browser** Browse server objects such as tables and stored procedures.

- **Diagram of the Showplan** This diagram shows the logical steps that are built into the execution plan of a SQL statement, and is intended to help you visualize the SQL statements and how they will execute. SQL Query Analyzer color-codes areas of your statements that need further attention. In addition, it provides a relative cost of the SQL query.

- **Index Tuning Wizard** This wizard analyzes a SQL statement and the tables it references to determine if additional indexes would improve the performance of the query.
- **Context-sensitive Transact-SQL statement help** Clicking a Transact-SQL statement displays syntax and option information on the command.

Running SQL Query Analyzer

The SQL Query Analyzer is installed by default when you install SQL Server. You can run it on the database server, or on any of your client machines.

After you install it, you can access SQL Query Analyzer by pointing to Start, Programs, Microsoft SQL Server 2000, and then clicking SQL Query Analyzer. You can also access it from the Enterprise Manager console on the Tools menu. A final method is to run it from a Windows command line by typing ISQLW and pressing Enter.

The Connection Process

After you start it, SQL Query Analyzer prompts you to enter the SQL Server alias to which you want to connect, as shown in Figure 16-1. The available SQL Server aliases are constructed from those specified in the SQL Server Client Network Utility. You can type a SQL Server alias in the text box, select one from the drop-down list, or click the ellipsis button (...) and select a SQL Server alias.

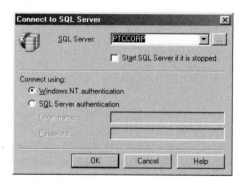

Figure 16-1. *The Connect to SQL Server dialog box.*

In the Connect using: section, specify either Windows NT or SQL Server authentication. If your database server is configured to accept Windows NT authentication, click the Windows NT Authentication option. This instructs your system to log on to the database using the user ID and password with which you are currently logged on. If your system is configured for SQL Server authentication, click the SQL Server Authentication option and enter your SQL Server login name and password in the appropriate boxes. Click OK to log on to your database system with the specified authentication.

The Query Window

After the logon process has completed, an empty window called Query appears. This is where you primarily interact with SQL Query Analyzer. The toolbar buttons in SQL Query Analyzer assist you in analyzing your queries and stored procedures, as detailed here:

 New Query The New Query toolbar button allows you to start another connection to the current database server. Clicking the button opens a new query window. Click the New Query down arrow to open the New Query drop-down menu. On the drop-down menu, click Blank Query Window to open a new query window or click Template to open a SQL template. See the Insert Template icon description for an explanation of the templates.

 Load SQL Script This toolbar button opens the Open Query File dialog box which allows you to open an existing script containing a SQL statement, batch, or stored procedure and display it in the current query window.

 Save Query/Result Clicking the Save Query/Result toolbar button allows you to save the query text in the query window or the results to a specified file. Just click in the window to indicate which one you want to save, then click the toolbar button. If you are saving the query, the Save Query dialog box opens. If you are saving the results, a Save Results or Save Grid Results dialog box opens. Choose the location and file name to save your query or results.

 Insert Template This toolbar button allows you to choose from various predefined SQL Server templates to guide you in writing the SQL for such things as creating a trigger, creating a database, creating a view, and more. Click this button to open the Insert Template dialog box and browse the available templates. Of course, you can create your own template as well and open it here when you need it. When you open a template, the SQL code appears in a query window, and you simply edit the parts that need changing. These parts are in red text.

 Clear Window The Clear Window toolbar button allows you to quickly delete all the text in a query window.

Parse Query Clicking this toolbar button directs SQL Query Analyzer to parse your SQL statements and identify any syntax errors. This command does not execute the statements.

 Execute Query The Execute Query toolbar button executes the SQL text in the query window. You can also execute the SQL code by pressing F5 or Ctrl+E.

 Cancel Query Execution This toolbar button allows you to cancel the currently executing query.

Execute Mode The Execute Mode toolbar button allows you to specify how the results of the query analysis are to be displayed. It has six options:

- **Results In Text** Display the query results as text without the execution plan
- **Results In Grid** Display the query results in a grid
- **Results In File** Save the query results to a file
- **Show Execution Plan** Display the execution plan with the result
- **Show Server Trace** Display the SQL Profiler trace information for the statements executed
- **Show Client Statistics** Display client statistics for the statements executed

You can select only one of the first three options—view results in either text, grid, or to a file—and you can also select one or more of the last three options—execution plan, trace, and client statistics. Each option you choose shows up in the results pane as a separate tab.

 Display Estimated Execution Plan Clicking this toolbar button displays the estimated execution plan(s) for the query text in the query window. It does not actually execute the query against the database.

 Object Browser Clicking this toolbar button displays the Object Browser in the left side of Query Analyzer. Click the button again to hide the Object Browser.

 Object Search Clicking this toolbar button opens the Object Search window, where you can search for a particular object, such as a table, and which displays information about that object once it is found.

Current Connection Properties Clicking this toolbar button opens the Current Connection Properties dialog box, where you can select various options for the current connection in Query Analyzer. If you open another query window (another connection) in Query Analyzer, these connection options will be set by default for that new connection.

 Show Results Pane This toolbar button allows you to show or hide the lower pane of the query window. This pane contains the results of the query text.

In addition to the buttons, the query window contains the Current Database drop-down list. This drop-down list contains all existing active databases on the database server to which you are connected. Selecting a database in this list is equivalent to executing the USE (*database name*) SQL statement.

Analyzing Queries

After you have connected to your database server, you can use the query window to enter the text of your SQL statements. You can open an existing query file, enter new SQL statements, or extract the SQL statements embedded in your applications. Once the query text is displayed in the query window, you can execute all or part of the query text. To execute the entire batch of SQL statements, either click the Execute Query button, press F5, or press Ctrl+E. To execute portions of the query text, simply select the SQL statements you wish to execute and then either click the Execute Query button, press F5, or press Ctrl+E.

In either instance, the results are displayed in the lower pane of the query window. Depending on the option you chose for displaying the results, you see any messages, any result sets, and any execution plans generated.

Execution Plans

One of the most important aspects of SQL Query Analyzer is its ability to display query execution plans. After you have opened your query text in the query window, select Show Execution Plan from the Query menu. When you execute the query, the results are displayed in the Results tab, and the execution plan is displayed in a graphical format in the Execution Plan tab.

Logical and Physical Operators

The logical and physical operators in the execution plan describe how a query or update is executed. The *physical operators* describe the physical implementation algorithm used to process a statement, for example, scanning a clustered index. Each step in the execution of a query or update statement involves a physical operator. The *logical operators* describe the relational algebraic operation used to process a statement, for example, performing an aggregation. Not all steps required to process a query or update involve logical operations.

SQL Query Analyzer uses icons to represent the different aspects of query execution. The most common ones are listed here.

 Assert The Assert logical and physical operator performs condition verification. It represents operations such as checking referential integrity constraints or performing any internal checks to ensure that a scalar subquery returns only one row. Each row is passed through the Assert operator, which evaluates the expression. If the expression evaluates to NULL, the Assert operator passes the row on. If it is a non-null value, the Assert operator raises an error condition.

 Bookmark Lookup The Bookmark Lookup logical and physical operator uses a bookmark (a row ID or clustering key) to look up the corresponding row in the table or clustered index. The operator includes an argument that contains the bookmark label used for the lookup, as well as the table name or the name of the clustered index in which the row was looked up. If the WITH PREFETCH clause appears in the argument, then the SQL Server query processor has determined that it is optimal to use asynchronous prefetching, or read-ahead buffering, when looking up bookmarks in the table or clustered index. A bookmark lookup occurs when the columns selected in the SELECT statement are not all found in the index itself (that is, the query is not covered). If all columns are found in the index itself, then a bookmark lookup is not necessary. For example, if you execute a SELECT statement that selects columns a, b, and c, and there is an index on columns a and b only, then a bookmark lookup is necessary to retrieve the data for column c. If the index was on columns a, b, and c, then the data would be retrieved directly from the index leaf node. In cases where the number of columns selected are few, and the tables are fairly large, covering the query by including all selected columns in the index can improve performance of the query. (For small tables a table scan or bookmark lookup may prove just as fast.)

 Clustered Index Delete The Clustered Index Delete physical operator deletes rows from the clustered index specified in the Argument column. If a WHERE:( ) predicate is present in the Argument column, only those rows that satisfy the predicate are deleted.

Clustered Index Insert The Clustered Index Insert physical operator inserts rows from the input into the clustered index specified in the Argument column. The Argument column also contains a SET:() predicate, which indicates the value to which each column is set.

Clustered Index Scan The Clustered Index Scan logical and physical operator scans the clustered index specified in the Argument column. If an optional WHERE:() predicate is present, only those rows that satisfy the predicate are returned.

If the Argument column contains an ORDERED clause, the query processor requests that the rows' output be returned in the order in which the clustered index has sorted them. If an ORDERED clause is not present, the storage engine determines the optimal way to scan the index. This last method does not guarantee that the output is sorted.

Clustered Index Seek The Clustered Index Seek logical and physical operator performs row retrieval through the clustered index. The Argument column contains the name of the clustered index used by the operator, as well as the SEEK:() predicate. The SQL Server storage engine selects only those rows that satisfy the SEEK:() predicate. This operator can include a WHERE:() predicate that further limits the scope of the seek. If the WHERE:() predicate is specified, the storage engine does not use the index.

If the Argument column contains an ORDERED clause, the query processor has determined that all the rows will be returned in the same order as the clustered index has sorted them. If an ORDERED clause is not present, the storage engine determines the optimal way to scan the index. This method does not guarantee that the output is sorted.

Clustered Index Update The Clustered Index Update physical operator updates rows in the clustered index specified in the Argument column. If a WHERE:() predicate is specified, only the rows that satisfy the predicate are updated. The SET:() predicate, if present, indicates the value to which each updated column is set. A DEFINE:() predicate indicates the list of values that this operator defines. These DEFINE:() values are referenced in the SET clause or elsewhere within the operator.

Collapse The Collapse logical and physical operator optimizes update processing. When the query processor performs an update, it can use a split option to break the update into a delete and an insert. If the Argument column contains a GROUP BY:() predicate and a list of the grouped columns, the query processor groups the set of columns and optimizes the update operations by not using any temporary or intermediate row changes.

Compute Scalar The Compute Scalar logical and physical operator evaluates an expression to produce a computed scalar value, which can be returned to the user or referenced elsewhere in the query.

 Concatenation The Concatenation logical and physical operator scans multiple inputs and returns each row scanned.

 Constant Scan The Constant Scan logical and physical operator introduces a constant row into a query. It returns either zero or one row, which usually contains no columns. The Compute Scalar operator is often used to add columns to the row produced by a Constant Scan operator.

 Deleted Scan The Deleted Scan logical and physical operator scans the special *deleted* table within a trigger.

 Filter The Filter logical and physical operator scans the input rows and returns only ones that satisfy the filter predicate. The filter predicate appears in the Argument column.

 Hash Match The Hash Match physical operator builds a hash table by computing a hash value for each row from its build input. A HASH:() predicate specifies a list of columns to be used to create a hash value. This predicate appears in the Argument column. For each probe row (as applicable), this operator computes a hash value and scans the hash table for matches. If a residual predicate is present in the Argument column, that predicate must also be satisfied for rows to be considered a match. This operator's behavior differs according to the actual logical operation that is being performed. The following list outlines the behaviors:

- If you are performing a join, the first input value is used to build the hash table, and the second input is used to probe the hash table. The output matches are dictated by the specified join type. If multiple joins use the same columns, the hashing operations are grouped for efficiency.

- For the Distinct or Aggregate operators, the input value is used to build the hash table. Duplicates are removed and aggregates are computed at this stage. After the hash table is built, it is scanned and all the rows are returned.

- If the Union operator is specified, the first input value is used to build the hash table, removing any duplicates as the table is built. The second input value, which must have no duplicates, is used to probe the hash table. All rows that have no matches are removed; the hash table is then scanned to return all the rows satisfying the Union operator.

Hash Match Root   The Hash Match Root physical operator coordinates all Hash Match Team, or grouped hash, operations directly below it. The Hash Match Root operator and all Hash Match Team operators directly below it share a common hash function and partitioning strategy. This grouping is for hash efficiency. The Hash Match Root operator always returns its output to an operator that is not a member of its team.

 Hash Match Team   The Hash Match Team physical operator is part of a team of connected hash operators sharing common hash function and partitioning strategy.

 Index Delete   The Index Delete physical operator deletes input rows from the nonclustered index specified in the Argument column. If a WHERE:() predicate is present, then only those rows that satisfy this predicate are deleted.

 Index Insert   The Index Insert physical operator inserts rows from its input into the nonclustered index specified in the Argument column. The Argument column also contains a SET:() predicate, which indicates the value to which each column is set.

 Index Scan   The Index Scan logical and physical operator retrieves all rows from the nonclustered index specified in the Argument column. If an optional WHERE:() predicate appears in the Argument column, then only those rows that satisfy the predicate are returned.

If the Argument column contains an ORDERED clause, it indicates that the query processor has determined that the rows returned will be in the order that the nonclustered index has sorted them. If the ORDERED clause is not present, then the storage engine determines the most efficient way to search the index. This last condition does not guarantee that the rows returned are sorted.

 Index Seek   The Index Seek logical and physical operator indicates row retrieval through the nonclustered index. The Argument column contains the name of the nonclustered index used by the operator, as well as the SEEK:() predicate. The SQL Server storage engine selects only those rows that satisfy the SEEK:() predicate. This operator can include a WHERE:() predicate that further limits the scope of the seek. If the WHERE:() predicate is specified, the storage engine does not use the index.

If the Argument column contains an ORDERED clause, the query processor has determined that all the rows will be returned in the order that the nonclustered index has sorted them. If an ORDERED clause is not present, the storage engine determines the optimal way to scan the index. This last condition does not guarantee that the output is sorted.

Index Spool The Index Spool physical operator contains a SEEK:() predicate in the Argument column. This operator scans its input rows, placing a copy of each row in a hidden spool file, which is stored in the tempdb database, and builds an index on the rows. This allows you to use the seeking capability of indexes to output only those rows that satisfy the SEEK:() predicate. The spool file exists only for the lifetime of the query. If the operator is rewound, such as by a Nested Loops operator, but no rebinding is needed, the spooled data is used instead of rescanning the input.

 Index Update The Index Update physical operator updates rows from its input in the nonclustered index specified in the Argument column. If a WHERE:() predicate is specified, only the rows that satisfy the predicate are updated. The SET:() predicate, if present, indicates the value to which each updated column is set. A DEFINE:() predicate indicates the list of values that this operator defines. These DEFINE:() values are referenced in the SET clause or elsewhere within the operator.

 Inserted Scan The Inserted Scan logical and physical operator scans the special *inserted* table within a trigger.

 Log Row Scan The Log Row Scan logical and physical operator scans the transaction log.

 Merge Join The Merge Join physical operator performs the inner join, left outer join, left semi-join, left anti-semi-join, right outer join, right semi-join, and right anti-semi-join, and union logical operations.

The Argument column contains the MERGE:() predicate if the operation is performing a one-to-many join. If the operation is a many-to-many join, then the Argument column contains a MANY-TO-MANY MERGE:() predicate. Within the predicates is a comma-separated list of the columns the query processor will use to perform the join. A merge join requires two inputs, both sorted on their respective columns. If required, an explicit sort is inserted into the query plan by the query processor.

 Nested Loops The Nested Loops physical operator performs the inner join, left outer join, left semi-join, and left anti-semi-join logical operations. This operator first performs a search on the inner table for each row of the outer table. This is typically done using an index, if available. The query processor decides, based on anticipated query costs, whether to sort the outer input. This sort is done to improve locality of the searches on the index over the inner input. Any rows that satisfy the optional predicate in the Argument column are returned.

Parallelism The Parallelism physical operator performs the distribute streams, gather streams, and repartition streams logical operations. The Argument column can contain a PARTITION COLUMNS:( ) predicate. This predicate contains a comma-separated list of the columns being partitioned. The Argument column can also contain an ORDER BY:( ) predicate with a list of the columns for which the sort order is preserved during partitioning.

 Parameter Table Scan The Parameter Table Scan logical and physical operator scans a table that is acting as a parameter in the current query. Typically, this is used for INSERT queries within a stored procedure.

 Remote Delete The Remote Delete logical and physical operator deletes the input rows from a remote object.

 Remote Insert The Remote Insert logical and physical operator inserts the input rows into a remote object.

 Remote Query The Remote Query logical and physical operator submits a query to a remote source. The Argument column contains the text of the query that is sent to the remote server.

 Remote Scan The Remote Scan logical and physical operator scans a remote object. The Argument column contains the name of the remote object to be scanned.

 Remote Update The Remote Update logical and physical operator updates the input rows in a remote object.

 Row Count Spool The Row Count Spool physical operator scans the input, counting the number of rows present and returning that many rows without any data in them. Use this operator when it is important to check for the existence of rows rather than the data contained in the rows. For example, if a Nested Loops operator performs a left semi-join operation and the join predicate applies to inner input, a row count spool might be placed at the top of the Nested Loops operator's inner input. Then the Nested Loops operator can look at how many rows are output by the row count spool (since the actual data from the inner side is not needed) to determine whether to return the outer row.

 Sequence The Sequence logical and physical operator drives wide update plans. The Sequence operator executes each input in sequence, from top to bottom. Each of the inputs is usually an update of a different object. Only those rows that come from its last or bottom input are returned.

Sort The Sort logical and physical operator sorts all incoming rows. The Argument column contains a DISTINCT ORDER BY:() predicate if duplicates are removed by this operation, or an ORDER BY:() predicate with a comma-separated list of the columns being sorted. Each of the columns is prefixed with the value ASC if the columns are sorted in ascending order, or the value DESC if the columns are sorted in descending order.

 Stream Aggregate The Stream Aggregate physical operator calculates one or more aggregate expressions returned by the query or referenced elsewhere within the query. It can perform a group by a set of columns before the aggregate is calculated. If the Stream Aggregate operator is performing a group by columns operation, a GROUP BY:() predicate and the list of columns appear in the Argument column. If the Stream Aggregate operator computes any aggregate expressions, a list of them appears in the Defined Values column of the output from the SHOWPLAN_ALL statement or the Argument column of the graphical execution plan.

 Table Delete The Table Delete physical operator deletes rows from the table specified in the Argument column. If a WHERE:() predicate is included in the Argument column, only those rows that satisfy the predicate are deleted.

 Table Insert The Table Insert physical operator inserts rows from its input into the table specified in the Argument column. The Argument column also contains a SET:() predicate, which indicates the value to which each column is set.

 Table Scan The Table Scan logical and physical operator retrieves all rows from the table specified in the Argument column. If a WHERE:() predicate appears in the Argument column, only those rows that satisfy the predicate are returned.

 Table Spool The Table Spool physical operator scans the input and places a copy of each row in a hidden spool table, which is stored in the tempdb database. The spool table exists only for the lifetime of the query. If the operator is rewound, such as by a Nested Loops operator, but no rebinding is needed, the spooled data is used instead of rescanning the input. This operator looks just like the Row Count Spool operator.

 Table Update The Table Update physical operator updates input rows in the table specified in the Argument column. If a WHERE:() predicate is present, then only those rows that satisfy this predicate are updated. If a SET:() predicate is present, it indicates the value to which each updated column is set. If a DEFINE:() predicate is present, it lists the values that this operator defines. These values may be referenced in the SET clause or elsewhere within this operator and elsewhere within this query.

 Top The Top logical and physical operator scans the input, returning only the first specified number or percentage of rows. The Argument column can contain a list of the columns that are being checked for ties. In update plans, the Top operator is used to enforce row count limits.

Interpreting Graphical Execution Plans

You read the graphical execution plan displayed in SQL Query Analyzer from right to left and from bottom to top. Each query in the batch that is being analyzed is displayed, including the cost of each subquery as a percentage of the total cost of the query batch. Figure 16-2 shows a sample graphical representation of an execution plan.

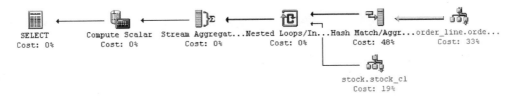

Figure 16-2. *An example of an execution plan displayed in SQL Query Analyzer.*

The execution plan diagrams use the following conventions:

- Each node in the tree structure is represented as an icon that specifies the logical and physical operator used to execute part of the query or statement.
- Each node is related to a parent node. All nodes with the same parent are drawn in the same column. An arrow connects each node to its parent.
- Recursive operations are indicated by an iteration symbol.
- Operators are shown as symbols related to a specific parent.
- When the query contains multiple statements, multiple query execution plans are drawn.
- The parts of the tree structures are determined by the type of statement to be executed.

SQL Query Analyzer breaks down a query into its components, each of which can be one of the five following types:

- **SQL statements and stored procedures** If SQL Query Analyzer determines that the statement is a stored procedure or Transact-SQL statement, it promotes it to the root of the graphical execution plan tree. A stored procedure can have multiple children that represent statements called by the stored procedure.
- **Data manipulation language statements** When the statement is determined to be a Data Manipulation Language (DML) statement, such as SELECT, INSERT, DELETE, or UPDATE, the DML statement is made the root of a tree. A DML statement can have up to two children. The first child is the execution plan. The second child represents a trigger if used.
- **Conditionals** When SQL Query Analyzer identifies a statement as a conditional statement, such as IF..ELSE, it divides it into three children. The IF..ELSE statement is the root of the tree. The "if" clause becomes a subtree node. The "then" and "else" clauses are represented as statement blocks. SQL Query Analyzer processes WHILE and DO-UNTIL statements in the same manner.

- **Relational operators** Operations such as table scans, joins, and aggregations are represented as nodes on a tree.
- **Cursor declarations** When SQL Query Analyzer encounters a DECLARE CURSOR statement, it promotes it to the root of a graphical execution tree, with its related statement as a child or node.

Once you have displayed the graphical execution plan in SQL Query Analyzer, you can put your cursor over a node and view the context-sensitive information related to that part of the query statement, as shown in Figure 16-3. The ToolTip can include the following information:

- **Physical operation** The physical operator used for the operation, such as Hash Join or Nested Loop.
- **Logical operation** The logical operator that matches the physical operator. If the logical operator is different from the physical operator, it is listed after the physical operator and separated by a forward slash.
- **Estimated row count** The number of rows output by the operator.
- **Estimated row size** The estimated size of each row output.
- **Estimated I/O cost** The estimated cost of all the I/O activity for the operation.
- **Estimated CPU cost** The estimated cost for all CPU activity for the operation.
- **Estimated number of executes** The number of times the operation was executed during the query.
- **Estimated cost** The cost to the query optimizer in executing the operation. This includes the cost of this operation as a percentage of the total cost of the query.
- **Estimated subtree cost** The total cost to the query optimizer in executing this operation and all operations preceding it in the same subtree.
- **Argument** The predicates and parameters used by the query.

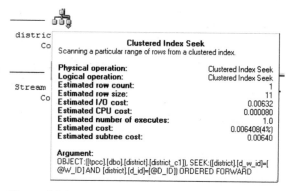

Figure 16-3. *Statement details.*

Example of Using SQL Query Analyzer

Let's look at a sample query in SQL Query Analyzer. This query is based on one of the transactions in the Transaction Processing Council's TPC-C benchmark. The query is not too complex, but it does provide an excellent example of what to look for with SQL Query Analyzer. The SQL text of the query is as follows:

```
CREATE PROC TPCC_STOCKINFO    @W_ID          SMALLINT,
                              @D_ID          TINYINT,
                              @THRESHOLD     SMALLINT
AS
DECLARE  @O_ID_LOW    INT,
         @O_ID_HIGH   INT
SELECT   @O_ID_LOW    = (D_NEXT_O_ID - 50),
         @O_ID_HIGH   = (D_NEXT_O_ID - 1)
FROM     DISTRICT
WHERE    D_W_ID       = @W_ID AND
         D_ID         = @D_ID
SELECT   COUNT(DISTINCT(S_I_ID))
FROM     STOCK
WHERE    S_W_ID       = @W_ID AND
         S_QUANTITY   < @THRESHOLD AND
         S_I_ID       IN (SELECT DISTINCT(OL_I_ID)
                          FROM     ORDER_LINE
                          WHERE    OL_W_ID  = @W_ID AND
                                   OL_D_ID  = @D_ID AND
                                   OL_O_ID BETWEEN @O_ID_LOW
                                   AND @O_ID_HIGH)

SET      ROWCOUNT 20
SELECT   DISTINCT(S_I_ID),
         S_QUANTITY,
         S_YTD
FROM     STOCK
WHERE    S_W_ID       = @W_ID AND
         S_QUANTITY   > @THRESHOLD AND
         S_I_ID       IN (SELECT DISTINCT(OL_I_ID)
                          FROM     ORDER_LINE
                          WHERE    OL_W_ID  = @W_ID AND
                                   OL_D_ID  = @D_ID AND
                                   OL_O_ID BETWEEN @O_ID_LOW
                                   AND @O_ID_HIGH)

ORDER    BY S_YTD DESC,
         S_QUANTITY ASC,
         S_I_ID ASC
SET      ROWCOUNT 0
GO
```

Let's look at each piece of the query and its associated graphical execution plan. The first SELECT statement,

```
SELECT   @O_ID_LOW      = (D_NEXT_O_ID - 50),
         @O_ID_HIGH     = (D_NEXT_O_ID - 1)
FROM     DISTRICT
WHERE    D_W_ID         = @W_ID AND
         D_ID           = @D_ID
```

uses a warehouse identifier and a district identifier (which are passed in) to select the last 50 orders. The graphical execution plan generated by SQL Query Analyzer for this query is shown in Figure 16-4.

Figure 16-4. *Graphical representation of the execution plan for the first SELECT statement in the example query.*

The first line of the text output gives you the relative weight of this query in the batch you presented to SQL Query Analyzer. In this example, with only one query active at a time, the query cost is 100 percent. The second line of the output displays the text of the query. The results pane displays the execution plan using an icon for each distinct part of the statement.

By placing the cursor over one of the icons, such as the Clustered Index Seek icon, you can get detailed information about that portion of the statement, as shown previously in Figure 16-3. This display indicates that the physical and logical operations being performed are clustered index seeks. The Estimated Row Count is 1, and the Estimated Row Size is 11. The Estimated I/O Cost gives you an indication of the I/O resources this portion of the query will use. The value in the example query, 0.006408, is acceptable. It takes into account that the columns used for the scan all have valid statistics and that there is a clustered index on the columns used. You should strive to keep I/O cost as low as possible. The appropriate use of index structures can help you achieve this goal.

The next statement is a little more complex. Figure 16-5 shows the execution plan that SQL Query Analyzer generates for the second part of our sample query batch. Several different icons are represented in this output. The query in question executes a clustered index seek operation, and then a hash match/aggregate operation. The result of the latter operation is then joined with the result of another clustered index seek. The Nested Loops/Inner Join icon represents this join. Following the join, an aggregate function is executed. Finally, the scalar computation is performed and the results are returned to the requestor.

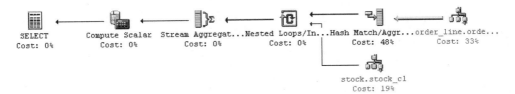

Figure 16-5. *Execution plan for the example query.*

This query also illustrates another feature of SQL Query Analyzer. The two clustered index seeks are color coded in red. When you move the mouse over the icon to display the operation details, a message appears that indicates that some statistics are missing for this table, as shown in Figure 16-6. If you want to create the missing statistics, right-click the icon and select Create Missing Statistics from the shortcut menu. SQL Query Analyzer then displays the Create Missing Statistics dialog box showing which column or columns in the table are missing statistics, as shown in Figure 16-7.

Figure 16-6. *A ToolTip indicating missing statistics.*

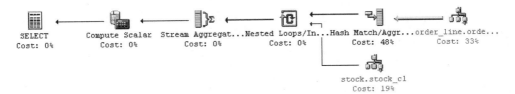

Figure 16-7. *The Create Missing Statistics dialog box.*

In our example, SQL Query Analyzer suggests that we generate statistics for the *ol_i_id* column of the *order_line* table. Before clicking OK, you can determine how much data is to be sampled. The default is to sample 25 percent of the rows in the table. This sampling allows the statistics creation to occur in a timely fashion. You can request that a different percentage of the rows be sampled, or have the statistics generated based on all rows. Be aware that creating statistics on all rows may require a great deal of time.

In addition, you can instruct SQL Server not to automatically recompute statistics. This option is not recommended for tables in which the data is dynamic. As you insert, delete, and update tables for which automatic recomputation of statistics has been disabled, the quality of the statistics degrades. This leads to decreased performance when seeking records in those tables. If you have tables that are static in nature, automatic recomputation of statistics is not necessary.

One other option you have in the Create Missing Statistics dialog box is to view and edit the actual Transact-SQL code that will be executed. After you have set your particular options, and when you are satisfied with the code, click OK to instruct SQL Server to generate the statistics. When the statistics have been computed, subsequent displays of the execution plan no longer show up in red.

Earlier we looked at each piece of the batch of our queries separately. In each of those cases, the query cost was 100 percent. When we display all the statements of our batch together, we can get a feel for which areas of our batch are the most expensive in relation to other queries in this batch. Figure 16-8 shows the output for the entire query batch of our example. In this example, 7.79 percent of the time is spent on the first query in the batch, and 92.21 percent is used on the second query. Using the relative costs allows you to focus your efforts on the most expensive parts of your query batch, giving you the most return on your time investment.

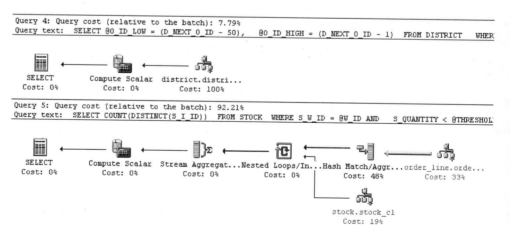

Figure 16-8. *Graphical representation of the execution plan for a complete SQL batch.*

Index Tuning Wizard

An integral part of SQL Query Analyzer is the Index Tuning Wizard. The Index Tuning Wizard allows you to select and create an optimal set of indexes and statistics for a SQL Server database without requiring an expert understanding of the structure of the database, the workload, or the internal workings of SQL Server.

The Index Tuning Wizard requires a workload as its input. A workload can consist of a SQL script or a SQL Profiler trace saved to a file. A SQL Profiler trace is the recommended input for the Index Tuning Wizard. The more closely the input represents your actual environment, the more accurate the Index Tuning Wizard's recommendations. Furthermore, the longer the trace duration, the better the end analysis. Bear in mind, however, that using a long SQL Profiler trace increases the time the Index Tuning Wizard requires for its analysis. See Chapter 7, "Using SQL Profiler," for more information.

Features of the Index Tuning Wizard

The Index Tuning Wizard offers the following features to assist you in your tuning efforts. It can

- Recommend the best mix of indexes for a database given a specific workload by using the query optimizer to analyze the queries in the workload. Bear in mind that the index mix recommended might not be optimal if the workload changes, even slightly, from that used in the Index Tuning Wizard.
- Analyze the effects of the proposed changes, including index usage, distribution of queries among tables, and performance of queries in the workload.
- Recommend ways to tune the database based on a small subset of queries used in your workload.
- Allow you to customize the recommendations by specifying advanced options such as disk space constraints.

After the Index Tuning Wizard completes its analysis, it presents several recommendations. A recommendation consists of SQL statements that can be executed to create new, more effective indexes and, if you want, to drop existing indexes that are ineffective. Once the Index Tuning Wizard has suggested a recommendation, you can implement it immediately, schedule it to be implemented later by creating a SQL Server job that executes a SQL script at a specified time, or save it to a SQL script so that it can be executed later, possibly on a different server.

Limitations of the Index Tuning Wizard

The Index Tuning Wizard has some limitations to keep in mind. To begin with, the wizard does not recommend indexes on the following:

- Tables referenced by cross-database queries that do not exist in the currently selected database
- System tables
- Primary key constraints and unique indexes

Furthermore, the number of tunable queries allowed in the workload is limited to 32,767. Any additional queries in the workload are not considered. Queries with quoted identifiers are also not considered for tuning.

Because the Index Tuning Wizard gathers statistics by sampling the data, successive executions of the wizard on the same workload may result in variations in the indexes recommended as well as variations in the improvements that result from implementing these recommendations. You may also encounter a condition in which the Index Tuning Wizard does not make any suggestions. Normally, this indicates either that there was not enough data in the tables sampled to come up with any meaningful recommendations or that the potential recommendations do not offer any significant performance improvements over the existing index structures.

If you encounter problems with excessive or unacceptable Index Tuning Wizard execution times, there are several things you can do to reduce the execution time:

- Clear the Perform Thorough Analysis option in the Select Server And Database dialog box. When you opt to perform a thorough analysis, you instruct the Index Tuning Wizard to analyze all the queries in the input stream. This results in longer execution times.
- Restrict the Index Tuning Wizard to a subset of the tables in your database. When performing index analysis from SQL Query Analyzer, the Index Tuning Wizard analyzes only the tables in the workload or query you opened. If you open the Index Tuning Wizard from Enterprise Manager, however, you can select a subset of your tables from the Tables object pane prior to starting the wizard.
- Reduce the overall size of the workload file.

If you select the Keep All Existing Indexes option, the Index Tuning Wizard does not recommend dropping any indexes. It only recommends new indexes. Clearing this option can result in a greater overall improvement in the performance of the workload. Additionally, the Index Tuning Wizard does not recommend dropping indexes on primary key constraints or unique indexes. However, it may drop or replace a clustered index that is not unique or currently created on a primary key constraint.

You can defer building the indexes recommended by the Index Tuning Wizard by saving the recommended SQL scripts using SQL Query Analyzer. You can then examine and edit the SQL statements. Once you've edited it, you can run the script at a more convenient time.

Using the Index Tuning Wizard

Let's look at an example of using the Index Tuning Wizard. We use the same SQL batch we used earlier in this chapter except that the clustered indexes have been deleted. After you have loaded the workload by selecting Open from the File menu, you can access the Index Tuning Wizard by clicking Index Tuning Wizard on the Query menu. You can also press the keyboard shortcut Ctrl+I.

Now the system analyzes the queries and the existing index structures. Depending on the complexity of the workload and the tables involved, this process can take a while. When the Index Tuning Wizard finishes its analysis, it displays a window that indicates the recommended index or indexes and the appropriate SQL statements for building them, as shown in Figure 16-9. You can click the Accept button to build the recommended index or indexes; or you can copy the SQL statements and execute them later.

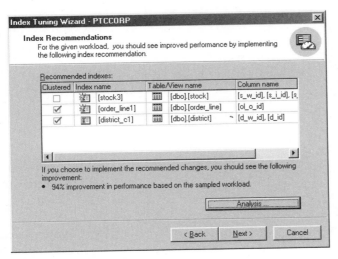

Figure 16-9. *Index Tuning Wizard results.*

Summary

In this chapter you learned about SQL Query Analyzer and the Index Tuning Wizard. You have seen how to use SQL Query Analyzer to view the graphical execution plan and to view the details of each subcomponent of your queries. In addition, you have seen how to use the Index Tuning Wizard to enhance your query strategy. Now that you have been exposed to the tools available to optimize and tune your queries, let's look at the techniques you can use to get the most performance from your SQL statements.

Chapter 17
Tuning SQL Statements and Stored Procedures

An important area of system performance involves the SQL statements used in your applications. In this chapter we explore techniques for effective application design, query design and tuning, and index design and tuning. Finally, we briefly look at the differences between ActiveX Data Objects (ADO) and Open Database Connectivity (ODBC), and some techniques you can use to better the performance of your applications that issue the same SQL queries many times.

Application Design

An efficient application design is critical to your system's performance. If you have purchased your application from a third party, it might be difficult or impossible to examine the database statements. If you have implemented the techniques and tips from other chapters in this book and still have performance problems, it would be wise to contact the provider of your application for assistance.

If your application is of your own design, or home grown, you have much more flexibility in tuning it and its associated queries. One way to think about your application is to view it and the client as a controlling entity. The application controls the flow of information and directs the Microsoft SQL Server database's actions. Your application tells SQL Server which queries to execute, when to execute them, and how to process the results. This has a major effect on the type and duration of locks, the amount of I/O, and the processing load on the server's CPU, and hence on performance.

Thus, it is important to make good decisions during the application design phase. A well-designed application allows SQL Server to support thousands of concurrent users. On the other hand, a poorly designed application prevents even the most powerful server platform from handling more than a few users.

Recommendations

You can easily analyze and correct several areas to improve performance of your system and applications that run on it. You should always strive to eliminate excessive network traffic between the clients and the SQL Server system. The network round-trips are the conversational traffic sent between SQL Server and the clients for every batch and results set. Generally, you can exploit SQL Server stored procedures to minimize the round-trips. We examine stored procedures later in this chapter.

Another area to look at in your applications is the size of the result sets returned. You should attempt to minimize this size because retrieving needlessly large result sets for browsing on the client adds processor and network I/O load. It also can make the application less capable of remote use and limit multi-user scalability. It is a good idea to design the application to prompt the user for sufficient input so queries are submitted that generate modest result sets. You can use several techniques to control the size of the result set returned. For more information on properly sizing result sets, see the "Efficient Retrieval of Data" section later in this chapter.

There are several SQL language best practices that can also benefit performance; the first of which is to avoid using wildcards, such as SELECT *, when you build your queries. Reducing the use of wildcards not only decreases the data retrieved, it also reduces the metadata flowing across the network for the client libraries. You should also consider using SQL statements such as TOP n [PERCENT] to limit the number of rows returned by the query. One advantage that TOP has over the traditional SET ROWCOUNT = n is that SQL Server has to satisfy only the first n rows and return, so CPU utilization is much less. In contrast, with SET ROWCOUNT, the statement must build the result set, and then return only the requested number of rows.

Another way to optimize queries is to use the EXISTS clause. The sample code below is typical of code found in IS shops anywhere. The result is a table or index scan that can generate a huge number of locks. So, rather than:

```
SELECT SUM(A.Col2) FROM MyTableA A
    WHERE (
        (SELECT COUNT(*) FROM MyTableB B
        WHERE B.Col1 = A.Col1) > 0)
```

Try:

```
SELECT SUM(A.Col2) FROM MyTableA A
    WHERE EXISTS(
        SELECT * FROM MyTableB B
        WHERE B.Col1 = A.Col1)
```

Using the EXISTS clause with the asterisk (*) or a single numeral allows SQL Server to select the best index for the job while eliminating bookmark lookups, because it will never hit the core table data as long as a covering index or combinations of indexes exist for the criteria. This results in latch locks, which are far less costly than typical table, page, or row locks.

You can also try to eliminate ad hoc queries from your client systems. Ad hoc queries are typically poorly constructed and return far more rows than necessary. Eliminating ad hoc queries can be a drastic step that provokes a user rebellion, but it can save an impressive amount of valuable server resources. If ad hoc queries are absolutely required, consider using a replicated reporting server, or even better, implementing an Analysis Services database with all the reporting data.

One area that is often overlooked is providing an application feature that allows a user to cancel a query and regain control of the processing. If a user or client makes a mistake, allowing them to cancel the query eliminates needless processing on the system. A simple Cancel button can work wonders for system performance. When this feature is overlooked, it can lead to performance problems that are difficult to detect and resolve. The most common data access libraries, including ADO, ODBC and DB-Library provide an API for query cancellation. If you do allow cancellation of a query, you should make sure that the application issues either a commit or rollback to ensure data integrity, because canceling a query does not automatically commit or roll back a transaction.

Another easy technique you can use is to always implement a query or lock timeout. This measure prevents miscoded queries from running indefinitely, a common problem in environments that allow ad hoc queries. SQL Server and ODBC provide functions and statements to regulate the duration of query and lock timeouts.

Another common area of effective application design is the selection of application generation tools. Though we do not cover the selection of these tools, we do have a recommendation concerning their features. Some application generation tools do not allow you to control explicitly the SQL statements generated and sent to SQL Server. Tools that transparently generate SQL statements sound inviting and are fantastic for prototyping an application. Such tools, however, can and do cause performance problems in production environments. Tools such as these normally do not provide mechanisms for query cancellation, query timeout, or overall transactional control. You can often encounter problems because of locking and transactional blocking, which, as we have seen in other chapters, are critical to overall system performance.

You should minimize the use of database cursors in your applications when possible. Cursors are useful tools but are usually more expensive to use than regular, set-oriented SQL statements. In set-oriented SQL statements, the client application tells the server to update the set of records that meet specified criteria. SQL Server figures out how to accomplish the update as a single unit of work. When updating through a cursor, the client application requires the server to maintain locking or version information for every row accessed in case the client asks to update the row after it has been fetched.

The state information that is retained on the server in a server side cursor, such as the current rowset, is very expensive in terms of overhead. This state information is usually maintained in temporary storage. With a small number of users, this is usually not a problem. As the user population grows, however, maintaining this state becomes an expensive use of valuable server resources. A better strategy is to use client side cursors, eliminating any need for client state information to be held at the server between calls. We examine techniques for efficient cursor use later in this chapter.

You should avoid intermixing online transaction processing (OLTP) and decision support queries on the same system. Each type of workload has different requirements and functions that might compete if they are on a single system. Consider implementing one or more systems for your OLTP workload, and having other systems that use offline data for your decision support queries. Decision support and OLTP systems are discussed in detail in Chapters 12, "Online Transaction Processing Systems," and Chapter 13, "Data Warehouses."

Additionally, you should attempt to keep the duration of transactions as short as possible to minimize blocking and improve concurrency. There are two major causes for long-running transactions, which are long-running queries and transactions waiting for user input. Many programmers attach a BEGIN TRANSACTION to the open event of a dialog box, and a COMMIT and ROLLBACK to the OK and CANCEL buttons respectively. While this might seem an intuitive use of transactions, in a multi-user environment, the cost is far too high, often leaving entire tables locked while the end user fetches another cup of coffee.

Likewise, a long-running query can block other queries. A DELETE or UPDATE operation that affects many rows can acquire many locks that might even escalate to table locks. These locks can prohibit other transactions from executing. You should look for ways to optimize a long-running query by changing indexes, breaking a large, complex query into simpler queries, or running the query during off hours or on a separate computer. Execution of SQL statements in SQL stored procedures or in prepared execution statements can also improve application performance. The most common instances of long-running queries typically include decision support queries. Remember that you should try not to mix your decision support and OLTP queries on the same database.

Finally, another important consideration for performance is the client library. SQL Server offers several, including DB-LIB, ODBC, OLE DB and ADO. A long held myth is that DB-LIB is faster than ODBC. This is based on experiences with Sybase and Oracle, and is not actually true. With Sybase and Oracle, the only native access was through

DB-LIB (CT-LIB today) and SQL-NET, respectively. Using Sybase and Oracle with a tool like ODBC, with its goal of transparent connectivity to multiple database vendors, required ODBC to be implemented on top of the native drivers, which had a definite impact on the driver's performance. Unlike those tools, SQL Server's ODBC driver actually reads and writes to the underlying tabular data stream (TDS). Because the ODBC driver is not required to call on any other application layer, the performance is comparable to that of any previously native driver.

Critical-Path Transactions

Before analyzing your applications and queries, you should attempt to identify the transactions that are in your critical path. These are the transactions or database operations that could affect your system the most if they perform poorly or block other transactions. After you have identified the critical transactions or operations, you can easily focus on the areas that can provide the most return on your time investment.

One way to analyze your critical transactions is to draw an execution matrix. Using a spreadsheet or graph paper, list the critical transactions or operations down the left side. Then for each transaction or operation, list the table and the type of access. Are you selecting, inserting, updating, or deleting rows? Also be sure to note if you are joining multiple tables in the transaction. Once you have your information plotted in the matrix, you can analyze it for concurrency or look for places where redundant data might be appropriate. If you find places where a transaction is doing a large join, for example, it might make sense to have redundant data in some tables to lessen the impact of the join. Figure 17-1 is an example of an execution matrix for two transactions. For each transaction, only those columns that are being accessed are displayed. This is done for readability in the example. For each column, the type of access is noted, as well as any joins that might be occurring. One caveat here is that in systems that are already I/O bound, using redundant data might exaggerate the problem, rather than help.

Transaction # 1	District			Order-Line				Stock		
	d_id	d_w_id	d_next_o_id	ol_w_id	ol_d_id	ol_i_id	ol_o_id	s_w_id	s_i_id	s_quantity
Stock Information	= local var.	= local var.	Select	Join (s_w_id	= local var.	Join (s_i_id)	= local var.	Join (ol_w_id)	Join (ol_w_id) Return Count	< local var.

Transaction # 2	Customer					History			
	c_last	c_w_id	c_d_id	c_id	c_ytd_payment	h_c_id	h_d_id	h_w_id	h_date
Payment		= local var.	= local var.	= local var.	Update =val + local var.	Insert = local var.	Insert = local var.	Insert = local var.	Insert = local var.

Figure 17-1. *An execution matrix.*

Using Stored Procedures

Most well-designed SQL Server applications are developed with stored procedures in mind. Stored procedures allow you to reuse queries on your system by simply specifying them by name and passing in the appropriate parameters.

A *stored procedure* is simply a group of SQL statements that are compiled into a single execution plan. SQL Server stored procedures can take input via input parameters and can return data in one of four ways: output parameters of either actual data or cursor variables, an integer return code, a result set for each SELECT statement, or a global cursor that can be referenced outside the context of the stored procedure.

Stored procedures allow you to achieve a consistent implementation of logic across all your applications. The SQL statements and logic needed to execute a commonly performed task can be designed, coded, and tested once and then reused. Each application that needs to perform the task can simply execute the stored procedure. In addition, traditional client/server application developers might gain greater control in ensuring that all clients are using the most current versions of business rules and procedures when the business logic is coded into stored procedures.

The use of stored procedures allows you to isolate your normal application logic from the database layout. If you have a stored procedure that returns some values to your application, you can modify the database layout and stored procedure without changing the underlying application, requiring a redistribution of the binaries. As long as you return the expected number and type of values, the application code does not have to change. Even modern n-tiered applications can benefit from reusing stored procedure code, because the procedures can provide a consistent interface for updates, deletes, and inserts, and act as a proxy for remote servers in a federated cluster.

Another benefit of SQL Server stored procedures for developers is the version information. In SQL Server you can place a semi-colon and a numeric identifier after the stored procedure name. You can use this numeric identifier as a versioning tool, which allows developers to stagger deployment throughout the enterprise. Essentially, if *sp_mystoredproc;2* is called by the newest version of the application while *sp_mystoredproc;1* (the ";1" is assumed if no number is given) is called, then both versions of the application might continue to work, even if the number of columns, result sets or data types expected differ.

Stored procedures also improve performance. Generally, an application performs a task as a series of SQL statements. The output of the first statement provides data for subsequent SQL statements, and a conditional expression determines which SQL statements will be executed. If you can combine these SQL statements and conditional logic into a stored procedure, they become part of a single execution plan on the server. This concept is illustrated in the following SQL code sample:

```
IF (@QuantityOrdered < (SELECT     QuantityOnHand
                        FROM       Inventory
                        WHERE      PartID = @PartOrdered))
      BEGIN
            <insert SQL Statements to do work if condition is true>
      END
ELSE
      BEGIN
            <insert SQL Statements to do work if condition is false>
      END
```

Even though there is a single execution plan now, you will still get some traffic between the client and the server. At the end of each SQL statement, SQL Server sends a response back to the client indicating the number of rows affected by the statement; these messages take up some network bandwidth. Once you are comfortable with the logic in your stored procedure, you can turn off these messages by issuing the SET NOCOUNT ON connection command. The results then do not have to be returned to the client to have the conditional logic applied; all the work is done on the server. This helps minimize the number of network round-trips required for execution.

Using stored procedures can also reduce network bandwidth because applications do not need to transmit all the SQL statements in the procedure. To execute the procedure, the application need only transmit either an EXECUTE or CALL statement containing the name of the procedure and the values of the parameters. Consider a scenario where your application requires a complex JOIN between multiple tables; using a single EXECUTE command and the associated procedure and parameters can dramatically reduce the amount of data being sent across the network.

SQL Server 2000, unlike versions of SQL Server prior to 7.0, does not save a partially compiled plan for a stored procedure when the procedure is created. A stored procedure is compiled at execution time like any other SQL statement or batch. SQL Server retains execution plans for all SQL statements in the SQL Server procedure cache, which despite the name, is not just for execution plans of stored procedures. SQL Server uses an efficient algorithm for comparing any new SQL statements with the SQL statements used in existing cached execution plans. If it determines that the new SQL statement matches the SQL statement of an existing execution plan, it reuses the plan. This reuse reduces the relative performance benefit of precompiled stored procedures by extending execution plan reuse to all SQL statements. The advantage is that each execution of the procedure considers the impact of the changes in the underlying data and on the effectiveness of the query plan. With SQL Server 2000 the distribution of the data causes a given query plan to be compared against the actual current distribution of data in the hopes that the additional cost of compiling the new query plan is lower than that of using an outdated plan.

It is the change in the underlying data distribution that causes a common problem in stored procedure development, which involves recompilation during execution. This occurs when the data within a table used by the stored procedure changes dramatically after the procedure begins, while the procedure and additional statements within the procedure work with that table. In this case, the entire procedure is recompiled. Because this happens most often with very large stored procedures, which might require several seconds just to compile, system performance might be dramatically reduced.

You can create stored procedures by either coding SQL statements within a CREATE PROCEDURE wrapper or by creating the stored procedure within the SQL Server Enterprise Manager. The following code sample shows the creation of a stored procedure using the CREATE PROCEDURE SQL statement:

```
USE SALES
IF EXISTS (SELECT     NAME
              FROM    SYSOBJECTS
              WHERE   NAME = 'REGION_INFO' AND
                      TYPE = 'P')
    DROP PROCEDURE REGION_INFO
GO

USE SALES
GO

CREATE PROCEDURE REGION_INFO @REG_NAME VARCHAR(40),
                             @BRAND VARCHAR(20)

AS
SELECT    REGION_NAME,
          UNITS_SOLD,
          SALES_BY_MONTH,
          BRAND_NAME
FROM      REGION_DATA
WHERE     REGION_NAME = @REG_NAME AND
          BRAND_NAME  = @BRAND
GO
```

Let's look at this code in detail. The first thing we want to do is to find out if there is an existing stored procedure by this name in our database. Since we want to give our users the most current version, if we find an existing version we drop that version of the procedure. Next we issue a CREATE PROCEDURE command. This command names the procedure and, in this case, defines two parameters that will be passed to the stored procedure as input. We then use these input parameters in the subsequent SELECT statement. You can see that the stored procedure consists of regular SQL statements with an additional wrapper around them.

If you choose, you can use the Stored Procedure Properties dialog box in SQL Server Enterprise Manager to build your stored procedure. To create a stored procedure within the Enterprise Manager, expand your list of databases in Enterprise Manager's console tree. Right-click the database you want, point to New, and then click Stored Procedure on the shortcut menu. The Stored Procedure Properties dialog box opens, as shown in Figure 17-2. Enter your stored procedure text in the Text box. At any time, you can click the Check Syntax button to quickly make sure that you have entered the correct syntax in your stored procedure. In addition, you can choose to save the text as a template for the development of future stored procedures. This feature allows you to create a stored procedure style for your applications and queries and then easily maintain that style across other stored procedures you create.

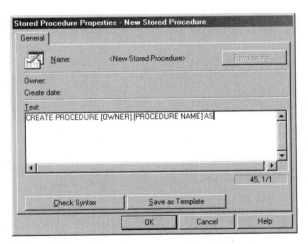

Figure 17-2. *The Stored Procedure Properties dialog box.*

Regardless of how you create your stored procedures, you will want to get data or result sets back from them. The code on the following page illustrates three ways that stored procedures can return data to your application.

```
USE NORTHWIND
GO

IF EXISTS (SELECT NAME FROM SYSOBJECTS WHERE NAME = 'ORDERSUMMARY')
    DROP PROCEDURE ORDERSUMMARY
GO

CREATE PROCEDURE ORDERSUMMARY @EMPID INT

AS
DECLARE @MAXQUANTITY INT
IF (@EMPID >= 0)
    RETURN 1
ELSE
    BEGIN
      SELECT    ORD.EMPLOYEEID,
                SUMMSALES = SUM(ORDET.UNITPRICE * ORDET.QUANTITY)
      FROM      ORDERS AS ORD
      JOIN      [ORDER DETAILS] AS ORDET ON (ORD.ORDERID = ORDET.ORDERID)
      WHERE     ORD.EMPLOYEEID = @EMPID
      GROUP BY  ORD.EMPLOYEEID

      SELECT    @MAXQUANTITY = MAX(QUANTITY)
      FROM      [ORDER DETAILS]

      SELECT    @MAXQUANTITY AS 'MAX QUANTITY'
    END
GO
```

To run the stored procedure, use the following line of code:

```
EXEC @ORDERSUM = ORDERSUMMARY @MAXQUANTITY = @LARGESTORDER OUTPUT
```

This sample stored procedure first checks to see if the input parameter, @EMPID, is greater than zero. If it is not, we consider this an error condition and the stored procedure exits and returns 1 to the calling application. If the input parameter is greater than zero, the stored procedure issues a SELECT statement that returns a result set summarizing the sales activity from the Orders and Order Details table grouped by employee where the employee ID equals the input parameter. Next, the stored procedure issues another SELECT statement that fills an output parameter called @MAXQUANTITY. This value is not returned to the user at this time. Finally, the stored procedure performs another SELECT statement that returns the @MAXQUANTITY value back to the user.

The Effect of Variables

To reduce the impact of recompiles on your server, consider minimizing the use of variables within your procedures. Not to be confused with parameters, *variables* are declared within the scope of the executing procedure or batch, and as such, their values are not available at execution time. If a value is not available when the query plan is being created, SQL Server's cost-based index selection makes educated guesses based on the standard deviation of the data within the index, rather than the number of steps. For example, consider a non-unique index with only two possible values, True or False. In the table, 10,000 rows match True and 5 rows match False.

```
—  ================================================
—  Create table with IDENTITY column
—  ================================================
IF EXISTS (SELECT name FROM sysobjects WHERE name = 'truefalse'
            AND type = 'U')
    DROP TABLE truefalse
GO

CREATE TABLE truefalse
    (tf_id int IDENTITY(1,1) PRIMARY KEY CLUSTERED,
    tf_true bit NOT NULL)
GO

INSERT INTO truefalse VALUES (0)
INSERT INTO truefalse VALUES (0)
INSERT INTO truefalse VALUES (0)
INSERT INTO truefalse VALUES (0)
INSERT INTO truefalse VALUES (0)

WHILE @@IDENTITY < 10000
BEGIN
        INSERT INTO truefalse VALUES (1)
END

CREATE INDEX idxtf_true ON truefalse (tf_true)

dbcc SHOW_STATISTICS ('truefalse', 'idxtf_true')
```
(continued)

(continued)

```
SELECT COUNT(*) from truefalse

- Batch'ed query
SELECT * FROM truefalse WHERE tf_true = 0

- Parameterized query
DECLARE
        @val BIT,
        @SQLString NVARCHAR(500)

SET @val = 0

SET @SQLString = N'SELECT * FROM truefalse WHERE tf_true = @val'
    exec sp_executesql @SQLString, N'@val BIT', @val
```

This code remarked by batched query will always generate an index scan, while a parameterized query will conclude that there are so few incidences of a 0 value that a simple seek is adequate. This resulted in only two logical reads using the parameterized views versus 20 without them. This particular example is an exaggeration, because the query optimizer in SQL Server 2000 is far better than the one in SQL Server 7.0 at locating parameters in even simple batches.

Using the batched query, SQL Server might not have the value of the variable during compile time, and will choose the index based upon the variance in the data, rather than the actual number of steps for that value. This generates overhead and reduces the opportunities for best index selection. Note that using a rules-based index, such as those in competing products almost never uses the "best" index, because the index chosen at compile time has little to do with the number of steps.

So, consider breaking your stored procedure into several smaller procedures. Alternatively, make use of the *sp_executesql* stored procedure, which can also make efficient use of the caching features in SQL Server. It eliminates the single execution plan, but minimizes the impact of recompiles while increasing opportunities for best possible index selections. If you use the multiple procedure approach, use the root stored procedure to create or delete any temporary tables, and return any result sets to the caller.

Caching Execution Plans

In addition to caching the execution plans of stored procedures, SQL Server 2000 caches the execution plans of queries that are not stored procedures. If your users issue ad hoc queries, SQL Server 2000 caches the execution plans. If a subsequent ad hoc query matches a cached plan, SQL Server 2000 will reuse the plan.

SQL Server 2000 enhances the automatic parameterization of queries that was available in SQL Server 7.0. SQL Server guesses which constants in a SQL batch are parameters. Subsequent SQL batches that follow the same basic template can use the same execution plan as the original batch. As an example of auto-parameterization, let's look at the two following queries:

```
SELECT BRAND, SW_UNITS, SW_SALES FROM REGION_SALES
    WHERE BRAND = 'WIDGET'
SELECT BRAND, SW_UNITS, SW_SALES FROM REGION_SALES
    WHERE BRAND = 'GIZMO'
```

These two queries will use the same plan for execution. SQL Server will internally parameterize the brand condition. To avoid any possible performance degradation with auto-parameterization, SQL Server will use the same execution plan only if the template is considered safe. The plan is safe if any change to the actual parameter will not change the execution plan.

Rather than relying on auto-parameterization, consider using tools such as the *sp_executesql* stored procedure and the ODBC SQLBindParameter function. These tools allow for the explicit parameterization of the SQL statement, increasing the reusability of the execution plan. While *sp_executesql* is a Transact-SQL feature for use within stored procedures and complex query batches, SQLBindParameter is available for client applications through ODBC, OLE DB and ADO. In fact, *sp_executesql* is used by OLE DB, ADO and ODBC when sending across parameterized queries. Even your stored procedures can benefit from the use of parameterized queries.

Coding SQL Statements as Transactions

If you use SQL statements appropriately, you will reduce the amount of data transferred between server and client. Reducing the amount of data transferred will normally reduce the time it takes to accomplish a logical task or transaction. Transactions with long execution times are adequate for a single-user system, but they will inhibit proper scaling when your system encounters multiple users. As we have seen, to support transactional consistency, a database system must hold locks on shared resources from the time they are first acquired within the transaction until the transaction commits. If another user needs access to the same resources, the user must wait. As your individual transactions get longer, the queue of other users waiting for locks gets longer and system throughput decreases. Long transactions also increase the chances of a deadlock, which occurs when two or more users are each waiting on locks held by the other.

Some techniques you can use to reduce transaction duration in your applications are as follows:

- Commit your transactional changes as soon as possible within the requirements of the application. If your application includes large batch-oriented jobs, such as month-end summary processing, you should break the entire job into individual steps that can be committed without compromising your data consistency. If you can commit the changes as quickly as possible, you minimize the duration of locks that must be held.

- Take advantage of SQL Server statement batches. Statement batches are a means of sending multiple SQL statements from your clients to SQL Server at one time. These batches minimize the number of round-trips between the client and server, which shortens the time that locks must be held to complete a transaction. If you are forced to go back to the client after each piece of the overall transaction, you will increase the lock duration.

SQL Server provides an excellent tool for determining if you are exploiting the SQL batches and not delaying a commit: SQL Profiler, which can be used to monitor, filter, and capture all calls sent from client applications to SQL Server. It will often reveal unexpected application overhead due to unnecessary calls to the server. SQL Profiler can also reveal opportunities for gathering into batches statements that are currently being sent separately to the server. You can find more information on SQL Profiler in Chapter 7, "Using SQL Profiler."

Efficient Retrieval of Data

With the SQL language you can filter data at the server so you return only the minimum amount of data to the client. This minimizes expensive network traffic between the server and client. You need to ensure that your WHERE clauses are restrictive enough to retrieve only the data that is required by the application. It is always more efficient to filter data at the server than to send it to the client and filter it in the application. This principle also applies to columns requested from the server. If an application issues a SELECT * FROM statement, the server is required to return all columns to the client even if the client application has not bound all the columns for use in the program. By selecting only the needed columns by name, you avoid unnecessary network traffic. As a result, your application is more robust in the event of table definition changes, because newly added columns are not returned to the client application.

SQL Server assumes that your application will fetch all the rows from a default result set immediately. Therefore, your application must use the client's resources to buffer any rows that are not used immediately, but might be needed later. This requirement makes it especially important for you to specify your SQL statements properly so you are not forced to buffer any unneeded data.

On the surface, it appears that requesting the default result set and having your application fetch rows as they are needed would be the most efficient means of getting your data. This is not normally the case. Unfetched rows from a default result can cause SQL Server to hold locks at the server, possibly preventing other users from updating the locked rows. This concurrency problem might not show up in small-scale testing, but it can appear later when the application is deployed and the user count increases.

Some applications cannot buffer all the data they request from the server. If an application queries a large table and allows the user to specify the selection criteria, it might return no rows or millions of rows. The user probably does not want to see millions of rows, so he or she will typically re-execute the query with narrower selection criteria. Thus, the application fetched and buffered millions of rows only to have them thrown away by the user, which wastes time and system resources.

Because there are many cases in which applications do need to select a large number of rows from large tables, SQL Server offers server cursors. These cursors allow an application to fetch a small subset or block of rows from an arbitrarily large result set. If the user wants to see other records from the same result set, a server cursor allows the application to fetch any other block of rows from the result set, including the next n rows, the previous n rows, or n rows starting at a certain row number in the result set. SQL Server fulfills each block fetch request only as needed and does not normally hold locks between these block fetches.

Server cursors also allow an application to do a positioned update or delete of a fetched row without having to figure out the source table and primary key of the row. If the row data changes between the time it is fetched and the time the update is requested, SQL Server detects the problem and prevents a lost update.

There is a downside to this cursor flexibility, however. If all the results from a given query will be used in your application, using a server cursor is more expensive than using the default result set. A default result set requires only one round-trip between client and server, whereas each call to fetch a block of rows from a server cursor results in a round-trip. Additionally, server cursors consume more resources on the server, and there are restrictions on the SELECT statements that can be used with some types of cursor.

For these reasons, you should use server cursors only when your application needs their features. If your particular task requests a single row by primary key, then by all means use a default result set. If another task requires an unpredictably large or updateable result set, use a server cursor and fetch rows in reasonably sized blocks. A good rule is to fetch a screen of rows at a time for user processing. You should also attempt to make use of fast forward–only cursors with the ODBC *autofetch* option enabled. These cursors can be used to retrieve small result sets with only one round-trip between the client and server, similar to a default result set.

Tuning SQL Queries

Most people with database system performance problems look at the system-level components: memory size, number and speed of processors, and so on. Tuning these components eliminates many performance problems, but might mask some underlying problems that can be alleviated by tuning the actual SQL queries your applications or users are issuing. The SQL queries can be contained in an application, generated by a third-party application development tool, or issued from an ISQL utility command prompt or SQL Query Analyzer.

As you start to look at tuning queries, it is helpful to understand how the SQL Server query optimizer parses and determines the execution plan for a query. First, the query optimizer parses each clause of the query and determines if the clause can be used to limit the amount of data that must be scanned for the query. Such a clause can be used as a search argument in an index. After the query is parsed for any search arguments, the query optimizer determines if an index exists for the search argument and decides the usefulness of the index. Next, the optimizer derives a query execution plan. Finally, the query optimizer estimates the cost of executing the plan to find the rows that satisfy the search argument.

The query optimizer determines the usefulness of an index based on the answers to the following questions:

- Is the first column of the index used in the search argument?
- Does the search argument specify an upper bound, lower bound, or both to limit the scope of the search?
- Does the index contain every column referenced in the query?

If the query optimizer finds an index that contains all the columns referenced in the query, referred to as a *covering index*, it uses it. This is normally the fastest data access. Because all the required information to satisfy the query is held in the index, the system does not have to access the actual data pages. This provides a large savings in physical I/O for this query.

Once the query optimizer determines that it has a useful index, it evaluates the index by using the index's statistics. SQL Server generates the index statistics automatically unless you disable the *auto update statistics* option. As the database ages, you might encounter a condition in which the statistics are out of date. When SQL Server detects this condition, it will update the statistics unless you have explicitly disabled the automatic statistics update feature. You can force an update by issuing the UPDATE STATISTICS command. The index statistics contain an even sampling of values associated with the index key. The query optimizer accesses the statistics from the *sysindexes* system table in SQL Server. In addition to the statistics information, the *sysindexes* table includes the number of pages in the table or index.

The last piece of information that the query optimizer uses is the *density*, or uniqueness, of the index. The more selective an index, the more useful it is. A unique index leads to greater density because each index item points to exactly one data item.

Once the query optimizer has gathered its data, it costs the access method for the data. Even though an index has been deemed useful, its relative cost might be higher than other indexes. The query optimizer evaluates the index to estimate the number of potential cache hits based on the density and step values in the index statistics. Once this value is determined, the query optimizer estimates how many rows qualify based on the search argument discussed earlier in this chapter. The query optimizer will analyze multiple indexes, if they exist, as well as performing a simple table scan. It will finally decide on the access method that results in the smallest number of logical reads. Table 17-1 shows the different access methods and their estimated costs.

Table 17-1. Data Access Methods and Their Estimated Costs

SQL Server Access Method	Estimated Cost in Logical I/Os
Table scan	The total number of data pages in the table.
Clustered index	The number of levels in the index plus the number of data pages to scan. (Data Pages to Scan = Number of Qualifying Rows / Rows per Data Page)
Nonclustered index on a heap	The number of levels in the index plus the number of leaf pages plus the number of qualifying rows.
Nonclustered index on a table with a clustered index	The number of levels in the index plus the number of leaf pages plus the number of qualifying rows times the cost of searching for a clustered index key.
Covering nonclustered index	The number of levels in the index plus the number of leaf index pages. Because this is a covering index, the actual data pages need not be accessed.

In addition to using SQL Server's SQL Query Analyzer and SQL Profiler, you can also check query performance by using the SET statement. With the SET statement, you can enable the SHOWPLAN, STATISTICS IO, STATISTICS TIME, and STATISTICS PROFILE options. Each of these options is described here.

- **SHOWPLAN** Displays the method chosen by the SQL Server query optimizer to retrieve data
- **STATISTICS IO** Reports information about the number of scans, logical reads, and physical reads for each table referenced in the statement
- **STATISTICS TIME** Displays the amount of time (in milliseconds) required to parse, compile, and execute a query
- **STATISTICS PROFILE** Displays a result set after each executed query that represents a profile of the execution of the query

Remember, you can also use the graphical execution plan option in SQL Query Analyzer to view a graphical representation of how SQL Server retrieves data. Chapter 16, "Using SQL Query Analyzer," discusses SQL Query Analyzer in detail.

With the information gathered by these options you can determine how the SQL Server query optimizer is executing a query and which indexes are being used. With this information, you can determine if performance improvements can be made by rewriting the query, changing the indexes on the tables, or perhaps modifying the database design when possible.

SQL Server creates statistics regarding the distribution of values in a column automatically on indexed columns. You can also create statistics on nonindexed columns either manually, by using SQL Query Analyzer or the CREATE STATISTICS statement, or automatically, by setting the *auto create statistics* database option to TRUE. The query optimizer also use statistics on the nonindexed columns to determine the optimal strategy for evaluating a query. Maintaining additional statistics on nonindexed columns involved in join operations can improve query performance.

Some queries are inherently resource intensive due to fundamental database and index issues. For example, highly nonunique WHERE clauses and queries returning large result sets can be resource intensive. These queries are not inefficient, because the query optimizer will implement the queries in the most efficient fashion possible; but they are resource intensive, and the set-oriented nature of SQL can make them appear inefficient. No degree of query optimizer intelligence can eliminate the inherent resource cost of these constructs. Although SQL Server will use the optimal available access plan, it is limited by what is fundamentally possible.

General Recommendations

You can put the query tuning information in this chapter to good use by following these guidelines.

- Add memory to the server. If the system runs many complex queries, this can improve general query performance. See Chapter 2, "SQL Server 2000 Architecture Fundamentals," for more information about memory management in SQL Server.

- Run SQL Server on a computer with more than one processor. Multiple processors allow SQL Server to make use of parallel queries. Chapter 4, "System Tuning," discusses this in more detail. (In an OLTP environment, however, you might be better off setting the maximum degree of parallelism to 1, eliminating the overhead of merging the processed data.)

- Consider rewriting the query if it uses cursors. Look into using a more efficient type of cursor.

- If your application uses looping, consider putting the loops inside the query. Often an application contains a loop that includes a parameterized query, which is executed many times and requires a network round-trip between the computer running the application and SQL Server. Instead, create a single, more complex query using a temporary table. Only one network round-trip is necessary, and the query optimizer can better optimize the single query.

- Do not use multiple aliases for a single table in the same query to simulate index intersection. SQL Server automatically considers index intersection and can make use of multiple indexes on the same table in the same query.

- Make use of query hints only if necessary. Queries using hints executed against earlier versions of SQL Server should be tested without the hints specified. The hints can prevent the query optimizer from choosing a better execution plan. For more information, see Chapter 19, "Using Hints in SQL Server."

- Make use of the *query governor cost limit* configuration option. This option can be used to prevent long-running queries from executing, thus preventing system resources from being consumed. By default, the *query governor cost limit* configuration option allows all queries to execute, no matter how long they take. However, the option can be set to a maximum number of seconds that all queries for all connections (or just the queries for a specific connection) are allowed to execute. Because the *query governor cost limit* option is based on estimated query cost, rather than actual elapsed time, it does not have any runtime overhead. It also stops long-running queries before they start, rather than running them until some predefined limit is hit.

Queries Using Joins

If you require joins or merge functions in your queries, there are additional techniques for analyzing and enhancing your queries. SQL Server performs sort, intersect, union, and difference operations using in-memory sorting and hash joins. For query plans that use these operations, SQL Server supports vertical table partitioning, sometimes called *columnar storage*. SQL Server supports nested loop joins, merge joins, and hash joins.

When one join input is quite small (10 rows or fewer) and the other join input is fairly large and indexed on its join columns, the index nested loops operation is the fastest join operation because it requires the least I/O and the fewest comparisons. If the two join inputs are not small but are sorted on their join column, then a merge join is the fastest join operation. If both join inputs are large and the two inputs are of similar sizes, the merge join with prior sorting and the hash join offer similar performance. However, hash join operations are often much faster if the two input sizes differ significantly from each other.

Hash joins can process large, unsorted, nonindexed inputs efficiently. They are useful for processing intermediate results in complex queries for the following reasons:

- Intermediate results are not indexed, unless explicitly saved to disk and then indexed, and often are not produced suitably sorted for the next operation in the query plan.

- The query optimizer estimates only intermediate result sizes. Because estimates can be wrong by an order of magnitude in complex queries, algorithms to process intermediate results not only must be efficient but also must degrade gracefully if an intermediate result turns out to be much larger than anticipated.

Hash joins reduce the need to denormalize the database. Denormalization is typically used to achieve better performance by reducing join operations, in spite of the dangers of redundancy, such as inconsistent updates and increased I/O. Hash joins allow vertical partitioning, which represents groups of columns from a single table in separate files or indexes.

Prepared Execution

The ODBC API defines *prepared execution* as a way to reduce the compiling overhead associated with repeatedly executing a SQL statement. The application builds a character string containing a SQL statement and then executes it in two stages. First, it calls SQLPrepare to have the statement compiled into an execution plan by the database engine.

Next, it calls SQLExecute for each execution of the prepared execution plan. This saves the compiling overhead on each execution. Prepared execution is commonly used by applications to repeatedly execute the same, parameterized SQL statements.

For most databases, prepared execution is faster than direct execution for statements executed more than three or four times, primarily because the statement is compiled only once, whereas statements executed directly are compiled each time they are executed. Prepared execution can also reduce network traffic because the driver can send an execution plan identifier and the parameter values, rather than an entire SQL statement, to the data source each time the statement is executed.

SQL Server 2000 reduces the performance difference between direct and prepared execution through improved algorithms for detecting and reusing execution plans from SQLExecDirect. This provides some of the performance benefits of prepared execution to statements that are executed directly.

SQL Server 2000 also provides native support for prepared execution. An execution plan is built on SQLPrepare and later executed when SQLExecute is called. Because SQL Server 2000 does not need to build temporary stored procedures on SQLPrepare, there is no extra overhead on the system tables in tempdb.

If you call SQLDescribeCol or SQLDescribeParam before calling SQLExecute, you generate an extra round-trip to the server. When SQLDescribeCol is called, the driver removes the WHERE clause from the query and sends it to the server with SET FMTONLY ON to get the description of the columns in the first result set returned by the query. When SQLDescribeParam is called, the driver calls the server to get a description of the expressions or columns referenced by any parameter markers in the query. This method also has some restrictions, such as being unable to resolve parameters in subqueries.

Excessive use of SQLPrepare with the SQL Server ODBC driver degrades performance, especially when the driver is connected to earlier versions of SQL Server. You should not use prepared execution for statements that are executed once. Prepared execution is slower than direct execution for a single execution of a statement because it requires an extra network round-trip from the client to the server. On earlier versions of SQL Server it also generates a temporary stored procedure.

In SQL Server 2000, prepared statements cannot be used to create temporary objects; this is also true in earlier versions of SQL Server if the option to generate stored procedures is active. With this option turned on, the prepared statement is built into a temporary stored procedure that is executed when SQLExecute is called. Any temporary object created during the execution of a stored procedure is dropped when the procedure finishes.

Some early ODBC applications used SQLPrepare any time SQLBindParameter was used. SQLBindParameter does not require the use of SQLPrepare; it can be used with SQLExecDirect. For example, use SQLExecDirect with SQLBindParameter to retrieve the return code or output parameters from a stored procedure that is executed only once. Do not use SQLPrepare with SQLBindParameter unless the same statement will be executed multiple times.

Summary

This chapter discussed techniques for ensuring that your applications and queries do not inhibit your system's performance. We looked at application design considerations, query design, and query tuning. We also explored how to use indexes and how the SQL Server query optimizer selects the appropriate index for your query. Finally, we looked at how you can use specific ODBC API calls to enhance performance in applications that issue the same SQL statements multiple times. Now that your SQL statements are optimized, we need to look in detail at the indexes in your database. The next chapter explores indexes and how to use and tune them.

Chapter 18
Using and Tuning Indexes

The use of indexes on your tables is critical to the performance of data operations. But you must understand how to use indexes to benefit from them. In this chapter, we discuss index fundamentals as well as the different types of indexes and when you should use them. We also give general guidelines for building indexes, show how to analyze and tune indexes for better query performance, and discuss how to form queries so they use the indexes you create.

Index Fundamentals

An *index* is an auxiliary data structure used to assist Microsoft SQL Server 2000 in accessing data. With SQL Server 2000, indexes are created on tables or views. One table or view can have more than one index that refers to its data. Depending on the type of index, the index data can be stored either with the table data or separate from it. All types of indexes work in fundamentally the same way. A database index is like an index in a book: you can look up the term in the index to quickly find the data instead of searching every page.

Without an index, all data is retrieved through table scans, which means that all the data in a table must be read and compared against the data you request. You should avoid table scans because they generate a lot of I/O (unless you want to select a high percentage of rows from the table). Large tables consume far too many system resources when a table scan is performed. By using an appropriate index, you can greatly reduce the number of I/O operations needed to find the correct data rows. This speeds up access to the data and frees system resources for other operations.

Indexes are typically structured as *B-trees*. The B-tree structure begins with a *root node*, which is the start of the index. The root node contains index rows (that is, rows of index data) that contain ranges of index key values and pointers to the next index nodes, which are called *branch nodes*. Branch nodes in turn contain index rows with further refined ranges of values that point to other branch nodes. Each level of branch nodes is called an *index level*.

The nodes in the lowest level of the index tree are called the *leaf nodes*. The leaf nodes contain the index key data and either information about where the referenced data resides or the data itself, depending on whether the index is nonclustered or clustered. (These two index types are described in the "Types of Indexes" section later in this chapter.) The number of index levels that must be traversed to reach a leaf node determines the number of I/Os necessary to find the requested row of data. Figure 18-1 illustrates the terms discussed so far. The nodes do not necessarily contain only two pointers each, as shown in Figure 18-1. Actually, each index row in a node contains a pointer to another node, as shown in Figure 18-2.

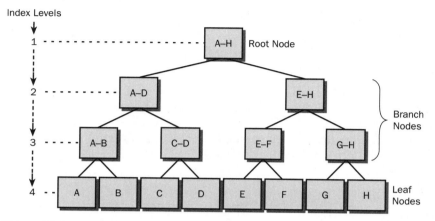

Figure 18-1. *A sample index.*

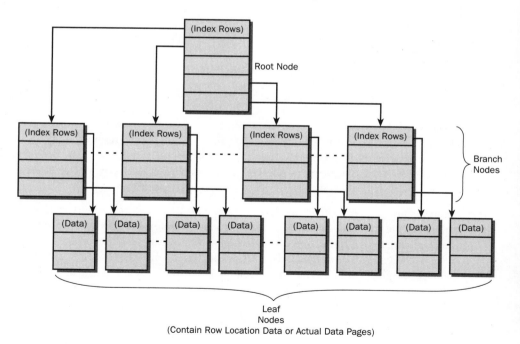

Figure 18-2. *An index structure.*

Indexes are helpful not only with SELECT statements, but with UPDATE and DELETE statements as well, because SQL Server must find a row before it can update or delete it. For the remainder of this chapter, when we discuss finding data or performing queries we are referring to any of these three types of operations.

Index Keys

Index keys are the columns for which an index is created. To access a row of data through the index, you must include an index key value or values within the WHERE clause of the SQL statement. You can create an index on one or more index key columns. New to SQL Server 2000, you can define the sort order for any index as ascending or descending. While we assume an ascending sort order in this chapter, you should carefully consider and choose the sort order on a case-by-case basis.

An index with only one index key is called a *simple index*. For example, a simple index might be created on the customer ID column of a customer table. This index is used for queries that search for a particular customer ID. Note that the customer ID must be included in the WHERE clause of the SQL statement in order for the index to be used.

An index with more than one key column is called a *composite index*. A composite index might be created on the last-name column and first-name column of the customer table. This index is used for queries that search for a particular customer by last name only, by first name only, or by last name and first name. For more information on index keys, see the "Choosing the Index Key Columns" section later in this chapter.

Types of Indexes

SQL Server supports two major types of indexes: clustered and nonclustered. For either type of index, you can specify whether the index should be a unique index. (A unique index is sometimes considered a third type of index, but it is actually a characteristic of a clustered or nonclustered index.) Another type of index, the *full-text index*, is more like a catalog. The full-text index has characteristics that differ from those of clustered and nonclustered indexes and so falls into a separate category. The following sections explain the characteristics of each type of index and discuss when each type is useful.

Clustered Index

A *clustered index* indicates the order in which table data should be physically stored. The table data is sorted and stored according to the key column or columns specified for the clustered index. This type of index is analogous to a dictionary, which stores information in alphabetical order and provides guide words to help locate the information quickly; the data is found on the same page as its guide words. The clustered index is similar in that it includes the index pages as well as the actual data pages, which make up the lowest level (the leaf node) of the clustered index, as shown in Figure 18-3 on the following page. Each row in the root node points to a branch node, whose rows can point to other branch nodes (only one set of branch nodes is shown in Figure 18-3). The last set of branch nodes point to the leaf nodes. When you get to the leaf nodes, you have reached the actual data page as well. Because the data is physically stored in a specific order, you can create only one clustered index per table.

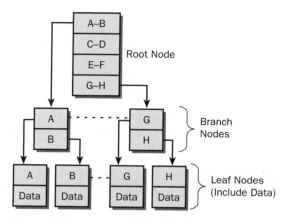

Figure 18-3. *The structure of a clustered index.*

Clustered indexes are very efficient when created on columns that will be searched for a certain range of values. For example, you might want to frequently retrieve all rows from a customer table that contain last names that start with letters *A* through *C*. When you use a clustered index on the last-name column, the data is physically stored in order of the last name. When the query is performed, the row with the first selected value is found (the first occurrence of a last name that starts with *A*); the subsequent rows are guaranteed to be physically adjacent. Therefore the rows are retrieved quickly until the last row containing a last name that starts with *C* is reached.

Another case in which clustered indexes are particularly efficient is when you frequently need to sort the data that is retrieved. If you create a clustered index on the column or columns that you would need to sort by, then the rows are physically stored in that order (and thus presorted), eliminating the overhead of sorting the data after it is retrieved.

Clustered indexes are also efficient when you frequently perform queries to find a row that contains a specific value for a column that contains all unique values, such as a customer ID column (assuming each customer has a unique customer ID). Creating a clustered index on that column provides the fastest path to retrieve a row in this case.

For reasons described later, as a general rule you should make clustered indexes unique, which means that no duplicates of that column can be inserted into the table. If the clustered index is unique, SQL Server provides an error message if you attempt to insert a duplicate value into the index key column or columns. If your clustered index is not unique, SQL Server generates a unique identifier for you. This unique identifier is not visible to the user.

Because you can have only one clustered index per table, you must look at what search conditions your queries will use (such as searching for a range of values or for a particular customer), how often they will be performed, and how much data is involved in each query (that is, the size of the table to be queried). You want to create the clustered index so that it will best benefit your situation. For instance, if you create the clustered index to service a particular query that is run only once each night, you might cause performance to suffer for other queries that run more often during the day by not building the clustered index to satisfy the more frequently run queries. On the other hand, the nightly query might take too much time to complete if the clustered index is not built to speed that query.

> **Note**   When you create a primary key constraint on a column, SQL Server creates a unique clustered index for that constraint if one does not already exist and if you do not explicitly specify that the index should be a unique nonclustered index. The main difference between a PRIMARY KEY and a UNIQUE CONSTRAINT is that a PRIMARY KEY can not contain any NULL values, while a UNIQUE CONSTRAINT can contain a single NULL value. (In stark contrast, an Oracle database allows multiple NULL values within a UNIQUE CONSTRAINT.)

Nonclustered Index

Unlike the clustered index, a *nonclustered index* does not contain the actual table data in its leaf nodes, as shown in Figure 18-4. Instead, the index itself is completely separate from the data, like a book with an index in the back—the index indicates which page to go to, but the data is not with the index itself. The leaf nodes of the nonclustered index contain index rows that hold index data and information that specifies the exact location of a row.

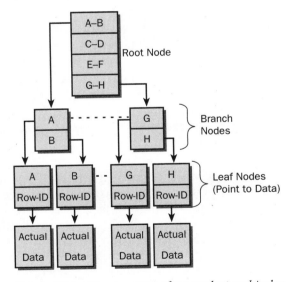

Figure 18-4. *The structure of a nonclustered index.*

The location information can be one of two types, depending on whether there is a clustered index on the table. If there is a clustered index, then for each row the key value of the clustered index is stored in the leaf node of the nonclustered index as the row locator. This value is used to locate the data, which resides in the leaf node of the clustered index. If the clustered index is not a unique index, SQL Server assigns an internal value to any duplicate index key values to make them unique for use with nonclustered indexes. The internal values are not visible to users. Because your clustered index key is appended to any nonclustered index, generally you should make your clustered index key as small as possible.

If there is no clustered index on the table, then each leaf node contains a row ID as the row locator, instead of a key value of the clustered index. The row ID is a pointer made up of the file ID, page number, and row number in the page. This pointer indicates exactly where the row is found, so that once the row ID is reached, only one more I/O is required to read the row of data. Figure 18-4 illustrates the structure of a nonclustered index.

SQL Server allows a maximum of 249 nonclustered indexes on a table. Remember that the more indexes you have, the more overhead is incurred during inserts, updates, and deletes because the index pages must be maintained to include those modifications as well. Thus you do not want to create unnecessary indexes.

Indexed Views

New to SQL Server 2000 is the ability to index a view. This is a dangerous ability because it can significantly increase the number of I/Os in the system, but it offers solutions to many of the most common query problems. If SQL Server recognizes that an indexed view satisfies a query request, even if SQL Server does not reference the view, it uses that view's index to satisfy the query.

One drawback to an indexed view is that you must create a clustered index on a PRIMARY KEY that you define on the view. This means that each view to be indexed must have a column or set of columns that are always unique. Many views are not designed to meet this requirement, so satisfying it might require some creative thinking.

Indexes on Calculated Columns

Also new to SQL Server 2000 is the ability to index a calculated column. Previous versions of SQL Server allowed the data architect to define a virtual column that resulted from a calculation based on one or more other columns in the same table. This was great until an unwary user attempted to query the table using the virtual column as the only criteria. Without an index on the calculated column, SQL Server had to perform a table scan and calculate every possible result to satisfy the query. As you can imagine, a table with a billion rows would significantly hinder the system performance. Such queries are common in data warehousing, where a fact table has a calculated measure. In such an environment, you might want to locate any customer that matches a given value. Because these are not highly volatile values, it can be extremely helpful to system performance to create an index against the calculated measure. Be aware, though, that changes to values of any of the base columns used to generate the calculated column force an index update.

Unique Index

A *unique index* is either a clustered or a nonclustered index that is created specifically to be unique. Values inserted in the key value column or columns must be unique; duplicates of the key values are not allowed. For composite keys, the combination of the values must be unique. For example, if you have a unique index created on the last-name and first-name columns of a customer table, no duplicate last-name and first-name pairs can be inserted; you can insert two or more rows with the same last name, but they must have unique first names and vice versa. You would want the unique index to be on only one column when you want a single column to be unique in itself, such as a column that contains social security numbers. You can create a unique index on that column to ensure that there are no duplicate social security numbers in the table.

You can also use another method to enforce uniqueness of data for certain columns—you can create a UNIQUE constraint. When you create a UNIQUE constraint, SQL Server creates a unique nonclustered index to enforce the constraint. Once you have a unique index on a table, SQL Server prevents duplicates from being entered into the table and displays an error message stating that a duplicate row insert was attempted.

Full-Text Index

The *full-text index* is more complex than the previously discussed indexes. The full-text index is actually like a catalog. Instead of simply searching in an ordered B-tree fashion, the full-text index allows you to search by groups of keywords. The full-text index is part of the Microsoft Search service. It is used extensively in Web site search engines and other text-based operations.

Unlike B-tree indexes, the full-text index is stored externally to the database, but is maintained by the database. This is done so that the index can maintain its own structure. The following restrictions apply to creating and maintaining full-text indexes:

- Full-text indexes can be created only on **char** and **varchar** column types.
- Only one full-text index is allowed per table.
- A full-text index is not automatically updated, unlike B-tree indexes.
- A full-text index is created, managed, and dropped using stored procedures or the Full-Text Indexing wizard.

The full-text index has a wealth of features that cannot be found in normal B-tree indexes. Because this index is designed to be a text search engine, it supports more than normal text search capabilities. With the full-text index you can perform the following types of operations:

- Searching for words or phrases
- Searching for single words or groups of words
- Searching for words that are similar to each other

> **Note** To use full-text indexing, you must have installed the Full-Text Search service with SQL Server Standard or Enterprise Edition. To select the option, you must choose the custom install.

See SQL Server Books Online for more information on the full-text index.

Tuning Indexes

An efficient index helps you to find data with fewer I/Os and less system resource usage than a table scan. Because an index involves traversing the B-tree to find an individual value, it is not efficient to use an index when you retrieve large amounts of data. A general rule is that for queries that access more than 20 percent of the rows in a table, it is better to do a table scan than to use an index.

Upon the execution of a query, the SQL Server query optimizer evaluates the costs of the possible methods of finding the data and chooses the method that is most efficient to use as the query execution plan. SQL Server determines whether to use an index and which of the available indexes to use. (If it is more efficient not to use an index to satisfy the query, SQL Server doesn't use one.) In versions preceding SQL Server 7.0, only one index could be used in a query execution plan. With SQL Server 7.0 and SQL Server 2000, an index intersection or index union can be performed to make use of more than one index to satisfy a query. SQL Server can also join two indexes defined on the same table to satisfy a query.

Basically, creating an appropriate and efficient index is the first step in tuning the index. You must make several decisions when creating indexes, including the following:

- Which column or columns to include in the index.
- Whether to add a PRIMARY KEY constraint or UNIQUE constraint to the table, which allow SQL Server to create an index for you. (You might have already done this at table creation.)
- Whether the index should be clustered or nonclustered.
- Whether or not the index should be unique.
- Whether to use a fill factor and, if so, what percentage to choose. (For more information, see the "Fill Factor" section later in this chapter.)

To help in making these decisions, you must look at your SQL statements to determine which tables and columns are being accessed and how they are being accessed. We discuss this in more detail in later subsections. But first, here are some general guidelines for creating indexes:

- Determine if most of the queries are SELECT statements, or if there are significant numbers of INSERT, UPDATE, or DELETE statements. As the number of indexes on a table increases, so does the amount of overhead required to maintain those indexes for INSERT, UPDATE, and DELETE statements. For queries with a lot of these statements, therefore, be conservative with the number of indexes you create on the modified tables. If your queries are mostly SELECT statements, then more indexes might allow better performance by providing SQL Server more indexes to choose from for its query execution plans. Usually you must find a balance between these two cases.

- You should attempt to build your indexes to aid specific queries—do not just generalize or guess about what columns to use as the index keys. After creating an index, you should check the execution plan for the query or queries for which it was built and verify that the index is being chosen by SQL Server as you expected. We explain how to do this in the "Using SQL Query Analyzer" section later in this chapter.

- Indexing very small tables can hurt performance, because it might be more efficient for SQL Server to perform a simple table scan. The query optimizer should detect this fact; however, it is not perfect, so be aware that SQL Server might try to use an index where one is available.

- Avoid having too many index keys in the index, because the greater the amount of data in the index, the more data must be updated when modifications are made to the table, thus causing more overhead. An index with one to a few key columns is called a *narrow index*; an index with many key columns is called a *wide index*. A narrow index takes up less space than a wide index and is preferable when possible.

- Avoid choosing columns with large data types as index keys. For example, an **integer** column type is a good choice for an index key, whereas a **varchar** column type is not a good choice because the **varchar** data can require a lot of space and therefore more overhead for maintenance.

Now we'll look at some guidelines concerning what type of data search clauses in queries will most benefit from indexes:

- **Searches that match a specific value** These queries will retrieve only a few rows that match a specific equality. For example: `WHERE customer_ID = 19`.

- **Searches that match a range of values** These queries will also retrieve a small number of rows. For example: `WHERE customer_ID BETWEEN 19 AND 22` or `WHERE customer_ID >= 19 AND customer_ID <= 22`.

- **Searches that are used in a join** Columns that are used as join keys often are good candidates for indexes. For example: `FROM customer_table as cust, customer_detail_table as cust_det WHERE cust.customer_ID = cust_det.customer_ID`.

- **Searches that retrieve data in a specific order** If you want the resulting data set to be sorted, you can use a clustered index on the column or columns by which you want to sort. Because the data is already sorted within the index itself, no sorting is required when the results are returned. An example is assuming a clustered index on customer_ID: `WHERE customer_ID < 100 ORDER BY customer_ID`.

Creating and verifying index usage is a continual process as your queries grow and change. In the next sections we discuss in more detail how to choose the index key columns for an index, how to use a fill factor, and how to use SQL Query Analyzer to determine the execution plan for a query by SQL Server.

Choosing the Index Key Columns

An index is most beneficial when you are searching for only a few rows. Therefore, you should design your indexes with good selectivity. The *selectivity* of an index is based on the number of rows per index key value. An index with poor selectivity is one that has multiple rows per key value, such as an index key on a gender column that holds one of two values: M for male and F for female. An index with good selectivity has one or a few values per index key, such as an index on a customer ID column. A unique index has the best selectivity.

Information about the selectivity of an index is stored within the index distribution statistics. An index with good selectivity is more likely to be used by the query optimizer than an index with poor selectivity. You can view the selectivity of an index by using the command DBCC SHOW_STATISTICS (*table_name, index_name*). The lower the density returned in the output, the higher the selectivity. Index statistics are updated automatically by default, but can be manually updated with the command UPDATE STATISTICS *table_name*. For more information about these two commands and their syntax, search for them by name in SQL Server Books Online.

The selectivity of an index can be enhanced by using a composite index. Several columns with poor selectivity can be joined together in a composite index to form one index that has good selectivity. Although a unique index provides the best selectivity, be sure to choose an index type that fits your data model. For instance, you should not create a unique index on a customer last-name column if duplicate last names are allowed in your table.

For a clustered index with a composite key, the order in which the key columns are listed in the CREATE INDEX statement is also important. In a clustered index, the data is sorted first by the first key, then by the second key, and so on, according to the order in which the columns were specified when you created the index. For example, if you create a clustered index for a customer table on the customer last-name column and then on the customer first-name column, the data is first sorted by last name; if there are any rows with the same last name, those rows are also sorted by first name. If there are 100 entries with the last name Smith, for example, the Smith duplicates are sorted in order of first names after the data is sorted by last name. Therefore, a query using this index is more efficient if either both last name and first name are included in the WHERE clause, or if only the last name is in the WHERE clause. A less efficient query would search for first name only, because all last names will have to be checked for the matching first name. In all three cases, the clustered index will be used to satisfy the queries, and each will be performed more efficiently than if there were no index on the table.

In contrast, the order in which the columns actually appear in the WHERE clause does not matter. (This is true for both clustered and nonclustered indexes.) For example, the following two queries use the index just described in the same manner (that is, they have the same execution plan):

```
SELECT CUSTOMER_ID FROM CUSTOMER
    WHERE LAST_NAME="SMITH" AND FIRST_NAME="PENELOPE"

SELECT CUSTOMER_ID FROM CUSTOMER
    WHERE FIRST_NAME="PENELOPE" AND LAST_NAME="SMITH"
```

It is also important when choosing your index keys to try to cover a query. *Covering* a query means to include each of the columns in the SELECT list as an index key within the same index, so that the data retrieved resides in the index keys themselves, and the actual data pages do not have to be read at all. The covered query needs to read data only from the index and can bypass the table data pages. For example, if a query selects only columns A and B, and a composite index on that same table has columns A and B as the index keys, then the query is covered. Even if the index is created on columns A, B, and C, the query is still covered. Also consider that if a nonclustered index exists for column B while a clustered index exists for column A, then the query is covered as the leaf node of the non-clustered index automatically contains the key value for A.

Fill Factor

As inserts, updates, and deletes are performed on a table that has indexes, the indexes must be updated to reflect the changes in the table. The index rows are stored in order based on the index keys. Therefore, particularly for inserts and updates, new index rows must be added in the appropriate location to maintain order in the index. As index pages fill up, space for additional index rows must be created. SQL Server does this by moving approximately half of the rows in the index page to a new page. This operation is known as a *page split*. Page splits result in increased system overhead because of the CPU usage and additional I/Os they incur. One way to avoid page splits is by tuning the fill factor of the index pages. The *fill factor* specifies the percentage of the page to fill when creating the index. This allows you to leave room in the index pages for additional index rows.

You can specify the fill factor on an index by using the FILLFACTOR option with the CREATE INDEX command or, if using Enterprise Manager, by opening the database diagram, right-clicking the table you want, and selecting Properties from the menu. Click the Indexes/Keys tab, select the index from the drop-down list, and enter the percentage you want in the Fill Factor section. The value of the fill factor varies from 0 to 100, indicating the percentage of the index page that should be filled upon index creation. If the fill factor is not specified, the system default (the value set for the SQL Server configuration option *fillfactor*) is used. This value is set to 0 when SQL Server is installed.

Note The fill factor parameter only specifies how the index is originally created. It has no effect once the index has been built.

When 0 is specified for the fill factor, the leaf pages are packed to 100 percent, but the branch nodes have some space left free. This is the SQL Server installation default, and it usually works well. A value of 100 for the fill factor specifies that all index pages are completely filled when the index is created. This is optimal for tables that never have new data inserted in them (that is, read-only tables). Both the leaf pages and upper-level pages are completely packed; thus, any insert will cause a page split. The benefit of packing the index pages is that the index requires less storage space.

Using a low value for the fill factor allows a great deal of space for inserts, but requires a lot of extra space in which to store the index. Unless you will be doing constant inserts to the database, a low value for the fill factor is usually not recommended. If you are experiencing a great many page splits, try decreasing the value for the fill factor by a small percentage, then recreate the index and see if the problem is solved.

The number of page splits per second that your system is experiencing is displayed in the SQL Server Page Splits/sec statistic. This value can be found using System Monitor in the Performance console and the SQLServer:Access Methods object. If this value is high, you might need to rebuild the index with a lower fill factor.

Using SQL Query Analyzer

SQL Query Analyzer has many functions, but we focus here on three particular functions that help with index tuning. First, we show how SQL Query Analyzer can be used to perform index analysis on a query; SQL Server will recommend a possible index to help with the execution of the specified query. Next, we show how SQL Query Analyzer can be used to display the estimated execution plan that SQL Server will use to execute a query, without actually executing the query. Finally, we show how to display the actual execution plan that SQL Server used to perform a query.

For the index analysis examples, we use our own sample database, salesdb. (We don't use the installed sample database because it contains so little data that SQL Server will not make any index recommendations.) You should be able to follow along and do similar testing with your own databases.

We use SQL Query Analyzer to help determine what indexes would be helpful for some queries to the *customer* table of our salesdb database. This table currently has no indexes and contains 300,000 rows of data. First we open SQL Query Analyzer and select salesdb as the database in the Current Database drop-down list on the toolbar. Then, in the Query window, we type in our query, which searches for all rows with a last name of "Smith," as shown in Figure 18-5. Next we select Index Tuning Wizard from the Query menu. The welcome page opens, as shown in Figure 18-6.

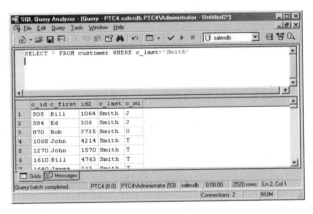

Figure 18-5. *SQL Query Analyzer.*

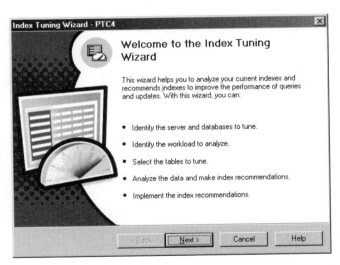

Figure 18-6. *The welcome page of the Index Tuning Wizard.*

Clicking the Next button displays the Select Server and Database page (see Figure 18-7), where you can select the server and table or tables that you want to analyze for index recommendations. You can also select whether to keep existing indexes or not, whether to include indexed views, and how thorough an analysis to do.

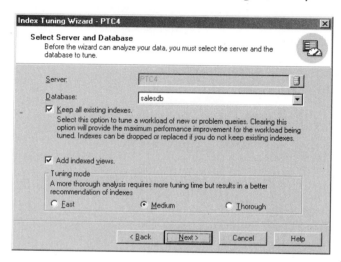

Figure 18-7. *The Select Server and Database page allows you to select the object to analyze and specify tuning settings.*

Click Next to view the Specify Workload page (see Figure 18-8), where you can specify whether to use the query defined in the SQL Query Analyzer, or another workload, such as from SQL Profiler, in order for the wizard to make tuning recommendations.

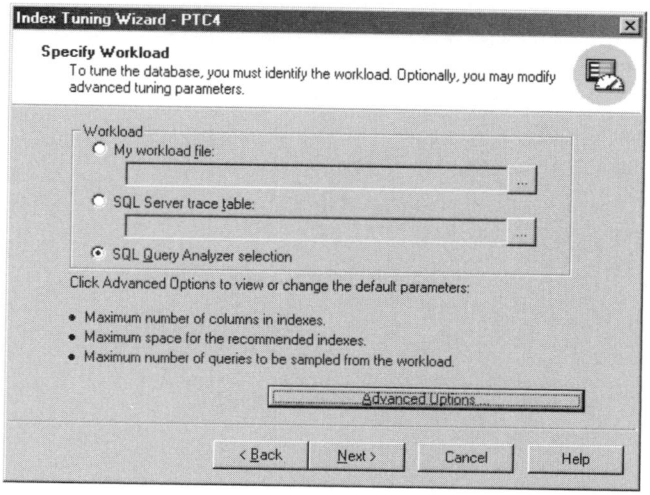

Figure 18-8. *The Specify Workload page.*

Click Next to display the Select Tables to Tune page, as shown in Figure 18-9. Here you simply select the table or tables that you want to get index recommendations on.

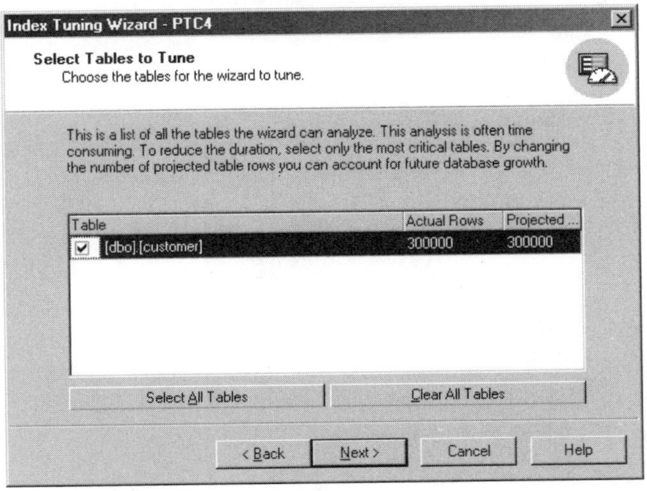

Figure 18-9. *The Select Tables to Tune page.*

Clicking Next begins the analysis process. This might take a few seconds, a few minutes, or longer depending on the amount of data to analyze. Once it has completed the status window closes and the Index Recommendations page appears, as shown in Figure 18-10.

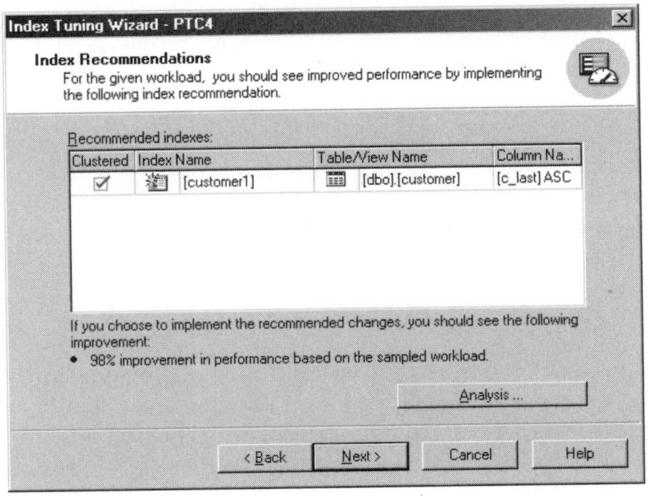

Figure 18-10. *Index recommendations after index analysis.*

The Index Recommendations page shows you the type of index the Index Tuning Wizard recommends and whether it is clustered. It also provides an estimate on improved performance. You can click the Analysis button to browse the statistics gathered in the analysis.

In this case, SQL Server recommends an ascending clustered index, named *customer1*, on the *customer* table, with *c_last* as the index key. Clicking Next advances the Wizard to the Schedule Index Update Job page, as shown in Figure 18-11. We can choose to accept the recommended index and let SQL Server create it, create an index creation script for later use, or cancel the wizard.

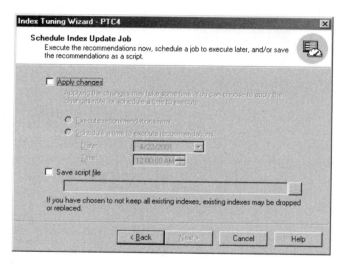

Figure 18-11. *The Schedule Index Update Job page.*

We choose to cancel this window so we can perform index analysis on another query. You probably should perform index analysis on more than one query before deciding which indexes to create. There might be another query, for example, that searches for the customer by last name and first name.

Before we create any indexes on our *customer* table, we'll look at the same query on *c_last* and *c_first* as before using the SQL Query Analyzer, but this time choose the Display Estimated Execution Plan option from the Query menu. This option displays the estimated execution plan without executing the query. This is helpful when you suspect that the query might take a long time to complete and you do not want to execute it, but you want to find out what execution plan SQL Server would choose if it did execute the query. The results of our query are shown in Figure 18-12.

To understand the output, you read from right to left (following the gray arrow) and from bottom to top (had there been more levels of information). As you see in Figure 18-12, SQL Server would perform a table scan to complete our query. A table scan is not desirable since it requires reading every row in the table, so we create a clustered index on the *c_id* column using the following command:

```
CREATE CLUSTERED INDEX cust_indx_1 on customer (c_last, c_first)
GO
```

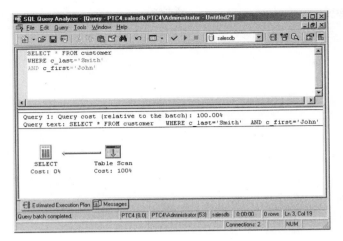

Figure 18-12. *The estimated execution plan for a sample query before creating an index.*

Now we display the estimated execution plan again, and we get the results shown in Figure 18-13. This time for its execution plan, SQL Server chose to use the index we just created. If you move the mouse over the icon and the name of the index in the displayed results, you will see statistics about the index operation, as shown in Figure 18-14. Move the mouse to point at the arrow between the SELECT and index icons, or above the SELECT icon, and you will see more statistics windows. See Chapter 16, "Using SQL Query Analyzer," and SQL Server Books Online for details on what the icons signify and what the statistics mean.

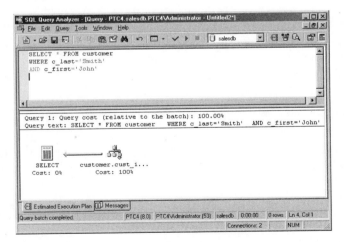

Figure 18-13. *The estimated execution plan for the same sample query after the index has been created.*

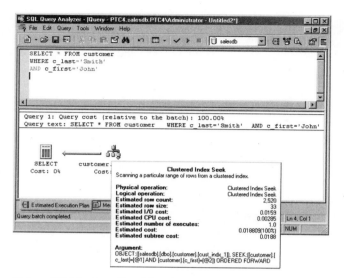

Figure 18-14. *Details of the clustered index seek.*

Now we'll actually run this query and see if the estimated execution plan is the same as the execution plan SQL Server really uses. First, we change the query to select only *c_last* instead of *, so that less data is returned. Next select Show Execution Plan from the Query menu, so that the icon to the left is highlighted in light gray (this indicates that it is enabled). Then we click the Run toolbar button (the green arrow) to run the query.

Once the query has been completed, the query results are displayed in the Results tab, and the execution plan that was used is displayed in the Execution Plan tab. We click the Execution Plan tab and see the results shown in Figure 18-15. If we hold the mouse over the index icon again, we see the query execution statistics for that index seek operation, as shown in Figure 18-16.

If we compare this set of actual statistics for the index operation with the set of estimated statistics shown in Figure 18-14, we can see that the row count is less and the row size is less. However, the actual cost of the index operation is the same in both cases (0.018809), so the estimate was fairly accurate.

Now that you have seen how to use SQL Query Analyzer, you should be able to display the execution plans for your queries to help you determine whether your indexes are being used or not, and if the right index is being used.

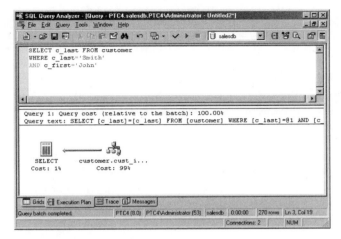

Figure 18-15. *The actual execution plan.*

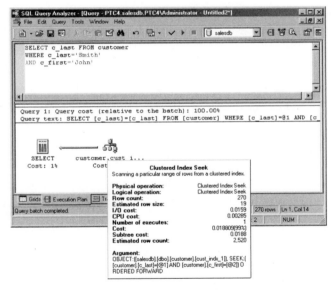

Figure 18-16. *Query execution statistics.*

Summary

This chapter focused on tuning SQL Server indexes. You first learned the fundamentals of indexes—the different index types and their structures. Then, as part of tuning, you learned that it is important to create your indexes properly and to test them for specific queries. Choosing the columns for the index keys should be based on the columns used in the search conditions of the queries for which you are creating the index. You should build indexes that are useful for your queries. We showed you how to use SQL Query Analyzer to determine the execution plan for a query and to recommend possible indexes for a query. Remember, index usage should be evaluated often to determine if indexes are being used properly, especially if new queries are added to your application, or new indexes are created. In the next chapter you will learn how to use hints to direct certain behaviors of SQL Server.

Chapter 19
Using Hints in SQL Server

With Microsoft SQL Server 2000 you can include hints that instruct the SQL Server query processor how to handle your query. You can override the normal processing to meet your specific needs. This chapter discusses the different isolation levels and what they mean. It also explains how to apply hints to your query statements to take advantage of these isolation levels.

Isolation Levels

Before you can start exploring the hints available in SQL Server, you must understand the isolation levels available. When you use locking as a concurrency control mechanism, you have solved the concurrency problems. The locking strategy, either at the table, page, or row level, allows all transactions to run in complete isolation from one another, although more than one transaction can run in SQL Server at any one time.

Isolation depends on *serializability*, a property of the database system that specifies that the state the database achieves after running a set of concurrent transactions must be equivalent to the state it would achieve if the set of transactions were executed serially in some order. This property ensures that all the data stored and retrieved from the database is correct and consistent. Without serializability, we could receive different answers to our concurrent queries depending on the order in which they were run. That would be unacceptable.

We can illustrate serializability with the analogy of several writers working on different chapters of the same book. Any author can submit chapters to the project at any time. After a chapter has been edited, however, an author cannot make changes to the chapter without the editor's approval. This way the editor can guarantee the accuracy of the project at any point in time, regardless of when new unedited chapters arrive.

Although serializability maintains data integrity, it does so at the expense of performance. To get around the performance problem and still maintain data integrity, database developers determined that some queries do not require full isolation to be acceptable. This led to the establishment of isolation levels. You can think of an isolation level as the threshold below which a transaction will not accept inconsistent data. When you run at a low isolation level, you gain higher concurrency at the expense of data correctness. Conversely, when you run at a higher isolation level you ensure data correctness, but your overall transaction concurrency is negatively affected. It is important to look at your transactions and determine the appropriate isolation levels required.

The SQL-92 standard defines four isolation levels, all of which are supported by SQL Server:

- **Read Uncommitted** The lowest level of isolation, which ensures that transactions are isolated just enough that they do not read corrupt data.
- **Read Committed** SQL Server's default isolation level, which ensures that transactions are isolated enough that they read only committed data.
- **Repeatable Read** This isolation level ensures that if a transaction reads the same item twice without updating it in the interim, the read returns the same value.
- **Serializable** The highest level of isolation, in which transactions are completely isolated from one another.

Next we'll look at the four concurrency problems that the four isolation levels help alleviate. Without locking and isolation, the following problems could occur:

- **The lost update problem (dirty write)** The lost update problem arises when two or more transactions select the same row and then update the row based on the value originally selected. Because each transaction is unaware of other transactions, the last update overwrites the updates made by the other transactions. Therefore, data is lost.

    Returning to our book-authoring example, suppose we have two editors who each make an electronic copy of the same document. Each editor changes his or her copy independently and then saves the changed copy, thereby overwriting the original document. The editor who saves his or her changed copy last overwrites changes made by the first editor. The first editor's work has been lost without anyone knowing it, causing problems later on. It would be better if the second editor could not make changes until the first editor had finished.

- **The uncommitted dependency problem (dirty read)** This condition occurs when a transaction modifies a data element and a second transaction reads the data before the first transaction commits the changes. If the first transaction performs a rollback of the change, then the second transaction will have used a value that was never committed and therefore might be incorrect.

    Using our book example, suppose an editor is making changes to an electronic document. During the changes, a second editor takes a copy of the document that includes all the changes made so far and distributes it to the intended audience. The first editor then decides the changes made so far are wrong and removes the edits and saves the document. The distributed document contains edits that are no longer valid and should be treated as if they never existed. It would be better if no one could read the changed document until the first editor determined that the changes were final.

- **The inconsistent analysis problem (nonrepeatable read)** This condition arises when a transaction reads a data element, and then a second transaction comes along and modifies or deletes the data element and performs a commit. If the first transaction were to reread the data element, it might receive a modified value or discover that the data element has been deleted.

  For example, an editor reads the same document twice, but between each reading, the author rewrites the document. When the editor reads the document for the second time, it has completely changed. The original read was not repeatable, leading to confusion. It would be better if the editor could read the document only after the author had completely finished writing it.

- **The phantom problem (phantom read)** The phantom read problem manifests itself when a transaction reads a set of values that satisfy some search criteria. A second transaction then generates additional data that also satisfy the search criteria of the first transaction. If the first transaction were to repeat its initial read with the same search criteria, it would obtain a different set of values.

  Once again, we can return to our book example to illustrate this problem. An editor reads and edits a document submitted by an author, but when the edits are being incorporated into the master copy of the document by the production department, they find that new, unedited material has been added to the document by the author. The document contains material that previously did not exist, leading to confusion and problems. It would be better if no one could add new material to the document until the editor and production department finished working with the original document.

Session-Level Isolation

Occasionally, your application might require more or less strict isolation than the default SQL Server read committed isolation level. If the entire SQL batch requires the same isolation level, you can override the SQL Server default setting for this session. You set the isolation level for a session by issuing the SET TRANSACTION ISOLATION LEVEL statement.

When you specify the isolation level, the locking behavior for all SELECT statements in the SQL Server session operates at that isolation level and remains in effect until the session terminates or until you specifically set the isolation level to another value. For example, if you want to set the transaction isolation level to Serializable, ensuring that no phantom rows can be inserted by concurrent transactions into a *Sales* table, you would execute the following SQL statements:

```
SET TRANSACTION ISOLATION LEVEL SERIALIZABLE
GO
BEGIN TRANSACTION
SELECT Monthly_Widget_SW FROM Sales
GO
```

You can also query SQL Server to determine what transaction isolation level is in effect by using the DBCC USEROPTIONS statement. The following SQL batch and its output illustrates this:

```
SET TRANSACTION ISOLATION LEVEL REPEATABLE READ
GO
DBCC USEROPTIONS
GO
```

The following output is produced:

```
Set Option         Value
Textsize           4096
Language           us_English
Dateformat         mdy
Datefirst          7
isolation level    repeatable read
```

SQL Hints

SQL Server provides several options and hints that you can set to affect the results and performance of your SQL statements. These options can affect SQL Server at the index or table level. To determine which option or hint takes precedence, SQL Server follows a hierarchical sequence. As we explore the different hints and options available, you should keep the following sequence in mind.

If the option or hint is available at more than one level, then SQL Server determines the level on which the option or hint will be applied. The base level consists of server options, which are set via the *sp_configure* stored procedure. Any database option, specified via the *sp_dboption* stored procedure, overrides a server option. The database option can be overridden by a SET command. Finally, a hint at the statement level will override a *set* option. This hierarchy allows you to specify which behavior of the server you want to be the default. You can then easily override that setting for special queries or SQL statements.

The most flexible method for providing hints is at the SQL statement level. Hints at this level override any option or hint set at any other level. SQL Server allows you to specify three different types of transactional hints: join hints, table hints, or query hints. We explore each of these in detail.

Caution The SQL Server query optimizer usually selects the best execution plan for a query. Incorrect or inappropriate join hints can have a negative impact on the performance of the system. For that reason join hints, query hints, and table hints should be used only as a last resort by experienced database administrators.

Join Hints

SQL Server 2000 provides a mechanism for modifying the default behavior during a table join operation through the use of join hints. For example, you can force SQL Server to use a hash join by specifying the following join hint:

```
SELECT Region_ID,
    Region_Name,
    Sales_YTD
FROM Sales INNER HASH JOIN Regions
    ON Sales.Region_ID = Regions.Region_ID
```

You can specify whether the SQL Server query optimizer should use a loop, hash, merge, or remote method for the join.

The *loop join*, also called *nested iteration*, uses one join input as the outer input table and one as the inner input table. The outer loop consumes the outer input table row by row. The inner loop, executed for each outer row, searches for matching rows in the inner input table. In the simplest case, the search scans the entire inner input table or index. A loop join is particularly effective if the outer input is quite small and the inner input is preindexed and quite large. In many small transactions, such as those affecting only a small set of rows, loop joins are far superior to both merge joins and hash joins. In large queries, however, loop joins are often not the optimal choice.

The hash join method has two inputs: the build input and the probe input. The query optimizer assigns these roles so that the smaller of the two inputs is the build input. Hash joins are used for many types of set-matching operations, such as inner joins; left, right, and full outer joins; left and right semi-joins; intersections; unions; and differences.

You can only use a hash join if there is at least one equality (WHERE) clause in the join predicate. Because joins are typically used to reassemble relationships (expressed with an equality predicate between a primary key and a foreign key), most joins have at least one equality clause. The set of columns in the equality predicate is called the *hash key*, because these are the columns that contribute to the hash function. Additional predicates are possible and are evaluated as residual predicates separate from the comparison of hash values. The hash key can be an expression, as long as it can be computed exclusively from columns in a single row. In grouping operations, the columns that appear in the GROUP BY clause are used as the hash key. In set operations such as intersection, as well as in the removal of duplicates, the hash key consists of all columns.

The merge join requires both inputs to be sorted on the merge columns, which are defined by the WHERE clauses of the join predicate. The query optimizer typically scans an index, if one exists on the proper set of columns, or places a Sort operator below the merge join. Because each input is sorted, the Merge Join operator gets a row from each input and compares them. For example, for inner join operations, the rows are returned if they are equal. If they are not equal, whichever row has the lower value is discarded and another row is obtained from the same input as the discarded row. This process repeats until all rows have been processed.

The merge join operation can be a regular or a many-to-many operation. A many-to-many merge join uses a temporary table to store rows. If there are duplicate values from each input, one of the inputs rewinds to the start of the duplicates as each duplicate from the other input is processed.

The merge join itself is very fast, but it can be expensive choice if it requires sort operations. If the data volume is large and the data you want can be obtained presorted from existing B-tree indexes, however, a merge join is often the fastest available join algorithm.

You should specify the remote join method only when you are explicitly performing a join between remote tables. Specifying a remote join when the tables are both local results in the SQL Server query optimizer ignoring the join hint.

Table Hints

One common place for passing hints to SQL Server is at the table level. These hints are specified in the SELECT, INSERT, UPDATE, and DELETE statements and allow you to override the locking scheme that SQL Server would use on the selected table.

Locking Hints

SQL Server provides a range of table-level locking hints. These locking hints tell SQL Server how to lock and access the table or tables used in a query statement. Remember that these table-level locking hints override any systemwide or transactional isolation levels. These hints modify the system behavior so you can exploit the system performance.

Generally, the SQL Server query optimizer automatically makes the correct table-locking determination. You should use these locking hints only when absolutely necessary. Specifying an incorrect or inappropriate table-locking hint can negatively affect the overall performance of your system.

The table-locking hints are specified in all data manipulation statements. For example, the following SQL statement accesses the table using a table-locking hint of HOLDLOCK:

```
SELECT Monthly_Widget_SW
FROM Sales (HOLDLOCK)
GO
```

The table-locking hints that SQL Server allows are summarized in Table 19-1.

Table 19-1. Table-Level Locking Hints

Locking Hint	Description
HOLDLOCK	This hint tells SQL Server to hold a shared lock until the transaction is completed instead of releasing the lock as soon as the required table, row, or data page is no longer required. HOLDLOCK is equivalent to SERIALIZABLE. HOLDLOCK can negatively affect concurrency of your system. No other concurrent transaction can access the locked table.
NOLOCK	The NOLOCK hint tells SQL Server not to issue shared locks and not to honor exclusive locks. When this option is in effect, it is possible to read an uncommitted transaction or a set of pages that are rolled back in the middle of a read. Dirty reads are possible. This table-locking hint applies only to the SELECT statement.
PAGLOCK	This hint tells SQL Server to use a page lock rather than a single table lock, which would normally be used.
READCOMMITTED	When you specify READCOMMITTED, SQL Server performs a scan with the same locking semantics as a transaction running at the Read Committed isolation level. By default, SQL Server operates at this isolation level.
READPAST	This table-locking hint tells SQL Server to skip any locked rows it encounters. This option causes a transaction to skip over rows locked by other transactions that would ordinarily appear in the result set, rather than to block while waiting for the other transactions to release their locks on these rows. The READPAST lock hint applies only to transactions operating at Read Committed isolation and reads only past row-level locks. It applies only to the SELECT statement.
READUNCOMMITTED	The READUNCOMMITTED table-locking hint is equivalent to the NOLOCK hint.
REPEATABLEREAD	This table-locking hint tells SQL Server to perform a scan with the same locking semantics as a transaction running at the Repeatable Read isolation level.
ROWLOCK	The ROWLOCK table-locking hint tells SQL Server to use row-level locks rather than the coarser-grained page-level and table-level locks.
SERIALIZABLE	Specifying the SERIALIZABLE hint tells SQL Server to perform a scan with the same locking semantics as a transaction running at the Serializable isolation level. This hint is equivalent to HOLDLOCK.
TABLOCK	The TABLOCK table-locking hint tells SQL Server to use a table lock rather than using finer-grained row-level or page-level locks. SQL Server holds this lock until the end of the statement. If you also specify HOLDLOCK, the table lock is held until the end of the transaction.

(continued)

Table 19-1. *(continued)*

Locking Hint	Description
TABLOCKX	The TABLOCKX table-locking hint tells SQL Server to use an exclusive lock on a table. This lock prevents other transactions from reading or updating the table and is held until the end of the statement or transaction.
UPDLOCK	The UPDLOCK tells SQL Server to use update locks instead of shared locks while reading a table. It also tells SQL Server to hold the locks until the end of the statement or transaction. UPDLOCK has the advantage of allowing you to read data (without blocking other readers) and update it later with the assurance that the data has not changed since you last read it.
XLOCK	XLOCK causes an exclusive lock to be set on all data affected by the transaction. XLOCK can be used with PAGLOCK and TABLOCK. XLOCK is a great way to prevent deadlocking if you apply it at the beginning of the transaction.

In addition to the table-locking hints, SQL Server provides other table hints, which are summarized in Table 19-2.

Table 19-2. Table Hints

Table Hint	Description
FASTFIRSTROW	The FASTFIRSTROW hint tells the SQL Server query processor to optimize the query for retrieval of one row. FASTFIRSTROW is currently supported for backward compatibility. Consider using OPTION (FAST *nrows*) instead.
INDEX =	When you specify the INDEX = table hint, you tell SQL Server to use the specified index or indexes for a table. This overrides the normal SQL Server index selection process. INDEX = has also been replaced with the more powerful INDEX(*index_num, ..n*). When used, INDEX(...) allows for the enforcement of index *ANDing*. The order of the indexes listed is important.

Query Hints

In addition to the table hints, you can specify query hints. These hints tell SQL Server to modify its default processing of a query. You specify the query hints by using the OPTION clause of SELECT, UPDATE, or DELETE SQL statements. The INSERT SQL statement does not allow query hints. The following SQL sample illustrates the use of query hints.

```
SELECT Region_ID,
    Region_Name,
    Sales_YTD
FROM Sales INNER HASH JOIN Regions
    ON Sales.Region_ID = Regions.Region_ID
    GROUP BY Region_ID
    OPTION (ORDER GROUP, ROBUST PLAN)
```

When you use query hints, you should keep several things in mind. You can specify a query hint only once. You can specify multiple query hints, but only one of each type. If you have multiple queries in your statement, you must use the OPTION clause on the outermost query. The query hint then affects all operators in your statement. If you happen to specify one or more query hints that cause the SQL Server query optimizer to generate an invalid execution plan, SQL Server recompiles the query and ignores your query hints. When this occurs, SQL Server issues a SQL Profiler event for debugging purposes. The query hints available in SQL Server are summarized in Table 19-3.

Table 19-3. Query Hints

Query Hint	Use with Clause	Description
HASH	GROUP	Tells SQL Server to use hashing when performing the aggregations specified in the GROUP BY clause of the query.
ORDER	GROUP	Tells SQL Server to use ordering when performing the aggregations specified in the GROUP BY clause of the query.
CONCAT	UNION	Tells SQL Server to use concatenation when computing a UNION set. If more than one UNION hint is specified, the optimizer selects the least expensive strategy from those hints specified.
HASH	UNION	Tells SQL Server to use hashing when computing a UNION set. If more than one UNION hint is specified, the optimizer selects the least expensive strategy from those hints specified.
MERGE	UNION	Tells SQL Server to use merging when computing a UNION set. If more than one UNION hint is specified, the optimizer selects the least expensive strategy from those hints specified.
HASH	JOIN	Tells SQL Server to use a HASH join on the given JOIN clause. If more than one JOIN hint is specified, the optimizer selects the least expensive strategy from those hints specified.
MERGE	JOIN	Tells SQL Server to use a MERGE join on the given JOIN clause. If more than one JOIN hint is specified, the optimizer selects the least expensive strategy from those hints specified.

(continued)

Table 19-3. *(continued)*

Query Hint	Use with Clause	Description
LOOP	JOIN	Tells SQL Server to use a LOOP join on the given JOIN clause. If more than one JOIN hint is specified, the optimizer selects the least expensive strategy from those hints specified.
REMOTE	JOIN	Tells SQL Server to use a HASH join on the given JOIN clause, causing the JOIN to be performed on the right table. This is useful if the left table has fewer rows than the right table, and the right table is on a remote server. If more than one JOIN hint is specified, the optimizer selects the least expensive strategy from those hints specified.
FORCE ORDER	FROM	Tells SQL Server to process the tables in exactly the same order specified in the FROM clause.
ROBUST PLAN	N/A	Tells SQL Server to use the query plan that will work for the maximum potential row size. This could force SQL Server to use a plan that might degrade performance. This option is useful when you have large VARCHAR columns. These columns can cause an overflow condition on SQL Server's internal rows that produces an error. The ROBUST PLAN eliminates any potential plans in which this condition could occur.

Though query hints can be useful and can enhance the overall system performance, you should use them with caution and only if necessary. If you are migrating queries using hints that you executed against earlier versions of SQL Server, you should test the queries without using the hints because incorrect or inappropriate hints can prevent the SQL Server query optimizer from choosing a better execution plan.

Bulk Copy Hints

In addition to the join, table, and query hints, SQL Server 2000 provides several hints to use for bulk copying data into your tables. These hints allow you to customize how the *bcp* utility loads your tables so that you can optimize the efficiency of the bulk copy process. You can combine two or more of the following hints to achieve the behavior you want:

- **ORDER (*column* [ASC | DESC], ...)** This hint notifies SQL Server of the sort order of data within specified columns in the input data file. The bulk copy performance is improved if the data being loaded is sorted according to the clustered index on the table. If the data file is sorted in a different order or there is no clustered index on the table, the ORDER hint is ignored. The names of the columns supplied must be valid columns in the destination table. By default, the *bcp* utility assumes the data file is unordered.

- **ROWS_PER_BATCH = *bb*** This hint allows you to specify the number of rows of data per batch (as *bb*). This option is generally used when the *[en]b* (batch size) parameter is not specified. If you do not specify ROWS_PER_BATCH or batch size, the entire data file is sent to the server as a single transaction. SQL Server optimizes the bulk load according to the value *bb*. By default, ROWS_PER_BATCH is not used, and the bulk copy is done as one transaction.

- **KILOBYTES_PER_BATCH = *cc*** This hint specifies the approximate number of kilobytes of data per batch (as *cc*). By default, KILOBYTES_PER_BATCH is not used.

- **TABLOCK** The TABLOCK hint tells SQL Server to acquire a table-level lock for the duration of the bulk copy operation. This hint significantly improves performance because holding a lock only for the duration of the bulk copy operation reduces lock contention on the table. When you specify the TABLOCK hint, a table can be loaded from multiple clients concurrently if the table has no indexes. By default, locking behavior is determined by the table option specified in the *table lock on bulk load* database option.

- **CHECK_CONSTRAINTS** The CHECK_CONSTRAINTS hint tells SQL Server to honor any constraints on the destination table. All constraints are checked during the bulk copy operation. Checking the constraints negatively affects bulk copy performance because each row copied must be verified against any existing table constraints. By default, constraints are ignored.

- **FIRE_TRIGGERS** Causes insert triggers to be fired during bulk copy operation. Without FIRE_TRIGGERS, no triggers are fired.

You specify hints on the *bcp* command line via the *-h* option. For example, the following command will bulk copy the SWSales.txt file into the *Sales* table in the Softdrinks database using the TABLOCK and ROWS_PER_BATCH hints:

```
bcp 'Softdrinks..Sales' in SWSales.txt -c -w -Usa -P
-h"TABLOCK,ROWS_PER_BATCH=200"
```

Summary

This chapter explored the hints available in SQL Server 2000. The hints range from those specified for joins and queries to those available for bulk copying data. Specifying hints is a powerful and flexible method for modifying the default behavior of SQL Server. This power and flexibility should be used with caution, however, because specifying the wrong hints can cause SQL Server to use inefficient execution plans or can affect the concurrency of the system.

Part V
Appendixes and Glossary

Appendix A
SQL Server
Configuration Options

This appendix lists the configuration options available with Microsoft SQL Server 2000. You can set these configuration options through the SQL Server Enterprise Manager or by using the system stored procedure *sp_configure*. To use Enterprise Manager, right-click the server you want to configure and then select Properties from the shortcut menu. To set a configuration option with *sp_configure*, use the following syntax:

```
sp_configure 'option_name', value
```

For example, you can set the worker threads configuration option to 200 with the following command:

```
sp_configure 'max worker threads', 200
Go
```

In order to make the configuration changes take effect immediately, the reconfigure statement must be run. Even with the reconfigure statement, some parameters require a SQL Server restart in order for configuration changes to take effect.

Note A complete description of these options can be found in the SQL Server Books Online.

Configuration Options

- ***affinity mask*** A bitmap variable that defines the number of the CPU on which SQL Server is allowed to run. The default value of 0 lets the Microsoft Windows 2000 scheduler determine which CPUs to use. Because the variable is a bitmap, the binary representation of the value determines the number of CPUs. The binary values are supplied as a bit mask as follows:

```
Processor 1 = 0001
Processor 2 = 0010
Processor 3 = 0100
Processor 4 = 1000
```

.
.
.

For example, when you are using a four-processor system, you can set the *affinity mask* option to 15 (1111 in binary) to allow SQL Server to run on all four CPUs.

- ***allow updates*** Allows users with sufficient privileges to update system tables directly. When allow updates is set to 0 (the default), the system tables can only be updated through the system stored procedures.

- ***AWE enabled*** Allows the use of the Address Windowing Extensions (AWE) option in Windows 2000. When *AWE enabled* is set to 1 the use of memory above 4 GB is allowed.

- ***c2 audit mode*** Enables C2 security mode auditing. This logs specific events in SQL Server to achieve the C2 security level.

- ***cost threshold for parallelism*** Specifies a cost to be used in determining whether parallelism should be used for queries. If the cost of the query in serial mode exceeds the value of *cost threshold for parallelism* the query is parallelized. The default value is 5.

- ***cursor threshold*** Specifies the minimum number of rows in the cursor set that will cause the cursor keysets to be created asynchronously. If the number of rows is less than the value of *cursor threshold*, the keysets will be created synchronously. The default value of –1 specifies that all cursor keysets are created synchronously.

- ***default full-text language*** Specifies the ID of the default language used by SQL Server Full-Text Indexing. The default of 1033 is English US.

- ***default language*** Specifies the ID of the default language used by SQL Server. The default of 0 is English.

- ***default sortorder id*** Specifies the ID of the sort order used by SQL Server. The value of *default sortorder id* is set when SQL Server is installed with the custom option.

- ***fill factor*** Specifies how densely SQL Server packs index pages when it creates them. A value of 1 specifies that pages are mostly empty, a value of 100 specifies that pages are completely packed. The default value of 0 specifies that leaf pages are fully packed but upper pages have some space left.

- ***index create memory*** Specifies the amount of memory for index create sorts. The default value of 0 specifies that SQL Server determines this value.

- ***lightweight pooling*** This TRUE (1) or FALSE (0) option specifies whether SQL Server uses Microsoft Windows NT fiber mode scheduling to reduce context switching. Context switching incurs a lot of system overhead and is reduced by allowing SQL Server to do its own scheduling. The default value is 0, which specifies that fiber mode scheduling is not used.

- ***locks*** Specifies the maximum number of locks. The default value of 0 allows SQL Server to dynamically allocate and deallocate locks. You can monitor the number of locks in the system with the Performance tool; if you see a lot of allocation and deallocation you may want to statically allocate locks. The default value of 0 is the recommended setting.

- ***max degree of parallelism*** Specifies the maximum number of threads that can be allocated for use in a parallel execution. The default value of 0 specifies that the number of CPUs in the system is used. A value of 1 disables parallel execution. Because parallelism can help in I/O bound queries, you may find that you can achieve better performance with a larger value for *max degree of parallelism*. The maximum value is 32.

- ***max server memory*** Specifies the maximum amount of memory that can be dynamically allocated by SQL Server. This option works in conjunction with *min server memory* to determine how much memory is used. If you want to reserve additional space for other processes, you can use this option. The default value of 0 specifies that SQL Server automatically allocates memory.

- ***max text repl size*** Specifies the maximum number of bytes of text and image data that can be added to a replicated column in a single SQL Statement.

- ***max worker threads*** Specifies the maximum number of Windows NT threads that SQL Server allows in its pool of worker threads. This option can be adjusted in order to allow more threads for processing within SQL Server. Too many threads can overload a Windows 2000 system.

- ***media retention*** Specifies the number of days that a backup medium is retained. SQL Server does not overwrite a backup medium until this time has been exceeded.

- ***min memory per query*** Specifies the minimum amount of memory that will be allocated for a query. The default value is 1024, but you can use a range of values. This option can help performance with large sorts and hashing operations by allocating the memory when the query begins.

- ***min server memory*** Specifies the minimum amount of memory that can be dynamically allocated by SQL Server. It is used in conjunction with *max server memory* to manually set the minimum and maximum amount of memory that SQL Server can use. The default value of 0 specifies that SQL Server automatically allocates memory.

- ***nested triggers*** Specifies whether a trigger can initiate another trigger. The default value of 1 signifies yes.

- **network packet size** Specifies the size of incoming and outgoing data from SQL Server. The default value of 4096 specifies a packet size of 4 KB. If many of the result sets are large, you may want to increase this value.

- **open objects** Specifies the maximum number of objects that can be opened at one time in the SQL Server database. The default number of open objects is 500.

- **priority boost** When enabled (set to 1), specifies that SQL Server runs at a higher Windows NT scheduling priority than it normally would. The default value of 0 disables priority boost. This option can improve SQL Server performance but can keep other processes from getting enough CPU time. If SQL Server is the only program running on the Windows 2000 system you can set this value. This option can cause erratic results if you are not careful; change it at your own risk.

- **query governor cost limit** Specifies the maximum time in seconds that a query can run. Before a query is executed, the optimizer will estimate the amount of time that the query will run. When set, this option prohibits large queries from running.

- **query wait** When there is insufficient memory for a query to run, SQL Server queues the query until the resources are available. By default, the wait time is 25 times the estimated cost of the query. By setting the *query wait* option, you can specify the timeout value.

- **recovery interval** Sets how often checkpoints occur by specifying the maximum amount of time that SQL Server can take in the event of a system failure. The default value of 0 lets SQL Server determine this value automatically.

- **remote access** Specifies whether remote logins from other SQL Server systems are allowed. The default value of 1 allows remote logins.

- **remote login timeout** Specifies how long a remote login waits before timing out. The default value is five seconds.

- **remote proc trans** When you set *the remote proc trans* option to 1, remote transactions with Distributed Transaction Coordinator (DTC) support ACID properties of the transactions.

- **remote query timeout** Specifies how many seconds must elapse before a remote query times out. The default value of 0 specifies that queries do not time out.

- **scan for startup procs** Specifies whether to scan for scheduled jobs at startup. The default value of 0 specifies not to scan for jobs.

- ***set working set size*** When the set *working set size* option is enabled (set to 1), it specifies that SQL Server memory does not get paged out, even when SQL Server is idle. If you are allowing SQL Server to allocate memory dynamically do not enable *set working set size* to 1. The default value of 0 disables *set working set size*. This option can be very important for performance and works in conjunction with *min server memory* and *max server memory*.

Show Advanced Options

When the *show advanced options* configuration option is set to 1, *sp_configure* displays the advanced options.

- ***two digit year cutoff*** Specifies Y2K behavior in SQL Server 2000.
- ***user connections*** Specifies the maximum number of users that can be connected to SQL Server. By default SQL Server dynamically adjusts the number of allowed user connections, but this causes additional overhead. This option allows you to statically set the number of allowed user connections.
- ***user options*** Specifies global defaults for all users.

Option Specification

Some of the configuration options are advanced options; to change these options, you must set *show advanced options* to 1 or use Enterprise Manager. Some options take effect immediately and others require a SQL Server restart. Table A-1 specifies which options require restarts as well as which are advanced options.

Table A-1. Characteristics of Configuration Options

Option	Advanced Option	Restart Required
affinity mask	Yes	Yes
allow updates	No	No
AWE enabled	Yes	Yes
cost threshold for parallelism	Yes	No
cursor threshold	Yes	No
default full-text language	Yes	No
default language	No	No
fill factor	Yes	Yes
index create memory	Yes	No
lightweight pooling	Yes	Yes
locks	Yes	Yes

(continued)

Table A-1. *(continued)*

Option	Advanced Option	Restart Required
max degree of parallelism	Yes	No
max server memory	Yes	No
max test repl size	No	No
max worker threads	Yes	Yes
media retention	Yes	Yes
min memory per query	Yes	No
min server memory	Yes	No
nested triggers	No	No
network packet size	Yes	No
open objects	Yes	Yes
priority boost	Yes	Yes
query governor cost limit	Yes	No
query wait	Yes	No
recovery interval	Yes	No
remote access	No	Yes
remote login timeout	No	No
remote proc trans	No	No
remote query timeout	No	No
scan for startup procs	Yes	Yes
set working set size	Yes	Yes
show advanced options	No	No
two digit year cutoff	No	No
user connections	Yes	Yes
user options	No	No

Changing Options with the Enterprise Manager

You can modify many of the configuration options through Enterprise Manager. You can set these options by right-clicking the server icon in the console tree of Enterprise Manager and selecting Properties on the shortcut menu.

General Tab

The initial tab of the SQL Server Properties dialog box is the General tab, as shown in Figure A-1. The General tab does not have any options associated with it, but you can select some autostart options here. You can also change some startup options, which you access by clicking the Startup Parameters button.

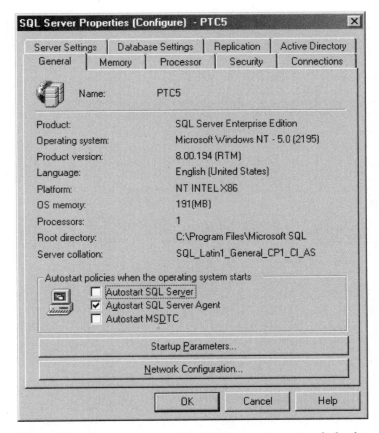

Figure A-1. *The General tab of the SQL Server Properties dialog box.*

Memory Tab

The Memory tab (Figure A-2) allows you to choose whether memory is dynamically allocated or statically chosen. You can set the amounts by moving slide bars. You can also set the minimum query memory used by SQL Server here.

The options you can set on the Memory tab are as follows:

- *min server memory*
- *max server memory*
- *min memory per query*
- *set working set size*

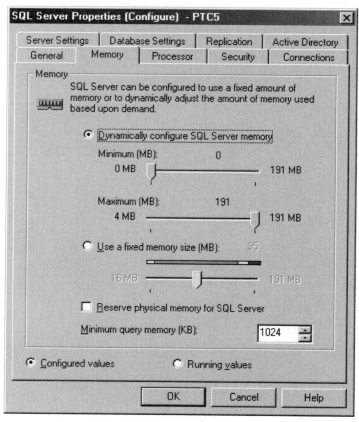

Figure A-2. *The Memory tab of the SQL Server Properties dialog box.*

Processor Tab

The Processor tab (Figure A-3) gives you the option of selecting CPUs that are available for SQL Server use. You can also set the maximum number of worker threads. Other check boxes allow you to boost SQL Server's scheduling priority and to use Windows NT fibers. Finally, you can specify how SQL Server parallelizes queries.

The options you can set on the Processor tab are as follows:

- *affinity mask*
- *max worker threads*
- *priority boost*
- *lightweight pooling*
- *max degree of parallelism*
- *cost threshold for parallelism*

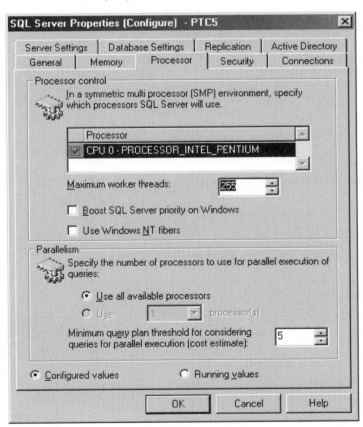

Figure A-3. *The Processor tab of the SQL Server Properties dialog box.*

Security Tab

The Security tab (Figure A-4) does not deal with tuning options. Instead you can specify the authentication method, the audit level, and the Windows accounts in which to start up and run SQL Server.

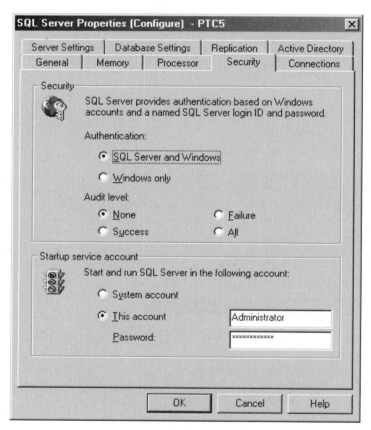

Figure A-4. *The Security tab of the SQL Server Properties dialog box.*

Connections Tab

The Connections tab (Figure A-5) provides a number of settings related to the user connections. Here you can set the maximum number of users and specify the level of constraint checking. You can also configure remote connection settings, such as allowing RPC connections, setting the query timeout, and enforcing distributed transactions.

The options you can set on the Connections tab are as follows.

- *user connections*
- *user options*
- *remote access*
- *remote query timeout*
- *remote proc trans*

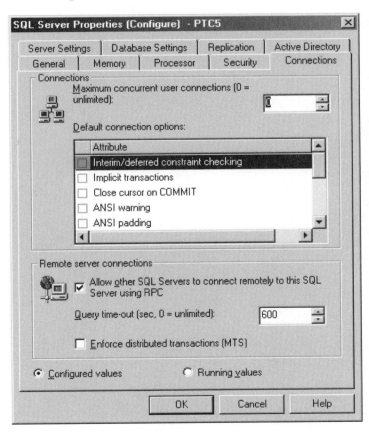

Figure A-5. *The Connections tab of the SQL Server Properties dialog box.*

Server Settings Tab

The Server Settings tab (Figure A-6) deals with general server options. Here you can set the default language for the user, as well as options to allow catalog modification, and to allow triggers to fire triggers. You can also set the query governor and configure the SQL mail profile and Year 2000 support.

The options you can set on the Server Settings tab are as follows:

- *default language*
- *allow updates*
- *using nested triggers*
- *query governor cost limit*
- *two digit year cutoff*

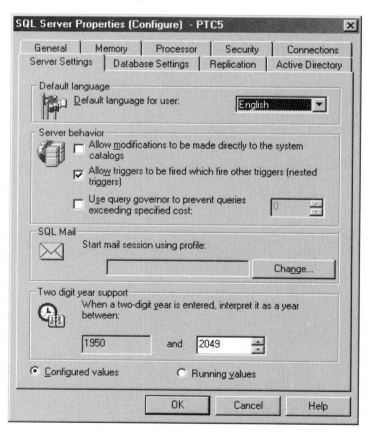

Figure A-6. *The Server Settings tab of the SQL Server Properties dialog box.*

Database Settings Tab

The Database Settings tab (Figure A-7) gives you the option of setting the database fill factor as well as backup options and the recovery interval.

The options you can set in the Database Settings window are as follows:

- *fill factor*
- *media retention*
- *recovery interval*

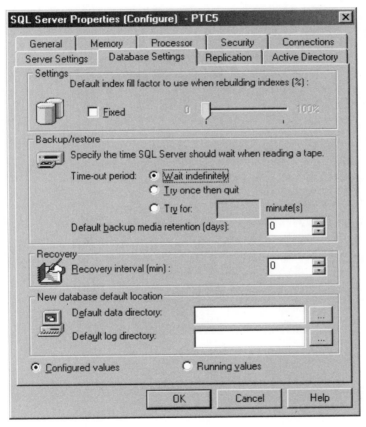

Figure A-7. *The Database Settings tab of the SQL Server Properties dialog box.*

Replication Tab

The Replication tab (Figure A-8) allows you to view and set replication publishing and distribution.

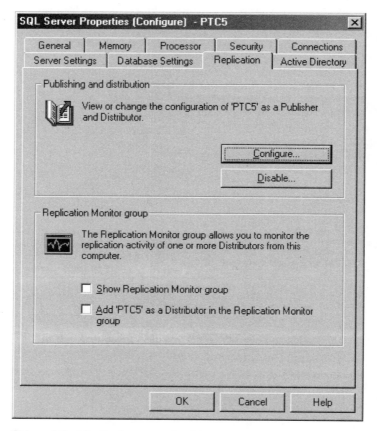

Figure A-8. *The Replication tab of the SQL Server Properties dialog box.*

Active Directory Tab

The Active Directory tab (Figure A-9) allows you to add the server along with its databases and publications to the Active Directory information repository. The tab also provides the functionality to refresh or remove the information maintained by Active Directory.

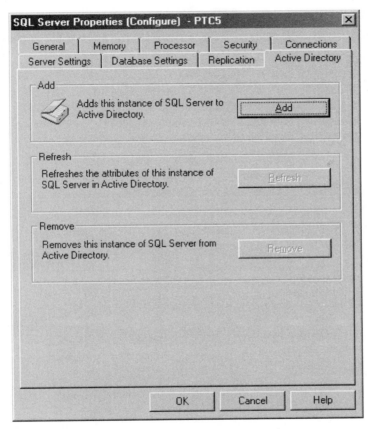

Figure A-9. *The Active Directory tab of the SQL Server Properties dialog box.*

Appendix B
SQL Server Monitoring

Microsoft SQL Server provides a number of counters that can be monitored by the Performance application of the Microsoft Management Console (MMC) snap-in. This appendix presents a reference to those objects and counters that SQL Server installs.

SQLServer:Access Methods

The performance counters under the SQLServer:Access Methods object represent different object access methods and properties. The counters include the following:

- **Extent Deallocations/sec** The number of extents released per second by SQL Server.
- **Extents Allocated/sec** The number of extents allocated per second by SQL Server.
- **Forwarded Records/sec** The number of records retrieved through forward record pointers.
- **FreeSpace Page Fetches/sec** The number of pages returned per second by free space scans.
- **FreeSpace Scans/sec** The number of scans done per second to find free space for record insertion.
- **Full Scans/sec** The number of full table or index scans per second. If this counter shows a value greater than 1 or 2, you should analyze your queries to see if table scans are really necessary and whether the SQL queries can be optimized.
- **Index Searches/sec** The number of times an index lookup is performed. This could be a single record lookup or the start of an index range scan.
- **Mixed Page allocations/sec** The number of pages allocated that are used to store the first eight pages of an extent or index.
- **Page Deallocations/sec** The number of pages deallocated per second.
- **Page Splits/sec** The number of page splits that result when an index page overflows.

- **Pages Allocated/sec** The number of pages allocated for index or data storage.
- **Probe Scans/sec** The number of scans performed to look up rows in base tables or indexes.
- **Range Scans/sec** The number of range scans through indexes.
- **Scan Point Revalidations/sec** The number of times that the scan point had to be revalidated before the scan could be continued.
- **Skipped Ghosted Records/sec** The number of ghosted records skipped during a scan.
- **Table Lock Escalations/sec** The number of times per second that a table lock was escalated.
- **Workfiles Created/sec** The number of workfiles (used in query execution) created per second.
- **Worktables Created/sec** The number of worktables (used in GROUP BY, ORDER BY and UNION operators) created per second.
- **Worktables From Cache Ratio** The percentage of worktables created when the initial pages were available in the worktable cache.

SQL Server:Backup Device

The single counter for the SQLServer:Backup Device object reports the performance of backup devices. Each instance has its own counter.

- **Device Throughput Bytes/sec** The number of bytes per second being transferred to a backup device during a backup operation. This counter is useful for both monitoring the throughput as well as the balance of I/Os through the various backup devices.

SQL Server:Buffer Manager

This object contains a number of counters related to the SQL Server buffer cache and how it is operating.

Note AWE (Address Windowing Extensions) is used to support physical memory above 4 GB. SQL Server makes special system calls in order to use this large amount of memory.

The counters are as follows:

- **AWE lookup maps/sec** The number of AWE map calls for pages in the buffer pool. AWE holds the pages in a window of memory; this is the mapping of that window.

- **AWE stolen maps/sec** The number of AWE map calls for pages stolen from the buffer pool.

- **AWE unmap calls/sec** The number of AWE unmap calls per second.

- **AWE unmap pages/sec** The number of AWE pages unmapped per second.

- **AWE write maps/sec** The number of AWE map calls made for writing data to disk.

- **Buffer cache hit ratio** The percentage of pages that were found in memory. This is an indicator of how well the SQL Server buffer cache is doing.

- **Checkpoint pages/sec** The number of pages written to disk by the checkpoint process, including those on behalf of other operations. The checkpoint process causes all dirty pages to be flushed to disk. If this counter constantly shows a large value you might be experiencing too frequent checkpoints. How often you checkpoint is based on your specific needs. Frequent checkpoints guarantee faster recovery time, less frequent checkpoints offer higher performance.

- **Database pages** The number of pages that currently make up the SQL Server cache. You can monitor this counter for constantly changing size. If it shows large swings during the day, you might want to fix the cache size by using the *min server memory* and *max server memory* parameters.

- **Free list stalls/sec** The number of requests per second that had to wait for a page to be freed before they could continue.

- **Free pages** The number of free (nonused, but allocated) buffers available in the buffer cache. Don't worry if this seems low. Remember that SQL Server dynamically creates more buffers as necessary.

- **Lazy writes/sec** Number of buffers per second written by the lazy writer. The lazy writer is used to free dirty buffers based on a LRU (Least Recently Used) algorithm.

- **Page life expectancy** The estimated number of seconds a page will stay in the buffer pool before written out (if not referenced).

- **Page lookups/sec** The number of requests to find a page in the buffer pool per second.

- **Page reads/sec** The number of physical database page reads issued per second.
- **Page writes/sec** The number of physical database page writes issued per second.
- **Procedure cache pages** The number of pages used for the procedure cache, which is where the compiled queries are stored.
- **Readahead pages/sec** The number of pages per second that are read in anticipation by SQL Server. These pages have not been requested by a user yet, but SQL Server is guessing that they soon will be, based on previous requests.
- **Reserved pages** The number of reserved pages in the buffer cache.
- **Stolen pages** The number of pages that have been stolen from the buffer cache to satisfy another memory request.
- **Target pages** The number of pages in the buffer pool that SQL Server considers optimal.
- **Total pages** The total number of pages in the buffer pool.

SQL Server:Buffer Partition

This object contains a number of counters related to the SQL Server buffer partition and how it is operating. The counters are as follows:

- **Free list empty/sec** The number of times a free page was requested per second when there were no pages to satisfy the request.
- **Free list requests/sec** The total number of times that a free page was requested per second.
- **Free pages** The total number of pages on all free lists.

SQL Server:Cache Manager

This object is used to maintain overall cache manager statistics. Each of the counters is available for the following instances: ad hoc SQL plans, miscellaneous normalized trees, prepared SQL plans, procedure plans, replication procedure plans, and trigger plans. The counters are as follows:

- **Cache Hit Ratio** The ratio between cache hits and misses. This is a very good counter for seeing how effective the SQL Server cache is for your system. If this number is low, you might want to add more memory.
- **Cache Object Counts** The number of cache objects in the cache.
- **Cache Pages** The number of 8-KB pages used by cache objects.
- **Cache Use Counts/sec** The number of times each type of cache object has been used.

SQLServer:Databases

The SQLServer:Databases object contains a set of counters for each database in the system. The instances represent the database that you can monitor and include master, model, msdb and tempdb as well as Northwind, pubs, and all your user created-databases. The counters are as follows:

- **Active Transactions** The number of currently active transactions in the database.
- **Backup/Restore Throughput/sec** The throughput of active backup and restore operations.
- **Bulk Copy Rows/sec** The number of rows per second currently being copied via a bulk copy operation.
- **Bulk Copy Throughput/sec** The number of kilobytes per second currently being copied via a bulk copy operation.
- **Data File(s) Size (KB)** The total size of all of the data files in the database.
- **DBCC Logical Scan Bytes/sec** The logical read scan rate for DBCC commands.
- **Log Bytes Flushed/sec** The number of log bytes that are flushed per second.
- **Log Cache Hit Ratio** The percentage of log reads that were satisfied from the log cache.
- **Log Cache Reads/sec** The number of log cache reads per second.
- **Log File(s) Size (KB)** The size of the log file or files in kilobytes.
- **Log File(s) Used Size (KB)** The amount of space currently used in the log file or files.
- **Log Flush Wait Time** The total wait time for log flushes in milliseconds.
- **Log Flush Waits/sec** The number of log flush waits per second.
- **Log Flushes/sec** The number of log flushes per second.
- **Log Growths** The number of log growths; that is how many times the log has extended itself.
- **Log Shrinks** The number of log shrinks; that is, how many times the log has shrunk itself.
- **Log Truncations** The number of times the log has truncated for this database.
- **Percent Log Used** The current percentage of the log that is used.
- **Repl. Pending Xacts** The number of pending replication transactions in this database.

- **Repl. Trans. Rate** The number of replication transactions per second.
- **Shrink Data Movement Bytes/sec** The rate data is being moved by an autoshrink operation.
- **Transactions/sec** The number of transactions per second for this database. This counter gives you a good idea of the activity in your system. The higher the value, the more activity is occurring.

SQLServer:General Statistics

This object represents some general user connection information about SQL Server, including the following:

- **Logins/sec** The number of logins per second.
- **Logouts/sec** The number of logouts per second.
- **User Connections** The number of users currently connected.

SQLServer:Latches

This object is used to show SQL Server latch statistics, including the following:

- **Average Latch Wait Time (ms)** The average wait time, in milliseconds, that a SQL Server thread has to wait on a latch. If this number is high, you could be experiencing severe contention problems.
- **Latch Waits/sec** The number of waits per second on latches. If this number is high, you are experiencing a high amount of contention on resources.
- **Total Latch Wait Time (ms)** The total amount of time, in milliseconds, that latch requests had to wait in the last second.

SQL Server:Locks

This object contains a number of counters that keep track of lock activity. These counters each keep track of the following SQL Server lock types: database locks, extent locks, key locks, page locks, RID (row locks) and table locks.

These counters give you a good idea of the types of locks and frequency of locks that are being used in the system. The counters are as follows:

- **Average Wait Time (ms)** The average time, in milliseconds, that a thread is waiting on this type of lock.
- **Lock Requests/sec** The number of requests for this type of lock per second.

- **Lock Timeouts/sec** The number of times per second that a lock could not be obtained by spinning. The number of times that a thread spins before timing out and sleeping is governed by the SQL Server configuration parameter *spin counter*.
- **Lock Wait Time (ms)** Total wait time for locks, in milliseconds, for the last second.
- **Lock Waits/sec** The number of times a lock request caused a thread to wait in the last second.
- **Number of Deadlocks/sec** The number of lock requests that resulted in a deadlock.

SQL Server:Memory Manager

This object contains information about SQL Server memory other than the buffer cache. The counters are as follows:

- **Connection Memory (KB)** The amount of memory, in kilobytes, that is used for maintaining connections.
- **Granted Workspace Memory (KB)** The amount of memory, in kilobytes, that has been granted to processes for sorting and index creation operations.
- **Lock Blocks** The current number of lock blocks in use on the server.
- **Lock Blocks Allocated** The total number of allocated lock blocks.
- **Lock Memory (KB)** The amount of memory, in kilobytes, that is allocated to locks.
- **Lock Owner Blocks** The number of lock owner blocks that are currently in use on the server.
- **Lock Owner Blocks Allocated** The number of lock owner blocks that have been allocated on the server.
- **Maximum Workspace Memory (KB)** The total amount of memory that has been allocated to executing processes. This memory can be used for hash, sort and index creation operations.
- **Memory Grants Outstanding** The current number of processes that have acquired a workspace memory grant.
- **Memory Grants Pending** The current number of processes waiting for a workspace memory grant.
- **Optimizer Memory (KB)** The amount of memory, in kilobytes, that the server is using for query optimization.

- **SQL Cache Memory (KB)** The total amount of memory that the server is using for the dynamic SQL cache.
- **Target Server Memory (KB)** The total amount of dynamic memory, in kilobytes, that the server may potentially consume.
- **Total Server Memory (KB)** The total amount of dynamic memory, in kilobytes, that the server is currently consuming. Because SQL Server dynamically allocates and deallocates memory based on what is available in the system, this counter is your view of what is currently being used. If there are large swings over the course of a day, or when special events occur, you may want to fix the amount of memory that SQL Server is using by setting the *min server memory* and *max server memory* parameters.

SQL Server:Replication Agents

This object displays information on the number of running replication agents. The following counter is available:

- **Running** The number of running replication agents.

SQL Server:Replication Dist.

This object is used to view information about distributors and subscribers. The counters are as follows:

- **Dist:Delivered Cmds/sec** The number of commands per second delivered to the subscriber.
- **Dist:Delivered Trans/sec** The number of transactions per second delivered to the subscriber.
- **Dist:Delivery Latency** The amount of time between when transactions are delivered to the distributor to when they are applied to the subscriber.

SQL Server:Replication Logreader

This object is used to view information about distributors and publishers. The counters are as follows:

- **Logreader:Delivered Cmds/sec** The number of commands per second delivered to the distributor.
- **Logreader:Delivered Trans/sec** The number of transactions per second delivered to the distributor.
- **Logreader:Delivery Latency** The amount of time between when transactions are applied to the distributor to when they are delivered to the distributor.

SQL Server:Replication Merge

This object pertains to the replication merge process. The counters are as follows:

- **Conflicts/sec** The number of conflicts per second occurring during the merge process.
- **Downloaded Changes/sec** The number of rows per second merged from the publisher to the subscriber.
- **Uploaded Changes/sec** The number of rows per second merged from the subscriber to the publisher.

SQL Server:Replication Snapshot

This object pertains to the snapshot replication process. The counters are as follows:

- **Snapshot:Delivered Cmds/sec** The number of commands per second delivered to the distributor.
- **Snapshot:Delivered Trans/sec** The number of transactions per second delivered to the distributor.

SQL Server:SQL Statistics

This object is very interesting in that it offers useful statistics on SQL statements that have been run. The counters are as follows:

- **Auto-Param Attempts/sec** The number of autoparameterization attempts per second.
- **Batch Requests/sec** The number of SQL batch requests per second that have been received by the server.
- **Failed Auto-Params/sec** The number of autoparameterization attempts that have failed per second.
- **Safe Auto-Params/sec** The number of safe autoparameterizations per second.
- **SQL Compilations/sec** The number of times per second that SQL compilations have occurred.
- **SQL Re-Compilations/sec** The number of times per second that SQL recompilations have occurred.
- **Unsafe Auto-Params/sec** The number of unsafe autoparameterizations per second.

SQLServer:User Settable

The SQLServer:User Settable object represents a set of user counters that you can define. These counters can be set from within any SQL statement by calling the system stored procedures *sp_user_counter1* through *sp_user_counter10* followed by an integer value to which you want to set the counter. You can read these counters through the Performance tool by viewing the following counter:

- **Query** Represents the user-settable value. This counter has 10 instances associated with it: User counter 1 through User counter 10. The value displayed is the value that your program or SQL statement has set.

Glossary

A

Active Server Pages (ASP) A Web page technology that creates HTML pages dynamically on the server. ASP is commonly used to access SQL Server from the World Wide Web.

ad hoc A term used to describe a spontaneous query. Typically an ad hoc query is not optimized and is typed into the SQL Query Analyzer, ISQL or OSQL, not used through an application. The Latin words mean "this is."

agent A program that runs independently within Windows 2000 to perform a service. Agents usually have a particular task, such as scheduling operations or performing replication tasks. The equivalent in the UNIX world is a daemon.

aggregate function Function that performs an operation on a set of values and returns a single value. The SQL Server aggregate functions are AVG, COUNT, DISTINCT, GROUP BY, HAVING, MAX, MIN, STDEV, STDEVP, SUM, VAR, and VARP.

API *See* application programming interface.

AppleTalk The Apple networking protocol.

application The code that provides the interface for the end user and communicates with the RDBMS.

application programming interface (API) The standard and documented interface that programs are coded to. By coding to an API one can create programs that use external functions, such as SQL Server access.

article A table or subset of data that is selected to be replicated.

ASP *See* Active Server Pages.

Asynchronous Transfer Mode (ATM) A network hardware protocol.

B

backup A duplicate copy of the contents of a SQL Server database to be used in the event of a system failure. The backup can be copied back into the database to return the database to the state it was in when the backup was performed.

bandwidth The throughput capacity of a device or system. This term is typically associated with a network device or computer bus.

batch processing system A system distinguished by scheduled loading and processing of data in groups. These long-running jobs are done offline with little or no user intervention.

BCP *See* bulk copy program.

bit The smallest unit of data. A bit is either on (1) or off (0).

block *See* page.

bottleneck A performance-limiting component. The term comes from an analogy to a bottle containing liquid: the narrowing of the neck slows the flow of liquid.

branch node An intermediate node in an index. Branch nodes are between the root node and the leaf nodes.

buffer cache *See* cache.

bulk copy A generic term relating to the act of copying large amounts of data to or from a SQL Server database. Typically a bulk copy uses the BULK INSERT Transact-SQL statement.

bulk copy program (BCP) A program provided with Microsoft SQL Server that is used for loading data from text files into the database.

BULK INSERT A way of copying large amounts of data from a data file into a SQL Server table from within SQL Server. Whereas BCP is an external program, BULK INSERT is a Transact-SQL command.

bulk load The act of loading the database using bulk insert operations, which can be done by using the BULK INSERT Transact-SQL statement or the *bcp* utility.

byte A sequence of eight binary bits. A byte is the basic unit of data used in computers. It is made up of bits (ones and zeros) that represent numbers, characters, and so forth.

C

cache Random access memory (RAM) used to hold frequently accessed data in order to improve performance. SQL Server contains its own cache made up of Windows 2000 memory used to hold commonly accessed pages. This is referred to as the SQL Server buffer cache or page cache. CPU chips contain their own on-board caches, and some I/O controllers also contain caches.

capacity planning Planning for increased use of the system and anticipating capacity that must be added. This task is performed to maintain the level of service expected by the user community while the load on the system is increasing.

capacity planning measurement A collection of performance statistics (counters) used to determine the resource consumption of a workload to plan for additional hardware resources. This type of measurement covers a period of longer duration than a performance measurement. Where performance measurements are usually minutes or hours, a capacity planning measurement can be hours or even a day.

Cartesian product The product of a join that does not have a WHERE clause. The size of the resulting data set is the number of rows in the first table multiplied by the number of rows in the second table. A Cartesian product is not usually an intentional result of a query.

central processing unit (CPU) The brains of the computer; that is, the chip that processes data.

checkpoint An operation performed to synchronize the data files with the current state of transactions to reduce the recovery time needed in the event of a system failure. The checkpoint process traverses the list of dirty pages and flushes them to disk.

client-server model The programming model where the user interface portion of the program resides in an executable program on your computer and accesses data in a database on a server. The application logic is divided between the client and the server.

cluster *See* clustered index, Microsoft Cluster Server.

clustered index A combination of index and table. The index is stored as a B-tree, and the data is stored in the leaf nodes of the index.

collision A collision occurs when two controllers attempt to use the network at the same time. Each controller detects the collision and waits a usually random amount of time before trying again. In a heavily utilized network, collisions can cause a performance bottleneck. This term is usually associated with an Ethernet network.

column A collection of corresponding fields in all rows of data in a table. Each column has a data type associated with it. All the columns in a row make up a database record.

COMMIT The SQL statement that finalizes a SQL transaction. Until the COMMIT statement has been issued the transaction can be undone by issuing the ROLLBACK statement.

Component Object Model (COM) COM technologies are a set of APIs and tools developed by Microsoft. These applications run under the control of Microsoft Transaction Server (MTS) on the server system and under the control of DCOM (Distributed COM) on client systems. COM clients are developed using platforms such as Visual Basic and Visual C++. Applications can also be made up of newer technologies such as ASP (Active Server Pages) and Internet Services Application Programming Interface (ISAPI).

composite index An index that is created on a combination of two or more columns.

configuration option A setting that allows you to change the behavior of SQL Server. These options are used to tune the SQL Server engine. Configuration options affect things such as SQL Server memory allocation, thread counts, and number of user connections.

constraint A restriction placed on a table to guarantee referential integrity.

CPU *See* central processing unit.

cube A multidimensional representation of both detail and summary data. Cubes are typically used in OLAP.

D

database A repository of data. This can be anything from a small list of names to a record of the entire population of the world.

database administrator (DBA) The person or persons responsible for maintaining the database. The DBA's role can vary depending on your company's needs.

database consistency checker (DBCC) A utility for finding and correcting problems in the consistency of the database.

database management system (DBMS) The programs, files, processes, and memory that make up the database. SQL Server is a relational DBMS (RDBMS).

database role A role helps in the assignment of permissions to users. Rather than assigning individual permissions to individual users, a role can be created that represents the permissions granted to a set of users. In this method, only the roles need be assigned to the users.

data definition language (DDL) SQL statements that are used in the definition or declaration of database objects. A DDL includes statements such as CREATE DATABASE and DROP DATABASE.

data file The physical operating system file that is used to hold the data associated with a filegroup and, in turn, the database. Under SQL Server this can be an NTFS file or a Windows NT raw device.

data integrity *See* integrity.

data manipulation language (DML) SQL statements that are used to insert, update, delete, or retrieve data from the database.

data mart A decision support system created from company online transaction processing (OLTP) data. A data mart differs from a data warehouse in that the former is typically used by one business segment, such as Accounts Receivable or Accounts Payable.

Data Transformation Services (DTS) The Microsoft SQL Server facility for transforming data between systems.

data warehouse A decision support system created from company online transaction processing (OLTP) data. A data warehouse is usually a very large system, which can reach terabytes.

DBA *See* database administrator.

DBCC *See* database consistency checker.

DBLIB Abbreviation of DB-Library; a SQL Server connectivity protocol.

DBMS *See* database management system.

DDL *See* data definition language.

decision support system A database system that is used to aid in business decisions based on data in the database. These decisions can be based on sales trends, product sales, and so forth.

differential backup A mode of backup that saves only the data that has changed since the previous backup. This mode can back up the database faster than a full backup, but usually takes longer to restore the database.

dirty page A page in the SQL Server cache that has been modified but has not been written to disk.

disk In this book, the term identifies a fixed disk drive. A fixed disk drive is a magnetic medium that is used to store data. A disk is persistent storage: data remains on the disk even after power is removed.

Distributed Transaction Coordinator (DTC) The Microsoft SQL Server facility that coordinates transactions between systems by performing two-phase commits.

distributor The intermediary component in SQL Server replication. A distributor takes replication data from a publisher and presents it to a subscriber.

DML *See* data manipulation language.

domain A Windows 2000 network group. Systems in a domain share the same user list and passwords.

DSS *See* decision support system.

DTC *See* Distributed Transaction Coordinator.

DTS *See* Data Transformation Services.

E

encryption Encoding data or stored procedures with password protection for security reasons.

enterprise A term for a system that services the entire company.

Enterprise Manager The main utility used to administer the SQL Server RDBMS.

equijoin A join that uses an equality operator in the WHERE clause of the SQL statement performing the join.

Ethernet A popular network hardware protocol.

execution plan The method that the parsed SQL Server statement uses to perform operations on the database.

F

fault tolerance The ability of a subsystem to continue functioning after a component has failed. This is done with redundant components. Fault tolerance is typically associated with the I/O subsystem and RAID controllers, but other subsystems, such as power supplies, can also be fault tolerant.

fiber or **fiber optics** A network hardware protocol.

fiber channel A new I/O protocol that operates using either copper wire or fiber optic connection hardware.

field *See* column.

filegroup A group of files that is used as a repository for SQL Server objects. A filegroup can be made up of one or more data files. When SQL Server objects are created they can be assigned to a specific filegroup.

filegroup backup A form of backup that backs up and restores filegroups, rather than the entire database, so that the database backup can be spread across several days.

foreign key A field in a table that is also a primary key in another table.

foreign key constraint A requirement that a foreign key is a valid primary key in the database. This type of constraint is typically used to verify that referenced data is available.

full backup A backup that saves all data in a database.

full table scan A select operation in which all rows in the table are read in order to find the data you want. A full table scan is not usually best because of the heavy I/O overhead involved.

G

gigabyte (GB) 2^{30} bytes, 1,024 megabytes, or 1,073,741,824 bytes.

graphical user interface (GUI) An interface that is graphical in nature in order to simplify the use of the application. A GUI can be used to show data in a format that is easier for the human mind to comprehend.

GROUP BY A SQL clause used to divide a table into groups of data. These groups can consist of column names or results in computed columns.

GUI *See* graphical user interface.

H

HBA *See* host bus adapter.

hint An addition to SQL statements to allow you to give the query optimizer information on how you would like the execution plan to be constructed.

host bus adapter (HBA) A computer adapter used to communicate with an I/O bus.

hub A hub is a passive network device that is used to connect the network cards from multiple systems. A hub is an electrical device that has no application logic, thus they are very fast.

I

index An auxiliary data structure used to speed access to data within the database.

index scan An operation that occurs when a group of index entries must be read to find the requested data. Such a scan is used when a composite index is accessed and not all the columns that make up the index are supplied in the WHERE clause.

input/output (I/O) The movement of data from one computer component to another. The term can describe the disk subsystem or other data transfer components.

integrity Data integrity ensures the quality of the database. It allows only valid (within the business model) data in the database.

I/O *See* input/output.

I/O capacity The amount of work that can be supported by the I/O subsystem. The I/O capacity is constrained by either the number of I/Os (if random seeks are the limiting factor) or throughput (if seeks are sequential).

IPX/SPX A network protocol used in Novell networks.

ISQL An application supplied by Microsoft that allows access into the SQL Server RDBMS. ISQL uses the DBLIB protocol; OSQL uses the ODBC protocol.

J

JBOD An acronym for "just a bunch of disks." A non-RAID disk configuration.

join An operation that allows you to retrieve data from two or more tables by taking advantage of the relationship between the tables.

K

key The column or set of columns that is used to define the access point into an index. If a composite index is made up of two columns, those two columns make up the index key.

kilobyte (KB) 2^{10} bytes, or 1,024 bytes.

L

latency The term used to describe the time a process spends waiting on an operation to complete. Most typically used to describe the time a thread waits on an I/O to complete.

lazywriter The thread that takes dirty blocks from the SQL Server cache and writes them to disk. It is called the lazywriter because it is a background process that operates on its own schedule and priority.

leaf node The lowest node in an index. The leaf node contains either a pointer to the row data or the data itself (in the case of a clustered index).

level 1 (L1) cache Memory built into a CPU chip that is used for holding data and instructions to speed access from the CPU. Usually 16 KB or 32 KB.

level 2 (L2) cache Memory that is either built into or external to a CPU chip and that is used in addition to the level 1 cache as an overflow.

lock An object that is used to allow only one thread to access a resource at a time. Locking can be very important, especially in an SMP system, because many threads may be trying to access resources simultaneously.

log *See* transaction log.

logical disk drive A virtual disk drive that appears to the operating system as a physical disk drive, but in reality is made up of two or more disk drives in a RAID system.

log writer The SQL Server thread that is responsible for reading the log buffer and writing the contents out to the transaction log.

M

measurement configuration The set of performance counters that is selected for the system to monitor.

medium (plural: **media**) An object to which data is written. Both physical disk drives and tapes are media.

megabyte (MB) 2^{20} bytes, 1,024 kilobytes, or 1,048,576 bytes.

memory A term used to describe random access memory (RAM) that is allocated and used by the operating system and SQL Server. The term *memory* in this book refers to main memory. The main use of SQL Server memory is as a database cache. Memory is not durable; its contents are lost upon loss of power.

merge replication Merge replication is similar to transactional replication in that it keeps track of the changes made to articles. However, instead of propagating transactions that have made changes, merge replication periodically transmits all changes that have been made to the database.

Microsoft Cluster Server (MSCS) An add-on to SQL Server that allows another SQL Server system to operate in standby mode for the primary server. In the event of a failure with the primary server, the secondary server would take over.

Microsoft Transaction Server (MTS) A framework for developing three-tiered distributed applications now integrated into Component Services.

mirroring A duplicate of the component is created, providing a redundant copy that can be used in the event that the original fails. Usually associated with I/O subsystems. Both RAID 1 and RAID 10 use mirroring.

N

named pipes A SQL Server net-library. Named pipes is required for SQL Server Windows NT installations. Named pipes is a secure net-library and supports several underlying network protocols, such as IPX/SPX, NetBUEI and TCP/IP.

network packet Data and control information that is transferred across the network as a unit. A SQL Server request may fit into one network packet, or multiple network packets may be required.

NWLINK The SQL Server network library that supports Novell's IPX/SPX network protocol.

O

ODBC *See* Open Database Connectivity.

OLAP *See* online analytical processing.

OLAP Services Microsoft OLAP Services is an add-on component to Microsoft SQL Server 7.0, designed to assist you with online analytical processing (OLAP); you can use it to access data in your data warehouses and data marts.

OLTP *See* online transaction processing.

online analytical processing (OLAP) The manipulation of data for analytical purposes. OLAP is usually associated with data marts or data warehouses.

online transaction processing (OLTP) Database processing characterized by many users accessing different data while waiting for that processing to be completed. These users are online and active; thus, response time is critical for OLTP systems.

Open Database Connectivity (ODBC) A Microsoft-designed database connectivity API that can be used to communicate from applications to a multitude of different RDBMSs.

optimizer *See* SQL Server query optimizer.

ORDER BY A clause that specifies the sort order of columns returned in a SELECT statement.

OSQL An application supplied by Microsoft that allows access into the SQL Server RDBMS. OSQL uses the ODBC protocol; ISQL uses the DBLIB protocol.

outer join An operation that returns all rows from at least one of the tables or views mentioned in the FROM clause, as long as those rows meet any WHERE or HAVING search conditions.

P

packet *See* network packet.

page The fundamental unit of data storage in SQL Server. This is the smallest unit of data that will be written to or read from disk or memory. The page size for SQL Server 2000 is 8 KB; it was 8 KB for SQL Server 7.0 and 2 KB for SQL Server 6.5.

page lock *See* lock.

paging Should Windows NT and SQL Server use more memory than is physically available, some of this data is temporarily copied to disk. This is known as paging. When paging occurs, the performance of the system is severely degraded. Also known as *swapping*.

parity Extra data (or pseudodata) that is used to validate or correct the base data. Typically parity refers to a bit that is used to force the underlying data bits to be either even or odd. By checking the data to determine if the data is even or odd, the system can validate that it is correct. RAID 5 uses parity to protect its data.

parse A process performed by SQL Server to break down a SQL statement into its fundamental components before passing it to the query optimizer.

partitioning Dividing a table or database into separate components to create smaller and more easily managed data sets.

peak utilization period The time the machine is most stressed during a measurement or a working day.

Performance console A Microsoft Management Console (MMC) snap-in that ships with the Windows 2000 operating system that allows you to look at various performance counters within the operating system and SQL Server.

performance counter A unit of collection that reflects resource usage.

performance measurement A collection of performance statistics (called performance counters) used to tune a computer system. This type of measurement is of short duration (usually seconds, minutes, or sometime hours) in order to capture anomalies in the system performance and correct them.

Performance Monitor (PerfMon) *See* System Monitor.

physical memory The chips that are used for memory within the system.

predictive analysis The use of mathematics in order to predict the outcome of a specific change to the system. Predictive analysis can be used to predict the effect of adding users to the system.

primary key A column or combination of columns whose values uniquely identify each row in the table. This column (or columns) is used to enforce the entity integrity of the table.

procedure cache The part of SQL Server memory used for caching stored procedures and parsed SQL statements. The procedure cache is used to improve SQL Server performance.

processor Another term for central processing unit (CPU); the brains of the computer. A standard computer system consists of one or more CPUs, main memory, and disk storage.

profiler *See* SQL Profiler.

publication A group of articles that is replicated from a publisher.

publisher The SQL Server system that is replicating its data to other systems. The receiver of the replication is called a subscriber.

pull subscription A form of replication in which the replication is initiated by the subscriber.

push subscription A form of replication in which the replication is initiated by the publisher or distributor.

Q

query A SQL SELECT statement that is used to retrieve data from the database. When this book refers to a *query,* we are talking about a read-only operation.

query analyzer *See* SQL Query Analyzer.

query optimizer *See* SQL Server query optimizer.

queue The list of processes, or threads that are awaiting processing. A queue is a list waiting to be processed.

queueing The act of waiting in line for processing. Queueing occurs throughout SQL Server, the Windows 2000 operating system, and in the hardware itself.

R

RAID (redundant array of inexpensive disks) A disk array that is used to form one large logical disk drive by partitioning or distributing the data across many physical disk drives. RAID controllers can be configured in different ways, each of which has different fault-tolerance and performance characteristics.

RAID level The identifier that is used to specify which RAID configuration is being used.

RAID 0 The RAID level that provides for data striping and no fault tolerance. This is the most economical and fastest RAID level, but it provides no tolerance for disk failures.

RAID 1 Commonly known as mirroring. RAID 1 volumes consist of two disk drives that are exact copies of each other.

RAID 5 Known as distributed parity RAID. This RAID level creates a parity for each stripe. It is very economical and provides fault tolerance.

RAID 10 The RAID level that combines both disk mirroring and disk striping. RAID 10 is sometimes referred to as RAID 0+1 or RAID 1/0.

random access memory (RAM) Nonpersistent storage that is used for data processing. RAM is faster than disk, but all data is lost upon the removal of power.

raw device A method of accessing a disk drive through a raw interface, that is, by bypassing the operating system file system.

RDBMS *See* relational database management system.

record A single row in the database.

recovery An operation in which SQL Server is restarted after a system failure; the transaction log is used to roll forward all committed transactions and roll back all noncommitted transactions in order to bring the database to the state it was in at the point of failure.

recovery interval How long it takes for SQL Server to recover in the event of a system failure.

referential integrity *See* integrity.

relational database management system (RDBMS) A database system that stores the data according to the relational data model. The hierarchy of the data is made up of relations between objects. SQL Server is one example of an RDBMS.

replication An add-on to SQL Server that allows you to automatically create copies of SQL Server objects or subsets of objects to other systems. Replication comes in three forms: snapshot, transactional, and merge.

response time The length of time that is experienced between when the user submits the request for data (executes the transaction) and when that data is returned to the user. Often the response time is used to judge the performance of the system.

restore To copy a SQL Server backup back into the SQL Server database. This operation takes the database back to its state when the backup was created.

roles *See* database roles.

ROLLBACK The SQL Server statement to undo a transaction. Prior to committing a transaction, you can issue a rollback statement that will undo all the activity performed by that transaction.

root node The top node in an index.

rotational latency The time it takes for the disk drive to rotate to where the requested data resides.

router A network devices that passes data from one subnet to another based on the network addresses.

row A single record in the database. A row or record of data represents one entry in the database. This entry is a set of a number different pieces of data known as columns or fields.

row lock *See* lock.

S

SAN *See* storage area network.

schema A collection of objects associated with a database. Schema objects consist of tables, indexes, views, and so on.

SCSI *See* Small Computer System Interface.

seek time The time it takes for the disk heads to move from the current track to the track where the requested data resides.

selectivity The ability of an index to identify objects. An index with very few unique values is said to have poor selectivity. A unique index has excellent selectivity.

self join A join of a table with itself.

service level agreement (SLA) A contract between the provider of computer or database services and the user of those services. This agreement specifies the minimal level of service that is guaranteed and usually is in the form of maximum response times for certain transactions.

sizing The task of determining the proper amount of hardware (CPU, memory, disks) for a computer system. The system needs to be sized before it is designed and built. After it has been in production, capacity planning is used to plan for future growth.

SLA *See* service level agreement.

Small Computer System Interface (SCSI) An I/O interface that is very popular in today's computer systems. SCSI disks are disks that use the SCSI interface.

SMP *See* symmetric multiprocessor.

SMS *See* System Management Server.

snapshot replication A form of replication in which the entire publication is periodically copied from the publisher to the subscriber.

snowflake schema A snowflake schema involves dimension tables that are joined with other dimension tables before being joined to the fact table. Several layers of dimension tables can be involved before joining to the fact table. The schema thus looks like a snowflake.

SPID *See* system process ID.

split seek A feature of RAID 1 and RAID 10 where both disks in a mirror can simultaneously seek for data.

SQL *See* structured query language.

SQL Server Microsoft's enterprise RDBMS product.

SQL Server Agent A program that performs background tasks, such as scheduling of SQL Server jobs and handling notification of problems within SQL Server. The SQL Server Agent scheduler is used for execution of other agents, such as the replication agents. The SQL Server Agent was formerly known as the SQLExecutive in SQL Server 6.5. Its primary functions are scheduling tasks and handling alerts.

SQL Profiler A SQL Server utility that is used to monitor server performance and activity. SQL Profiler is a useful tool for tracking events within SQL Server.

SQL Query Analyzer The SQL Query Analyzer has replaced ISQL-W (ISQL Windows Version) as the preferred tool for ad hoc SQL Server access. SQL Query Analyzer allows you to type in SQL statements and view the results in another pane; it also allows you to debug SQL statements by displaying the execution plan.

SQL Server query optimizer An internal component of SQL Server that analyzes SQL Server and object statistics to determine the optimal execution plan. Users do not access the query optimizer; instead, the parser passes parsed SQL statements to the query optimizer.

staging table A temporary table in which to insert data so that it can then be extracted or transformed and copied into permanent tables. Using staging tables is a common way of transforming data within a database.

star schema A single fact table surrounded by dimension tables. The dimension tables are used to form the basis of the analysis of the data in the fact table. Each of the dimension tables is joined to a column in the fact table. If you imagine a fact table surrounded by dimension tables you can see how it resembles a star. A star schema is very common for data warehouses.

steady state The average utilization factor of a machine for either a measurement or a working day.

storage area network (SAN) An I/O subsystem in which multiple computer systems can share the same RAID subsystem.

stored procedure One or more Transact-SQL statements compiled into a single execution plan. This compiled plan is stored in the SQL Server database.

striping Spreading data among two or more disk drives in equal chunks. With RAID controllers, data is distributed among all the drives in the logical volume in equal pieces.

structured query language (SQL) A common language used with relational databases. Standards for SQL are defined by both the American National Standards Institute (ANSI) and the International Standards Organization (ISO). Most modern DBMS products support the Entry Level of SQL-92, the latest SQL standard (published in 1992).

subscriber The recipient of SQL Server replication data.

swapping *See* paging.

switch A network device in which the path from one connector to another is electronically connected based on network addresses. This differs from a hub, in which all connectors see all traffic, and from a router, in which packets are modified.

symmetric multiprocessing (SMP) system A system with multiple CPUs that each share the same memory and that function equivalently. Each CPU in an SMP system typically has cache memory, but no main memory associated with it.

system administrator The person or persons responsible for maintaining the hardware and operating system. The system administrator's role can vary depending on how a company is organized.

System Management Server (SMS) Microsoft's enterprise management platform.

System Monitor The portion of the Performance console which can be used to graphically monitor performance counters. System Monitor provides statistical information relating to the performance of various system components. This information can then be used to tune the system to avoid bottlenecks and achieve optimum performance. This utility was called Performance Monitor (PerfMon) in Windows NT.

system process ID (SPID) A unique integer (smallint) assigned to each user connection when the connection is made. The assignment is not permanent.

T

table lock *See* lock.

table scan An operation in which all rows in the table are read before the data you want is found. A table scan is not usually a good way to perform a query.

TCP/IP *See* Transmission Control Protocol/ Internet Protocol.

terabyte (TB) 2^{40} bytes, 1,024 gigabytes, or 1,099,511,627,776 bytes.

thread A feature of Windows 2000 operating systems that allows application logic to be separated into several concurrent execution paths. All threads are part of the same process and share the same memory.

throughput The data capacity of a data conduit such as a network or CPU bus. The term is used to describe how much data can pass through that bus or network hardware in a particular time.

Token Ring A popular network hardware protocol developed by IBM.

transaction A set of SQL statements that ends with either a COMMIT or ROLLBACK statement. The term *transaction* is usually used for those statements that modify data, and the term *query* is usually used for SELECT (read-only) statements.

transactional replication A form of replication that operates by duplicating on the subscriber each transaction that has run on the publisher.

transaction log A file in the database that is used to record all modifications to the database. Information on the transaction that performed each modification is also kept in the transaction log. The transaction log stores enough information to undo the transaction (in case of a rollback) or to redo the transaction (in case of a roll forward).

Transact-SQL The procedural SQL language that is used by SQL Server. Transact-SQL is a superset of SQL.

Transmission Control Protocol/Internet Protocol (TCP/IP) A popular network protocol.

trigger A special type of stored procedure that fires or runs automatically whenever a predefined event occurs. This event can be an UPDATE, INSERT, or DELETE statement executed on a table.

truncate Truncating a table removes all rows from an object without deleting the object itself. A table can be truncated with the TRUNCATE TABLE command. The transaction log can also be truncated.

T-SQL *See* Transact-SQL.

two-phase commit A protocol used to coordinate a transaction between two in dependent systems by guaranteeing an all-or-nothing approach to the commit. The two-phase commit splits the commit operation into two parts. The first part is the prepare phase; the second part is the commit phase. These phases are initiated by a COMMIT command from the application.

U

UNION A SQL statement used to combine the results of two or more queries into a single result set consisting of all the rows that are returned from all the queries in the union statement.

unique A value with no duplicate values. SQL Server can be used to enforce unique-ness by either creating a constraint or a unique index.

Universal Naming Convention (UNC) name A full Windows NT name of a resource on the network. The UNC name conforms to the following syntax: \\servername\sharename. Here *servername* is the name of the network server, and *sharename* is the name of the shared resource. The UNC name can and usually does include the directory path under the name; for example, \\servername\sharename\ directoryname\filename.

UPDATE The SQL statement used to modify a record in the database.

V

view An auxiliary data structure that is used to create a virtual table. This virtual table is defined by a SQL statement that makes the table appear as either a subset or superset of the underlying objects.

virtual memory Allows Windows NT to ac-cess more memory than is actually present in the system through the use of paging and swapping. Only a portion of the virtual memory is actually in physical memory at any one time.

W

WHERE A clause in a SQL statement used to define the conditions for the data that you want. It is used to refine search criteria to access specific data.

wizard A user-friendly tool provided in most Microsoft applications to simplify the process of administering the system and performing configuration tasks.

working set The amount of memory that is currently being used by a process.

Index

A

Edward Whalen Mr. Whalen is founder and vice-president of Performance Tuning Corporation (*www.perftuning.com*), a consulting company specializing in database performance, administration, and backup/recovery solutions. Prior to Performance Tuning Corp., Mr. Whalen worked at Compaq Computer Corporation in the capacity of OS developer, and then as database performance engineer. He has extensive experience in database system design and tuning for optimal performance. His career has consisted of hardware, OS, and database development projects for many different companies. Mr. Whalen has published with Marcilina Garcia several books on SQL Server, such as *Microsoft SQL Server 7.0 Administrator's Companion, Microsoft SQL Server 7.0 Performance Tuning Technical Reference, Microsoft SQL Server 2000 Administrator's Companion*, as well as two books on the Oracle RDBMS, *Oracle Performance Tuning and Optimization* and *Teach Yourself Oracle8 in 21 Days*. In addition, he has worked on numerous benchmarks and performance tuning projects with Microsoft and Oracle. Mr. Whalen is recognized as a leader in database performance tuning and optimization.

Marcilina Garcia Mrs. Garcia is a senior consultant of Performance Tuning Corporation (*www.perftuning.com*), a consulting company specializing in database performance, administration, and backup/recovery solutions. Prior to Performance Tuning Corp., Mrs. Garcia worked at Compaq Computer Corporation in Houston, Texas, as a database performance engineer. As a consultant, she has worked for many companies in the areas of database performance benchmarks, SQL Server performance and database design, and system configuration and tuning. She and Edward Whalen have written three other SQL Server books for Microsoft Press, and Marcilina has written several whitepapers and a magazine article.

Steve Adrien DeLuca Program Manager responsible for developing performance tools at Microsoft Corporation since 1998, Mr. DeLuca is currently developing performance and capacity planning solutions for Microsoft's Distributed Management Division. While at Microsoft Corporation, Mr. DeLuca has written three other books and has filed for eleven patents for work in capacity planning and performance. Prior to working at Microsoft, Mr. DeLuca worked as an architect engineer at Oracle Corporation, where he co-invented and developed the Oracle System Sizer. In addition to his work at Microsoft and Oracle, Mr. DeLuca has performed the function of performance engineer specializing in sizing and capacity planning for such organizations as DEC, Tandem, Apple, and the U.S. Air Force. Mr. DeLuca has been participating in performance benchmarks, developing performance tools, and lecturing about them around the world since 1980.

Michael Dean Thompson Dean Thompson has worked as a Senior Consultant for Performance Tuning Corporation and as a Technology Specialist with Microsoft for SQL Server in the Gulf Coast District. Prior to Microsoft, Dean was an application development consultant in Dallas with over 13 years of experience. Currently, Dean is working as a contract database analyst and data architect in the Houston area. When he is not working on SQL Server, he is developing Web applications in ASP and Perl, or performance tuning his Ford Mustang. Dean can be reached at *dean@txsqlusers.com*. His Web site is *http://www.txsqlusers.com*.

Jamie Reding A performance engineer with the SQL Server team at Microsoft Corporation, Mr. Reding is responsible for developing and maintaining the Transaction Processing Council (TPC) benchmark kits and analyzing SQL Server system performance. Prior to Microsoft, Mr. Reding worked at the Compaq Computer Corporation in the capacity of database performance engineer. Mr. Reding has been participating in performance benchmarks and systems analysis since 1984. In addition to his work at Microsoft and Compaq, Mr. Reding spent 11 years with the IBM Corporation.

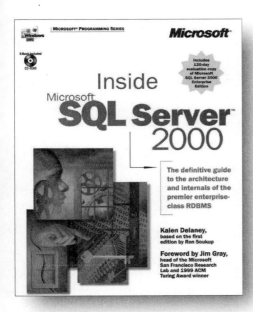

Learn SQL programming

the easy way with this practical, step-by-step guide!

U.S.A.   **$49.99**
Canada $72.99
ISBN: 0-7356-1142-4

Whether you're new to databases or familiar with Microsoft Access, Oracle, and other relational databases, MICROSOFT® SQL SERVER™ 2000 PROGRAMMING STEP BY STEP is the ideal way to learn how SQL Server can work for you. Written by an experienced database developer and author and replete with examples and exercises, this book will help you quickly get up to speed on creating and maintaining databases with the interactive tools provided by SQL Server 2000 Personal, Standard, and Enterprise Editions. This book is a must-have resource for anyone who wants to create and maintain databases and program with Transact-SQL. Included on CD-ROM with the book are sample database files and sample script code in Transact-SQL.

mspress.microsoft.com

Get a **Free**
e-mail newsletter, updates,
special offers, links to related books,
and more when you
register on line!

Register your Microsoft Press® title on our Web site and you'll get a FREE subscription to our e-mail newsletter, *Microsoft Press Book Connections.* You'll find out about newly released and upcoming books and learning tools, online events, software downloads, special offers and coupons for Microsoft Press customers, and information about major Microsoft® product releases. You can also read useful additional information about all the titles we publish, such as detailed book descriptions, tables of contents and indexes, sample chapters, links to related books and book series, author biographies, and reviews by other customers.

Registration is easy. Just visit this Web page and fill in your information:

http://www.microsoft.com/mspress/register

Microsoft
